The Politics of the Irish Civil War

The Politics of the
Irish Civil War

BILL KISSANE

OXFORD
UNIVERSITY PRESS

OXFORD
UNIVERSITY PRESS

Great Clarendon Street, Oxford OX2 6DP

Oxford University Press is a department of the University of Oxford.

It furthers the University's objective of excellence in research, scholarship,
and education by publishing worldwide in

Oxford New York

Auckland Cape Town Dar es Salaam Hong Kong Karachi
Kuala Lumpur Madrid Melbourne Mexico City Nairobi
New Delhi Shanghai Taipei Toronto

With offices in

Argentina Austria Brazil Chile Czech Republic France Greece
Guatemala Hungary Italy Japan Poland Portugal Singapore
South Korea Switzerland Thailand Turkey Ukraine Vietnam

Oxford is a registered trade mark of Oxford University Press
in the UK and in certain other countries

Published in the United States
by Oxford University Press Inc., New York

British Library Cataloguing in Publication Data

Data available

Library of Congress Cataloging in Publication Data

Data available

Typeset by SPI Publisher Services, Pondicherry, India
Printed in Great Britain
on acid-free paper by
Biddles Ltd., King's Lynn, Norfolk

ISBN 978–0–19–927355–3 (Hbk.)   978–0–19–923765–4 (Pbk.)

1 3 5 7 9 10 8 6 4 2

In memory of my grandparents

Acknowledgments

Writing a relatively balanced book on one of the most divisive episodes in Irish contemporary history has proven a formidable challenge in view of the perennial nature of the issues that divided the two sides in 1922. This book makes no claim to be providing a transcendent interpretation, but mainly goes into detail on aspects of the conflict that have not received sustained attention. Such a book could not have been written, but for the excellent archival resources available to researchers on the Irish state, as well as the professional way they are administered. I thank the staffs of the Irish National Archives, the UCD Archives, the National Library of Ireland, the British Library's newspaper library at Colindale, the Public Record Office at Kew, and the British Library of Political and Economic Science for their help. I also acknowledge the receipt of a teaching replacement grant from Sticerd at the LSE in 2003, and am grateful to Daragh Minogue of Queen Mary's Strawberry Hill for substituting for me. Thanks also go to the editors of *Civil Wars*, *The Journal of Political Ideologies*, and *Irish Political Studies* for allowing me to publish longer versions of articles originally published by them as Chapters 3, 5, and 6. They are now all part of the Taylor and Francis Group, which can be found at hhtp://www.tandf.co.uk/journals. This book was a long time in gestation and I thank Professor Brendan O'Leary, now at the University of Pennsylvania, for suggesting that I write it, and for guidance on what it should consist of. Much of the actual writing of the book was done under the convenorship of Professor Dominic Lieven of the LSE, who proved to be an inspired head of department in this period. Beyond that Mark Boden, Shelley Deane, and Nick Sitter commented on parts of the manuscript, and I am grateful for their criticisms, alongside those of Oxford University Press's internal readers. In addition, Fred Halliday, Jim Hughes, John Hutchinson, John Madeley, Peter Mair, John McGarry, Eunan O'Halpin, and Joan O'Mahony have all helped in various ways. Anne Gelling at Oxford University Press has been positive from the outset and I am grateful for her efficiency and enthusiasm. Responsibility for what follows is mine alone.

Contents

List of Figures

List of Tables

1

Introduction

It is a remarkable reflection on Irish political history in the twentieth century that the first substantive decision to be taken by an independent Irish parliament led to civil war. That war began on 28 June 1922 and ended on 30 April 1923. Over a thousand lives may have been lost in the conflict, but the records do not allow for a precise estimate. The material cost, in terms of damage to the infrastructure of the new state, was immense.[1] At issue was the Anglo-Irish Treaty, signed on 6 December 1921, but supporters of the Treaty also believed that the military opposition to the settlement called into question the proper basis of social and political order in Irish society. Paradoxically, a point in Irish history that should have been seen as a triumph of national unity revealed the deep divisions within Irish nationalism and its capacity for internal discord. Indeed the protagonists could not even agree on how to characterize the events of 1922–3. Pro-treatyites often resented the appellation 'civil war', since they believed that it gave their opponents a degree of legitimacy their cause did not entitle them to. The fighting was merely a reassertion of law and order in the wake of a disorderly War of Independence.[2] Anti-treatyites, in contrast, did not believe that independence had been achieved by the Treaty, and liked to describe the fighting as a continuation of the War of Independence against the British, which had begun in 1919.[3] Neutrals accepted that it was a civil war, an avoidable and destructive conflict brought about by an irresponsible and embittered national leadership.

THE CIVIL WAR AS A PUBLIC EVENT

It is by now a truism in the comparative study of civil wars that not all such conflicts need have a public character. Kaldor outlines the typical features of the 'new wars' of the post-cold war era, which often blur the distinction between war, organized crime, and massive human rights violations.[4] In these conflicts, the

---

[1] D. Fitzpatrick, *The Two Irelands, 1912–1939* (Oxford, New York, 1998), 134. For a higher figure see M. Hopkinson, 'Civil War and Aftermath, 1922–4', in J. R. Hill (ed.), *A New History of Ireland volume 7, 1921–84* (Oxford, 2003), 54

[2] E. Neeson, *The Irish Civil War* (Dublin, 1989), 222.

[3] *The Case of the Republic of Ireland*, republican pamphlet issued in response to Bishops pastoral (UCD, de Valera Papers, 150/1653).

[4] M. Kaldor, *New and Old Wars: Organised Violence in a Global Era* (Cambridge, 2001), 2.

objective of the protagonists is not always to win the military conflict by gaining control of the state, and given the diminishing importance of the state in an era of globalization, it may be surprising if they do.[5] Nonetheless, the Irish civil war still commands attention precisely because it was a public conflict, with the issue of state legitimacy a key variable, and where both sides fought with the aim of victory. The fact that the civil war was preceded by a nationalist revolution in which constitutional and military methods were conjoined in the Sinn Fein movement (1917–22), obviously predisposed the movement to see the military divisions of 1922–3 in constitutional terms, and this factor also explains the relative ease with which military divisions became party political divisions after 1922.

Indeed the identities of the main two political parties in the Republic of Ireland, the institutions of the state, and, for a long time, the governing personnel themselves all have their origins in the civil war. A 1946 book called *Politicians by Accident* demonstrated that twelve of the fourteen members of the then Fianna Fail government had fought on the losing side in 1922, with over three-quarters of them seeing out the conflict in the government's prison camps in 1923.[6] The pattern of politics that followed the war, 'civil war politics' in Irish parlance, lasted long after the issues that caused the initial division had lost their salience. In 1948 the attempt to form the first coalition government in the state's history almost came to ground because of one party leader's insistence that Fine Gael's Richard Mulcahy be prevented from becoming prime minister, because of his involvement in the Provisional Government's execution policy during the civil war. Then as now, Irish politics south of the border were dominated by three parties; the nationalist Fianna Fail; the less nationalist Fine Gael (which priori-tizes economic development over the redress of nationalist grievances); and the Labour Party, which believes that the rivalry between the first two obstructs the more important pursuit of social justice.[7] Eighty-two years after the civil war, it is hard to see what has really changed. Fianna Fail and Fine Gael have yet to form a coalition government together, despite the fact that both enter coalitions with a range of ideological partners.

The pivotal role played by the civil war in Irish political development derives in the first instance from the character of the fighting in 1922–3, which amounted to more than the large scale riot or faction fight sometimes depicted by Irish historians.[8] To be categorized as a civil war a conflict must meet a number of conditions. Firstly, it must involve armed clashes that result in a significant number of deaths. Although the conventional phase of the conflict lasted only a month, armed clashes between the National Army and the anti-treaty IRA lasted almost a year, and took the form of a guerrilla war from August 1922 on. Although

---

[5] D. Keen, 'Incentives and Disincentives for Violence', in M. Berdal and D. M. Malone (eds.), *Greed and Grievance: Economic Agendas in Civil Wars* (Boulder and London, 2000), 26.

[6] L. Skinner, *Politicians by Accident* (Dublin, 1946).

[7] See K. Gilland Lutz, 'Irish Party Competition in the New Millenium: Change or Plus Ca Change?' *Irish Political Studies*, 18/2 (Winter 2003), 40–60.

[8] See T. Garvin, *1922: The Birth of Irish Democracy* (Dublin, 1996), 45.

some analysts suggest that the National Army's casualties may have been around 800, it is certain that the overall figures were higher.[9] Secondly, a civil war must feature a government fighting an organized opposition that seeks to replace it through armed victory. The National Army was clearly under the sole control of the Provisional Government established by the Treaty, whereas from October 1922 onwards, the activities of the IRA were sanctioned by a Republican Government, which claimed continuity with the revolutionary governments that orchestrated the independence movement from 1919 on. Thirdly, the fighting must take place within a recognized political unit or a state. Although the boundaries of the Irish state had only been established by the Government of Ireland Act in 1920, and although both sides were committed to ending partition, neither side operated across the northern border, and the contest was essentially over control of the 26 counties of southern Ireland. Indeed it had an east–west core–periphery aspect and, significantly, the most intense fighting was in the south-west, the region furthest removed from the northern border. A final criterion for civil war is that both sides must expect the political unit to continue in the future, since the issue of who controls the state and determines its international status is only meaningful in a relatively permanent entity. The intensity of civil war derives from this fact.[10] Although the victory of the government gave undoubted permanence to the Irish Free State created by the Treaty, their efforts to negotiate a future role for their opponents in the system floundered on a rock of mutual distrust in May 1923.

Although the existence of a coordinated campaign of violence, sanctioned by a section of the national political elite, and aimed at undermining the authority of the recognized state, is ultimately what gives the conflict its status as a civil war, the polarization inherent in the concept also increased as the war wore on. The first phase to consider is between 6 December 1921, when the Treaty was signed, and the attack on the Four Courts on 28 June 1922, when the general drift to violence was accompanied by constant efforts to prevent the Treaty split culminating in all-out civil war. In the conventional phase that followed, between June and September 1922, atrocities were not commonplace and resistance to the state was half-hearted. Once guerrilla war set in, however, this restraint was removed, and both sides resorted to more extreme measures in this third phase. The Provisional Government's use of (77) official executions to discourage resistance, and its tolerance of the murder of many more prisoners, was matched by a destructive campaign of intimidation, arson, and assassination on the part of the IRA, which was designed to prevent the government from functioning, to drive the landowning class (principally Protestant) from the country, and to reduce the economic life of the country to ruin, especially through the destruction of railway lines.[11] In this phase, both sides largely turned their backs on any

---

[9] See M. Hopkinson, *Green against Green: The Irish Civil War* (Dublin, 1988), 273.
[10] See R. Licklider, 'The Consequences of Negotiated Settlements in Civil Wars, 1945–1993', *American Political Science Review*, 89/3 (1995), 681–90.
[11] D. O'Sullivan, *The Irish Free State and its Senate: A Study in Contemporary Politics* (London, 1940), 99.

thought of compromise, and the brutality of method was matched by polarization on constitutional issues.

Although this linkage between military and ideological factors was clearly key to the public character of the war, the formative nature of the conflict still requires further explanation. On the one hand, it may be precisely because the fighting was so limited that it was possible to institutionalize the division into conventional party politics afterwards. Hart shows that the counties of Galway, Longford, Westmeath, Kings, Kildare, Kilkenny, Monaghan, Wicklow, Meath, Cavan, Leitrim, Roscommon, Clare, and Donegal were hardly affected by the fighting.[12] Where the deaths were more extensive, as in Finland in 1918, silence has been the preferred way of dealing with the memory of civil war.[13] On the other hand, if the violence really was so limited, and if a degree of desultory violence inevitably follows any violent revolution, why make so much of what some regarded as nothing more than an army mutiny? Kalyvas suggests that the variation in violence in civil wars is almost always determined by local factors, and several Irish studies also suggest this.[14] According to Hart, in 1922 the Cork IRA were not just defending an Irish national Republic, but the Cork Republic as well as innumerable parish republics. By the time of the truce with the British in July 1921 each unit was in undisputed control of their territory, 'and the reality of local power was as difficult to surrender as the ideal of a purified and untrammelled Ireland'.[15] In Kerry the leaders of all three IRA brigades, and the overwhelming majority of activists, took the anti-treaty side, despite the fact that Kerry public opinion and its political representatives were split.[16] In Connacht O'Gadhra suggests that the influence of the local IRA commanders was more important that that of elected politicians in shaping the attitudes of volunteers. The first western division, under Commandant Michael Brennan, covered Clare and South Galway and went pro-treaty. The second western division, under Tom Maguire, covered South Roscommon, South and East Mayo, and North Galway, and went anti-treaty.[17] Wexford was another county where there was more fighting during the civil war than during the War of Independence, and a crucial factor was again that the north Wexford and south Wicklow brigade, under Commandant Joseph Cummins, supported the Treaty, while the south Wexford brigade under Commandant Thomas O'Sullivan opposed it.[18] In Longford Coleman suggests that the relative lack of activity during the civil war there is explained by the decision of Sean MacEoin, who

[12] P. Hart, *The IRA at War, 1916–1923* (Oxford, 2003), 41.

[13] See the essays by Alapuro, Peltonen, and Lehto in K. Christie and R. Cribb (eds.), *Historical Injustice and Democratic Transition in Eastern Asia and Northern Europe* (London and New York, 2002).

[14] S. Kalyvas, 'The Ontology of "Political Violence": Action and Identity in Civil Wars', *Perspectives on Politics*, 1 (2003), 465–94.

[15] Hart, *The IRA at War*, 269.

[16] T. Ryle Dwyer, *Tans, Terror and Troubles: Kerry's Real Fighting Story 1913–23* (Cork, 2001), 339.

[17] N. O'Gadhra, *Civil War in Connacht 1922–1923* (Cork, 1999), 13.

[18] S. MacSuain, *County Wexford's Civil War* (Wexford, 1995), 46.

had close links with Collins and GHQ, to support the Treaty.[19] In Sligo the IRA were determined to maintain the degree of independence they had obtained during the truce from central encroachment.[20]

These studies suggest that we distinguish between causes of the civil war that operated at the national level and those that operated at the local level, and imply that opposition to the Treaty may not have been primarily ideological.[21] Of the twelve anti-treaty veterans Hart interviewed in Cork none could remember exactly why they opposed the settlement, and the Republic had nothing to do with politics for most of them.[22] Indeed for Fitzpatrick, differences of principle were relatively unimportant in Ireland, and gained their importance only because the civil war created a powerful retrospective need for them, particularly on the anti-treaty side. He notes that compromises such as the Treaty tend to provoke the reassertion of principle anyway, and that personal and factional conflicts often surface after the withdrawal of a common antagonist. It was these personal and factional differences that determined Ireland's post-revolutionary line-up.[23] They were expressed most clearly in the rivalry between elites over control of the IRA, and in the split between the Barrett and Brennan families in Clare, an example of how territorial jealousy was elevated into high-minded principle.[24] The feuds between the Hanniganites and the Manahanites in east Limerick, and the Sweeneys and the O'Donnells in Donegal, are other examples.[25] Once the imperative for public solidarity was removed, like a family feuding over a contested inheritance, the survivors of the War of Independence 'tore each other and their legacy asunder'.[26]

The problem, however, is that if factional and local rivalries were key, their violent expression might have been curtailed 'by more systematic repression, or defused by more effective conciliation'.[27] Here the key pro-treaty argument is that de Valera was to blame for giving political dignity to this family quarrel: as one pro-treaty TD, Michael Hayes, put it, the civil war would have been no more than a riot were it not for de Valera putting his 'political cloak over it'.[28] Curran also suggests that if de Valera had denied the anti-treaty IRA his prestige and support, the civil war would not have assumed the proportions it did.[29] Coogan also argues that if de Valera had thrown in his lot with the Provisional Government in trying to work the Treaty, opposition to it in the country would have been nothing like that which he helped generate.[30] Younger believes that if de Valera

[19] M. Coleman, *County Longford and the Irish Revolution, 1910–1923* (Dublin, 2003), 167.
[20] M. Farry, *The Aftermath of Revolution: Sligo 1921–23* (Dublin, 2000), 49.
[21] Hart, *The IRA at War*, 31.
[22] P. Hart, *The IRA and Its Enemies: Violence and Community in Cork 1916–1923* (Oxford, 1999), 114.
[23] Fitzpatrick, *The Two Irelands*, 124.
[24] D. Ftizpatrick, *Politics and Irish Life: 1913–1921* (Dublin, 1977), 191.
[25] Hart, *The IRA and Its Enemies*, 266.
[26] Fitzpatrick, *The Two Irelands*, 134.
[27] Ibid., 125.
[28] Quoted in C. Younger, *Ireland's Civil War* (London, 1968), 464.
[29] J. Curran, *The Birth of the Irish Free State 1921–1923* (Mobile, Ala., 1980), 280.
[30] T. P. Coogan, *De Valera: Long Fellow Long Shadow* (London, 1993), 309.

had stuck to his constitutional guns, the IRA garrison in the Four Courts would have become bored with their occupation in time, and the government's attack on 28 June would not have been necessary.[31]

In effect the microanalysis still has to return to the macrolevel to explain the public nature of the civil war. On the one hand, it is hard to resist the argument that had the President of Sinn Fein cooperated with Collins in working the Treaty, the civil war would have appeared no more than an army mutiny. On the other hand, de Valera was also representative of his followers, and his reasons for opposing the Treaty were consistent with the objectives of the Sinn Fein movement that had swept the polls in the 1918 general election. The Treaty split clearly transformed the tension between central and local authority that existed during the War of Independence, and it is too simplistic to suppose that what happened in 1922 was merely the result of a complex power struggle within an unwieldy nationalist movement unable to sort out clear lines of authority. Given the aims of Irish nationalism after 1916, it was predictable that the Provisional Government were going to have to use some force to carry the day for the Treaty, and given the older traditions of Irish nationalism, it was no surprise that the arguments would have a wider resonance.

The Irish conflict also occurred at a time when the break up of empires led to fighting in many European countries after 1917. The democratization of the suffrage, the promise of self-determination, and the Russian revolution led many within Sinn Fein to believe that what were once honourable but hopeless aspirations could soon be realized. What followed, with the creation of Northern Ireland in 1920 and the Irish Free State in 1921, put paid to such optimism, and should be considered part of the wider politics of 'bourgeois defence' in 1920s Europe.[32] As a result, the radicals were forced to square their idealized vision of Ireland with the prosaic reality of two conservative polities either side of the border, and this readjustment proved too difficult for many. In 1929 the writer Sean O'Faolain commented on the old disease of Irish nationalism, which was to imagine Ireland as a living being, a woman in fact, which 'changed her name to suit the particular character of the politician that courts her'.[33] The victory of the Free State in the civil war, and the prosaic record of the independent administrations, largely put paid to that tendency for good, but occasioned a disturbance in Irish society in 1922–3 that can only be considered a civil war.

THE COMPARATIVE STUDY OF CIVIL WARS

If the public character of the civil war and its formative role in Irish political development are its two most remarkable features, for social science the issue is

---

[31] Younger, *Ireland's Civil War*, 509.
[32] Kissane, *Explaining Irish Democracy* (Dublin, 2002), 21.
[33] Liam O'Flaherty, *Tourists Guide to Ireland* (London, 1929), 66–8.

what the conflict tells us about general theories of civil war. Manifestations of conflict are usually explained either by the motives of which the quarrelling parties are conscious of as the occasion of their quarrel, or by those objective situations and processes that underlie these processes, and in which both parties are involved ('or proceeding analytically', as Buber suggests, 'we try to explore the unconscious complexes to which these motives relate like mere symptoms of an illness to the organic disturbances themselves').[34] The comparative literature on civil wars of the past decade has overwhelmingly pursued the second approach, to the extent of actually adopting this medical analogy by describing the various phases of civil wars as 'onset, duration, and termination'.[35]

This literature is largely of a socio-economic nature and instead of focusing on the 'triggering events' that lead to the outbreak of the fighting in each case, it tries to relate the variation in civil war to countries' longer term social, economic, and institutional features.[36] Levels of economic development, socio-economic inequality, the distribution of natural resources, the nature of the political system, and ethnic and religious diversity have all been invoked to explain why some countries experience civil war and others do not. However, by implying that civil wars are caused by factors that straddle both the 'onset' and 'duration' phases, this literature often fails to distinguish between factors that bring a conflict into being, and those that help keep it in place. On the other hand, some authors acknowledge that civil wars are fuelled partly by the circumstances that account for the initial resort to violence, and partly by forces generated once violence has started and that tend to perpetuate it.[37] Political processes, such as those described in the previous section, may explain the 'onset' of civil war, but structural factors, such as deep-seated inequality, may perpetuate it.

The same approach has been adopted for Ireland. For Garvin, elite rivalries over control of the new administration and the IRA enabled the fighting to break out in 1922, but sociological factors gave the conflict much of its bite. Irish Catholics, he argued, saw democracy as a tolerable rather than ideal form of government, and believed that there were truths that the majority had no right to flout. This conditionality was a prime cause of the civil war.[38] Moreover, much of the energy of the civil war was provided by a residual land hunger among bands of anti-treatyites who either feared that the Treaty would deprive them of an opportunity to acquire land or hoped to exploit the turmoil of 1922 to do so.[39] This land hunger was to be expected in a political culture whose zero-sum mentality was 'a major conditioning factor in the civil war'.[40] If young men could not inherit land or a small business, or if their educational qualifications

---

[34] M. Buber, *The Way of Man* (London and New York, 2002), 20.
[35] See H. Hegre, 'The Duration and Termination of Civil War', *Journal of Peace Research*, 41/3 (2004), 243–52.
[36] P. Collier, *Breaking the Conflict Trap* (Washington, DC, 2003), 54.
[37] Ibid., 53.
[38] Garvin, *1922: The Birth of Irish Democracy*, 34.
[39] Ibid., 44
[40] Ibid., 154.

were not sufficient to secure a clerkship in an office, fighting in the IRA or emigration could appear as the only positive choices. Garvin cites statistical evidence to suggest that anti-treaty voting was strongest in areas of high emigration, notably in counties far from Dublin.[41] Finally, the kind of nationalism espoused by the anti-treatyites emphasized the primacy of ethnic ties and the absolute nature of the commitments deriving from it.[42] In April 1922 fourteen Protestants were killed in revenge for the death of an IRA officer in West Cork, prompting a local exodus.[43]

The problem is that other studies have generally failed to support these theses. Hart tested whether the distribution of republican activism between 1917 and 1923 correlated statistically with variables such as poverty, a local history of agrarian agitation, emigration, or rurality, but found only that exposure to cultural nationalism was statistically significant. His conclusions challenge the view that the civil war was one of social as well as political disaffection.[44] In Longford Coleman attributes IRA activism during the revolutionary period to the existence of a nationalist tradition going back to 1798, the absence of parental controls, the suspension of emigration during the First World War and the politicization of the county in the 1917 by-election. Land hunger, class resentment, sectarianism, or a particularly unfortunate history of emigration did not matter.[45] Farry's work on Sligo clearly refutes the notion that there was a hidden class basis to the civil war, since the social backgrounds of anti-treaty internees and government recruits were similar over the whole county. Moreover, there was no correlation between IRA activity and previous patterns of agrarian agitation, and for a county adjacent to Northern Ireland, there was no coordinated campaign of intimidation aimed at removing Protestants from the county.[46] Once again the sociological hypotheses are spectacularly unconfirmed.

Nevertheless, since the Irish conflict lasted less than a year, whereas the normal length of contemporary civil wars is more than seven years, the absence of sociological cleavages explains a lot about the duration of the civil war. Collier and Hoeffler's approach focuses on the situations in which people are able to rebel, rather than those in which they want to rebel.[47] If we separate the onset from the duration phase of the civil war, it may well be that economic viability is the best predictor of the duration of any civil war. In Ireland, the anti-treatyites were unable to exploit natural resources, attract the same degree of financial donations from the Irish diaspora as during the War of Independence, or receive military backing from the neighbouring government. The skewed nature of resource distribution hugely favoured the Provisional Government, which was backed by

---

[41] Garvin, *1922: The Birth of Irish Democracy*, 155.
[42] Ibid., 143.
[43] Hart, *The IRA and Its Enemies*, 115.
[44] P. Hart, 'The Geography of Revolution in Ireland, 1917–1923', *Past and Present*, 155 (May 1997), 163.
[45] Coleman, *County Longford and the Irish Revolution*, 178.
[46] Farry, *The Aftermath of Revolution*, 296.
[47] P. Collier and A. Hoeffler, *Greed and Grievance in Civil War* (Washington, DC, 2000), 16–17.

the British government, the banks, and the Catholic Church, and which, at one stage in the summer of 1922, was recruiting 1,000 men a day to its 'mercenary' army.

Fearon and Laitin also suggest that opportunity for prolonged insurgency usually exists only in weak states, with rough mountainous terrain, poor communication and transport systems, and dispersed populations. Like many of their cases, in 1922 the Irish Free State was a newly independent state, which had suddenly lost the coercive backing of the Empire, and whose military capacities were new and untested.[48] On the other hand, it was not a weak state, and the fact that the IRA tried to destroy the rail system to prevent it governing effectively is testimony to the importance of these environmental factors. By March 1923 IRA activity in anything like column strength existed only in the mountainous parts of the south and west.[49] In many 'new wars' of the post-cold war era, the inability of the state to provide basic services and physical protection for its citizens allows for the emergence of private armies that devise new systems of profit, power, and protection.[50] In Ireland, however, the swift victory of the Free State in conventional fighting ensured that this did not happen. Thus while ideological grievances remained strong, the opportunity for sustained civil war in such a small state was weak. Indeed it could be argued that it was a misperceived opportunity for rebellion that led to the intensification of the IRA challenge in the autumn of 1922, and this was rooted in the unviability of their campaign and their lack of public support. When more realistic leaders took over after Liam Lynch's death in April 1923, the war was quickly brought to an end.

However, grievances were still to affect the third phase, that of 'termination', when months of peace efforts in 1923 did not lead to an agreed settlement. Walter suggests that settling a civil war is unlike ending an interstate war, precisely because the adversaries cannot continue to possess rival armies, if they wish to coexist in a democratic state.[51] The problem is that the rebels cannot risk laying down their arms when no legal government and no impartial legal institutions can enforce the terms of peace on both sides. For this reason the Irish government's insistence on decommissioning proved to be a major hurdle in peace talks throughout the civil war. However, an external power need not be the only guarantor of post-civil war peace, if the victorious government can develop institutions not identified with its political party, and if the rebels can find a way of reconciling their political perspective to the state without decommissioning. In these respects, the 'termination' phase of the Irish civil war took over fifteen years.

In summary, although the onset of the Irish civil war can only be explained in terms of the issues discussed in the first section, the comparative literature can be

---

[48] J. Fearon and D. Laitin, 'Ethnicity, Insugency and Civil War', *American Political Science Review*, 97/1 (2003), 81.

[49] 'Report on the Military Situation, 31 March 1923' (NA, D/T, S3361).

[50] D. Keen, 'Incentives and Disincentives for Violence', 27.

[51] B. Walter, 'The Critical Barrier to Civil War Settlement', *International Organisation*, 51/3 (1997), 337.

applied to explain why, when the issues themselves were so intractable, the conflict ended relatively quickly. We can accordingly distinguish between the intensity and the violence of the civil war. A conflict is of great intensity if the cost of victory or defeat is high for the participants. The more importance the participants attach to the issues underlying the conflict, the more intense it is. The violence of a conflict, on the other hand, relates to its manifestations rather than its causes; it concerns the weapons chosen by the belligerents to express themselves. In this regard the Irish civil war was an intense rather than a violent conflict.[52] Indeed O'Halpin describes the actual fighting as no more than 'a succession of haphazard and indecisive scuffles' between two badly disorganized and poorly motivated groups of men.[53]

On the other hand, it is crucial to separate the phases of onset, duration, and termination from each other, and there is no simple structural explanation to explain why the Irish civil war occurred in 1922. The only plausible theory of this kind is a core–periphery one, but the regional distribution of the fighting may also be a function of opportunity, since the IRA remained active in 1923 largely in remote areas. Indeed part of the significance of this case is that the grievances were and remained powerful on both sides, and could only be absorbed within the political system over a period of two decades or more. Democracy is clearly a double edged sword. Although democratization from 1918 on helped destabilize the island as a whole, it was the strength of democratic values that enabled the civil war divide to be transcended south of the border. Had the civil war occurred in a milieu with less consensus on other issues, it is quite possible that 1922 would now be regarded as the graveyard rather than the cradle of Irish democracy.

THE STRUCTURE OF THE BOOK

It follows that the structure of this book should distinguish between the origins and the course of the civil war, and also pay attention to the manner in which the civil war division was absorbed within democratic politics, after peace negotiations had failed in May 1923. The first two chapters focus on the origins of the civil war. Chapter 2 locates the civil war in the comparative context of decolonization in the twentieth century, and tries to explain why a relatively generous post-imperial settlement proved so divisive for Irish nationalists, leading to a conflict with few parallels in the post-colonial world. Chapter 3 then goes into greater detail on the proximate causes of the war, and examines how the Treaty split was affected by the fixation on Ireland's right to self-determination after the First World War. It suggests (paradoxically) that the civil war can be seen as a conflict between the rival claims of democracy and self-determination, and in this sense one set of rights was opposed to another in 1922.

---

[52] R. Dahrendorf, *Class and Class Conflict in Industrial Society* (London, 1959), 208.
[53] E. O'Halpin, 'A Savage Chaos', *The Irish Review*, 6 (1989), 148.

The next three chapters are concerned with what happened in the civil war. Chapter 4 describes the course of the fighting, dividing it into the three phases already described. It emphasizes the unwanted nature of the civil war, and the weakness of the IRA's challenge once civil war became a reality. The limited nature of the fighting is explained not simply as the result of the scruples of the combatants, but as a consequence of the inequality of resources available to both sides. Nonetheless, the intractability of the civil war split, particularly when conventional fighting had ended in August 1922, is the subject of Chapter 5, which traces the fate of the various peace initiatives that accompanied the fighting from beginning to end. In the same vein, Chapter 6 discusses the role of 'neutral' organizations, and suggests that there was a second dimension to the conflict, which pitted Irish civil society against both sides of the nationalist elite over the desirability of the civil war.

The final three chapters are concerned with how the civil war has been interpreted by the actors themselves, and by historians. Chapters 7 and 8 examine how the civil war was incorporated into the self-understandings of the two civil war parties. Chapter 7 shows how central a Victorian conception of the state was to the pro-treatyite project, and how the resolute defence of central authority was combined with the protection of individual rights. Chapter 8 discusses the anti-treaty interpretation of 1922, and how it was modified under the leadership of Fianna Fail after 1932. It questions whether this interpretation was really undemocratic, since it was mainly constitutional, although fundamental ambiguities about popular sovereignty were resolved only in the long term. The final chapter is concerned with how Irish historiography has tackled the civil war, and revisits some of the issues discussed in this introduction at greater length.

In effect this book examines, in empirical detail, the three phases (the origins, the course, and the aftermath) of the Irish civil war. It provides mostly a political rather than a military history of the conflict, on the grounds that there was no correlation between the amount of the fighting in 1922–3 and the overall impact of the civil war. In this sense the rupture was primarily ideological. Wood has suggested that formal and agent-based models of civil war are not good at illustrating the emergence of ideologically motivated actors, whose behaviour may not be influenced by values that are part of the usual social science repertoire of material interest.[54] In Ireland the initial personalization of the Treaty conflict between two articulate national figures like de Valera and Collins helped give the split a public character, and once the fighting began, a clear shift in the underlying conditions of the conflict also occurred. For this reason much of the following chapters are devoted to analysing the process of ideological polarization that took place after June 1922.

The book is not intended to judge which of the Treaty sides had the more right on their side in 1922. However, a number of aspects of this study may inform

---

[54] E. J. Wood, 'Civil Wars: What We Don't Know', *Global Governance*, 9/2 (2003), 253.

value judgements; the centrality of self-determination to the Sinn Fein movement after 1917, and the extent to which the case made for it meant that acceptance of dominion status was an impossible compromise for many; the fact that no one ultimately wanted the civil war, which was a product of the force of circumstances as much as anything else; the total inequality in power resources once the fighting began, which explains why the Provisional Government survived the death of their two most prominent leaders in August 1922; the polarization of views on the constitutional issues once conventional fighting had ended, which problematized the relationship between de Valera and Liam Lynch on the anti-treaty side; and the skill with which both sides were able to represent their position in democratic terms after 1923. Finally, my research into Irish civil society suggests that the middle ground between the two Treaty positions was stronger among the public than a focus on the political elites would suggest, and this was another key reason why Irish democracy survived the civil war.

Nevertheless, if there is a core argument, it is that the civil war division was not simply a case of Tweedledum facing Tweedledee.[55] There was an ambiguity within Sinn Fein on certain core issues, and once the fighting started, a clear process of ideological polarization took place. The positions adopted in 1922 reflected older traditions within Irish nationalism, although the presence of dexterous politicians like Collins and de Valera suggested they could, at first, be bridged. These older traditions can be considered the 'root causes' that form the precondition of the crisis situation that developed in 1922 and also help explain the war's enduring impact on Irish political culture. On the other hand, the Treaty was also an essential catalyst that worked upon these root factors to increase their level of significance. Without such a divisive settlement it is unlikely that a southern civil war would have occurred, regardless of the differences within the nationalist movement. To use a causal analogy of Karl Popper's—when a weight of two pounds is put on a piece of thread that then breaks from the strain, both the universal hypothesis that strings will break when a certain weight is put on them and the concrete fact that a two-pound weight was put on a certain string at a given time have causal properties.[56] In Ireland, both the underlying precondition for conflict—the existence of rival traditions within Irish nationalism—and the proximate catalyst, the Treaty settlement, which touched on the nerve centre of the movement, must have causal status.

Nevertheless, the 'trigger' for the civil war was provided by the assassination of Field Marshal Sir Henry Wilson on 22 June 1922, and the resulting ultimatum given to the Provisional Government by their British counterparts. The full facts about the decisions taken in those final days will never be known, but the fighting can only be seen as the culmination of a process of events that had taken place over the previous months. By 28 June 1922 Collins had run out of peaceful options regarding the anti-treaty IRA, and although neither side entered into the conflict

---

[55] M. Hopkinson, *Green against Green: The Irish Civil War* (Dublin, 1988), 272.
[56] K. Popper, *The Poverty of Historicism* (London and New York, 2002), 113.

with much enthusiasm, months of diplomacy had failed to resolve their differences. As a result, the course of the conflict confirms van Clausewitz's insight that war is often simply politics continued by other means, and the fighting did resolve issues that had proved intractable during the truce. The civil war did nothing to counter the old image of a nation congenitally unfit for self-government, but short of one side capitulating to the other's perspective in 1922, it is not clear what more the political elite could have done to avoid it.

2

Decolonization and Civil War
in Comparative Perspective

In the 1950s the German scholar Erhard Rumpf was told by a native authority on Irish politics that 'there was no sociological, sectarian, or class problem or angle in the Sinn Fein movement, or any part of it, from beginning to end'.[1] The comment would seem especially appropriate to the Irish civil war, which has been attributed by one leading historian to native genius rather than to the inescapable logic of universal historical circumstance.[2] Certainly, since 1922 no scholar has convincingly argued that the conflict emerged out of objective social and political conditions, so it is impossible to subsume it under a general 'covering law' developed from a study of other conflicts. Yet if structural factors are to be discounted entirely, the problem becomes one of how to avoid analysing Irish nationalism entirely in terms of its own rhetoric. A compromise would be to view the civil war as the product of a unique combination of typically causative factors, but here the historian has to select those factors in the first place. In what follows I select one—decolonization—and assess the extent to which the Irish conflict may have parallels with the new states of Asia and Africa. Such an approach may either clarify the historical specificity of the Irish case or qualify the view that only native genius can explain the civil war. Either way, since the correlation between post-colonial status and civil war is still an intriguing one for the social scientist, a comparative approach is an obvious point of departure.[3]

DECOLONIZATION AND CIVIL WAR

In 1966 the historian, T. D. Williams, reflected that there was nothing peculiarly Irish about political and ideological divisions resulting from a compromise with a departing colonial power.[4] By locating the Irish conflict as part of a universal

---

[1] A. C. Hepburn, 'Introduction', in E. Rumpf and A. C. Hepburn, *Nationalism and Socialism in Twentieth Century Ireland* (Liverpool, 1977).

[2] J. Lee, *Ireland, 1912–1985* (Cambridge, 1989), 68.

[3] J. D. Fearon and D. D. Laitin, 'Ethnicity, Insurgency and Civil War', *American Political Science Review*, 97/1 (2003), 88.

[4] T. D. Williams, *The Irish Struggle 1916–1926* (London, 1996), 117–18.

experience, comparative analysis may absolve the Sinn Fein political elite, and the political culture that nurtured them, from responsibility for the civil war. However, detailed comparisons with other colonial conflicts have never been made, and the analogies made by Irish nationalists at the time were with the First World War. In September 1922, Sinn Fein's public organ, the *Irish Bulletin*, reflected that the Irish troubles did have their counterpart in other countries where freedom had recently been won, but the comparison it made was with North America in 1776.[5] Moreover, the analogies that have recently been made with the other European states formed out of the collapse of empires during the First World War suggest that there may have been something specifically Irish about violent conflict following a treaty with a departing colonial power.[6] The issue becomes even more crucial when we consider the fact that the vast majority of the British and French colonial territories completed the transition to independence after the Second World War peacefully—in two stages—with a treaty of association of some sort preceding full independence.

The relationship between decolonization and civil war has been explained in three ways by historians. Firstly, post-colonial civil wars may be rooted in the nature of the colonial relationship itself: the greater the degree of colonial domination, it is argued, the greater the violence that decolonization will unleash. In Algeria for example, where the disintegration of the FLN led to a situation amounting to civil war in the summer of 1962, elite discord and the disorder that resulted from it have been seen as the product of the obliteration of native institutions by 'a total colonial system'.[7] Secondly, post-colonial civil wars may be a product of an empire's strategy of delaying its departure by pursuing policies of divide and rule, which then breaks the unity of the nationalist movements. A similar logic may thus lie behind the emergence of civil wars and the introduction of partition, since the latter has often been justified as a response to the former. India is a case in point. Thirdly, since anti-colonial nationalism is often imitative in nature, the colonial administrative and military structures of control and repression may become duplicated when the elite of the independent state becomes faced with the problem of imposing order after independence, provoking a counter-response. The long history of attempts to impose order in post-colonial Indonesia involved a process of this kind.

At first glance, these arguments also apply to Ireland. Under the Union Ireland had been governed directly by Westminster, and despite the introduction of democratic local government in 1898, the delay in implementing Home Rule meant that moderate Irish nationalism did not establish its ascendancy through a native parliament, and was eclipsed when the effects of the First World War killed the Home Rule agenda. As it turned out, few members of the civil war elite had substantial experience in local or central government, and most entered politics

---

[5] *The Irish Bulletin*, 6 September 1922.

[6] J. Jorstad, 'Nations Once Again—Ireland's Civil War in European Context', in D. Fitzpatrick (ed.), *Revolution? Ireland 1917–1923* (Dublin, 1990), 159–73.

[7] E. Hermassi, *Leadership and National Development in North Africa: A Comparative Study* (Berkeley, 1972), 132.

during the revolutionary phase between 1916 and 1921. In their eyes constitutional politics had become identified with fractiousness, incompetence, and corruption, and the Irish Parliamentary Party had discredited themselves by receiving their salaries from the imperial coffers of the British treasury.[8] As a result, the Sinn Fein movement became predicated on what Fanon saw as the classic features of anti-colonial nationalism: the rejection of reformist and legalistic methods, the arrival of a determined revolutionary elite, and the mobilization of the peripheral elements in society against the standards of the centre.[9]

Secondly, it was a standard assumption of the Sinn Fein generation that the British Empire had sustained itself in Ireland through a policy of divide and rule, and that the ethnic and religious divisions that led to partition would be overcome if Britain stood aside. Thus, during the Treaty negotiations, on 17 October 1921 Griffith urged the British to stand aside on the issue of partition, and let the representatives of Irish nationalism deal directly with the Unionists in the North.[10] Ironically, it was then Griffith's opponents who maintained that he and his colleagues had been morally contaminated by their exposure to the ways of Westminster in 1921.[11] It would be too strong to argue that by imposing dominion status on Sinn Fein, the British government deliberately created the civil war, but they were aware of the possibility. On 22 June 1922 Lloyd George wrote to the Irish Provisional Government that British aid had been given to various dominions in the past when rebels challenged their authority, and it was available to the Irish in the form of artillery or other assistance.[12] The Irish case can thus be seen as an early example of a key feature of British counter-insurgency policy in the twentieth century, which was to encourage the emergence of a moderate nationalist elite that could mobilize the masses as a counter to undesirable radicalism.[13]

Thirdly, the stern measures the Provisional Government took to defeat the 'irregulars' in 1922–3, and the permanent repressive legislation put on the statute book to deal with the post-civil war IRA after 1931, have been seen as an example of a counter-hegemonic nationalist movement turning its back on its core values.[14] Once the civil war entered its guerrilla phase, the Free State's responses, through executions, internment, and official and unofficial reprisals, were all reminiscent of the worst phase of the War of Independence. Once the executions began, the British journal *The Nation* remarked that 'it seems as if the new I.F.S. government is taking over the spirit as well as the men who occupied it for so many centuries against the will of the Irish people'.[15] Indeed, the repressive powers acquired by the Irish state after 1921 exceeded anything deployed by the

---

[8] R. Bourke, *Peace in Ireland: The War of Ideas* (London, 2003), 126.
[9] See Hermassi, *Leadership and National Development in North Africa*, 128–9.
[10] Bourke, *Peace in Ireland*, 119.
[11] See T. Garvin, *1922: The Birth of Irish Democracy* (Dublin, 1996), 133.
[12] J. Curran, *The Birth of the Irish Free State, 1921–1923* (Mobile, Ala., 1980), 225.
[13] N. J. White, *Decolonisation: The British Experience since 1945* (London and New York, 1999), 98.
[14] D. Lloyd, *Anomalous States: Irish History and the Post-Colonial Moment* (Dublin, 1993), 3.
[15] *The Nation*, 6 December 1922, 595.

British during the War of Independence, and exceeded in brutality those used against nationalists in Northern Ireland between 1920 and 1972.[16] The clampdown was often accompanied by the application of British stereotypes about the Catholic Irish to describe the anti-treaty IRA—Collins himself remarking that 'they are the rebble and rough-necks from all quarters'.[17]

However, although all three hypotheses are relevant to Ireland, they are based on studies of individual countries, and not having been tested against a wide sample of cases, they have an ad hoc quality about them. Moreover, they relate to factors that have been present in many colonial cases, but civil war has only rarely been the immediate result of decolonization in the twentieth century. If all three had been established out of the Irish experience in the 1920s, they would have had little predictive power when it came to the post-1945 wave of decolonization. Alter lists a total of 124 cases of decolonization between 1922 and 1993, covering territories that became independent as a result of the collapse of the Tsarist, Ottoman, British, French, German, Dutch, Portuguese, and Soviet Empires.[18] Of these cases there are many that subsequently disintegrated into civil war, such as Sierra Leone, but few that experienced civil wars immediately after independence. At first glance, the only comparable cases were Finland (1918), the Phillipines (1946), Burma (1948), Indonesia (1949), Sudan (1956), Cyprus (1960), Nigeria (1960), Algeria (1962), Yemen (1968), Mozambique (1974), Timor (1975), Angola (1975), Georgia (1990), Tajikistan (1991), and Bosnia (1991). Including Ireland, this amounts to only 15 cases out of a sample of over 120, and of these 15, nearly half were ethnic conflicts. The sample of intranationalist civil wars is very small. Indeed in the 60 or so states created by the decolonization of the British Empire, between the creation of Jordan in 1946 and the return of Hong Kong to China in 1997, civil war occurred only in Yemen, although the transfer of power was violent elsewhere: such as in Aden, Kenya, and Malaya.

Small's compendium *Resort to Arms* lists a more extensive set of post-colonial conflicts, which includes Iran (1908), Morocco (1911), Afghanistan (1924 and 1928), Iraq (1958), Zaire (1960), Laos (1963), Uganda (1966), and Cambodia (1970), but nearly all these civil wars occurred well before or well after independence. Indeed, the typical post-colonial pattern may well be for serious internal conflicts to emerge only after a period of time, once frustrations with self-rule come to the surface.[19] Small also lists a number of other post-colonial conflicts that do not satisfy all the criteria of civil wars, such as Cuba (1917), Lithuania (1927), Bulgaria (1933), India (1946), South Korea (1948), Thailand (1951), Haiti (1956), Oman (1957), Jordan (1958), Rwanda (1959), Cameroon (1959), Tanzania (1964), Kenya (1964), Gabon (1965), and Zambia (1964).[20] The point is that of these fifteen cases

---

[16] See C. Cambell, *Emergency Law in Ireland, 1918–1925* (Oxford, 1993).

[17] Quoted in P. Hart, *The IRA and Its Enemies: Violence and Community in Cork 1916–1923* (Oxford, 1999), 135.

[18] P. Alter, *Nationalism* (2nd edn.: London, 1994), Table 4.2., 85.

[19] D. Lieven, *Empire: The Russian Empire and Its Rivals* (London, 2000), 378.

[20] M. Small, *Resort to Arms: International and Civil Wars 1816–1980* (Beverly Hills, 1982), 222–330.

only one, Cameroon, experienced something like civil war at the time of independence. In effect, the sample where something like the Irish pattern was later
replicated still consists of only seven cases, Indonesia (1949), the Philippines
(1946), Yemen (1948), Algeria (1962), Mozambique (1974), Angola (1975), and
Timor (1975). Two earlier cases were the Spanish Philippines, where internal
fighting followed the declaration of a republic in 1898, and Finland, where the
move away from Russia in 1917 also resulted in civil war the following year. Of
these nine cases only the Philippines, Finland, Indonesia, Algeria, Mozambique,
Angola, and Timor are clear examples of civil war resulting from internal
divisions within the nationalist movement. Moreover, in only two of these
cases, Algeria and the Philippines, was a treaty of sorts at issue, and here the
comparisons may still be misleading. In short, there may have been something
Irish about political and military divisions following a treaty with a departing
colonial power.

The contrast with Algeria also suggests this. The FLN was a broadly based
nationalist movement that, like Sinn Fein, first proved capable of subsuming
internal differences in favour of a general commitment to decolonization, but
which disintegrated immediately after independence. Between the ceasefire of
19 March 1962 and the election of Ben Bella as Algerian President on 26 September
1962, a crisis of authority within it was resolved only by something close to a civil
war in which 3,000 people died. Some aspects of the Algerian situation—the
belief of those who bore the brunt of the fighting that they should dictate the
future shape of the country, the use of the peace agreement to further personal
ends, the politicians' struggle for control of the army, and the role of personal
loyalties in shaping alliances—have their counterpart in Ireland.

Here, however, the parallels end. Firstly, Algerian public opinion itself was not
divided on the terms of peace. In the Evian Accords of 1962, France recognized the
sovereignty of the Algerian state over the fifteen *departements* of Algeria and the
Sahara, the civil and property rights of the European population were guaranteed,
France would retain military bases for some time, and close economic cooperation between the two states was envisaged.[21] In a referendum held on 1 July 1962,
voters chose independence rather than association with France, by 5,975,581 votes
to 16,534, so there was no basis for the emergence of rival political parties.
Secondly, the issue of civilian control of the military was not crucial in the
Algerian case. During the long war with the French the FLN had never aspired
to govern Algeria in a practical way, and there was no parallel to the electoral
campaigns of Sinn Fein between 1918 and 1921. By the spring of 1962 power had
become divided between four factions, none of which had the power to impose
central authority on their own: the Government Provisoire de la Republicque
Algerienne (GPRA), the Bureau Politique, the provincial leaders of the interior
army, and the army of the Frontier, based in Tunisia and Morocco. Among
these bodies there was no distinction between civilian forces and armed

---

[21] C. R. Ageron, *Modern Algeria: A History from 1830 to the Present* (London, 1991), 124

forces.[22] Thirdly, ideology played little role in the power struggles that followed Evian. In the absence of strong norms governing the distribution of power within the nationalist institutions, and given the lack of a constitutionalist dimension to the struggle, post-independence loyalties were entirely shaped in terms of alliances, clienteles, and personal ambitions.[23] Finally, the rate of intra-elite conflict among the FLN was much greater than that in Ireland, where the violence was of limited duration and scope. As young men moved up within the ranks during the war, the authority of the FLN declined, and by 1962 the founders of the FLN were no longer prominent in the organization. Indeed Hermassi estimates that between 1954 and 1970 around 87 leaders occupied leading roles for an average of two years.[24]

In effect, the 'total' nature of French colonialism, which obliterated most native public institutions, left a legacy of political underdevelopment with no parallel in Ireland. Indeed Lustick's comparison of the two cases suggests that because the Anglo-Irish were unable to prevent the mobilization of Irish nationalism within the parliamentary arena in the nineteenth century, in 1922 a bourgeois nationalist leadership, well-schooled in the arts of compromise and accommodation, was able to establish its hegemony over the radical wing of the nationalist movement in 1922.[25] The counter-argument, however, may simply be that there was no basis for the emergence of a bipolar division over Evian simply because the FLN got what it wanted in 1962. Here a comparison with the Philippines may be more instructive. Their war of independence had begun in earnest in 1894 when the nationalist leader, Andres Bonifacio, activated the *Katipunan* movement and committed it to independence from the Spanish crown. Three years later in 1897 a constituent assembly of Filipino nationalists declared separation from Spain and began the process of establishing a Philippine Republic, which was declared the following year.[26] However, the nationalist movement was divided between the radical Bonifacio and the more moderate Emilio Aguinaldo, and in December 1897, at the pact of Biak-na-bato, the latter accepted a compromise with Spain, involving a form of autonomy within the Empire alongside vague promises of social and political reforms.[27] Fighting nonetheless continued and by the time of the Treaty of Paris (on 10 December 1898), when Spain ceded sovereignty over the Philippines to the USA, the Spanish controlled only a few isolated outposts in the country. In May the following year Aguinaldo and other members of the *illustrado* elite decided to accept an American offer of autonomy.

---

[22] B. Stora, *Algeria 1830–2000: A Short History* (Ithaca, NY and London, 2001), 76.
[23] Hermassi, *Leadership and National Development in North Africa*, 141
[24] Ibid.
[25] See I. Lustick, *Unsettled States, Disputed Lands: Britain and Ireland, France and Algeria, Israel and the West Bank* (Ithaca, NY and London, 1993), 434.
[26] U. Mahajani, *Philippine Nationalism: External Challenges and Filipino Response 1565–1946* (St Lucia, 1971), 121.
[27] R. Constantino, *A History of the Philippines: From the Spanish Colonization to the Second World War* (New York and London, 1975).

Hostilities between the Filipinos and the Americans then broke out on 4 February 1899, and resistance continued for another ten years.

One Filipino historian attributes the internal divisions that resulted from the compromises with the Spanish, and then the Americans, to the basically assimilationist and reformist character of the Spanish-speaking *illustrado* elite who wanted an accommodation with the colonial powers in order to enhance their economic interests and secure their social and cultural aspirations.[28] A similar analysis has been made of the pro-treaty elite in Ireland, who wanted to 'arrest the decolonisation process at the point where it assumed control of the state apparatus left vacant by the off-shore power'.[29] However, there are clear differences between the two cases. Firstly, in Ireland the results of the 1922 election showed a broad swathe of public opinion in favour of abandoning the politics of Ireland's revolutionary era, so a divergence between elites and masses cannot explain the outcome. Secondly, in the Philippines there was no general and clear-cut condemnation of the elite who had compromised with the Spanish at the pact of Biak-na-bato, whereas in Ireland the split was immediate and long-lasting. Thirdly, American troops were used to crush the continued Filipino insurgency, whereas in Ireland British intervention was not necessary to defeat the republicans.[30] Finally, in the Philippines, enduring political organizations did not emerge from the conflict in the oligarchic political system that evolved after 1900. The territory was linguistically and geographically diverse, and were it not for American intervention, the War of Independence could easily have resulted in the creation of three *caudillo*-ridden states with the internal politics of nineteenth-century Venezuela or Ecuador.[31]

It may be that these comparisons merely reflect the fact that our understanding of past events is shaped more by rival historiographical traditions than what actually happened on the ground, but this does not affect the basic point that these conflicts took place in very different societies. The old adage about Irish politics—'in the beginning was the Treaty'—cannot be applied to the Philippines or Algeria, where the category of civil war has not always been applied to their post-colonial conflicts, and where the internal divisions were not institutionalized in a competitive party system afterwards. A comparison could also be made with the end of the Boer War where the treaty of Vereeniging, signed on 31 May 1902, created the Transvaal and the Orange Free State as republics within the British Empire. The loss of status this involved did not produce a deep split within the Boers, partially because they were exhausted by warfare, but also because the vast majority of delegates chosen to represent the commanders in the field accepted the need for compromise after a three-day debate at Vereeniging. In Ireland the equivalent debate in January 1922 produced a split

---

[28] Constantino, *A History of the Philippines* 55.
[29] G. Smyth, *Decolonisation and Criticism: The Construction of Irish Literature* (London, 1998), 92.
[30] Constantino, *A History of the Philippines*, 241.
[31] See B. Anderson, *The Spectre of Comparisons: Nationalism, Southeast Asia and the World* (London and New York, 1998), 200.

of sixty-four for and fifty-seven against compromise, so it is hard not to avoid the conclusion that Irish nationalism was culturally predisposed to a division of this kind. A comparison could also be made with Ben Gurion's attempts to incorporate the rival Zionist paramilitary organizations into the Israeli Defence Forces in 1948. This involved the deaths of sixteen members of a dissident paramilitary faction, the IZL, during the *Altalena* affair, and the formation of a new political party, Herut, out of Begen's National Military Organization. However, Ben Gurion's violent suppression of what he regarded as, potentially, an armed coup did not lead to a full-scale civil war, or the emergence of a bipolar party system on the Irish model.[32]

Comparative analysis does help identify those broad factors that were conducive to post-colonial conflicts, but it took the Treaty to provide the catalyst for the Irish civil war, and to give shape to its post-conflict development. Clearly critics of the post-colonial paradigm have a point. Post-colonial studies developed a vocabulary for analysing conditions in Africa, India, and the Middle East, but Ireland is a recognizably European country whose basic socio-political cleavage before 1921 was rooted in the seventeenth-century wars of religion. Moreover, Britain has not been an imperial force in Ireland in the same way it was in India, and to compare Anglo-Irish relations with those between Belgium and the Congo occludes the fact that Ireland was an integral part of the core of the British Empire for over 120 years.[33] Moreover, the Irish experience of violence and dislocation has been nowhere as destructive as that of the Third World colonies, with Hart putting the number of revolutionary deaths in Ireland (1916-23) at just over ten thousand.[34] In contrast, in Algeria the War of Independence left one million dead with two million imprisoned in concentration camps. In Ireland, in the whole period between 1916 and 1923, the main victims of the violence were the small Anglo-Irish minority in the south and the Catholic population in Belfast. Extreme violence was not generalized.

On the other hand, post-colonial theorists might argue that Ireland's deviance from the wider colonial pattern may be due to the fact that some colonial relationships were more deep-rooted in Ireland than in the Third World. The British government was willing to go to great lengths to keep Ireland within the Empire, and only moved to negotiation in 1921 when domestic opinion became critical of its counter-insurgency campaign. By that time it had already created two subordinate legislatures in Ireland, and an amendment to the Government of Ireland Act of 1920 also made it necessary for candidates seeking election to either Irish parliament to take an oath of allegiance to the King. The Irish conflict could be compared to the Kenyan and Malayan cases where the British government opposed nationalist movements in order to ensure that the successor regimes

[32] J. Heller, *The Birth of Israel 1945–1949: Ben-Gurion and His Critics* (Florida, 2000), 277.
[33] D. Donoghue, 'Fears for Irish Studies in an Age of Identity Politics', *Chronicle of Higher Education*, 21 November 1997.
[34] P. Hart, *The IRA at War 1916–1923* (Oxford, 2003), 30.

preserved British strategic and commercial interests.[35] Moreover, to the extent of encouraging unionist resistance to Home Rule after 1885, and partitioning Ireland in 1920, British conservative elites encouraged domestic resistance to the nationalist movement, and when that resistance took the form of paramilitary organization with the formation of the Ulster Volunteer Force in 1913, Irish nationalists followed suit. The result of this confrontation between a local majority on the island of Ireland and a local majority in Ulster was a crisis of parliamentary authority in the whole of the UK, which was resolved only by the establishment of two 'ethnic-majority' Irish states in 1920–2.[36] This impacted on another factor, which was that apart from some separate governing institutions, Ireland had no clear governmental status before 1921, and the inexperienced elites who inherited power in January 1922 were not in control over most of the territory of the new state. As Bulmer Hobson, a pro-treatyite writer, later reflected: 'during the preceding struggle the entire machinery of government had been disorganised, and respect for law had disappeared in the absence of law which could command respect'.[37] Some violence was thus inevitable, and the resulting civil war was fought more to restore central authority than to overthrow it.

Culturally, it was a measure of the challenge faced by Irish nationalists that the anglicization that they countered had penetrated every layer of Irish life by 1900, a situation rather different from that in Africa or Asia, whose emerging peoples were generally not so deeply penetrated by the culture of the colonizer.[38] In such a context a movement away from British rule was clearly parasitical on a well-developed sense of identity, and since the type of Irish nationalism that triumphed between 1916 and 1921 was in ways an anti-colonial nationalism, this made a settlement with the British Empire all the more difficult to achieve. However, even if the civil war was rooted in the nature of the Anglo-Irish relationship, the nature of that relationship must be understood on its own terms first, and the civil war might not reflect a general connection between decolonization and civil war. After all violence, personal rivalries, and collective identities have meaning only in the context of a given culture, and in 1921 the Irish cultural context was fairly unique.

IRISH NATIONALISM AND BRITISH RULE

If the utility of any cultural argument about the nature of British rule must lie chiefly in its ability to explain the resonance of the Treaty divide, the problem of looking back to a point in history when such schism became possible lies in the fact that before the Parnell split, Irish nationalism was known for its ability to gloss over internal differences in the interests of maintaining a united front.

---

[35] White, *Decolonisation: The British Experience since 1945*, 98.
[36] Hart, *The IRA at War 1916–1923*, 90.
[37] B. Hobson, 'Introduction' to *Irish Free State Official Handbook* (London, 1932), 15–16.
[38] D. Kiberd, *Inventing Ireland: The Literature of the Modern Nation* (London, 1996), 252.

However, the argument that the Treaty was a sufficient source of division in itself fails to explain the resonance of the divide in Irish political culture. On the one hand, although it is impossible to predict individual reactions to the Treaty on the basis of prior involvement in cultural organizations, the rhetoric of the anti-treatyites in 1922 does suggest the violation of a version of Irish nationality that had developed within them over the previous decades. On the other hand, the split also enabled the restoration of elements of moderate nationalism that had been bypassed during the First World War, and the construction of the new state along principles clearly central to the mainstream brand of parliamentary nationalism before 1918.[39] Attitudes to Empire then resurfaced as a kind of litmus test of responses to the Treaty, with one side seeing membership as a negation of Irish nationality, and the other finding in it a promise of equality.

For most of the nineteenth century mainstream Irish nationalism was constitutional in methods and ameliorative in aspiration. After the formation of the Irish Republican Brotherhood (IRB) in 1858, however, there was clear rivalry between the constitutional and physical force wings of Irish nationalism, but the movement with the greatest influence of the governing elite of the new state was actually the Gaelic Revival, which was in itself part of a wider mobilization of civil society that occurred towards the end of the nineteenth century.[40] In this period the Gaelic Athletic Society (1884), the Gaelic League (1892), the Feis Ceoil (1897), the National Literary Society of Ireland (1892), and the Irish Industrial Development Organisation (1903) were all formed, and as it turned out, over a third of the political elite of the new state had been members of the Gaelic League or the GAA in their youth.[41] The significance of these developments lays not only in providing a rationale for independence, but in inculcating a theory of nationality at odds with Ireland's continued membership of the Empire, and parasitic as that identity was on a sense of history, it gave cultural themes an unusual importance in political debate. It would be too strong to say that a preoccupation with Irish cultural distinctiveness led inevitably to separatism, but elsewhere in Europe at the time the currency of cultural nationalism was increasingly being converted into a political medium.[42]

The outstanding fact about the revival nevertheless was that it emerged only after the traditional culture of Gaelic Ireland had been undermined by the twin forces of emigration and modernization. Through its educational system and other policies, the British state had effectively confined the Irish speaking part of the country to the impoverished western hinterlands, and the language would never recover from its association with poverty and backwardness: by 1900 only one person in a hundred was a fluent Irish speaker. While Britain continued to

---

[39] See A. O'Day, *The English Face of Irish Nationalism: Parnellite Involvement in British Politics 1880–86* (Dublin, 1977).
[40] See B. Kissane, *Explaining Irish Democracy* (Dublin, 2002), 103–12.
[41] A. S. Cohan, *The Irish Political Elite* (Dublin, 1972), 40.
[42] See M. Hroch, *Social Conditions of National Revival in Europe: A Comparative Analysis of the Social Composition of Patriotic Groups among the Smaller European Nations* (Cambridge, 1988).

expand in wealth, power, and influence after the Famine, Ireland in contrast appeared to be a dying country, with its *Gaeltacht* dramatically shrinking in size, and with her people emigrating in millions to the United States.[43] The Famine and the subsequent emigration had altered Irish national character by making it more amenable to modernization and assimilation. What was left therefore was a struggle for identity, and this struggle could only be carried out in the cultural field, where the society's resources could not be monopolized by the imperial centre.[44] As Chatterjee remarks, this was a crucial strategy of many anti-colonial movements:

By my reading, anti-colonial nationalism creates its own domain of sovereignty within colonial society well before it begins its political battle with the imperial power. It does this by dividing the world of social institutions and practices into two domains—the material and the spiritual. The material is the domain of the 'outside', of the economy and of statecraft, of science and technology, a domain where the west had proved its superiority and the east had succumbed. In this domain, then, Western superiority had to be acknowledged, and its accomplishments carefully studied and replicated. The spiritual, on the other hand, is an 'inner' domain bearing the 'essential' marks of cultural identity. The greater one's success is imitating Western skills in the material domain, therefore, the greater the need to preserve the distinctiveness of one's spiritual culture. This formula is, I think, a fundamental feature of anti-colonial nationalisms in Asia and Africa.[45]

In the struggle for identity, a sense of Irish distinctiveness could only be asserted in opposition to the core values of Victorian Britain, and this was combined with a determination to show the Celts as one of the formative peoples of western Europe, rather than an offshoot of British imperial culture.[46] This attempt to ignore the present in favour of the past led to a central dilemma that could only be overcome by an effort of will. As Deane argues:

Even though the Famine totally weakened any argument in favour of Ireland's being a beneficiary of the Union and immeasurably strengthened the case for some form of independence, it was still difficult to maintain the position that a traditional culture had been destroyed while making the integrity of that culture the basis of a claim to independence. The difficulty was, nevertheless, overcome by an intensification of the claim to Irish difference, an intensification largely achieved in the literature of the Irish revival by the remarkable feat of ignoring the Famine and rerouting the claim for cultural exceptionalism through legend rather than through history. The modernisation of Irish society after the Famine was, therefore accompanied by the archaicizing of the idea of Irish culture.[47]

---

[43] J. Hutchinson, *The Dynamics of Cultural Nationalism: The Gaelic Revival and the Creation of the Irish Nation State* (London, 1987), 114

[44] S. Deane, *Strange Country: Modernity and Nationhood in Irish Writing since 1790* (Oxford, 1997), 50.

[45] P. Cahatterjee, 'Whose Imagined Community?', in G. Balakrishnan (ed.), *Mapping the Nation* (London and New York, 1996), 217.

[46] Hutchinson, *The Dynamics of Cultural Nationalism*, 197.

[47] Deane, *Strange Country*, 50–1.

As part of this 'archaising' of the idea of Irish culture, there emerged certain dichotomies intended to provide the Irish with a sense of moral superiority over the English. Against the hegemonic urban class society of Britain, nationalists contrasted the organic folk community of Celtic Ireland. In opposition to the mass industrial society of Victorian Britain, nationalists celebrated the more democratic rural society based on the conservative virtues of a prosperous peasant proprietary. Against British utilitarian and commercial values were posed Ireland's heroic and visionary qualities. Although the late nineteenth century was a dark day for native culture, cultural nationalists still celebrated the golden age of Celtic culture, which preceded the development of European civilization in the feudal era.[48]

There were two clear political implications of the use of these dichotomies. In the first place, if there were only two antagonistic cultures in Ireland, the Gaelic and the English, this implied a rejection of any synthesis of the two by representatives of the Anglo-Irish tradition.[49] Secondly, since what was considered 'essentially Irish' was that which was not British, it became imperative that the Irish community be portrayed as one that was impossible to recruit into the nineteenth-century normalizing narrative of progress and economic development.[50] As a result, the revival became an offshoot of an essentially German romantic tradition: it became a fight 'of the periphery against the centre, of country against town, of the genuine against the cosmopolitan, of natural virtues against modern decadence'.[51]

As with any fixation on a past golden age, the problem was how to explain the intermediary stage, where the values of the imperial centre seemed unchallenged by native society. As Deane suggests, it was easier to portray national character in legend rather than through history, where awkward facts could not be avoided by conscientious scholars.[52] There were two ways out of this conundrum. Firstly, the nationalist character of past revolts was emphasized, and history seen precisely as a history of nationalism that made sense, just like the stops on any train journey, only with the destination of full independence in mind. During the civil war, the anti-treaty leadership published an open letter, written by 'Padraig O'Brian' of the 'irregular' forces to his former comrade 'Pat O'Brien', and stated that whereas the IRA man would die for the old cause, 'your name and cause will fade like last year's snow, for that is ever the fate of the Imperialist in this country, whether he calls himself a Cromwellian, a Yeoman, a Constabularyman, or a National soldier'.[53] Second was the attempt to present the period of British rule in colonial terms, as a period of cultural vandalism, in which the British Empire deliberately

---

[48] See Hutchinson, *The Dynamics of Cultural Nationalism*, 114–41.
[49] Ibid., 175.
[50] Ibid., 146.
[51] M. Golding, *Faith of our Fathers* (Dublin, 1981), 127–8.
[52] Deane, *Strange Country*, 51.
[53] 'Open letter from Padraig O'Brien of the "Irregular" Forces to his former friend and Comrade, Pat O'Brien of "the National Army"' (n.d.), NIC 13, NL.

attempted to destroy all signs of a vital and older indigenous culture. During the War of Independence, Sinn Fein published a pamphlet under the title 'National Spirit Never Broken', which represented the Irish past in this way:

From their first appearance till the present day every effort was made to break up the national organisation, to destroy Ireland's unity, to exterminate or expatriate her people, to root out her language and culture. But the tenacity of the race, its resistance to assimilation, its marvellous recuperative power, defied all the efforts of the invader, and the Irish people remain to this day unsubdued, unassimilated, a coherent and organised whole who repudiate the right of England to possess or rule their country. Centuries of slaughter and spoliation, deliberately planned massacres, wholescale schemes of deportation, soul-crushing penal laws, enforced emigration, religious divisions fostered by England for the purpose of weakening the Irish people, all failed to break the national spirit or the national unity.[54]

Since the history of the British–Irish relationship was crucial to the nationalists' sense of identity, the issue of cultural representation thus became central for a culture that wished to defend its autonomy on the basis that it had not been and could not be represented in colonial-imperial form, and must therefore find alternatives more suited to it.[55] The new self-image that emerged rested on three arguments: (a) that Ireland was a culturally distinct nation; (b) that it had been mutilated beyond recognition by British colonialism; and (c) that it could nevertheless rediscover its lost features and thereby recognize once more its true identity. The latter could only be accomplished by an act of will in the cultural field, where adaptation to the revival's alter ego—the commercial, the economic, the religiously conformist version of the contemporary Irish—was derided as a betrayal of that heroic force that had animated Irish history.[56] In December 1922 a republican newsletter asked:

What is the argument for the Treaty? Is it not materialism, root and branch? Was it not openly said that we are getting the practical things, the essentials of freedom, the resources of the country, the power over education, industry, police, judiciary? And what are we asked to give in exchange? Nothing, a shadow, an oath of allegiance. 'All these will I give thee if falling down thou shalt adore me'. Do you think that a state rooted in materialism can evolve anything but a bitter materialism?[57]

Since the essence of this tradition lay in its uncompromising refusal to countenance any form of British/Irish partnership, it must be asked how it related to the mainstream tradition in Irish nationalist politics, which worked the channels of representation at Westminster precisely in order to achieve the kind of progress not prized by some cultural nationalists. Garvin suggests that because the Gaelic Revival had emerged at a time when the agrarian motor of discontent with British

---

[54] Sinn Fein, *The Case of Ireland* (n.d.), Sinn Fein Series no. 12 (UCD, Eamon de Valera Papers, P150/578).
[55] Deane, *Strange Country*, 54.
[56] Ibido., 53.
[57] IRA Daily Bulletin, no. 27 (30 December 1922).

rule was being assuaged by wholesale reform, the kind of progress that might be achieved by the parliamentary party was itself a threat to the revivalists' object-ives.[58] A series of state reforms, such as the 1881 Land Bill, the opening of civil service positions to competitive entry in 1870, and the expansion of post-primary education, were all clearly designed to the same end: the creation of a progressive educated middle class eager to participate, like the Scots and the Welsh, in the running of the British Empire.[59] So there was no natural sympathy between the cultural and political movements, and many cultural nationalists were critical of the belief that all problems could have political solutions. Eoin MacNeill, a President of the Gaelic League, was convinced by his studies of the Irish past that just as their Celtic ancestors had resisted the might of imperial Rome, alone of the European nations the Irish now resisted the profane worship of the state and the material power associated with it.[60]

Of course cultural and political nationalism were not necessarily opposed in practice: the alliance between the two to make Irish a subject in the university curricula after 1900 is an obvious example of cooperation. Where they differed substantially was in their ideal of the future. As Hutchinson argues, the aim of the revival was the rebirth of a distinct Irish community, whereas the goal of political nationalists was the normalization of Ireland's place among the nations of the world by the regaining of her independent statehood.[61] The touchstone of the former was a distinct identity; the aspiration of the latter, political equality. The practical implication of the cultural tradition was isolation if not autarchy, whereas the assimilationist logic of its rival was that an autonomous Ireland modelled on British imperial lines be given its proper status as an equal partner in the British imperial mission.[62] It is not hard to conceive of the split in 1922 as a conflict between these two visions of the future.

Key to the liberal approach was that the Irish question could be solved in the context of the overall progress of the Empire, and Irish nationalists saw the link between British democratization and improved conditions for Ireland. They shared, in other words, the Victorian assumptions of the age.[63] The record of the Parnellite group in the House of Commons does show a strong reformist tendency—in favour of more democracy and land reform, for example—but this was one that was compatible with the existing social order.[64] Indeed for all their identification with its subject peoples, they looked on the Empire with a mixture of pride and enthusiasm.[65] Although their claims for Irish independence could be compared with the demand for decolonization elsewhere, the parliamentary elite saw progress, not in terms of separating Britain and Ireland, but in terms of bringing Irish conditions into line with those elsewhere in Britain.[66] In other

[58] T. Garvin, 'The Anatomy of a Nationalist Revolution: Ireland, 1858–1928', *Comparative Studies in Society and History*, 28 (1986), 468.
[59] Hutchinson, *The Dynamics of Cultural Nationalism*, 115.
[60] Ibid., 126.   [61] Ibid., 152.   [62] Ibid.
[63] O'Day, *The English Face of Irish Nationalism*, 89.
[64] Ibid., 157.   [65] Ibid., 163.   [66] Ibid., 174.

words, they wanted self-government for Ireland, but did not seek to isolate it culturally or economically from the rest of the English-speaking world.[67] It was a future clearly at odds with the neo-traditionalist strand within Irish nationalism, and one that had clear implications when such a future was put on offer in 1921. Certainly, by 1926, William Cosgrave, the first genuinely pro-treaty prime minister, was in no doubts as to which vision of the future he found more attractive. On 5 November 1926 he told an audience in Manchester that

Your country and mine, separated for centuries by a tragic series of events, which have now happily come to an end, are giving an example to the world of what can be achieved by free association between nations. My colleagues and myself have the most profound conviction that the relations between us will ripen into a bond of sincere and lasting nature.... The whole world is striving for peace and we should be very short-sighted not to realise what a powerful instrument for that purpose is contributed by the people settled in the vast spaces of London, and Australia and New Zealand.[68]

In effect what occurred with the Treaty was precisely the 'restoration' of the values and status hierarchies of the Home Rule generation, and the triumph of pragmatism over dogma in Irish nationalist politics. The role of former Home Rulers in brokering a settlement based on dominion status, the dominance of former Unionists in the new Senate, and the abandonment of Griffith's ideas of economic protectionism in the 1920s suggest as much.[69] Once the shock of civil war was over, the priority in Anglo-Irish relations was also a return to normality, this time on the basis of bonds of friendship and equality. On 27 June 1923 Cosgrave wrote to Stanley Baldwin that

The statesmen on both sides who negotiated and concluded the Treaty between Great Britain and Ireland, believed that they were closing the long struggle between the two countries and that they were putting their hands to something great and constructive from which a new relationship of friendship between the two countries would emerge... the nation as a whole endorsed the Treaty and all that it stood for.[70]

The argument thus far has suggested that the resonance of the Treaty divide can only be understood in relation to the different traditions of Irish nationalism that existed before the First World War. In the end, although the sample of intranationalist conflicts is small, the existence of rival traditions within one movement is not a surprise. As a concept, self-determination is normally claimed on two bases. On the one hand, the right to self-determination is claimed on the basis of distinctiveness, and here the Gaelic Revival provided the essential ballast for the Sinn Fein view that Ireland was culturally a distinct nation. On the other hand, self-determination is also claimed on the basis of similarity with other nations, and here the liberal tradition provided the necessary argument that Ireland was as

---

[67] O'Day, *The English Face of Irish Nationalism*, 181.
[68] William Cosgrave, speech on receiving Freedom of Manchester, 5 November 1926 (NA, D/T, S5983/4).
[69] See P. Maume, *The Long Gestation: Irish Nationalist Life 1891–1918* (Dublin, 1999), 218.
[70] Cosgrave to Baldwin, 27 June 1923 (NA, D/T, S3135).

worthy of the same degree of self-government as subject peoples anywhere. Garvin argues that the pro-treatyites wanted to be recognized as leaders of an ancient European nation, but they also wanted to be seen as modern democratic leaders who could meet the leaders of the nations of the white English-speaking world on terms of equality.[71]

As Smyth has argued, the distinction is that 'liberal decolonization' refers to a form of nationalism in which the subordinate people seeks equality with the dominant power, and is concerned to raise the status of its nation up to the standards of the colonial centre. Not for nothing did Arthur Griffith term the Treaty 'a treaty of equality'.[72] 'Radical decolonization' on the other hand, entails the use by the subject of his differential status as the basis of both a repudiation of metropolitan values and a concomitant celebration of a national identity characterized as unique and authentic.[73] Austin Stack, an anti-treaty TD for Kerry, remarked that even if the Treaty did give the new state the same powers as Canada, he would reject it because Ireland had never been 'a child of England's'.[74] The Treaty, in other words, offered to some a chance to show that the Irish were as worthy of self-government as anybody else, while to others it amounted to an abandonment of their national birthright. For Collins it provided the Irish with one of the finest chances they ever had to mould the national destiny, and if they failed in that task they would have shown themselves and their nation unworthy of the task.[75] De Valera, in contrast, likened the Treaty to a plague and thought it was his duty to save the people from its effects.[76] In a curious way, for both sides the good reputation of the Irish nation was now at stake. For pro-treatyites, the growing disorder of 1922 affronted their determination to vindicate the Irish capacity for self-government, whereas for anti-treatyites acceptance of the Treaty was a betrayal of Ireland's tradition of heroic resistance to British rule.

THE CHOICE

If the split in 1922 was a profoundly formative event, the argument must then be that the existence of these traditions was a precondition for the civil war, with the Treaty being its essential catalyst. However, even if the small elite that prosecuted the civil war after Collins' death in August 1922 were genuine pro-treatyites, the majority of those that voted for the Treaty in the Dail debate were motivated by pragmatic considerations.[77] The nature of the settlement was clearly crucial. A less or more generous Treaty would have seen Sinn Fein united, in either rejection or

[71] Garvin, *1922: The Birth of Irish Democracy*, 68.
[72] Quoted in R. English, *Armed Struggle: A History of the IRA* (Basingstoke and Oxford, 2003), 31.
[73] Smyth, *Decolonisation and Criticism*, 54.
[74] English, *Armed Struggle*, 32.
[75] Collins to Chartres, 5 May 1922 (NA, D/T, S9242).
[76] Untitled manuscript, 26 December 1927 (UCD, de Valera Papers, P150/1604).
[77] F. S. L. Lyons, 'The Great Debate', in B. Farrell (ed.), *The Irish Parliamentary Tradition* (Dublin, 1973), 247.

acceptance, and one cannot point back to a period before the truce with the British in July 1921 to a time when violent internal conflict became likely.[78] In other words, however strong the connection between responses to the Treaty and the older traditions of Irish nationalism, the fallout in 1922 must also be understood in the context of Ireland's 'revolutionary' era, with the Treaty being seen either as the fulfilment of the Irish revolution or as a counter-revolution that negated its achievements. For Collins, with the Treaty Ireland was to be a fully constituted nation after 750 years.[79] The anti-treatyites, in contrast, labelled the Provisional Government as 'a military junta set up and armed by England', which was waging a war of aggression against the forces of the Irish Republic.[80]

Certainly, the sequence of events beginning with the 1916 Rising did nothing to undermine radical nationalists' belief in a heroic national character. The romantic nature of the Rising, the executions of 15 people, and the shift in public opinion afterwards clearly spelt disaster for the constitutional traditions of the Home Rule era. If Home Rule had been tarnished on account of its dependence on a liberal alliance productive of corruption and compromise, violence gave the illusion of an independent assertion of Irish rights.[81] That the Rising was also undertaken without a democratic mandate had clear implications for the self-image of the physical force men. In 1919 the IRA newsletter, *An tOglach*, reflected that the leaders of the Rising felt they were truly interpreting the wishes of the people of Ireland, and the course of events since then had proven that they were right. In what Hart calls 'a fascinating formulation', the democratic authority of the Dail was recognized, whereas the army's sovereign right to act in the name of the Republic, as in 1916, was reserved.[82] This attitude had clear practical consequences. At the beginning of the civil war, one anti-treaty leader, Robert Barton, consoled himself with the view that the deaths of republicans in the civil war would reverse majority opinion for the Treaty, and 'inspire the vast majority of our countrymen to fight until independence is achieved'.[83]

Yet Barton's belief in the ultimate popularity of the republican cause was also rooted in the electoral history of those years. Although elections to Westminster had become national events in Ireland in the 1820s, these elections had taken place on a restricted suffrage, and the first really democratic election took place in 1918. In that year Britain's decision to extend the suffrage to most adults led to a dramatic increase in those entitled to vote in Ireland, from less than 700,000 to almost 2,000,000. Of those 2,000,000 people entitled to vote in the 1918 election it has been estimated that only 360,00 had previously voted in a parliamentary

[78] M. Hopkinson, 'From Treaty to Civil War', in J. R. Hill (ed.), *Ireland, 1921–84: A New History of Ireland*, vol. 11 (Oxford, 2003), 7.
[79] M. Collins, 'Article on Treaty Negotiations' (Lifford, 1931).
[80] 'Statement issued by the Publicity Department, IRA, and addressed to each T.D. on 7 September 1922' (UCD, de Valera Papers, P 150/1648).
[81] M. Mulholland, review of E. O'Halpin, *Defending Ireland: The Irish State and Its Enemies since 1922*, H-Net Reviews in the Humanities and the Social Sciences (February, 2000).
[82] Hart, *The IRA at War*, 96.
[83] J. F. Homan 'Memorandum of Ambulance Work and Efforts for Peace' (NA, D/T, S8138).

election.[84] The result was that almost four decades of electoral dominance by the Home Rule party was ended when Sinn Fein won 69 out of 72 seats in the future area of the Irish state. Indeed, over the following three years Sinn Fein encountered little political opposition outside of Ulster, and even the representatives of the small Anglo-Irish minority were forced to come to terms with it.[85]

The fact that the push for independence coincided with democratization is clearly important, since successful secessions have generally happened a few years after the introduction of universal suffrage. Secession, as opposed to decolonization, is an extremely rare event in world politics, and requires two perceptions—confidence in the outcome of secession, and fear in the Union—to be present at the same time. In the 1918 general election fear of conscription and the promise of recognition at Versailles conspired to produce a mandate for secession in Ireland. Nevertheless, secessions are still improbable in well-established democracies because the two perceptions are unlikely to exist simultaneously at a high level of intensity.[86] As there was strong domestic and external resistance to Sinn Fein between 1918 and 1921, confidence in secession in Ireland was bound to waver, especially when the prospect of international recognition receded with the end of the Versailles talks. On the other hand, since the general direction of British legislation, after the disestablishment of the Church of Ireland in 1869, also benefited Catholics, intense fear in the Union was unlikely to be a long-term factor either.

For these reasons, short-term catalysts, such as the prospect of recognition at Versailles and the threat of conscription in 1918, were necessary in order for secessionists to convince a majority to vote for them. British counter-insurgency measures also had a radicalizing effect. According to Hart, in the 1920 elections to rural district councils Sinn Fein won over 70 per cent of the seats, compared to only 30 per cent of the seats or urban councils.[87] The following year the British government held elections to the 'parliament of southern Ireland' created by the Government of Ireland Act of 1920, but Sinn Fein candidates were returned unopposed in all constituencies, and instead attended the Second Dail, a parliament that remained unrecognized by the British. This combination of electoral victories fundamentally affected Sinn Fein's self-image. In November 1921 its message to Pope Benedict XV stated that 'the independence of Ireland has been formally proclaimed by the regularly elected representatives of the people of Ireland, and ratified by subsequent plebiscites'.[88]

The representative nature of these landslides has been questioned by historians, but few could argue that Sinn Fein had concealed its intentions from the public, or

---

[84] J. Coakley, 'The Election That Made the First Dail', in B. Farrell (ed.), *The Creation of the Dail: A Volume of Essays from the Thomas Davis Lecture* (Dublin, 1994), 36.

[85] P. Buckland, *Irish Unionism 1885–1922* (London, 1973), 39.

[86] S. Dion, 'Why is Secession Difficult in Well-Established Democracies? Lessons from Quebec', *British Journal of Political Science*, 26 (1996), 271.

[87] Hart, *The IRA at War*, 53.

[88] *Irish Bulletin*, 6/2 (21 October 1921).

that the public was ignorant of the choices being presented to them.[89] What seems
to have happened instead is that once the Treaty was signed, public opinion was
transformed, precisely because of the factors identified by Dion. Fear of the Union
was reduced when the Treaty gave the 26 counties a status comparable to that of
Canada, and also opened up a peaceful route to full independence in an increasingly democratic Commonwealth. On the other hand, confidence in secession was
lowered with the partition of the country in 1920, and diminished further when it
became clear that it could only be accomplished through 'terrible and immediate
war', with even less international sympathy than before. As a result of the failure of
Irish diplomacy, what was once presented to the world as a classic case of
decolonization came increasingly to have all the connotations of secession. By
1922 the short-term catalysts had receded into the background, and the peace
enjoyed during the truce increased the gulf between public opinion and the elitist
traditions of the IRA. Republicans have argued that the shift in public opinion was
essentially 'manufactured', especially by the press, but the spontaneous nature of
the change in favour of peace, especially at the local level, where the vast majority
of governing bodies supported the Treaty, has impressed historians.[90]

Either way, rival interpretations of the nature of this turnabout would clearly
affect attitudes to the Treaty, which in turn raised issues about the location of
status and influence in the new state. Since the formation of the Catholic
Commercial Club in 1881, Catholics had been making inroads into the associ-
ational life of the country, and since in this period the effects of expansions in
education were being felt, a native upper middle-class Catholic elite, largely
assimilated into the values and structures of the Anglo-Irish minority, was now
being formed. Paseta documents the ambiguous relationship this Catholic elite
had with the preoccupations of the Gaelic Revival, but concludes that they saw
the future in terms of a Home Rule and imperial settlement and aspired to play a
leading role in that order.[91] However, 1918 had seen a shift in sentiment away from
the Home Rule party among those sections, such as the business elite, the large
farmers, and the clergy, that were traditionally the dominant forces in Irish
politics. When these groups withdrew their support for the republican cause in
1922, their reversal of fortune was dramatic. Although the Treaty was only
narrowly accepted by the Dail on 7 January 1922, by 64 votes to 57, this only
suggests that the Dail was more radical than the electorate as a whole. As Regan
remarks, because most of its deputies had originally been elected in the 1918
general election, during which the IRB conspired to ensure the new assembly
would be drawn from the militarist-republican wing, the Dail over represented
the radicals within Sinn Fein.[92] Indeed, the poor performance of the anti-treaty

[89] Hart, *The IRA at War*, 25.
[90] Lyons, 'The Great Debate', 255.
[91] S. Paseta, *Before the Revolution: Nationalism, Social Change and Ireland's Catholic Elite, 1879–1922* (Cork, 1999), 148.
[92] J. M. Regan, *The Irish Counter-revolution 1921–36: Treatyite Politics and Settlement in Independent Ireland* (Dublin, 1999), 40

candidates in the 'pact election' on 16 June 1922 led the Provisional Government to interpret the election as giving a clear mandate to implement the Treaty. The republican position, upheld by 124 members in the Second Dail, would only be represented by 36 members out of 128 in the Third Dail.

The pro-treaty view of this turnaround was that the elections between 1918 and 1921 were irregular elections, producing 'manufactured' majorities, and that the 1922 election had simply returned a more representative body. Since 1917 Sinn Fein itself had been divided between moderates and radicals, with a large section, perhaps a majority, believing that the Republic was no more than a synonym for independence. De Valera admitted as much in March 1923:

> When I speak of the group which Mr Griffith represented, I do not at all of course mean his old followers—'the intellectual Sinn Feiners', as you call them—they were negligible almost. But to my mind he could be taken as largely representing the residue of nationalism when the Fenian and Volunteer elements were taken out of it. This residue was all the time conscious that it was numerically the stronger group and was constantly under the temptation of trying its strength in this respect to make its own view prevail. Certain of the Bishops in particular never ceased to be busy urging that disastrous policy. The Fenian element—the young fighting men—were the point of our spearhead, and to fling these aside or put them into antagonism ought to have been obvious as national madness.[93]

Pro-treatyites believed that the anti-treatyites' problem with the Treaty in 1922 was simply that democratization had generated too much pluralism, something at odds with the monopolistic traditions of Irish nationalism as it had developed over the previous fifty years. Popular support for the Treaty showed that the nation was really composed of different elements, each with its own agenda and interests, as opposed to the myth of the unified nation that had been erected after 1916.[94] Once the results of the 1922 election became known, the issue of democratic legitimacy then became crucial for the pro-treaty self-image: during the civil war Kevin O'Higgins, the Minister for Home Affairs, wrote that 'the fanatics and pseudo intellectuals, who would murder it (the nation) for a formula, must be met and beaten by those who have a democratic mandate to control its destiny'.[95]

Yet the shift of public opinion in 1922 raises a crucial question. If Dion's rational choice framework does explain the turnaround, the question is why pro-treaty arguments were not persuasive for the whole movement, in the way that Commonwealth membership was the rational option for decolonizing British territories after 1945. Put another way: how did it happen that the people who had fought the War of Independence, and whose admiration for Collins was unbounded, failed to see the force of his arguments in support of the Treaty?[96] On the one hand, the anti-treaty response to the Treaty was intimately linked to their

---

[93] De Valera to O'Brien, 16 March 1923 (UCD, NA, P150/1622).
[94] Kissane, *Explaining Irish Democracy*, 149.
[95] Typescript copy of an article to a US newspaper by Kevin O'Higgins, 1922–3 (UCD, P35C/160).
[96] A. Clifford, *The Constitutional History of Eire/Ireland* (Belfast, 1987), 299.

belief that the Irish public did not possess a particularly strong nationalist consciousness: in his inaugural speech at the founding of the Irish volunteers Padraig Pearse had actually said that the history of Ireland in the nineteenth century was the desperate attempt of a mob trying to recreate itself as a nation.[97] Heroic leadership had succeeded in galvanizing public support behind the Republic in 1916 where constitutional methods had failed. The corollary of this belief was that such a consciousness would be further weakened when normal political conditions returned. Like Franz Fanon, the anti-treatyites felt that their nation was 'an empty shell, a crude and fragile travesty of what it might have been', and that the assimilative power of the Empire could not be reversed under the terms of the Treaty.[98] The anti-treaty explanation for the electoral turnaround in 1922 had been that the rising and the elections that followed had disturbed the traditional power relationships in Irish society, which were then reasserted when the Treaty was signed, and the press and the clergy in particular played a key role in browbeating the public into supporting it. In 1922 the anti-treatyites had a very definite fear that this old order was re-establishing itself, which would put a brake on their aspirations for the future. In November 1922 their leadership addressed the following message to their troops:

They tell some of you that the Free State is to be only a stepping stone to the Republic. Surely you are not fools—such fools as to believe them. Allow the 'Free State' once to be set up and Irishmen in future who try to secure the Republic will be branded as rebels, as we are branded now, and will be shot down by the King's 'Free State' troops, as we are being shot down now. The Unionists, the Churches, the Press, and all who will have secured vested interests in the new regime will unite together to crush those who would stand for the Republic, just as they are uniting in their efforts to crush us. You have only to look around you to see the national demoralisation that has already set in. The Gaelic outlook is disappearing, and jobbery, corruption, and West Britonism everywhere in the ascendant. Make no mistake about it, those who will in the future re-establish the Republic if it be lost now, will need another Gaelic revival and will have to face another revolution and a new civil war, in which England will again side with the enemies of the Republic. The moral position will be more obscure, and their difficulties in every way be ten times what ours are.[99]

Yet this pessimism with regard to the prospects of Irish nationalism under the Treaty also reflected differences in the geo-political contexts. When the other former colonies of the British Empire were faced with the choice of whether to become members of the Commonwealth after 1945, the question was also whether memories of conquest and a sense of past exploitation would carry them to an independence beyond the confines of the Empire?[100] For various reasons, the

---

[97] B. Clifford, *The Irish Civil War: The Conflict That Formed the State* (Cork, 1993).

[98] F. Fanon, *The Wretched of the Earth* (London, 1963), 119.

[99] 'Address from the Soldiers of the Army of the Republic to Their Former Comrades in the Free State Army and the Civic Guard—signed on Behalf of the Soldiers of the Republic, Liam Lynch and Eamon de Valera—November 23 1922' (Dublin, 1922, NL Ir 320, p. 114).

[100] N. Mansergh, *The Commonwealth Experience, volume 2: From British to Multi-racial Commonwealth* (London, 1982), 163–201.

leaders of these new states were able to distinguish between the Commonwealth as a multiracial ideal and the British Empire, with its associations with racial superiority and economic exploitation. Britain after all had not generally opposed the independence projects in these colonies, and sought rather to influence them in a democratic direction. For British elites the Commonwealth ideal softened their opposition to decolonization, whereas in Ireland Tory opposition to Home Rule was of recent memory, and the civil war was seen by the anti-treatyites as a continuation of the War of Independence. Much was made, for example, of Lord Birkenhead's remark in the House of Lords on 8 March 1922 that the Treaty could be implemented with 'an economy of English lives'.[101] Moreover, for the colonies in Asia and Africa, the imperial centre was a distant land separated from the peripheries by thousands of miles, so (unlike in Ireland) the Commonwealth was not seen simply as an expression of Britishness.[102] A formula that guaranteed the freedom of Canada could not be applied to Ireland, whose fate was more closely bound up with that of the imperial heartland. Finally, the post-1945 colonies had in India a powerful example of a large colony that had chosen the Commonwealth of its own free will, and then played much the same role in democratizing the organization that the Irish Free State did in the 1920s and 1930s.

In other words, the choice the Irish were faced with in 1922 was a much more invidious one. The anti-treaty republicans were not able to make a distinction between the Empire and the Commonwealth, whereas the pro-treaty elite accurately predicted the latter's long-term direction of development: famously Collins argued that the Treaty was a 'stepping stone' to greater freedom. Much depended on the question of trust. Kevin O'Higgins conceded that the threat of force that lay behind the Treaty meant that the status between the two islands was not really equal, but it could in time evolve into that position. In contrast, Erskine Childers, the constitutional thinker on the anti-treaty side, argued that Ireland's close geographical proximity to Britain meant that equality of status could never exist on the Canadian model.[103] With regard to the 26 counties, O'Higgins was proved ultimately right, but in 1922 the only available precedent similar to that of India after 1945 was Canada, but here the conception of nationality also mattered. Lloyd George had never denied the existence of a distinct Irish nationality, but thought that it could only find expression in a British context where the geographical contiguity of the two islands and their economic and strategic interdependence were obvious facts. He denied the Irish not a separate culture, but a separate history.[104] Sinn Fein, on the other hand, rejected his analogy with the southern states of the United States, on the grounds that the appropriate parallels for Ireland were European. Its organ, the *Irish Bulletin* argued:

---

[101] 'The Drama of Eight Days' (UCD, de Valera Papers, P150/1628).
[102] White, *Decolonisation: The British Experience since 1945*, 100.
[103] N. Mansergh,, *The Unresolved Question: The Anglo-Irish Settlement and its Undoing 1912–72* (New Haven and London, 1991), 206.
[104] *Irish Bulletin*, 5/34 (18 July 1921).

The attempt of the Prime Minister of England to draw an analogy between the case of the southern States and Ireland shows how desperately necessary England feels it to be to stand well with the opinion of America. There is no analogy. The Southern states formed an integral part of one nation and have never enjoyed a separate existence. Ireland and England are different nations, and Ireland enjoyed for fourteen hundred years a separate political existence. That existence England has attempted to crush by force of arms. England holds Ireland as Russia held Poland—not as the United States held its constituent elements. The analogy of Ireland is not the Southern states but Poland. The analogue of England's Prime Minister is not Abraham Lincoln but the Russian Czar.[105]

From this perspective, a Treaty that suggested that Ireland had a permanent place in an Empire united by the British Crown clearly involved a rejection of those symbols that expressed Irish aspirations to be a European nation.

Ultimately, responses to this settlement were influenced by the rival traditions that dated back to before the First World War. De Valera later remarked that the problem with the Treaty was that it ignored the sentiment that made the revolutionary struggle possible.[106] On the other hand, the type of nationalism that triumphed in the civil war saw the Commonwealth as an appropriate arena for the pursuit of Irish national interests, and for the expression of Ireland's distinct identity. Notoriously, Kevin O'Higgins told the Dail that the Irish could go into the Empire with their heads held up.[107] What triumphed in 1922 (after Collins' death), in other words, was not so much Irish nationalism, but a particular form of liberalism that had its roots in the Home Rule era. Without the Treaty, the contrary tendencies within the movement might never have found open expression and a fatal choice might have been avoided, but the 1921 settlement clearly touched the nerve centre of a movement that had imagined its past and future in non-colonial terms. From this vantage point, Irish nationalism and British imperialism were bound to collide, not simply because of the imbalance in power between the two, but because both hung onto very different versions of the same history.

CONCLUSION

The problem with looking back before the 1916 Rising to find a root cause for the civil war in the different traditions of Irish nationalism is that there was nothing inherently incompatible between these traditions. The fact that a noted *gaelgoir* such as Eoin MacNeill should accept the Treaty for much the same reasons as Kevin O'Higgins suggests as much. However, the presence of essentially pragmatic attitudes on the pro-treaty side should not obscure the fact that given the conception of Irish identity that had developed during the revival, there was much less room for variation in the anti-treaty argument. Indeed, once the

---

[105] *Irish Bulletin*, 22 June 1920.
[106] De Valera to Loftus, 31 October 1922 (UCD, de Valera papers, P150/1647).
[107] Regan, *The Irish Counter-revolution*, 84.

fighting began, and once the 'stepping-stone' perspective lost its influence with the death of Collins, the polarity of views, and the extent to which they reflected older political traditions, is striking. Take away their limited enthusiasm for the Irish language, and the thought categories and values of the Cosgrave administration were entirely Victorian. Of course distinguishing between 'root causes', which form the preconditions of crises, and 'catalysts', which work upon these root causes to increase their level of significance, is open to the objection that it obscures the complexity of a civil war situation. Nevertheless, the evidence suggests that the Treaty touched the nerve centre of a nationalist movement with long-standing differences on the question of Empire.

Does this mean then that the civil war can be attributed to a universal process, that of decolonization, and that the role native genius played in creating the Irish conflict has been overplayed by historians? On the one hand, the fact that dominion status was offered to Sinn Fein in 1921 when freedom generally meant separation from the Empire rather than free association forms a counterpoint to the largely consensual experience of British decolonization after 1945. The relevant analogies were with the white Commonwealth, but these were at odds with Sinn Fein's conception of its own history. The crucial point is that the pro-treatyites were able to distinguish between the Empire and the Commonwealth in the way that the post-1945 colonies did, and with the benefit of hindsight they have ultimately won the Treaty argument. During the Dail debates Collins remarked that they had got rid of the word 'Empire' in the Treaty, since in it the Empire was called (for the first time) 'the Community of Nations known as the British Empire'.[108] Yet this only underscores how central the imperial context was to the Irish divisions, and it is no surprise that a minority of what was in many ways an anti-colonial nationalist movement saw in the Treaty not the cradle, but the graveyard of Irish national aspirations. On the other hand, the comparison with Algeria and the Philippines also shows that the proclivity to internal conflict in Ireland was pronounced. The Irish civil war was clearly a more 'public' conflict, partly because Irish national identity was much more developed in 1922, but also because Irish nationalist elites could better claim to be representative of public opinion.

This in turn raises another issue. Did the democratization of Ireland under the Union make it easier to resolve the Irish question, or did it prepare the way not only for partition and the subsequent dislocation, but also for the southern civil war? It is usually thought that the advent of democracy brings with it a diffusion of pacific norms, which then guide societies through periods of crisis, even in the absence of strong institutions.[109] The problem in Ireland, however, was that in 1914 majority rule was to be applied in a society where regular elections, the growth of civil society, and mass mobilization had already sharpened rather than

---

[108] See N. Mansergh, *The Unresolved Question*, 204.
[109] R. Axelrod, 'An Evolutionary Approach to Norms', *American Political Science Review*, 80 (1986), 1095–111.

blurred conflicting identities.[110] Indeed Hart argues that without the communal
mobilization between nationalists and unionists before 1914, and the paramilitary
politics it gave rise to, the southern civil war may well have been averted in 1922.[111]
Clearly democracy is no panacea in divided societies. Majority rule, the normal
decision-making rule in a state where membership of the political community
has been settled, can only be allowed to decide which group can exercise sovereignty over a territory, at the cost of alienating minorities. As Richard Bourke
suggests, a democratic state cannot credibly be presented 'as the property of some
part of its membership, however large'.[112] When its exercise does imply ownership
of a state, as it did in both parts of Ireland after 1921, the result is the alienation of
the ethnic minority. Nonetheless, Irish democracy could only work when power
and security was ceded, north and south, to ethnic majorities.[113] In both cases this
process was accompanied by something like civil war.

[110] Lieven, *Empire: The Russian Empire and Its Rivals*, 365.
[111] Hart, *The IRA at War*, 107.
[112] See Bourke, *Peace in Ireland*, Introduction.
[113] Hart, *The IRA at War*, 109.

3

The Doctrine of Self-determination and the Treaty Split

The doctrine of self-determination has been exposed to a variety of critiques, ranging from the charge that it is philosophically incoherent, to the argument that it cannot work in practice, to the claim that groups that exercise a right to self-determination invariably deny it to others.[1] More recently, it has been argued that no state has ever been formed out of a democratic exercise of self-determination, but this at least is not true.[2] Norway is a classic example, and the legitimizing principles of the Irish state were also couched in the language of self-determination: indeed the right of the Irish people to self-determination is written into Article 1 of the 1937 constitution. Speaking to the League of Nations on 16 September 1935 de Valera remarked that 'we find ourselves restored again as a separate recognised member of the European family to which we belong'.[3] Yet the 'restoration' was not so painless. It involved partition in 1920 and the civil war in 1922–3. By December 1921 faith in self-determination had waned so much that during the debates on the Treaty nobody mentioned the concept at all. On the other hand, the establishment of the Irish Free State under the terms of the Treaty has been seen as an exercise in self-determination, although republicans have always maintained that Ireland had been denied the right to self-determination since the 1918 general election.[4] The civil war that resulted from the Treaty was a conflict that exposed the fault line between these two contrary views. Despite this, there has been little effort by historians to unearth what exactly was meant by self-determination between 1918 and 1921, whether it was reducible to the demand for an Irish Republic, or to assess the extent to which the civil war reflected what Woodrow Wilson called the 'metaphysical tragedy' inherent in the concept. After reviewing the political background in which the claim was first made, what follows analyses the case made for Irish self-determination up to 1921, and the extent to which it had practical consequences once the Treaty was signed.

[1] See A. Cobban, *The Nation State and National Self-Determination* (London and Glasgow, 1969), 163.
[2] E. Hobsbawm, *The New Century: In Conversation with Antonio Polito* (London, 2000), 23.
[3] E. de Valera, *De Valera: Peace and War* (NL, IR 94109 D27), 46.
[4] A. Carty, *Was Ireland Conquered?: International Law and the Irish Question* (London 1996), 113. For the republican view, see G. Adams, *Free Ireland: Towards a Lasting Peace* (Dingle, 1995), 236.

THE POLITICAL BACKGROUND

In December 1921 Arthur Griffith, the founder of Sinn Fein, alluded to a time before the First World War when the cause of complete independence for Ireland was kept alive only by a few dozen people.[5] However, in the period between the Easter Rising of 1916 and the conclusion of the War of Independence in June 1921, the political landscape was transformed by the rise to dominance of Sinn Fein, which renounced a century-old tradition of attendance at Westminster, and committed the country to complete independence. Although a number of domestic factors may explain how the party arrived at that position—the delay in implementing Home Rule before the war, the executions of the leaders of the Rising, and the democratization of the franchise in 1918—arguably a chief catalyst for the radicalization of nationalist demands was an external one: the convening of a peace conference in Paris in January 1919 and Woodrow Wilson's desire to base the new international order on principles that were fair to small nations. What followed in Ireland was a heightening of expectations, a glut of political propaganda, and the systematic mobilization of all those ties of affection and purpose that united Ireland with its diaspora in the English-speaking world. Paradoxically, Sinn Fein, literally meaning 'ourselves alone', placed its prospects of success on its ability to win international support.[6] So much so that it was claimed by some that Sinn Fein could be accurately translated as 'self-determination'.[7]

On 3 March 1917 *Nationality*, the newspaper edited by Griffith, declared:

The political objective of Ireland today is admission to the Peace Conference. Nothing else political now matters. Mr O'Connor's Free Institutions, Mr Redmond's Home Rule on the Statute Book and their Masters' Imperial Conference are of no account to Ireland. Ireland is out of the corner where for generations she had been hidden away from the world. She is no longer an island lying behind England—she is again politically, as well as geographically, part of Europe.[8]

Going back as far as the summer of 1915 Irish nationalists had attended a conference held by the *Union des Nationalites* in Paris and gave their assent to a resolution supporting the right to self-determination for small nationalities. The conference was attended by representatives from Alsace-Lorraine, Armenia, Belgium, Bohemia, Bulgaria, Catalonia, Denmark, Finland, Ireland, the Lebanon, Lithuania, Rumania, and Serbia alongside Jewish representatives and some Letts.[9] One of the attractions of such company was that it allowed Irish nationalists to claim that Ireland was a European island with claims no less well founded than those of Europe's other nationalities.[10] *Nationality* pointed out that

    [5] A. Griffith, *Arguments for the Treaty* (Dublin, 1922), 13.
    [6] D. McCartney, 'De Valéra's Mission to the United States 1919–20', in A. Cosgrove and D. McCartney (eds.), *Studies in Irish History Presented to R. Dudley Edwards* (Dublin, 1979), 304.
    [7] *Nationality*, 2 December 1918.
    [8] *Nationality*, 3 March 1917.   [9] *Nationality*, 14 August 1915.
    [10] 'Sinn Fein Statement to the International Socialist Conference at Stockholm, December 1917', His Majesty's Stationary Office (HMSO), *Correspondence Relating to the Proposal for Her Majesty's Government for an Irish Settlement* (London, 1921), Appendix B, 57

Three years ago Poland had no National Government, no Parliament, no free political institutions. The Russian bureaucrats governed Poland from the Castle at Warsaw, by edict, by order in council, by proclamation. The Polish language was banned and the Polish past ignored in the teachings of the schools. Save that the Russian Government in Poland did not diminish the Polish population by artificial famine and destroy Poland's industries in the interests of the Russian manufacturers it would be possible to believe that Poland was an island in the Atlantic Ocean.[11]

In June 1917 'the Irish Provisional Government' contacted the American and Russian governments declaring that it was willing to have the Irish issue decided by a democratic plebiscite, provided that it was supervised by their representatives.[12] During the conscription crisis of that year, representatives of Labour, the Irish Parliamentary Party, and Sinn Fein signed a declaration protesting that the British government's plans to impose conscription on the Irish contravened the general principle of self-determination, thus enabling a purely domestic British issue to become one of international rights and justice.[13] At the Volunteer convention held in Dublin on 17 October 1917, de Valera, President of Sinn Fein, told the audience that his policy was to appeal to the Peace Conference, and should that appeal fail they would achieve their objectives by force. In December of the same year, Sinn Fein presented a statement to the International Socialist Conference at Stockholm, appealing to the Great Powers to recognize that the complete independence of Ireland was also 'an essential and indispensable' condition for the liberty of the seas.[14] On 12 December 1918 the Foreign Affairs Committee of the House of Representatives heard statements from prominent Irish-Americans requesting the American commissioners to the Peace Conference to present the Irish case to the Paris Peace Conference. In 1919 both the Senate and the House of Representatives passed motions supportive of the Irish case for a hearing at Versailles.

What galvanized the Irish case for self-determination, however, was not a diplomatic coup in the wider world, but Sinn Fein's dramatic victory at the 1918 general election, where it virtually wiped out the Parliamentary Party, and secured three-quarters of the seats in the future area of independent Ireland. De Valera recalled in 1921:

Five years ago men and women who knew the mind and understood the heart of our nation proclaimed this Republic. Within three years their judgement was put to the test, was definitely passed upon and confirmed by the overwhelming majority in a national plebiscite. The Republic in 1916, provisional and open to question before the elections of December 1918, was by these elections placed on a foundation of certitude either in point of fact or of moral right. Those who question the moral validity of the Republic now must challenge the foundations of Democracy and the constitutional rights of people everywhere.[15]

---

[11] *Nationality*, 28 August 1917.　　[12] HMSO, op. cit.
[13] M. Moynihan (ed.), *Speeches and Statements by Eamon de Valera 1917–1973* (Dublin, 1980), 52
[14] HMSO, op. cit.
[15] 'President de Valera States the National Position—Interview with Representative of "International News" and "Universal Service"', 30 March 30 1921 (NL, 11B 300 P2).

Sinn Fein had promised voters in 1918 that if elected it would withdraw its MPs from Westminster, form an alternative assembly in Dublin, and use every means possible to end British rule in Ireland. Gavan Duffy, Sinn Fein's Minister of Foreign Affairs, also informed the American President that should Ireland's case be ignored in Paris, violent conflict would inevitably ensue.[16] The tactic of abstentionism and the claim for self-determination were also inextricably linked. Voters during the 1918 election were told by Sinn Fein that if the people voted for the Parliamentary Party, President Wilson would refuse to hear the Irish case at Versailles.[17] It was essential to Sinn Fein that Ireland be no longer treated as 'a domestic problem of the British Empire', and 'Self-Determination for Ireland Leagues' emerged in Australia, Britain, Canada, Newfoundland, New Zealand, and some South American countries, to that end.[18] Sinn Fein's election manifesto in 1918 had promised to appeal to the Peace Conference for the establishment of Ireland as an independent nation, and in January 1919, after declaring independence for the 32 counties, its message to the free nations of the world also demanded that Ireland be allowed to face England at the Peace Conference. The Declaration itself asked for 'the recognition and support of every free nation in the world'. Three delegates, de Valera, Count Plunkett, and Griffith, were appointed by the Dail to make Ireland's case to the conference, and Sean T. O'Kelly was sent to Paris as an accredited envoy of the Republic to negotiate a hearing for the Irish delegates.[19]

Self-determination is primarily a doctrine of how international society should be organized, but since it became current only during the First World War, it did not function as a clearly worked-out ideology in Irish nationalist politics. After 1918 Sinn Fein's propaganda was directed more at the international than the domestic audience, and nearly all the documents attesting to the importance of the doctrine in the movement attest to this fact.[20] Nevertheless, within the broad church of Irish nationalism there was consensus on the precise meaning of self-determination. The Parliamentary Party defined it as meaning 'that all nations, large and small, should have free self-determination as to their form of government and that no people should be ruled and dominated even in their own internal affairs by arbitrary and irresponsible force instead of their own will and choice'.[21] The Irish Labour Party told the international socialist conference at Berne in February 1919 that it supported the self-determination of peoples 'in choosing the sovereignty and form of government under which it will live', and

---

[16] G. Duffy, 'An Urgent Preliminary Note for the Information of the President of the United States of America with Regard to Ireland and the Peace Conference', 28 December 1918 (NA, Gavan Duffy Papers, 1125/15/2).

[17] Untitled Sinn Fein poster (NL IR 94109, 109).

[18] *Nationality*, 2 December 1918.

[19] McCartney, 'De Valera's Mission', 304.

[20] K. Inoue, 'Propaganda 11: Propaganda of Dail Eireann, 1919–1921', in J. Augusteijn (ed.), *The Irish Revolution, 1913–1923* (Basingstoke, 2002), 87–102.

[21] 'Ireland's Appeal to President Wilson: Irish Parliamentary Party Reiterates the National Claim', 5 November 1918, NL.

this choice should be exercised 'without any military, political, or economic pressure from outside'.[22] Patrick McCarten, official Sinn Fein envoy to the United States, told the Foreign Affairs Committee of the House of Representatives in December 1918 that self-determination meant 'leaving to the Irish people themselves the decision as to the form and character of the government they want to live under'.[23] In January 1920 a meeting of the Catholic Bishops at Maynooth declared that the only way to resolve the Anglo-Irish conflict was to allow an undivided Ireland to choose its own form of government.[24] The Canadian, South African, New Zealand, Australian, and British Self-Determination Leagues together approved a formula giving Ireland the choice 'to choose freely, without coercion or dictation from outside, their own governmental institutions, and their political relationship with other States and peoples'.[25] In 1920 de Valera declared that the Irish case for self-determination rested on three moral bases: (1) that the people of every nation had a right to choose the governmental institutions under which they should live, (2) that Ireland was a nation, and (3) that the Irish people had, in fact, determined their government and declared their will in an unmistakeable manner.[26]

The external version of the doctrine implies a right for people to chose the sovereignty under which they live, whereas the internal version means the right of people to chose their own form of government.[27] In Ireland it was not possible to disentangle the two strands, since, as Regan puts it, republicans believed that sovereignty was a prerequisite for the Irish electorate expressing itself freely.[28] This view lay behind the compromise position on policy adopted by the Sinn Fein *Ard Fheis* on 26 October 1917. Hardliners wanted a commitment to the isolated Republic proclaimed in 1916, while moderates like Griffith, who had earlier advocated the Hungarian Dual Kingdom as a model for Anglo-Irish relations, thought that it would be a mistake to make a republic their aim. As Laffan remarks, some Sinn Feiners understood the goal of the Republic in the literal sense: their mission was to make real the Republic declared in 1916. For others republican status was no more than a synonym for independence.[29] The compromise that ensued reflected the spirit of the 1916 Proclamation, whose leaders

[22] 'Statement of International Aims Presented by the National Executive of the Irish Labour Party and Unanimously Endorsed by the Special Congress at its Sitting on Friday 1 November 1918', *Ireland at Berne: Being the Report and Memoranda Presented to the International Labour and Socialist Conference Held at Berne, February 1919* (Dublin, 1919).
[23] *The Irish Question: Hearings before the Committee on Foreign Affairs, House of Representatives Sixty-fifth Congress, Third Session, 12 December 1918* (Washington, 1919), 87.
[24] (UCD, de Valera Papers, P150/643).
[25] R. Davis, 'The Self-Determination for Ireland Leagues, and the Irish Race Convention in Paris, 1921–22', *Tasmanian Historical Research Association—Papers and Proceedings*, 24 (1977).
[26] E. de Valera, 'The Moral Basis of the Claim of the Elected Government of the Republic of Ireland for Official Recognition', a speech delivered at Worcester, Mass., 6 February 1920 (New York).
[27] B. Neuberger, 'National Self-Determination: Dilemmas of a Concept', *Nations and Nationalism* 1 (1995), 298.
[28] J. Regan, *The Irish Counter-revolution* (Dublin, 1999), 69.
[29] M. Laffan, 'Sinn Fein from Dual Monarchy to the First Dáil', in B. Farrell (ed.), *The Creation of the Dáil* (Dublin, 1994), 25.

had assumed the mantle of a Provisional Government but committed themselves to allowing the people to elect their own government once the franchise was democratized. In 1917 Sinn Fein declared its aim to be the securing of international recognition of Ireland as an independent Irish Republic, but once that status was achieved, the Irish people may by referendum freely chose their own form of government.

However, if the bedrock of self-determination was the freedom to chose your own form of government, the belief that the choice of Ireland would inevitably be for a republic became equally well founded. One Sinn Fein MP, Mary MacSwiney, told the American Commission on Conditions in Ireland in 1919 that the 1918 election had been more 'an anti-parliamentary party election' rather than 'a pro-republican election', but that the 1920 local elections had resolved the issue.[30] The British press had suggested that the 1918 election result was not due to public support for separation, but to the fear of conscription and other causes arising from the war. However, for the elections to local bodies in January and June 1920, over a year after the war, the British government introduced PR to fragment the Sinn Fein vote, and out of the total number of local boards republicans apparently won 83.1 per cent. As de Valera put it, the Irish Republic had been founded 'in the vote of the people'.[31] Nevertheless, when Sinn Fein addressed a message to the free nations of the world in January 1919 it spoke of the 1918 election as 'ratifying' the proclamation of the Republic in 1916. During his tour of the United States in 1920, de Valera also carried with him a pamphlet called *The Testament of the Republic*, containing the proclamation of the Republic in 1916 alongside the texts of the declaration of independence, the constitution of Sinn Fein, and other documents.[32] So although he declared on 23 June 1919 that he was head of a republic 'established by the will of the people, in accordance with the principle of self-determination', others maintained that it was the 1916 Rising not the democratic 1918 election that had established this Republic.[33] This was to remain the hardline republican interpretation of what happened.[34]

If Ireland had been a European isle far removed from the British mainland, these ambiguities would not have mattered, but further afield there was no consensus on the wisdom of aiming for the isolated Republic. In the dominions the Self-Determination Leagues adopted a policy in favour of self-determination that was capable of securing the support of nationalists who were not enthusiastic about Sinn Fein's tactics, and naturally enough, in Australia, Canada, New Zealand, and South Africa, self-determination was not seen as incompatible with membership of the Commonwealth.[35] The main Irish-American pressure group was the Friends of Irish Freedom formed in 1916. It too was in favour of

[30] M. MacSwiney, *The Background of the Irish Republic* (Chicago, 1921), 33.
[31] E. de Valera, *The Foundation of the Republic of Ireland in the Vote of the People* (Melbourne?, 1919).
[32] E. de Valera, *The Testament of the Republic* (NL LO P101).
[33] Moynihan, *Speeches and Statements*, 29.
[34] *Oglaigh na h-Eireann* (June 1932; NL LO P101).
[35] Davis, 'The Self-Determination for Ireland Leagues'.

Irish self-determination, but Irish-American opinion became so split on the issue of the isolated Republic that in 1920 de Valera ended up founding the American Association for the Recognition of the Irish Republic, which had upholding 'the existing Republic of Ireland' as its chief aim.[36] This split over whether the republican principle should give way to a more accommodating interpretation of self-determination also reflected the hopelessness of the Sinn Fein strategy. Sinn Fein won only an Irish victory in the 1918 general election, but the Conservative-Unionist Party had also won 338 seats in the House of Commons, and Lloyd George remained dependent on their support for his coalition.[37] Lloyd George himself believed that ceding a Republic to Sinn Fein would create the impression that the British government had lost grip on the Empire, and he revealed his preference for an offer of dominion status to the cabinet only in 1921.[38] The Peace Conference opened at Paris on 18 January 1919, but the two Irish envoys failed to get a hearing. In May 1919 the signing of the Covenant of the League of Nations, in so far as it guaranteed the territorial integrity of its members, effectively undermined Ireland's claim.[39] In America de Valera failed to achieve the recognition that Thomas Masaryk and Ignace Paderewski had got for Czechoslovakia and Poland in 1918. The Irish Race Convention held in Philadelphia in February 1919 had appointed a committee of twenty-five to use all honourable means to secure for Ireland her right to self-determination.[40] President Wilson met with two of their representatives on 11 June 1919 and stated that he could not raise the Irish issue officially but promised to pursue the Irish case unofficially.[41] Privately he confessed his first impulse was to tell the representatives 'to go to hell'.[42] Peace was signed at Versailles on 28 June 1919. In a journal kept by Thomas Jones, Lloyd George's cabinet secretary during the Versailles talks, only two entries for the whole of 1919 mention the Irish question.[43]

The freedom to chose one's own form of government was an aspiration bound to resonate internationally, since it was written into the American Declaration of Independence, but Sinn Fein was divided on whether the aim of self-determination was true internationally recognized sovereignty, i.e., the Republic, or the establishment of a political system that possessed the consent of the governed. The very ambiguity of the doctrine was an asset for those, like de Valera, who wanted to maintain a united front. De Valera also believed in 1917 that 'the only banner under which our freedom can be won at the present time is

---

[36] 'Constitution of the American Association for the Recognition of the Irish Republic' (NL P2167).

[37] I. Lustick, *Unsettled States: Disputed Lands: Britain and Ireland, France and Algeria, Israel and the West Bank-Gaza* (Ithaca, NY and London, 1993), 226.

[38] R. Wilson, 'Imperialism in Crisis: The Irish Dimension', in M. Langan and B. Schwarz (eds.), *Crises in the British State 1880–1930* (London, 1985), 169.

[39] McCartney, 'De Valera's Mission', 306.

[40] *Report on Conditions in Ireland with Demand for Investigation by the Peace Conference* (Paris, 1919).

[41] Anonymous, *Sinn Fein and the Peace Conference: Promises and Performances* (Dublin, 1919).

[42] Cobban, *National Self-Determination*, 66.

[43] Lustick, *Unsettled States*, 231.

the republican banner', since a lesser claim would have undermined the Irish case at Versailles.[44] The tragedy was that as the prospect of international recognition receded, and as the military clampdown intensified, the results of the 1920 local elections and the 1921 general election strengthened the republican case. Indeed it was later argued that the Sinn Fein landslide in the 1921 general election was effectively a protest vote against British counter-insurgency measures.[45] The Republic had initially been chosen because of the need to unify Sinn Fein in 1917, along with the belief that Sinn Fein would 'get all that Ireland has a right to' at Versailles, whereas the Parliamentary Party was determined only 'to take what they get'.[46] However, later elections convinced many that the Republic was more than a tactic, but a symbol itself of the democratic entitlement of Ireland to self-determination. To republicans the 1920 local elections supported that view.

The Irish use of the doctrine of self-determination between 1917 and 1921 shows how the geo-political context shapes the use of nationalist ideas, and the fact that nobody would mention the doctrine at all during the Dail debates on the Treaty is a dramatic illustration of this. Critics might consider Sinn Fein's decision to base its chances of success on a claim for international recognition as naive, but the ultimate attraction of self-determination was that it allowed Sinn Fein to represent itself to the world as more than just a physical force party.[47] It was the acceptable face of the Irish revolution. From the outset Sinn Fein's propaganda had been reluctant to highlight the violent side of its campaign, and the domestic audience had already been won over in 1918.[48] The resort to the language of self-determination was logical in these circumstances. Moreover, self-determination enabled the party to paper over fundamental policy divisions, and in 1923 de Valera recalled that it was his special role to mediate 'the vast fundamental differences' between the ideals of men like Cathal Brugha and Arthur Griffith.[49] Nevertheless, the inherent ambiguity of the concept would resurface with the Treaty split. Was external recognition (i.e., the Republic) really a necessary precondition for the freedom to chose your own form of government, or could Irish self-determination be exercised within the Empire? Standpoints on these issues were always going to be interpreted through the prism of history, and Sinn Fein's version of that history, not the doctrine itself, was the movement's basic ideology.

THE CASE FOR SELF-DETERMINATION

The paradox of nationalism, we are told, is that nations are objectively modern but subjectively ancient. One speaker before the US House of Representatives in

[44] Moynihan, *Speeches and Statements*, 8.
[45] Griffith, *Arguments*, 18.
[46] 'Self-Determination' (election poster 1918), Sinn Fein series, no. 12 (NL IR 94109 P90, 108).
[47] E. de Valera, *Ireland and India* (New York, 1920), 16.
[48] Inoue, 'Propaganda of Dail Eireann', 92.
[49] De Valera to O'Brien, 16 March 1923 (UCD, de Valera Papers, P150/1622).

1918 remarked that Ireland was a nation before Christ was born, after remarking that 'they have a nation over there now'.[50] Indeed a mass separatist movement had emerged only after the traditional social structures of the indigenous society had been destroyed, expressed most clearly by the decline of the Irish language to such an extent that it was spoken only by one person in a hundred in 1900. A remarkable feature of all the propaganda documents produced by Sinn Fein was that none mentioned the collapse of the Irish language. The decline had clearly weakened the objective case for separation but was, during the Gaelic Revival, compensated for by the assertion in legend of Irish national character as a heroic force that could recreate the Gaelic world.[51] This basic reflex to the cultural tragedy of the nineteenth century provided the essence of the separatist ideology, and was to influence hugely the case Sinn Fein made for the Republic, since a lesser status might suggest that Ireland was not a European nation at all, but 'a domestic province of cockneydom' that would have to be legislated for by the British parliament.[52] Ireland's claim, in other words, was not based simply on having been oppressed, or on the possibility that Irish independence would secure the freedom of the seas, but on nationality.[53] Self-determination may have been a doctrine for a new world order, but in Ireland it was interpreted through the prism of history, and Sinn Fein's version of that history had little place for compromise.

It became vital for Sinn Fein not only to show that an Irish nation existed before the Norman invasion of 1169, but also to show that the conquest had never been accepted. To argue otherwise would have made it impossible to base the claim to independence on the grounds of an illegal or illegitimate conquest.[54] At a dinner organized by the 'Friends of Freedom for India' in February 1920 de Valera responded sharply to the suggestion that Ireland had also been conquered, saying that a nation is conquered only when it abandons its cause and this the Irish had never done.[55] In his view the Irish had never accepted a partnership or union with Britain, but had at all times resisted British rule.[56] On the other hand, to isolate the period since the Act of Union in 1800 as a particularly disastrous period of British rule would be to base the claim only on the British government's breach of certain principles of government, and leave the separatist cause vulnerable to the empirical claim that reform was still possible.[57] The nationalist response to this dilemma was to represent the period of the Union as an intensification of the inherent malevolence of British rule. In 1921 de Valera spoke of Ireland surviving

[50] Statement of Revd Philip J. O'Donnell, *The Irish Question*, 28.

[51] S. Deane, *Strange Country: Modernity and Nationhood in Irish Writing since 1900* (Oxford, 1997), 53.

[52] A. de Blacam, *Towards the Republic: A Study of New Ireland's Social and Political Aims* (Dublin, 1918), 5.

[53] *Nationality*, 25 January 1919.

[54] Carty, *Was Ireland Conquered?*, 41.

[55] De Valera, *Ireland and India*, 5.

[56] E. de Valera, 'The Irish People Exercised the Right of Self-Determination and Declared for an Independent Republic', typescript (n.d., UCD, de Valera Papers, P150/687).

[57] See T. H. Jordan, *Pampered Ireland: Fact not Fiction* (Belfast, 1919).

'centuries of attempted assimilation' despite the fact that this really only happened in the nineteenth century.[58]

The basic assumption of the Irish case was that Irish statehood long preceded the Norman invasions of the twelfth century, in fact by a thousand years. It was argued that Ireland was recognized as a sovereign state by the European powers at the Council of Constance in 1417. There the question of precedence arose between the legates of the Charles the Sixth, King of France, and the legates of Henry the Fifth, King of England, and the latter made good of the case of the Irish nation and kingdom to be considered the third in precedence of the four ancient nations of Europe.[59] Sinn Fein also emphasized Ireland's outstanding contribution to European culture between the fall of Rome and the rise of the Carolingian Empire, and the development of a national civilization and culture long before the present nationalities of Europe had taken shape.[60] Since the beginning of the sixteenth century, however, England had been attempting to destroy all literary and historical traces of Ireland's ancient greatness and the result was centuries of resistance. By 1914 it was considered 'a solemn charge and tradition' that each generation would attempt to regain for Ireland her ancient rights. Since Ireland had never surrendered her sovereignty, no power possessed title to Ireland by conquest, contract, or treaty, 'and therefore the sovereignty of Ireland exists in suppression, the exercise of it being prevented by external force'.[61] A sovereign Irish nation had existed since before the Norman invasions and no subsequent acts by persons claiming to be the leaders of the Irish people were valid if these involved a surrender of Irish sovereignty.[62] The issue of consent was crucial. The British and Irish sides were keen to mobilize American support for their positions in advance of negotiations, and Lloyd George maintained that Sinn Fein's position was analogous to that of the Confederate States during the civil war. Sinn Fein rejected the analogy, stating that the crucial fact of Irish history had been the continuous opposition, constitutional or otherwise, to the British connection. The southern states, on the other hand, had freely accepted the Union, and sought subsequently to withdraw from it. Their position could be described as secessionist.[63]

For this reason there was consensus among radical nationalists that the conditions under which the Act of Union was passed in 1800 were so shameful that the Union could not be regarded as a voluntary contract between two islands. Like Hungary under the Hapsburgs, Griffith maintained that Ireland had had an 'ancient constitution' rooted in Grattan's parliament (1782–1800), which was

---

[58] De Valera, *Peace and War*, 46.

[59] 'Extract from a Statement of Ireland's Case before the Powers to be Assembled at a Peace Conference', *Report on Conditions in Ireland with Demand for Investigation by the Peace Conference* (Paris, 1919).

[60] Sinn Fein, *The Case of Ireland*, Sinn Fein Series No. 12 (1919; IR 94109 P90, NL).

[61] 'Extract from a Statement of Ireland's Case', op. cit.

[62] J. Coakley, 'Competing Conceptions of Legitimacy and the Creation of the New State', *Etudes Irlandaises*, 21 (1995), 60.

[63] *Irish Bulletin*, 5/34 (18 July 1921).

formed by a treaty between Ireland and the United Kingdom, the 1782 Renunciation Act. The Act of Union, which abolished that parliament, was unconstitutional and any Irish politicians who had attended Westminster after 1800 had been wrong tactically and legally.[64] However, critics observed that the majority of the Irish parliament had voted for the Union and even Griffith was aware that the general direction of British legislation since Catholic Emancipation in 1829 benefited Catholics.[65] Griffith's way out of this problem was to argue that reform bills such as the Church Disestablishment Act of 1869 and the Land Bill of 1881 were all a consequence of the Irish unconsciously carrying out the Hungarian policy of 'passive resistance', with occasional excursions into the domain of 'active resistance'. There was also the problem of those nationalist politicians who had attended Westminster since 1829, thus 'misrepresenting the Irish position to the world'.[66] It was countered that although the Irish would have been willing to accept Home Rule before 1914, it was only as an experiment that, had it been successful, would have led to complete independence.[67] In 1917 de Valera stated that the Irish people had always been prevented from expressing their views by England.[68] The outcome of the 1918 election, the first time the mass of the Irish people had exercised their vote, seemed to corroborate that claim. Griffith's paper also represented the election as an exercise of 'the inherent right to self-determination'. Comparing the effect of the election with the Hungarian Restoration Act of 1861, which left Hungary tied to the Austrian Empire only by a common monarch, it argued that the 1918 election had also brought the Union to an end;[69] hence the policy of withdrawing Irish MPs from Westminster.

However, the Union was also seen as a particularly disastrous period for Ireland, involving, Sinn Fein claimed, four artificial famines and 27 partial famines.[70] Since the eighteenth century it had been a common assumption in both Anglo-Irish and Gaelic nationalist thought that there was an inextricable link between economic decline and the absence of a native parliament. After 1800 the contrast between an increasingly industrialized and expansionist Britain and a relatively backward and stagnant Ireland served to focus nationalist complaint on the Act of Union itself as the main source of Irish economic backwardness.[71] It was argued that Grattan's parliament had overseen a time of extraordinary economic progress, forcing the English to introduce the Act of Union through bribery and corruption.[72] The catastrophes of the nineteenth century—the Great

---

[64] P. Maume, 'The Ancient Constitution: Arthur Griffith and His Intellectual Legacy to Sinn Fein', *Irish Political Studies*, 10 (1995), 125.

[65] Statement of Mr. George C. Fox, *The Irish Question*, 61.

[66] A. Griffith, *The Resurrection of Hungary: A Parallel for Ireland* (Dublin, 1904), 91–2.

[67] Statement of Mr.Charles J. Daly, *The Irish Question*, op. cit., 29.

[68] By-election speech in East Clare, 1917, in Moynihan, *Speeches and Statements*, 8.

[69] *Nationality*, 18 January 1919.

[70] Sinn Fein, *The Case of Ireland*.

[71] G. O Tuathaigh, 'De Valera and Sovereignty: A Note on the Pedigree of a Political Idea', in J. P. O'Connell and J. A. Murphy (eds.), *De Valera and His Times* (Cork, 1983), 63–4.

[72] Irish Self-Determination League of Great Britain (pamphlet) (NL ILB 300 P7, 41).

Famine, the fall in population, and the decline in native industry—would never have happened if there had been in existence an Irish parliament, responsive to its people and their needs. When Sinn Fein made its appeal to the US Congress for recognition, it compiled a lengthy document containing several statistical tables showing how retarded Ireland's comparative position had become since 1800.[73] De Valera was in no doubt that this was due to British rule:

Had Ireland been under a Kaiser, Emperor or Czar, its population would have doubled or trebled as the population of the three divisions of Poland, of Bohemia, of Alsace Lorraine have been. Our population should normally have increased from eight millions to sixteen. Instead our population, though we are the second most fecund race in the world, has decreased through English rule from eight million to four.[74]

On the other hand, if British rule was rejected simply because it had been disastrous, what of those on the island for whom the nineteenth century had not been traumatic? Sinn Fein made a detailed case that Ulster had also shared in the economic decline and demographic disaster of the nineteenth century, and insisted that there was no grounds for the 'two nations theory'.[75] Sinn Fein also rejected Lloyd George's view that they could not demand self-determination for the whole of Ireland, and deny the same right to Ulster. Griffith justified this stance by saying that the principle applied to nations and peoples, 'not to parishes and shires'.[76] However, some argued that if there was no such thing as a homogenous Ulster, neither was there a homogenous Ireland.[77] Generally, Irish nationalists subscribed to an ethnic if not racial conception of their national identity. Mary MacSwiney told the American Commission on Conditions in Ireland that America had less reason to secede from the British Empire, because Ireland was 'a distinct race'.[78] Sinn Fein, in its address to the Free Nations, remarked that 'nationally the race, the language, the customs, and traditions of Ireland are radically distinct from the English'.[79] Indeed on 22 August 1921 de Valera told a secret session of the Dail that some northern counties could democratically opt out of the Irish state on the basis that they did not want to be dominated by a state 'whose sentiments, ideals, and religion were different'.[80] This implied a clear modification of Sinn Fein's commitment in their 1921 election manifesto, to achieve unity first, and then to allow the North only some form of devolution.[81] Later, de Valera, who in 1922 claimed that Ireland was a nation 'ethnically, historically and by every other standard of political science', remarked that his

[73] Sinn Fein, *Ireland's Request to the Government of the United States of America for Recognition as a Sovereign Independent State* (Dublin, 1919).
[74] E. de Valera, Press Statement, New York, 23 June 1919, in Moynihan, *Speeches and Statements*, 30.
[75] Sinn Fein, *Ireland's Request to the Government of the United States of America for Recognition as a Sovereign Independent State*, 67–80.
[76] *Irish Bulletin*, 22 June 1920.
[77] P. Bew, *Conflict and Conciliation in Ireland 1890–1910* (Oxford, 1987), 219.
[78] MacSwiney, *The Background*, 34.
[79] De Valera, 'The Moral Basis of the Claim'.
[80] *Dail Eireann*, 22 August 1921.
[81] *Irish Bulletin*, 4 May 1921.

people were 'unmistakably delimited by the ocean'.[82] Either way, nationalists were still unanimous that their traditions were not sectarian—one speaker to the House of Representatives said that 'Ireland was the only nation in the world that never persecuted the Jews', despite the Limerick pogrom of 1904.[83]

Given the version of history subscribed to by most nationalists it was surprising that Third World analogies were never used to buttress the Sinn Fein case. The language used to describe the Irish experience of British rule—conquest by force, a plundered nation, and forced assimilation—was clearly colonial:

The nation which we represent enjoyed for over a thousand years the life of an independent sovereign State among the States of Europe. Then a neighbouring nation, England—which had received the benefits of civilisation and education first from our hands, lost to gratitude and honour and burning with lust for our possessions, burst in upon us as a conscienceless invader, and through the course of many generations strove to subvert our polity, annihilate our language and our culture, suppress our industry, ruin our agriculture, steal our trade and our commerce, deprive us of the advantages of our geographic position, cut us off from our ancient intercourse with other people, rob our revenues, and erase our name from the roll call of nations.[84]

Nevertheless the analogies remained European.[85] Sinn Fein noted that there were eleven small nationalities in Europe—Holland, Sweden, Norway, Denmark, Romania, Serbia, Switzerland, Montenegro, Bulgaria, Belgium, and Greece—who were independent, and four—Poland, Finland, Bohemia, and Ireland—that were not. Of the eleven sovereign nations Ireland exceeded five in extent, four in population, and ten in revenue. Of the nonsovereign small nations Ireland was third in extent, third in population, and second in revenue. Since the First World War the Poles, the Ukrainians, the Estonians, and the Finns had all gained their freedom, but none had as glorious a national past as Ireland and their oppression was never as 'awful'. In fact by 1919 Ireland was the only small nation in Europe without its own legislature. Its claim to independence was thus better-founded than many nations already free and some aspirant nations such as the Letts, the Czechoslovaks, and the Ruthenians were not regarded as nations at all by Sinn Fein but 'nationalities'.[86]

Of course much of European state building was itself colonial—British rule was no different from that of Germany in Poland, or of Austria in Bohemia—but the Irish felt their situation was the worst of all worlds. *Nationality* remarked that the Empire 'has meant purely and simply English domination over every phase of our national life, a domination more bitter and more unfortunate, than any experienced by small nations within the Austro-Hungarian Empire'.[87] De Valera

---

[82] Press interview, 15 January 1922, in Moynihan, *Speeches and Statements*, 94; de Valera, *Peace and War* (NL IR 94109 D 27), 46.
[83] Statement of Judge Kickam Scanlan, *The Irish Question*, 8.
[84] *The Struggle of the Irish People*, Address to the Congress of the United States Adopted at the January Session of Dail Eireann, 1921 (Washington, 1921).
[85] On analogies, see S. Howe, *Ireland and Empire* (Oxford, 1999), 58.
[86] Sinn Fein, *The Small Nations* (NL, 1R 94109 P90, leaflet S).
[87] *Nationality*, 2 December 1918.

remarked that rule by a foreign despot was a terrible thing, but rule by a foreign democracy was the worst of all, since it clouded the issue of responsibility.[88] Another writer remarked that countries such as India were frankly spoken of as possessions, and their populations recognized as subject peoples held by force, but the domination of Ireland by England 'has been verbally veiled as inclusion in the British Empire'.[89] De Valera believed that Ireland was not a colony, but British rule in Ireland had been based on the same principles by which the older European states ruled their colonies, namely the exploitation of those territories regardless of the rights and wishes of their inhabitants.[90] It is perhaps surprising then that Third World analogies were not resorted to, but there were obvious reasons for this reluctance. Ireland was not a province, or a dominion, but 'a Mother Country', which sent a large part of its population overseas.[91] Its status could not be compared to those of the white dominions and it wanted much more. De Valera informed an American audience that Ireland's case for independence was stronger than theirs, because 'you were only an English colony', whereas Ireland was an old nation of 'independent formation'.[92] Racist attitudes also existed. In 1918 Gavan Duffy had told his constituents that the fundamental question in the general election was whether Ireland 'alone of the white race' was to forgo its claim to self-determination.[93] In 1919 Sean T. O'Kelly remarked that 'the blacks and yellows, all colours and races, may be heard before the conference, except the Irish'.[94]

In summary, the Irish case for self-determination was that it was an ancient European nation, subjected to all the exploitation suggested by the term colonialism, but which had never consented to membership of the Empire. This perspective had practical consequences. During the Great War, British military and economic dependence on the USA had forced the British government to take the Irish question seriously, and a reasonably generous offer to Irish nationalists afterwards would create enthusiasm for an imperial bargain between the two powers.[95] Mounting press criticism of the Black and Tans at home, accusations abroad that it was denying the rights of small nations, and a general reluctance to govern Ireland as a crown colony forced the British cabinet in May 1921 to accept Lloyd George's judgement that the time for negotiation had come.[96] By the summer of 1921 Lloyd George was confident that an offer of dominion status to Irish nationalists would satisfy his conservative supporters, and ensure that US

---

[88] De Valera, *Ireland and India*.

[89] J. H. Bright, *What's Wrong with Ireland* (Dublin, 1919), 5.

[90] E. de Valera, typescript text of an article on Ireland's right to independence (UCD, de Valera Papers, P150/68).

[91] R. F. Spedding, *The Call of Democracy: A Study of the Irish Question* (Dublin, 1919), 16.

[92] S. Priollay, *Ireland in Rebellion* (Dublin, 1922), 18.

[93] G. Duffy, 'To the Electors of South County Dublin', 6 December 1918, (NA, Gavan Duffy Papers, 1125/29/1).

[94] Anonymous, *Sinn Fein and the Peace Conference*.

[95] Wilson, 'Imperialism in Crisis', 169.

[96] Lustick, *Unsettled States*, 234.

public opinion would be on his side in the negotiations.[97] Once Lloyd George had made the overall contours of the British offer known, rumours then began circulating in the British press that de Valera was considering accepting dominion status. However, de Valera publicly repudiated these claims, stating that the Irish position rested on the sole principle of self-determination, and that dominion status was incompatible with this principle.[98]

Furthermore, in correspondence with Lloyd George that summer, de Valera insisted that only an invitation to negotiations that treated his representatives as plenipotentiaries of a separate and foreign power was acceptable. Lloyd George for his part refused to accept that Anglo-Irish relations could be compared to the relationship between Belgium and Germany, and argued that the 'geographical propinquity' of Ireland to the British Isles was a fundamental fact. A century of Irish representation at Westminster, Irish service in the British army, and the loyalty of great numbers of Irish people to the throne, attested to this reality.[99] Moreover, de Valera, in rejecting allegiance to the Crown and loyalty to the Commonwealth was advancing claims made by none of the great Irish leaders from Grattan to John Redmond.[100] Indeed he maintained that the Sinn Fein position was more comparable to that of the Confederate States in the American south. The principle of 'government by the consent of the governed', if taken to de Valera's extreme, 'would undermine the fabric of every democratic state and drive the civilised world back into tribalism'.[101] For his part de Valera refused to accept that Sinn Fein's policy was one of secession, since the Union had never existed.[102] In addition, Sinn Fein continued to deny that the principle of self-determination could be applied to the Northern counties, and de Valera labelled the 1920 partition as an example of the 'tribalistic' interpretation of the principle of self-determination.[103]

In effect, Lloyd George refused to accept that the principle of self-determination could be applied to Ireland without reference to geographic and historical facts. Sinn Fein, on the other hand, maintained that Lloyd George's position was not 'a mere limitation' of self-determination, as he claimed, but a repudiation of the principle in itself.[104] During the latter stages of Sinn Fein's campaign, a number of concessions had been made by de Valera, which suggests that he accepted that the old concept of self-determination had to be adapted to meet the 'new imperialism' represented by the Commonwealth, but none involved a compromise on the Republic.[105] Association with the Crown as head of the

---

[97] D. G. Boyce, 'How to Settle the Irish Question: Lloyd George and Ireland 1916–21', in A. J. P. Taylor (ed.), *Lloyd George: Twelve Essays* (London, 1971), 157.

[98] *Irish Bulletin*, 5/37 (21 July 1921); 5/39 (25 July 1921).

[99] Lloyd George to de Valera, 13 August 1921, HMSO.

[100] Lloyd George to de Valera, 24 August 1921, HMSO.

[101] Lloyd George to de Valera, *Dail Eireann*, 7 September 1921.

[102] Moynihan, *Speeches and Statements*, 68.

[103] *Irish Bulletin*, 5/79 (20 September 1921).

[104] *Irish Bulletin*, 5/66 (1 September 1921).

[105] Spedding, *The Call of Democracy*, 16.

Commonwealth was acceptable only if freely given, allowing Northern counties to decide their fate by plebiscite was permissible only after independence had been recognized, and accepting a Monroe Doctrine for Ireland was likewise subject to status. External self-determination was still claimed as an absolute right—once accepted by Britain, compromise would follow. By the summer of 1921, 'plebiscite after plebiscite' had demonstrated the Irish public's preference for a Republic, and for de Valera, 'the degree to which any other line of policy deviates from it must be taken as a measure of the extent to which external pressure is operative and violence is being done to the wishes of the majority'.[106] In de Valera's letter to Lloyd George, accepting the offer of talks on 15 September, there was no mention of the principle of self-determination, but a declared willingness to negotiate on the principle of 'government by the consent of the governed'. However, in public statements de Valera clung to the position that Sinn Fein's simple demand was for a recognition of Ireland's right to self-determination. As late as 11 November 1921 he told the Canadian Self-Determination for Ireland League that a denial of this right would never be acquiesced in.[107]

Nevertheless, de Valera had tried to prepare the ground for compromise within his movement by trying to shift attention away from the goal of 'the isolated Republic' in 1921. He thought that the British government would not resort to war for the difference between dominion status and his formula of a Republic 'externally associated' with the Empire, and he was willing to risk a resumption of war to verify that assumption. Regan argues that cabinet unity was essential to de Valera's strategy of 'consolidation through unity'. Having got the British to concede external association in negotiations, de Valera hoped to get the cabinet to accept this formula, the cabinet would carry the Dail, and the Dail would carry the army. His tactics were scuppered by Britain's stubborn refusal to accept external association in the talks. The cabinet had accepted external association as an objective to be pursued in July 1921, but de Valera's insistence that Collins and Griffith make it their bottom line in the negotiations ultimately lost him the confidence of his two chief negotiators.[108] The weakness of de Valera's scheme of 'consolidation through unity' was that any break in his chain of command would send confusing messages to the rank and file, and the leadership prove unable to control the outcome of their divisions. This is essentially what happened. Liam Deasy believed that 90 per cent of the pre-truce IRA were against any kind of a split, but unity could not be maintained if the national elite became divided.[109] Collins, on the other hand, had secured the support of the majority of the IRB Council for the Treaty on 3 December 1921, but may have misjudged how representative of republican opinion the organization was, and overestimated its potential as a unifying factor.[110] By upstaging de Valera, whose personal authority

---

[106] De Valera to Lloyd George, ibid., 10 August 1921, HMSO.
[107] *Irish Bulletin*, 6/14 (8 November 1921).
[108] Regan, *The Irish Counter-revolution*, 10–23.
[109] L. Deasy, *Brother against Brother* (Cork, 1998), 54.
[110] Regan, *The Irish Counter-revolution*, 31.

was key to any settlement, Collins ensured that there would be no consensual response in the cabinet, the Dail, or the IRA.[111]

THE TREATY SPLIT

The Anglo-Irish Treaty signed on 6 December 1921 gave 26 counties of Ireland a generous measure of practical freedom, but denied the new Irish state the symbolic apparel that might have made it legitimate in the eyes of most republicans. The virtue of the settlement in the eyes of pragmatists was that it allowed Ireland full self-determination in internal affairs, while leaving Britain and Ireland a unit in military terms. Its flaw for republicans was not only that it denied the litmus test of sovereignty since 1917, external recognition as a republic, but that it was, they maintained, the first time Irish nationalists had assented to inclusion in the British Empire. It may be that without the earlier push towards self-determination questions of status might not have mattered, but conceptions of history and of status were intimately interlinked. Iceland, for example, was content under a common monarch with Denmark after 1918, but then Iceland had never been colonized by Denmark. What marked the Irish case out from the start was the bitterness of the intranationalist rift and the intense preoccupation with status. The arguments that followed ranged from the democratic, to the pseudo-democratic, to the blatantly undemocratic, but the Irish were caught in a dilemma only partially of their own making. Lloyd George's invitation to negotiate was premised on the belief that Irish national aspirations would find full expression in the Commonwealth, but de Valera was only willing to associate with, not be in the Commonwealth. For some the difference was not worth fighting for. The Irish Race Convention took place in Paris on 21 January 1922, and the delegates from the white dominions came out in favour of the Treaty, while voting for de Valera as President. Sinn Fein managed to send a unified delegation, but pro- and anti-treatyites travelled separately.[112] Revealingly, one delegate, Eoin MacNeill, had long believed that nineteenth-century conceptions of independence were obsolete and that in a world of interdependence there need be no conflict between Ireland and England.[113] Another, Mary MacSwiney, had remarked in September 1921 that compromise would mean that they 'acknowledge themselves a domestic question of England and would have accepted a position of inferiority for the first time in their history'.[114]

Behind these two positions were fundamentally different estimates of the prospects of Irish nationalism under the Treaty. Michael Collins promoted the Treaty as 'a stepping stone to greater freedom':

[111] Ibid., 34.
[112] D. Keogh, 'The Treaty Split and the Paris Irish Race Convention, 1922', *Etudes Irlandaises*, 22 (1987), 165–71.
[113] *The Irish Question*, 44.
[114] *Dail Eireann*, 14 September 1921.

Britain knows well that she can keep world opinion without conceding a Republic. She believes now, as she believed in July last, that she cannot afford to concede it. That it would break up the Commonwealth—that it would destroy her security and prestige if she were to acquiesce in a forcible breaking away, which would show her so-called Empire to be so intolerable, or herself so feeble as to be unable to prevent it. But she will acquiesce in the ultimate separation of the units, we amongst them, by evolution, which will not expose her and not endanger her.[115]

Much depended on taking advantage of the de facto position that the Treaty created, even if this meant abandoning the *de jure* claims of the Republic. The 1917 compromise had been that Sinn Fein would achieve external self-determination first; the form of government would be decided later. Now the sequence was reversed. Accept dominion status for the moment, Griffith argued, and in time full independence would be achieved—much in the same way that Norway opted out of its union with Sweden in 1905.[116] In the summer of 1921 Jan Smuts had also advised de Valera to leave Northern Ireland alone for the moment, and 'through a successful running of the southern state and the pull of economic and peaceful forces' eventually bring the North into the southern state.[117] Since Northern Ireland had a right under the Treaty to opt out of the Free State, Alfred O'Rahilly, a pro-treaty academic, argued that as the declaration of a republic would permanently alienate the North, there was a clear argument for 'gradual evolution' rather than 'forceful revolution'. The Irish must aim at the achievement of a united people first, 'prior to the final effort to secure for Ireland her rightful place among the nations of the world'.[118] In contrast, Mary MacSwiney had told the Dail on 14 September that up to a few years previously the majority in the country were 'West Britons', and if compromise were accepted, that West-Britonism would be re-established.[119] Erskine Childers, the constitutional expert on the anti-treaty side, believed that the new Governor General would become 'a centre and focus for anti-national reactionary influences in Ireland', much in the same way that the Viceroy had in the nineteenth century.[120] Another anti-treatyite remarked that as you go down the road of expediency, 'you will find leafy bowers and sycamore trees and mossy banks and happiness and luxury—the flesh pots of Egypt'.[121] The final loss of the North, the abandonment of the Republic, the involvement of Ireland in British wars—even the reoccupation of Ireland—could all follow. It is tempting to conclude that such fears reflected a lack of worldly experience on the part of some republicans, but even de Valera believed that the Treaty would 'begin the same history that the Union began'.[122]

[115] M. Collins, *The Substance of Freedom*, 5 March 1922 (NL LO P102), 14.
[116] Griffith, *Arguments*, 25.
[117] Smuts to de Valera, 4 August 1921, HMSO.
[118] A. O'Rahilly, *The Case for the Treaty* (NL LO P102), 22.
[119] *Dail Eireann*, 14 September 1921.
[120] E. Childers, *What the Treaty Means* (Dublin, 1922).
[121] Mr. Etchingham, *Dail Eireann*, 17 December 1921.
[122] *Dail Eireann*, 19 December 1921, 87.

Pro-treatyites also believed that dominion status placed the Irish state on an equal footing with other peoples of the Commonwealth, and although a certain amount of legal phraseology implied the subordination of the dominions to the British parliament, in practice they were fully independent. Moreover, a case could be made that the Treaty settlement was not all that different from the Irish constitution of 1782. Although that parliament was admittedly dominated by an English Executive, if it had been allowed to develop, the gradual democratization of British imperial institutions in the nineteenth century would have meant that the Irish parliament would have come to resemble those of the white dominions.[123] Griffith argued that Irish nationalism had not been about a particular form of government in any case, 'but a matter of getting the real independence of the Irish people achieved'.[124] O'Rahilly believed that under the Treaty the Irish had full 'internal sovereignty' and for certain portions of their 'external sovereignty' they would meet for joint discussion at imperial conferences.[125] The powers granted to the Free State were nonetheless extensive:

Meanwhile we have all the really important powers required for our normal political, social, and economic life. We can form our own constitution, we can embody therein the referendum, and the principal of federalism, thus practically abolishing bureaucracy and party system. Social legislation, so terribly needed and so long delayed is now within our powers. We can at last make education really national and really efficient. The Irish language, with all its historical, cultural, and spiritual associations, can be saved from extinction. We shall no longer be dependent on imported officials and alien Boards in striving to explore and develop our national resources and to foster our agriculture and industries. We can frame our own tariff policy and regulate our taxes and finances. We can appoint consular agents abroad and conclude commercial treaties with other countries. The Free State can enact legislation to exclude from the country any person it thinks fit to exclude, including British subjects. It can regulate the coinage and settle the conditions on which British coinage may be used in Ireland. It could forbid the use of titles in Ireland or could empower the grant of locally valid titles of honour.[126]

Hugh Kennedy, the Chief Law Officer, argued that political institutions were of two kinds, those derived from the people and those whose existence flowed from an external authority. Since a treaty could only be signed by two sovereign states, it followed that its very title indicated Irish sovereign statehood.[127] However, these institutions were bound to raise difficulties in a treaty agreed between republicans and an empire wedded to the concept of 'the crown in parliament'. During the negotiations the British government had insisted on the importance of the crown as the symbol of all that kept the nations of the Empire together.[128] However, although de Valera had told the 1917 Sinn Fein *Ard Fheis*

[123] Carty, *Was Ireland Conquered?*, 115.
[124] A. Griffith, 'The Gamblers Choice', 5 March 1922, in Griffith, *Arguments*, 28.
[125] O'Rahilly, *The Case for the Treaty*, 11.
[126] Ibid., 17.
[127] T. Garvin, *1922: The Birth of Irish Democracy* (Dublin, 1996) 177.
[128] Wilson, 'Imperialism in Crisis', 173.

that 'we do not wish to bind the people to any form of government', he ruled out a monarchy in which the House of Windsor would be the monarch.[129] Moreover, the fact that TDs would have to take an oath of allegiance to the Free State constitution, and of fidelity to the King as Head of the Commonwealth, created a false position, whereby Irishmen would be giving allegiance and obedience to an authority that they had already repudiated.[130] The stipulation that the constitutional position of Ireland was to be analogous to 'the constitutional usage and practice' of Canada for example, was no guarantee to an island that was not thousands of miles away from Westminster, and which had suffered 'centuries of racial oppression' by England.[131] In his correspondence with Lloyd George, de Valera had insisted that the freedom of the dominions would be illusory in Ireland, and stated that the most explicit guarantees, including the right to secede, would be necessary for Ireland to secure an equal degree of freedom.[132] The Provisional Government decided to pressurize the British into allowing the legislative practice obtained in Canada to be written into the Irish constitution, rather than the letter of the law, but the British refused.[133] Indeed there was no specification in the Treaty of who would interpret the Free State's powers should a dispute arise, and the overall tenor of the document was that the Free State's obligations were very precisely worded, whereas its freedoms were left open to interpretation. Legally, the Privy Council was the arbiter of all questions arising as to the interpretation of the Treaty.

There was also disagreement over the status of the new Irish state—the self involved in the concept of self-determination. The first stumbling block was the proposed name of the state, the Irish Free State. Lloyd George had pointed out to the plenipotentiaries that it was the direct English equivalent of *Saorstat*, the Irish Sinn Fein had used for Republic since 1919.[134] However, Childers remarked that there had been only two other Free States in history, the Congo Free State, a model of imperial exploitation, and the Orange Free State, now a minor province within South Africa.[135] For Collins, membership of the Commonwealth would guarantee Irish independence since any loss of Ireland's legislative power would be opposed by the other dominions. In contrast, Childers pointed out that Clause 1 of the Treaty used the phrase 'the British Empire' not 'the Commonwealth', and gave Ireland 'a parent nation with a distinct racial identity' the same constitutional status 'as four distant British colonies'.[136] The combined effect of Articles 1 and 2 was that the Irish voluntarily accepted for the first time 'to enter the British Empire as a colony and to accept the British King and the authority of the

[129] Moynihan, *Speeches and Statements*, 8.
[130] E. Childers, *Dail Eireann*, 15 December 1922.
[131] Childers, *What the Treaty Means*.
[132] De Valera to Lloyd George, 10 August 1921, HMSO.
[133] Provisional Government Minutes, 6 June 1922 (NA G1/1).
[134] T. Garvin, 'Democratic Politics in Independent Ireland', in J. Coakley and M. Gallagher (eds.), *Politics in the Republic of Ireland* (London and New York, 1992), 351.
[135] Childers, *What the Treaty Means*.
[136] Ibid.

British government over Ireland'.[137] The Treaty was not an international contract but operated because an Act of Parliament gave it force of law.[138]

Yet such a diminution of status might have been accepted as a logical consequence of their failure to achieve international recognition at Versailles, and the pro-treatyites claimed that the Treaty was also consistent with the principle invoked by both de Valera and Lloyd George in advance of the negotiations— 'government by the consent of the governed'. De Valera's immediate response to the Treaty was that it was in violent conflict with the wishes of the electorate, as expressed at repeated elections over the previous four years, but Patrick Hogan, a pro-treaty TD, denied that a mandate had ever been given for a form of government, since during the 1921 election 'the word republic was conspicuous by its absence' in his constituency. De Valera countered that Sinn Fein's election manifesto in that year had read 'for the confirmation of the legitimacy of the Republic', and all members of the Dail had taken an oath to the Republic in 1919.[139] Although the Sinn Fein victories were disputed by some observers, the British had never questioned Sinn Fein's interpretation of the various elections between 1918 and 1921, and during the negotiations Lloyd George told the House of Commons that the Sinn Fein leaders were duly and fairly elected.[140] However, ambiguity was still evident when de Valera referred to the Republic 'as it was established—as it was proclaimed in 1916—as it was constitutionally established by the Irish nation in 1919'.[141] Remarkably, all the anti-treatyites who spoke during the Dail debates accepted that the Treaty would be accepted by the people in the next election, but anti-treaty TDs believed that they would be voting under 'duress', under threat of war. The division between the two sides now rested on a narrow but profound difference of principle. In July 1922 the Provisional Government would tell its troops that they were still fighting for the same principles that they had fought for against the British: the right of the Irish people to be masters in their own country, and to decide for themselves the way in which they shall live and the system by which they shall be governed.[142] In contrast, de Valera would tell an aide that the simplest way to peace would be to secure the recognition of the right of the Irish people, 'to decide freely without threat of war, internal or external, how they should be governed and what should be their political relations, if any, with Great Britain and the British Empire.'[143] In other words, at issue were the rival claims of democracy and self-determination.

Indeed the sudden shift in public opinion, apparent to anyone that returned to their constituencies during the Christmas recess, forced most anti-treatyites to

[137] E. Childers, *Clause by Clause: A Comparison between the Treaty and Document No. 2* (Dublin, 1922).
[138] H. Harrison, *Ireland and the British Empire, 1937: Conflict or Collaboration?* (London, 1937), 43–4.
[139] *Dail Eireann*, 17 December 1921.
[140] *Irish Bulletin*, 6/9 (1 November 1921).
[141] *Dail Eireann*, 19 December 1921.
[142] 'Government Statement Circulated for the Information of all Officers and Ranks, July 15 1922' (UCD, Mulcahy Papers, P7/8/29).
[143] De Valera to O'Caoimh, 22 November 1922 (UCD, de Valera Papers, P150/1647).

disavow the democratic process entirely. *Poblacht na hEireann* remarked that the people's will was only the expression of one generation, and had no power over the people's sovereignty, which was the expression of the life of the race, from beginning to end.[144] Mary MacSwiney announced that 'it was the strong uncompromising minority who made today possible', and stated that the people were not able to judge the issues, because they had been in 'slavery for 120 years and longer'.[145] In April de Valera himself declared that the Irish Republican Army would be right to prevent a new election taking place, in order to prevent Britain getting 'an appearance of popular sanction for his usurped authority'.[146] Griffith, on the other hand, argued that should they 'muzzle' the people in this way, they would be renouncing the platform they were all elected on in 1918.[147] Collins believed that the Irish people had always fought for 'the democratic right to rule themselves' and the departure of the British army from Ireland, not the Republic, was the real recognition of that right.[148] Irish nationhood sprung from the Irish people 'and not from any equality—inherent and acquired—with any other people'—as clear a renunciation as any of the doctrine of self-determination.[149]

As time went on, the idea that the Provisional Government was the guardian of the people's right to determine their own destiny was added to the case for the Treaty, but the anti-treatyites strenuously denied that this was true. In September 1922, the Labour leader, Thomas Johnson, remarked that with one side claiming to be defending the will of the people, and with the other claiming to be defending the will of the people if Britain's threat of war was removed, it was difficult to be anything other than confused.[150]

The thesis that what was at issue in the resulting civil war was the electorate's right to determine its future has become accepted wisdom among Irish historians. The pro-treatyites claimed that a democratic government had been established under the terms of the Treaty, but de Valera had interpreted the principle of consent to mean the right of nations 'that had been annexed to empires against their will to free themselves from the grappling hook'.[151] External self-determination was thus invoked as the basic anti-treaty position. However, by December 1921 the pro-treatyites had given up on the concept of self-determination and based their claim on moral right, 'not on positive international law'.[152] Collins himself argued that Ireland's status as 'a mother country' was more important than any argument 'basing the claim of our historic nation on any new-found idea'.[153] An argument has been made that the pro-treatyites achieved something

---

[144] See J. M. Curran, *The Birth of the Irish Free State 1921–1923* (Mobile, Ala., 1980), 231.
[145] *Dail Eireann*, 17 December 1921.
[146] *Republic of Ireland*, 20 April 1922.
[147] Griffith, *Arguments*, 18.
[148] M. Collins, 'The Right of the People', 12 March 1922, 19
[149] M. Collins, *The Path to Freedom* (Dublin, 1996), 37.
[150] T. Johnson (NL, Thomas Johnson Papers, Mss. 17, 139).
[151] De Valera to Lloyd George, 12 September 1921, *Dail Eireann*, 89.
[152] O'Rahilly, *The Case for the Treaty*, 10.
[153] Collins, *The Path to Freedom*, 37.

like 'internal self-determination' for Ireland, which left foreign policy and defence to the crown, but fell short of secession. According to Knirck, Kevin O'Higgins believed that self-determination could be separated from republicanism, and his government's defence of the people's right to decide on the Treaty was in itself a defence of the right.[154] However, not only did O'Higgins never use the term to justify the pro-treaty position, before 1921 all shades of nationalist opinion had maintained that self-determination had to be exercised free from dictation from outside. Collins maintained that he did not sign the Treaty under 'duress', but because he would not commit the Irish people to war without the Irish people committing themselves to war.[155] However, it was clear from the account of the negotiations given by Gavan Duffy in the Dail on 21 December 1921 that negotiations were at breaking-point when Lloyd George issued his threat of 'terrible and immediate war'. According to Gavan Duffy, a member of the negotiating team, 'everyone who heard the British Prime Minster believed beyond all reasonable doubt that this time he was not playacting'.[156] The Treaty, in short, had been accepted under duress, and as Griffith remarked in the Dail debates on 15 December, the main issue facing the people was peace or war.[157] The population of the 26 counties had a clear right to say yes or no to the Treaty, but for the anti-treayites the June election, irregular as it was, was no exercise in self-determination. O'Rahilly argued that the people were never asked in the past to choose 'between a Republic as the outcome of the evolution of the Free State, and a Republic to be fought for here and now', but republicans argued that this choice was in itself an imposition.[158] As Liam Mellowes remarked, the people had had 'the ground cut from under their feet'.[159]

CONCLUSION

One of the most commonplace observations about the Treaty debates is that although little attention was paid to the issue of partition, questions of status were absolutely paramount. This was not surprising. Acceptance of the Treaty, however construed, clearly implied a negation of every argument made in the Sinn Fein case for self-determination: that Ireland was a European nation not a British colony, that its status should be derived from international recognition not from an Act of Parliament, and that the conquest of Ireland had never been consented to by the Irish people. De Valera argued that the Treaty meant that the Irish people 'voluntarily abandon their independence and the republican form of

[154] J. Knirck, 'Afterimage of the Revolution: Kevin O'Higgins and the Irish Revolution', *Eire-Ireland*, 38 (Fall/Winter 2003), 222.
[155] *Dail Eireann*, 19 December 1921.
[156] R. Barton, *The Truth about the Treaty: A Reply to Michael Collins* (Dublin, 1922), 6.
[157] *Dail Eireann*, 15 December 1921.
[158] O'Rahilly, *The Case for the Treaty*, 6.
[159] *Dail Eireann*, 17 December 1921.

government which enshrined it', and opposition to the June election on the part
of the anti-Treatyites was ultimately motivated by a desire to deny the British
Empire the veneer of popular assent.[160] Once again they could claim that Irish
sovereignty existed in suppression, its true expression being prevented by external
force. Acceptance of the Empire, in other words, meant acceptance of the original
conquest, and with it the authority of 'an Empire built on the ruins of Irish
freedom'. Moreover, under the Treaty, the relationship of Ireland and England, as
Kevin O'Higgins, a leading pro-treatyite, admitted, was not one of equals, despite
de Valera's demand that the negotiations be between 'our island and yours'.[161] At
the first meeting of the second Dail in August 1921, de Valera had told his
followers that dominion status did not give equality of status with Britain, but
a position of inferiority that no self-respecting nation could accept.[162] In time the
relationship would become equal, but of the three constitutional drafts submitted
by the Provisional Government to the British in May 1922, the British chose the
one least favoured by the Irish, insisting that the first clause contain a statement
that any future amendment inconsistent with the Treaty's terms would be void
and inoperative.

On the other hand, in order to make the case they did, Collins and his
supporters could not have fully believed in the version of history that Sinn Fein
had propagated, which assumed that the Anglo-Irish nexus could only work to
Irish disadvantage. All of a sudden the much-derided parliamentary tradition was
not suspect, and the Home Rule leader Parnell, who took an oath of allegiance to
further the nationalist cause, was invoked to justify the change in attitude. The
Irish nationalist tradition was redefined by Collins as fighting for 'the greatest
measure of freedom attainable at that time', as opposed to the republican tactic of
exploiting international circumstances in order to make the maximum demand.[163] However, there is no connection between the longevity of a tradition
and the inherent justice of a cause, and their case for the Treaty was not totally out
of sync with the arguments advanced between 1917 and 1921. Griffith was clear
that the Treaty definitely ended the Act of Union, and pro-treatyites were in no
doubt that the degree of legislative independence afforded by the Treaty would
allow them to undo the effects of the Union, a possibility hinted at by Lloyd
George in his sparring with de Valera in the summer of 1921.[164] Collins rewrote
history when he said that Irish history had not been a long struggle for the ideal of
freedom symbolized in the name Republic, but a 'story of slow, steady, economic
encroachment by England', but his attitude was undoubtedly more realistic
than his opponents'.[165] The word Republic was studiously avoided in Collins'

[160]   Press Interview, 15 January 1922, in Moynihan, *Speeches and Statements*, 94.
[161]   Quoted in Carty, *Was Ireland Conquered?*, 84. De Valera quotation in Moynihan, *Speeches and
Statements*, 52.
[162]   *Irish Bulletin*, 5/55, 12 August 1921.
[163]   Collins, *The Path to Freedom*, 28.
[164]   Griffith, *Arguments*, 20.
[165]   *Dail Eireann*, 19 December 1921, 4.

numerous speeches before his death, but the restoration of 'the Gaelic state', again a theme of earlier propaganda, was often alluded to as a possible outcome of the Treaty. The pro-treatyites, in short, were still nationalists who differed from their opponents not simply in the intensity with which they believed in the Sinn Fein version of Irish history, but in their capacity to see the long-term trend of events.

By 1921 Sinn Fein had become prisoner of its own rhetoric, and there was a clear parallel between the view that Irish sovereignty had never been surrendered in the past and de Valera's argument that the Irish Republic could not be disestablished by the Treaty. On the eve of his execution by the Provisional Government on 19 November 1923, Childers wrote that 'I have fought and worked for a sacred principle, the loyalty of the Nation to its declared independence in repudiation of any voluntary surrender to conquest and inclusion in the British Empire'.[166] To those, like him, who believed that British rule was based on an illegitimate conquest, any compromise on sovereignty was also bound to involve a loss of nationality, whereas a less normative approach would evaluate the Treaty principally in terms of whether it reversed the effects of the Union. Nationalist Ireland was now torn apart by the question of empire. Sinn Fein had refused to depict the Irish experience as a colonial one, but centuries of collaboration, Anglicization, and the reality of Ulster Unionism could not be wished away. Modern Ireland was a product of colonial rule. The fear of republicans that cooperation within the Empire would mean a loss of Irish nationality showed how far the process of absorption had actually gone. Paradoxically, Sinn Fein's propaganda had been aimed at a country whose own traditions had associated self-determination with self-government rather than national self-government per se. However, in Ireland self-government within the Empire was considered by many as being incompatible with the country's national traditions. Sinn Fein wanted to believe that its nation had withstood 'centuries of assimilation', so that the original nation still existed, its sovereignty unsurrendered, and its aspirations unbounded by imperial horizons. In de Valera's words, it possessed 'an intensity of national consciousness corresponding to its antiquity'.[167] Nobody within Sinn Fein would have disagreed with the sentiment behind these claims, but when it came to compromise, the refusal to accept Ireland's colonial past had explosive consequences. Acceptance of a treaty shrouded in the language and symbolism of empire could be justified on pragmatic grounds, but to others it was simply a denial of history.

---

[166] 'Souvenir Programme: Erskine Childers Commemoration Concert: Theatre Royal, Dublin 2 December 1923' (NL P2167).

[167] De Valera, 'The Moral Basis of the Claim'.

4

The Course of the Civil War

The disintegration of the Sinn Fein movement into two armed camps between the signing of the Treaty on 6 December 1921 and the outbreak of civil war on 28 June 1922 was once one of the great unknown stories of Irish political history.[1] From one point of view, since the question of whether the Treaty fulfilled or denied Irish aspirations to statehood could only be answered positively or negatively, only a civil war could have resolved the issue.[2] From another point of view, Fitzpatrick argues that differences over principle were usually relatively unimportant in generating conflict in Ireland so the civil war must be considered a predictable but not inevitable consequence of the Treaty split.[3] There was also once a hidden community of interest between the professional historians' reluctance to explore the period on the grounds of unsatisfactory source material and political elites' own neglect of a time where their willingness to compromise on matters of principle was at odds with the standpoint they later took in the civil war.[4] Either way, the release of new archival material and the subsidence of civil war passions generally should focus renewed attention on the efforts made to avoid civil war in the first part of 1922. After all the history of Irish nationalism before 1921 was usually one of glossing over internal differences, so the outbreak of fighting in 1922 can only be regarded as an aberration.

The question of whether Irish political elites could have averted civil war is also related to the broader issue of the performance of the revolutionary elite after 1921. The establishment of a viable party system, the consolidation of democracy more generally, and the elite's ability to project an Irish identity in international affairs can all be interpreted as the fruits of an uncommonly able revolutionary elite.[5] On the civil war itself historical judgement is more mixed. The year 1922 is

---

[1] The most thorough accounts are found in J. M. Curran, *The Birth of the Irish Free State, 1921–1923* (Mobile, Ala., 1980); M. Hopkinson, *Green against Green: The Irish Civil War 1922–23* (Dublin, 1988); B. Kissane, *Explaining Irish Democracy* (Dublin, 2002), 115–40; J. M. Regan, *The Irish Counter-revolution 1921–36: Treatyite Politics and Settlement in Independent Ireland* (Dublin, 1999), 35–75; M. Valiulis, *General Richard Mulcahy and the Founding of the Irish Free State* (Dublin, 1992), 111–72.

[2] See H. Roberts, *The Battlefield: Algeria 1988–2002—Studies in a Broken Polity* (London and New York, 2003), 116.

[3] D. Fitzpatrick, *The Two Irelands 1912–1939* (Oxford, 1998), 124.

[4] See D. Williams, 'Origins of the Civil War: Prof Williams on Scarcity of Documents', *Irish Press*, 6 June 1966.

[5] For an example see F. Munger, *The Legitimacy of Opposition: The Change of Government in Ireland in 1932* (Beverly Hills, 1975).

said to have induced a nervous breakdown in de Valera, whereas Regan's portrait of Kevin O'Higgins concludes that he was in some ways quite disturbed.[6] Although the failure of Sinn Fein to hold the two parts of the movement together has often been attributed to the force of circumstances, it is widely believed that the actual conduct of the civil war did not reflect credit on either side. In its aftermath William O'Brien wrote that 'the lack of magnanimity on the winning side and the criminal desperation of the losers constitutes a page of history which no unbiased Irishman can read without aching eyes and cheeks of shame'.[7] In a sense the two issues are inter-related, since it was the disappearance of the one person with the desire to be all things to all men, Michael Collins, that led to the descent into bitterness and extremism on both sides. How elites perform under the strain of conflict is a key issue in the analysis of any civil war, but in Ireland the conventional phase of the civil war between June and September 1922 was less traumatic than what followed. Guerrilla warfare, terrorism, and systematic executions punctuated the last phase, and although a military solution was in sight by the new year, political relationships were more polarized than ever. In October 1922 a British journal remarked that 'Ireland's failure strengthens the cause of those who believe in strong imperial government rather than democracy'.[8] So much for the integrative movements of the nineteenth century, when the presence of a common foe put a premium on solidarity and the harmonization of political differences.

The analysis of the course of the civil war offered here revolves around a number of paradoxes, chief among them the fact that the intensity of the conflict in ideological terms seemed unconnected to the extent of the fighting, which was limited. This was partially due to the reluctance with which IRA men joined the fray, but also to the fact that the pro-treaty leadership proved far superior in strategic terms to the republican side. In terms of its impact on the Irish polity as a whole the civil war was a profound experience, but it was a controlled if bitter phenomenon. Despite the range of potential oppositions to the Free State effective resistance was provided by only one organization, the IRA, which largely managed to retain its authority over its rank and file, even after its ceasefire. Crucially, the anti-treatyites retained the support of a large and constant minority within the civilian population that later became the basis for the rise of Fianna Fail. Although there is evidence to suggest that the war was fought over the heads of the general public, in the areas where the fighting was prolonged, the polarization of the electorate behind the two civil war parties was an obvious feature of the 1923 general election. In other words, the way that the war was fought reveals why it was possible to institutionalize the split into a party political system after 1923, and the ultimate paradox was that despite military factors clearly

---

[6] On de Valera see T. Garvin, 'Introduction', in P. S. O'Hegarty, *The Victory of Sinn Fein* (Dublin, 1998), 13. On O'Higgins, see Regan, *The Irish Counter-revolution*, 181–2.

[7] W. O'Brien, 'The Irish Free State: Secret History of its Foundation' (NL, William O'Brien Papers, MS 4201).

[8] *The Nation*, 25 October 1922.

determining the outcome, by the end of the fighting civilian leaders were in the ascendancy on both sides. With regard to their civil war the Irish have long and bitter memories, but the fact remains that for all the intransigence, it was a disciplined form of intransigence, and this is a good a description of 'civil war politics' as anything else.

THE DRIFT TO CIVIL WAR

In the period between the Treaty and the civil war Irish political elites were subject to two contrary pressures. On the one hand, since the possibility of a civil war on the Treaty was recognized from the outset, both sides recognized that only a constitutional *via media* could avert civil war. This put a premium on concili-ation and the Sinn Fein party as a whole did not formally split on the question of the Treaty before the June election. On the other hand, since the British govern-ment had insisted that an election take place on the Treaty in the first half of 1922, both sides were aware that their respective interpretations of the Treaty would be put to the test of popular approval so there was an impetus towards competitive behaviour too. With pressures both ways, it is not surprising that the outlook of someone like Collins should seem inconsistent as a result. In contrast to the well-worn juxtaposition between the cerebral de Valera and the impulsive Collins, de Valera's strategy was actually to delay the decision on the Treaty, whereas Collins sought to demonstrate that the Treaty was compatible with republicanism. On this difference rests the issue of democratic legitimacy, since delaying a popular verdict on the Treaty in the interests of avoiding civil war was regarded as a denial of popular sovereignty, whereas Collins' compromises on matters of principle were at odds with the pro-treaty rhetoric after the fighting had begun. Either way both men were operating in an increasingly compressed political space, and although there is a vast literature on the role elites can play in resolving conflicts, there is also a sizeable literature on the conditions that allow them to do so. By any measure these conditions were absent in 1922 and good will was a weak substitute for effective political authority.

The Dail vote on the Treaty took place on 7 January. As Regan has remarked, four weeks was a short time for Collins to get everyone to make the transition from the republican ideal to the reality of Commonwealth membership and the result was close: 64 members voted for the agreement while 57 voted against.[9] A few days earlier a scheme to avoid the Dail vote and allow de Valera to remain president of the Dail had already failed, largely due to de Valera's insistence that his document no. 2 should provide a basis for rejecting the Treaty. The problem for de Valera was that his 'external association' formula did not have the symbolic appeal of either the Republic or dominion status and it got little support in the debate. After the Dail vote he attempted to have himself re-elected as president of

---

[9] Regan, *The Irish Counter-revolution*, 44.

the Dail, and having failed by a margin of two votes, led his side in a walkout. His loss of authority may well be the best explanation for his occasionally reckless behaviour over the following months, and led to William Cosgrave's charge that he was trying to pervert constitutional practise whereby a minority in the assembly would form the government.[10] As a result of the vote Arthur Griffith became president of the Dail, and Collins became chairman of the Provisional Government, which was elected on 14 January by 'the parliament of southern Ireland' created by the Government of Ireland Act of 1920. The anti-treatyites refused to accept that this government had replaced the Dail government or that the Dail had the authority to disestablish the Republic, which could only be done by the votes of the people. The Provisional Government, chaired by Collins, consisted of William Cosgrave (local government), Eamon Duggan (home affairs), Patrick Hogan (agriculture), Kevin O'Higgins (economic affairs), Fionan Lynch (education), Joseph McGrath (labour), and J. J. Walsh (post and telegraphs).

The narrow acceptance of the Treaty by the Dail has been attributed to Collins' manipulation of the threat of war with Britain should the Treaty be rejected, whereas Hopkinson describes the public's acceptance of the Treaty in the June election generally as one of resignation rather than enthusiasm.[11] According to Mary MacSwiney, without the machinations of the Irish Republican Brotherhood led by Collins, the Treaty would not have been supported by 5 per cent of the TDs.[12] In 1989, Commandant Thomas Maguire of the second western division, which went anti-treaty, recalled that when the back-bench TDs from the Second Dail arrived in Dublin to debate the Treaty, they were met by Collins' IRB men at railway stations and put under pressure to vote for the settlement.[13] However, the Dail had been in recess from 22 December to 3 January and during the break many TDs had been swayed in favour of the Treaty by public opinion in their constituencies. At the same time the vast majority of local government bodies and the Catholic hierarchy had also come out in favour of the Treaty. The clergy based their case for the Treaty on the grounds that the majority of the people would accept it, but they themselves were shaping that opinion.[14] In contrast, the first southern division of the IRA, the largest in the country, unanimously rejected the Treaty before the Dail's vote, citing inclusion in the Commonwealth, the oath, and Britain's possession of Irish ports as its reasons.[15]

Although the Dail vote had been narrow, as time progressed, both the pro-treatyites and the British government were increasingly confident that there was a majority for the Treaty in the country. Nevertheless, at the Sinn Fein *Ard Fheis*

[10] R. Fanning, *Independent Ireland* (Dublin, 1983), 7.
[11] On the threat of force see Regan, *The Irish Counter-revolution*, 46–8; Hopkinson, *Green against Green*, 111.
[12] Mary MacSwiney, 22 January 1924 (UCD, Moss Twomey Papers, P69/15/ (66)).
[13] N. O'Gadhra, *Civil War in Connacht 1922–23* (Cork, 1999), 13–14.
[14] P. Murray, *Oracles of God: The Roman Catholic Church and Irish Politics, 1922–37* (Dublin, 2000), 44.
[15] Valiulis, *General Richard Mulcahy*, 113.

held in the Mansion House on 22/23 February Collins and de Valera agreed to delay the election on the Treaty for three months, by which time the public would have the new constitution before them. The former wanted time to achieve unity among the army on the basis of his interpretation of the Treaty, whereas the latter wanted time to get his opponents to revise it. Yet three months was a long time to allow events to drift, and with a divided elite and a confused authority structure (whereby the revolutionary Dail government partially overlapped with the Provisional Government), what transpired on the ground fed into unease about the direction of events. The evacuation of British troops and of the Royal Irish Constabulary also led to a power vacuum in the countryside and localized violence became sporadic.[16] Moreover, as O'Higgins later remarked, the economic situation was that there were 130,000 people out of employment in the spring, and the economic life of the county was ebbing.[17] Meanwhile, the Provisional Government were faced with increasing social disorder:

The habit of civic discipline had been eroded in the War of Independence, there were plenty of guns and gunmen and no trained policemen outside Dublin, and there were many grievances to be ventilated. Attacks on British troops and on ex-Royal Irish Constabulary (RIC) men, some simply acts of local vengeance, others calculated to provoke a British military response, caused acute embarrassment to the administration and increased British pressure on it to take firm action against the republicans. Frequent robberies and seizures of property, whether for the cause of the republic or for strictly private gain, emphasized the provisional government's lack of civil authority. Republican attacks on southern protestants, sometimes in reprisal for those on Catholics in Northern Ireland, sometimes in furtherance of agrarian grievances, sometimes, to use the language of an Irish-American document of April 1923, in pursuit of an exclusively 'Republican, Catholic' and 'Gaelic' Ireland, called into question the new state's ability and will to protect its religious minorities. To anyone not at the bottom of the rural heap, widespread land seizures appeared to threaten the entire social fabric. Labour unrest, including fitful use of the red flag and red rhetoric, seemed deeply menacing despite the enduring modesty of most of the labour movement's demands, methods, and aims.[18]

As the British withdrew from the country, army barracks were occupied by local brigades of the IRA, regardless of attitudes towards the Treaty. The Provisional Government, unsure of its military strength, allowed this to happen, leaving a country divided between armed camps, with most areas under the control of anti-treaty commanders.[19] Hopkinson suggests that from February 1922 onwards the anti-treaty IRA was hardly influenced by the politicians, and on 26 April Richard Mulcahy told the Dail that assaults on private individuals, attacks on government troops, and the seizure of stores had become common currency for the anti-treaty IRA.[20] As O'Halpin suggests, the anti-treaty IRA had a vested

---

[16] Regan, *The Irish Counter-revolution*, 58.
[17] K. O'Higgins, typescript copy of an article or letter to a US newspaper, 1922–3 (UCDA, Mulcahy Papers, P35 C/160).
[18] O'Halpin, *Defending Ireland: The Irish State and Its Enemies since 1922*, (Oxford, 1999) 2.
[19] Hopkinson, *Green against Green*, 52–109.
[20] Ibid., 57; Valiulis, *General Richard Mulcahy*, 140.

interest in the growing disorder since it underlined the Provisional Government's lack of practical authority in the country.[21] From February on, the establishment of governmental authority over the area of the 26 counties would automatically involve civil war unless a solution was found to the constitutional differences.[22]

On 24 February 1922 a meeting of the divisional and brigade commandants of the IRA requested that Richard Mulcahy, minister for defence, hold an army convention with a view to establishing a new army council. They hoped the convention would show the Provisional Government that the majority of the IRA were against the Treaty. Earlier in the month a stand-off between pro- and anti-treaty brigades of the IRA in Limerick had seen Mulcahy allow the anti-treaty mid-Limerick brigade to remain in control of the city, a decision that led Griffith to state that failure to stand up to the IRA would leave them with the reputation of being the 'greatest poltroons in Irish history'.[23] On 15 March Mulcahy's decision to allow the IRA convention to go ahead was reversed by the cabinet, Griffith's objection being that the purpose of the convention was to remove the army from the control of the elected government. The banned convention met on 26 March anyway, with over two-thirds of IRA brigades represented. The convention consisted of 223 delegates representing sixteen IRA divisions.[24] It unanimously agreed that the army 'shall be maintained under an Executive appointed by the convention'.[25] The IRA was no longer under the authority of the Ministry of Defence and on 13 April the Executive occupied a number of buildings in Dublin, including the Four Courts. Asked whether this occupation constituted a *coup d'état*, Rory O'Connor first remarked that 'you can take it that way if you like'. The following day he denied it and announced there would be no revolution in Ireland.[26] The move was clearly a decisive step in the drift towards civil war. On the one hand, it strengthened the intransigent elements within the IRA since the government would be forced to deal with them directly. On the other, the occupation showed that Mulcahy's strategy of maintaining the unity of the IRA by dealing with its moderate elements had clearly failed, which in turn strengthened the hand of those within the government who wanted no compromise.[27]

Differences over the election reached a head when a conference convened by Archbishop Byrne and the Lord Mayor of Dublin, Laurence O'Neill, was held at Dublin's Mansion House between 13 and 29 April. The Provisional Government proposed that in keeping with the February agreement, 'a plebiscite on the issue of acceptance or rejection of the Treaty shall be taken within a month', but the anti-treaty delegates rejected the proposal. On 14 April the army council of the

---

[21] O'Halpin, *Defending Ireland*, 3
[22] Hopkinson, *Green against Green*, 58.
[23] Valiulis, *Richard Mulcahy*, 132.
[24] C. Townshend, *Ireland: The Twentieth Century* (London, 1999), 111.
[25] Ibid., 66.
[26] *Irish Independent*, 15 April 1922.
[27] Valiulis, *General Richard Mulcahy*, 139.

IRA had already informed the Provisional Government of the terms under which they were prepared to discuss the unification of the pro- and anti-treaty IRA. These included demands that the existing Republic be upheld, that the IRA be under the control of an elected independent executive, and crucially that no election on the Treaty be held while Britain's threat of war existed.[28] All members of the Dail were given a copy of these terms in order to give them an opportunity of taking the initiative away from the cabinet.[29] At the conference Labour also proposed that the Provisional Government be replaced by a Council of State with the minster of defence elected by the delegates entitled to attend the banned IRA convention of 26 March. This was supported by de Valera, who promised to try to get the IRA Executive to accept the scheme, but the Provisional Government refused to continue with the conference.[30] Instead, the Provisional Government announced that it 'has now cast upon it the duty of seeing that the people of Ireland who are and must be the sovereign authority shall be free to vote their approval or disapproval of the Treaty'.[31]

Consensus on the election only came after a meeting was held in the Oak Room of the Mansion House in the middle of May. Representing the Provisional Government were Arthur Griffith, Michael Collins, Richard Mulcahy, and Eoin O'Duffy. Eamon de Valera, Liam Lynch, Cathal Brugha, and Rory O'Connor represented the anti-treatyites. Five men from the North also attended the meeting, and stressed the importance to the others of maintaining unity in view of the situation developing in the six counties. As a result of their plea, talks focused on the conditions under which 'an agreed election' could be held in the south. Progress was initially stalled on Collins' insistence that he retain a working majority in the new Dail. However, on 17 May Collins finally agreed that both Treaty sides could be represented on the joint panel for the new Dail in the same proportion as they were represented in the existing Dail. This concession on Collins' part, which gave the anti-treatyites the share of representation they had demanded on an earlier Dail peace committee, broke the impasse.[32] The next day de Valera and Collins formally agreed at University College Dublin to put forward a united slate of candidates at the election and to form a coalition government afterwards. On 20 May the Dail approved the agreement. The pact was also approved by a general convention of Sinn Fein held on 23 May. Collins told the audience that if unity could only be got at the expense of the Treaty, the Treaty would have to go.[33] Humphrey Murphy, the Kerry IRA leader, recalled that in the negotiations leading to the pact, Collins was convinced that the split between the IRA in the south and those in the Four Courts would ensure that civil war would not happen.[34]

[28] Secretary Army Council to Secretary Dail Eireann, 14 April 1922 (NA, Dail Eireann, 4/11/66).
[29] B. P. Murphy, 'The Irish Civil War 1922–1923: An Anti-treaty Perspective', *The Irish Sword*, 20/80 (1997), 296.
[30] *Freeman's Journal*, 1 May 1922.
[31] Ibid.
[32] Aiken to O'Donoghue, 9 March 1953, (UCD, Frank Aiken Papers, P104/1304 (2)).
[33] Murray, *Oracles of God*, 62.   [34] C. Younger, *Ireland's Civil War* (London, 1968), 396.

It soon became clear, however, that the British Government was not happy with the pact. The Provisional Government were to meet them on 27 May and their policy was to stress the fact that the pact was agreed to 'to enable the Provisional Government to carry out the terms of the Treaty and to restore order'.[35] When the two sides met in Downing St, Churchill pointed out that Article 17 of the Treaty obliged all members of the Provisional Government to sign a declaration of adherence to the Treaty. There was no requirement in the pact that the four republican ministers would sign the Treaty. Churchill stated that if Clause 17 did not apply 'the process of transfer of function does not go forward anymore'. On the other hand, the British did not want to be seen to be interfering in the internal affairs of a dominion. Their acceptance of the pact was subject to one fundamental condition: the conference agreed that acceptance of the pact did not prejudice the British government's right 'to raise any question of non-conformity between the constitution and the Treaty'.[36] On 1 June Churchill then told the House of Commons that ratification of the Treaty would be upheld if an Irish government were formed including members who had not signed the declaration under Article 17.[37]

On the election day, 16 June, Collins' new constitution was published. As early as 12 December 1921 the leadership of the IRB had sent a circular to their members stating that the Treaty would have to be judged on the substance of the constitution it produced.[38] An army council founded on 11 January, consisting of four members of the IRA's GHQ's staff and many commanders in the field, had also agreed to postpone military action until the constitution was published.[39] However, it is unlikely that anything more than a handful of voters had seen the constitution before the election, and if it had been published earlier, it would clearly have led to the breakdown of the pact. Collins' original draft had contained no references to the Treaty, no mention of the oath of allegiance to the Crown, and the role played by the governor general was given to 'the President of Ireland'.[40] However, the British had severely amended it, and the final draft contained a clause stipulating that if in any respect the constitution conflicted with the Treaty, it would be 'void and inoperative'. Under such a constitution there was no way that those who supported the Treaty and those loyal to the isolated Republic could coexist in one government.[41] Collins later blamed his political opponents for this:

A few months ago, we could have got a Constitution on practically definitely Gaelic lines. The first was made impossible by the actions and attitude of the Opposition. Suspicions of the British were aroused, and, more unfortunately, our weakness fully shown up. If the

[35] P.G. Decision, 25 May 1922 (NA, D/T, S2942).
[36] Conference on Ireland, 10 Downing St, London, 27 May 1922 (NA D/T, S2942).
[37] F. Pakenham and T. P. O'Neill, *Eamon de Valera* (Dublin, 1970), 189.
[38] Regan, *The Irish Counter-revolution*, 32.
[39] Murphy, 'The Irish Civil War 1922–1923', 296.
[40] Draft constitution (NA, D/T, S1125/15).
[41] Valiulis, *General Richard Mulcahy*, 153.

whole of nationalist Ireland had had the simple honesty to accept the Treaty for what it was worth I believe we could have got a Gaelic constitution based on the fact of our freedom and our general authority, that the British would have to acquiesce.[42]

Since early May negotiations on army unity had also been going on between the Ministry of Defence and officers of the first southern division. After the pact was signed, an army council was set up to consist of Richard Mulcahy, Gearoid O'Sullivan, and Eoin O'Duffy on the pro-treaty side, and Liam Lynch, Liam Mellowes, Rory O'Connor, and Sean Moylan on the anti-treaty side. Initially, the army council unanimously agreed to accept de Valera as the Minister of Defence, but this was rejected by the Provisional Government.[43] As a basis of unity a GHQ staff memo proposed that a unified Army Council would be periodically elected by an IRA convention. This council would have the right to ratify the government's choice of minister of defence, and taken with the assumption inherent in the pact, that the minister of defence would be a representative of the army's interests, it would clearly contravene democratic precepts.[44] Eight members of the council were proposed by Mulcahy, four from each Treaty side. The overall scheme of army organization was agreed to by the Four Courts Executive on 9 June, but they demanded that the chief of staff would be chosen by them.[45] The demand was accompanied two days later by a warning that negotiations could not be prolonged after 12 June.[46] On 11 June the Four Courts Executive debated the Provisional Government's proposal to appoint the minister of defence and the chief of staff themselves and voted by 14 votes to 4 to reject the proposals.[47] The IRA Executive would hold another convention on June 18.

Mulcahy believed that the anti-treatyites wanted Rory O'Connor as chief of staff and suggested Eoin O'Duffy as an alternative.[48] On 12 June he replied to the IRA Executive that the original list of members was only a probable one, subject to overall agreement. As early as 5 June the cabinet was concerned at the 'excessive representation' given to the IRA Executive on the proposed Army Council, and Mulcahy's cabinet colleagues were unenthusiastic about the scheme.[49] Now Mulcahy informed the IRA Executive that his side had 'gone in this matter as far as it is possible for us to go'.[50] He believed that five members of the proposed Army Council were prepared to agree to his proposals, and two of those from the IRA Executive were prepared to recommend to the IRA convention on 18 June

---

[42] 'Difficulties of the Constitution', n.d. (UCD, Mulcahy Papers, P7/B/28).
[43] 'Incidents in Connection with IRA That Had Bearing on Outbreak of Civil War', n.d. (UCD, Frank Aiken Papers, P104/1253 (3)).
[44] Valiulis, *General Richard Mulcahy*, 152.
[45] O'Malley to Mulcahy, 10 June 1922 (UCD, Mulcahy Papers, P7/B/192).
[46] Ibid.
[47] Valiulis, *General Richard Mulcahy*, 151.
[48] *Cork Examiner*, May 29 1922, 'Chronology of Events Leading to Civil War' (UCD, Mulcahy Papers, P7/B/192). On proposal of O'Duffy, see Richard Mulcahy, 'Memorandum', 8 September 1922, Mulachy Papers, ibid.
[49] P.G. Decision, June 5 1922, 'Army Negotiations for Unification 1922' (NA, D/T, S1233).
[50] Mulcahy to O'Malley, 12 June 1922 (UCD, Mulcahy Papers, P7/B/192).

that unification be proceeded with on the proposed basis. On 14 June, however, the IRA Executive rejected the proposals by 14 votes to 5, and informed the Ministry of Defence that not only were negotiations to cease, but the IRA Executive had resolved to take 'whatever action may be necessary to maintain the Republic against British aggression'.[51] On 17 June it was then indicated that because of objections on the part of Sean Moylan and Liam Lynch to portions of the draft constitution, the proposals would not be recommended to the IRA convention.[52]

On 14 June, the day the IRA rejected the scheme for army reunification, Collins seemed to renounce the pact in Cork, stressing that 'the country must have the representatives it wants'.[53] The election returned pro-treaty Sinn Fein as the largest party with 58 seats out of a 128, while the anti-treatyites got 36, a loss of 22 seats. The results gave their government a moral authority it had previously lacked and strengthened the position of those who believed, pact or no pact, that a duly constituted government could not tolerate a rebellion in their midst.[54] However, the anti-treatyites had only accepted the election provided that no issue was being determined under the pact. They saw the result as a mandate for the coalition government idea. Revealingly, the work of the Dail peace committee had been bedevilled by the pro-treaty delegates' insistence that their counterparts recognize that there was a majority for the Treaty in the country, whereas the anti-treatyites' overall strategy was to engage in negotiations in the hope that their opponents would eventually be converted to their outlook.[55] Although the pact held in all but two constituencies, the fact that transfers under the STV system were generally made within the two Treaty sides where there was a second pro- or anti-treaty candidate to receive them endorses George Gavan Duffy's view that it was impossible to hold an election in 1922 that would not be seen as a plebiscite on the Treaty.[56] De Valera had advised voters to vote first for their preferred Treaty or anti-treaty candidate, and give their second preference to a candidate from the other side, but generally this happened only where there was no second pro- or anti-treaty candidate to receive them.[57] According to Costello, the choice in the June election was simply between war or peace, with the mood of the electorate more in favour of maintaining the peace with each passing month. With the anti-treaty vote at less than a quarter of the poll, it now became easier for the government to characterize resistance to Treaty as opposition to the will of the people.[58]

---

[51] 'Resolutions Passed at Executive Meeting Held on June 14 1922' (NA, D/T, S1233).

[52] Richard Mulcahy, 'Memorandum', 24 June 1922 (UCD, Mulcahay Papers, P7/B/192).

[53] *Cork Examiner*, 15 June 1922; A. Mitchell and P. O'Snodaigh (eds.), *Irish Political Documents* (Dublin, 1985), 136.

[54] Valiulis, *General Richard Mulcahy*, 153.

[55] See Kissane, *Explaining Irish Democracy*, 131.

[56] M. Gallagher, 'The Pact General Election of 1922', *Irish Historical Studies*, 21 (1979), 405.

[57] See Michael Hayes' discussion of the issue in UCD Hayes Papers, P53/304/(97).

[58] F. Costello, *The Irish Revolution and its Aftermath 1916–23* (Dublin, 2003), 300–1.

On 18 June a motion was put to the IRA army convention that unless Britain withdrew from the island within seventy hours, resumption of war should occur. This proposal originated with Tom Barry, who was afraid that Liam Lynch would put the Beggar's Bush proposals to the convention. Lynch, Sean Moylan, and Liam Deasy opposed the motion, while Barry, Rory O'Connor, and Liam Mellowes argued in its favour.[59] The convention was divided between those who felt that further negotiations on army unity were futile and that peace moves only gave their opponents a chance to prepare for war and the delegates of the IRA's first southern division, who followed Lynch in his belief that negotiations should continue. In general the Four Courts men preferred to force national unity by renewing the conflict with Britain, whereas the first southern men felt that unity could be based on the coalition government to be established on 1 July. The majority of the Executive and a slim majority of the delegates seemed to back war, but on a second ballot the motion was narrowly defeated. It was opposed by the majority of the delegates of the first southern division. After that, the defeated minority walked out and returned to the Four Courts.[60] According to Sean MacBride, there was a fundamental policy difference among the IRA Executive at this stage, with those close to Lynch ultimately willing to accept the Beggars Bush proposals, and Tom Barry and his allies hoping to renew the conflict with Britain rather than let this happen.[61] The existence of this split probably played a role in the Provisional Government's decision to attack the Four Courts. According to Valiulis, at the time of the peace agreement of 4 May Mulcahy's aim was to ensure that the IRA in the south would not take up arms in support of the Four Courts men, and the possibility remained that whatever fighting occurred would be confined to Dublin.[62]

This decision to begin shelling the Four Courts on 28 June was prompted by the assassination of Field Marshal Sir Henry Wilson on 22 June and Lloyd George's subsequent demand that the sham government in the Four Courts no longer be tolerated. Two days later the election results were published. On 26 June Lloyd George warned that further tolerance of the men in the Four Courts would mean the Treaty would be 'formally violated' and the British government would resume 'liberty of action'. Arguments about what triggered the government's attack on 28 June would form the basis for the two sides' interpretations of the civil war in the months and years to come. According to O'Higgins, civil war was necessary because the 'mutineers' set themselves energetically to prepare a *coup d'état* that would plunge the country back into a death struggle with Britain.[63] In contrast, the anti-treatyites saw British pressure as the decisive variable, one

---

[59] 'Extract from a Notebook, the Property of Sean McBride, Which was Seized at Newbridge Barracks, July 1923' (UCD, D/T, S1233).

[60] E. Neeson, *The Irish Civil War 1922–1923* (Cork, 1966), 109.

[61] 'Extract from a Notebook, the Property of Sean McBride' (NA, D/T, S1233).

[62] Valiulis, *General Richard Mulcahy*, 144.

[63] K. O'Higgins, typescript copy of an article or letter to a US newspaper, 1922–3 (UCD, Mulcahy Papers, P35C/160).

document citing a speech by L. Worthington Evans in Colchester on 29 June where he stated that the British government had told the Provisional Government that they had to govern or simply go.[64] The only documentary evidence on this ultimatum was a reply to Lloyd George signed by a legal official, Diarmuid O'Hegarty, in the absence of Collins on 23 June, asking the British to place whatever information they had on Wilson's assassination in the hands of the Provisional Government, so that the new parliament, which would meet on 1 July, would be able to take whatever measures might be considered adequate. De Valera later took this to mean that the Provisional Government's initial reaction to Lloyd George's ultimatum was to 'temporise'.[65] Either way the fact that invitations to the first session of the new parliament were being issued as late as 26 June suggests that the decision to attack the Four Courts came late in the month, but no later than the following morning.[66]

A key feature of civil wars is that they usually occur when the relevant sides lose their belief in the capacity of politics to produce consensus. Labour later suggested that the split could have been avoided but for the matter of one job, but the failure of the army negotiations was not simply due to personalities: the IRA Executive wanted to provide the chief of staff to ensure that the army would not be used to undermine the Republic, whereas Collins argued that allowing the opposition to have this post would definitely be breaking the Treaty position.[67] More generally, for the Provisional Government the disorder that elapsed between the Dail vote and the June election, the anti-treatyites tactics over the pact, and the IRA's decision to provoke British intervention on 14 June were enough to justify civil war. Michael Hayes, the first speaker of the Third Dail, later maintained that the only way to avoid civil war had been for the IRA to acknowledge the verdict of the Dail on 7 January, and de Valera was blamed for putting a political cloak around those who wanted to use force to resist it.[68] However, as Hopkinson suggests, the Provisional Government's decision to go to war before convening the Dail shows that their collective enthusiasm for democracy was also limited, but by 28 June the alternative to civil war was probably British intervention, in which case the whole pro-treaty project would be jeopardized.[69] For the anti-treatyites, the Provisional Government's reneging on their promise to maintain the IRA as the army of the Republic, Collins' duplicity over the constitution, and his renunciation of the pact were clear evidence that the government's desire to implement the Treaty was greater than their willingness to accommodate the anti-treaty perspective. Their organ, *Sinn Fein*, argued that if the pact had been adhered to, peace and an Irish constitution would have been possible, but at

---

[64] 'Who Caused the Civil War: Extracts from Some Speeches, Documents and Records, Which Free State Ministers Forget' (Dublin, n.d.), NL.

[65] E. De Valera, *Dail Debates*, 1 March 1939, 2490.

[66] P.G. Minutes, 27 June 1922 (NA, G1/1).

[67] Lynch to de Valera, 20 December 1922 (UCD, de Valera Papers, 1749).

[68] Hayes to Boland, n.d. (UCD, Michael Hayes Papers, P53/279 (4)).

[69] Hopkinson, *Green against Green*, 111.

England's bidding the pact was broken and the result was war and an English constitution.[70]

On the eve of the civil war Kevin O'Higgins sent an apocryphal memo to the cabinet asking how his army of 'raw lads' with no experience of fighting were to cope with hardened units of the IRA that saw themselves as custodians of the republican ideal.[71] Not for the last time, the catastrophic impulse in O'Higgins' imagination was no guide to reality. Indeed it is a strange reflection on Ireland's 'revolutionary period', from 1916 to the truce of July 1921, that when it came to a military contest between the conservative and radical wings of the Sinn Fein movement in 1922, it took the former just over a month to defeat the anti-treaty IRA in conventional warfare. On the one hand, this casts doubt on Hart's thesis that the civil war was the last gasp in a revolutionary process set in train by the leaders and principles of 1916.[72] If it had been, in key areas the resistance to the Free State should have been ferocious, but in the summer the anti-treaty IRA in Castlebar, Limerick, Clonmel, Cork, and Waterford had no real stomach for a conventional fight.[73] By 11 August 1922, when Fermoy fell to government troops, they were no longer in possession of a single military installation in the country, and apart from a week's fighting in the Killmallock area, their efforts to resist the Free State in conventional warfare were feeble. On the other hand, Hart's perspective helps explain why the IRA's resistance was so weak. He argues that its members were still influenced by the traditions of the Irish Volunteers, whose strategy before 1919 was basically a deterrent one.[74] In 1922 the anti-treaty IRA had thought that merely by existing they could preserve the national honour by blocking the establishment of the Free State, but when faced with the need for an aggressive strategy, many quickly capitulated.[75] Nevertheless, the total failure of the anti-treaty IRA to defend 'the Munster Republic' suggests that the sprit of the GPO had left the nationalist movement. Individual examples, such as the suicidal Cathal Brugha were exceptions, but overall 'the singing flame', as Ernie O'Malley put it, seemed to have stopped burning in 1921.

At the outset the military advantage did seem to lie with the anti-treaty forces who dominated the provinces of Ulster, Connacht, and Munster, three-quarters of the country. A mere seven of a total of sixteen IRA divisions were loyal to the Ministry of Defence and the largest IRA divisions, the first and second southern,

---

[70] *Sinn Fein*, 13 August 1923.
[71] O'Higgins to Executive Council, n.d. (NA, D/T, S6696).
[72] See P. Hart, 'Definition: Defining the Revolution', in J. Augusteijn (ed.), *The Irish Revolution* (Basingstoke, 2002), 26.
[73] Hopkinson, *Green against Green*, 129.
[74] P. Hart, *The IRA at War 1916–1923* (Oxford, 2003), 101.
[75] Ibid., 105.

under Liam Lynch and Ernie O'Malley respectively, were anti-treaty. They contained a third of the total force of the IRA.[76] Of the old IRA provincial leadership only Michael Brennan in Clare and Sean MacEoin in Athlone were the sole supporters of the Provisional Government, and there were doubts about the former's reliability.[77] Since the IRA convention of 18 June Liam Lynch had not acted as chief of staff, but owing to the attack on the Four Courts, Lynch took up his post once more on 29 June.[78] Although the leadership of the IRA Executive was composed of men who had been prominent in the War of Independence, a large number of young men had joined the IRA after the truce, when the organization's prestige was at its height, and were known derisively as 'trucileers'. Many older IRA men, as many as 10,000 in Cork, according to Lynch, remained neutral in the civil war.[79] Nevertheless, Hart's study of Cork suggests that those who remained to fight the Free State were by and large those who had fought against the British.[80] The nucleus of the Free State army was taken from the Dublin Guard, but the bulk of its recruits were young men attracted either by material benefits or by a sense of adventure. On 3 July 1922 a force of 20,000 men was authorized; this was raised to 30,000 men in August, and by the end of the war the army had grown to approximately 55,500 men and 3,500 officers.[81] Lyons suggests that with 150,000 men unemployed, recruitment in the summer grew to 1,000 a day.[82] This massive growth, coupled with a constant supply of arms from the British, meant that an anti-treaty victory could only be achieved in the early stages of the war. By September 1922 27,400 rifles, 6,606 revolvers, and 246 Lewis guns had been supplied by the British to the Provisional Government.[83]

Digging in in the Four Courts, however, was not the ideal way to achieve that quick victory. Some within the IRA would have preferred to adapt guerrilla tactics and it was later maintained by Paddy Morrissey, an IRA commander, that if the Four Courts garrison had come out to fight in Dublin they would have obtained an easy victory.[84] The IRA's GHQ staff preferred to make a symbolic gesture of resistance rather than take the offensive, with the result that the elite of the IRA spent the rest of the civil war in prison.[85] A plan drawn up by the Four Courts commander, Paddy O'Brien, and Oscar Traynor, commander of the first Dublin brigade, whereby the National Army's positions would be attacked from the rear and subjected to constant sniping, was never put into practice as the IRA Executive did not want to be the first ones to open fire. As a result the Free

---

[76] P. V. Walsh, *The Irish Civil War, 1922–23*—A NYMAS Fulltext resource.
[77] M. Hopkinson, 'The Civil War from the Pro-treaty Perspective', *The Irish Sword*, 20/80 (1997), 289.
[78] Lynch to all units, *Poblacht na h Eireann*, 4 July 1922.
[79] Lynch to Director of Organisation, 26 January 1923 (UCD, de Valera Papers, P150/1793).
[80] P. Hart, *The IRA and Its Enemies: Violence and Community in Cork 1916–1923* (Oxford, 2003), 267.
[81] Walsh, *The Irish Civil War, 1922–23*, 7.
[82] F. S. L. Lyons, *Ireland since the Famine* (Glasgow, 1983), 463.
[83] Hopkinson, *Green against Green*, 125.
[84] See T. Garvin, *1922: The Birth of Irish Democracy* (Dublin, 1996), 31.
[85] F. M. Blake, *The Irish Civil War and What It Still Means for the Irish People* (Dublin, 1986), 33.

State troops were allowed to surround the Four Courts without interference.[86]
Liam Deasy reflected that the IRA's failure to devise a plan to relieve the Four
Courts men reflected their unwillingness to fight a civil war at this stage.[87] As it
turned out, despite the use of heavy artillery supplied by the British government,
it took three days and nights of heavy shelling, followed by a full-scale assault,
before the garrison surrendered on Friday 30 June. By Monday most of the IRA
positions south of the Liffey had also been taken and the Free State Army
concentrated its efforts on a section to the east of O'Connell street, known as
'the block', consisting of the Gresham, Crown, Granville, and Hammam Hotels.
Realizing the futility of holding fixed positions against superior firepower, on
Monday Traynor ordered what remained of his first Dublin brigade to escape and
by Wednesday evening the last of the IRA strongholds had been taken. An army
report on 5 July reported that only stragglers and snipers were left in the city.[88]
A total of sixty-five men had been killed on both sides, including Cathal Brugha,
who fought to the end in the Granville Hotel. There may have been as many as 250
civilian casualties.[89]

After being allowed to leave the city by Mulcahy on the grounds that he would
remain a voice for peace Liam Lynch travelled south, intending to establish 'a
Munster Republic' that would be defended by the Limerick–Waterford line and
show the limited authority of the Free State in the south. The line consisted of,
moving from east to west, the city of Waterford and the towns of Carrick-on-Suir,
Clonmel, Fethard, Cashel, Golden, and Tipperary, ending in the city of Limerick
where Lynch established his headquarters. To the south lay the first and second
southern divisions. Limerick was a strategically vital city since if the republicans
retained control of it they could consolidate their grip on the south and the west.
On the other hand, if the Free State gained control they would cut off the
republicans in Connacht and Munster from each other and use the city as a
base for attacks on both areas. However, Lynch's strategy was basically defensive
and he signed a ceasefire with his opponents in Limerick on 4 July, which he
hoped would enable him to negotiate with the government. GHQ, however,
rejected the agreement on 11 July and after over a week's fighting captured the
city on 20 July. The Kerry IRA leader, Tom McEllistrim later recalled that he knew
the civil war was over once they left Limerick.[90] By 20 July Lynch had moved his
headquarters to Clonmel and then to Fermoy and was already contemplating
adopting guerrilla tactics.[91] His peace agreement had only served to give GHQ
time to send men and arms to Limerick in preparation for a fight and was one
more example of the procrastination that had deprived the IRA of its military
advantage in the spring.

[86] Walsh, *The Irish Civil War*, 9.
[87] L. Deasy, *Brother against Brother* (Cork, 1998), 63.
[88] 'Report from the Adjutant General at 1.45 pm on July 5 1922' (NA, D/T, S3361).
[89] Walsh, *The Irish Civil War*, 12.
[90] T. Ryle Dwyer, *Tans, Terror and Troubles: Kerry's Real Fighting Story 1913–23* (Cork, 2001), 354.
[91] Ibid., 14.

It was clear that the anti-treaty IRA was ill-prepared for military conflict and was bereft of any clear strategy apart from falling back to defend its local areas. So convinced had many been that the Treaty split would not result in civil war that when the fighting began they were slow to react.[92] When republican positions on the defensive line between Waterford and Limerick came under attack from government troops there was no attempt to defend them. Moreover, after the fall of Limerick, the anti-treaty commands were now clustered in the north-east, Connacht, and the south, and these regions were separated by divisions loyal to the Ministry of Defence.[93] The rationale of the IRA campaign was to provoke counter-productive coercion, arouse popular indignation, and destabilize the state to the point of collapse, but the consequences of their lack of conventional military successes were pointed out by one observer:[94]

The Provisional Government must inevitably succeed in advancing and conquering the South, even though it is quite possible to keep up guerrilla warfare for several years and thus make government and social peace possible in large districts. Meanwhile, the Provisional Government will be hailed as saviours of the people, they will receive a great accession of power and authority. The national defences of Ireland will be handed over to those who are the weakest nationally. The best fighters and strongest leaders will be killed, jailed and scattered; they will have lost all place in public life and all influence with the people. The greatest blow against the Republic is the coming exclusion of Republicans from what the vast majority of Ireland will regard as the Irish Army and the Irish Parliament.[95]

The comments proved prophetic. Waterford fell to government troops in the second week of July after an IRA plan to relieve their comrades from the west never materialized. Government troops landed by sea on the coasts of counties Kerry and Cork on 2 and 8 August, respectively, and the anti-treaty forces had to abandon their defences in Kilmallock, south of Limerick, after over a week's conventional fighting. The collapse of Cork soon followed, with the Cork anti-treaty IRA failing to put up much of a fight. After naval landings at Fenit and Tarbert, the population centres of Kerry, where the majority of the IRA also went anti-treaty, were occupied by the Free State forces by mid-August. The naval landings were of tremendous psychological impact since if the IRA could not hold Tralee for even a day, it was one more indication that they could not win the civil war.[96] According to Francis Blake, the IRA should have attempted some open fighting while it was still strong and sufficiently supported, instead of waging a hopeless guerrilla campaign against men who were familiar with their tactics and local environs.[97] This rapid succession of defeats in the south also led to a

---

[92] Hopkinson, *Green against Green*, 128.
[93] Fitzpatrick, *The Two Irelands*, 128.
[94] Ibid., 132.
[95] 'The outcome of Present Position', Confidential Memo, handwriting supposed to be of Barry Egan of Cork, n.d. (UCD, Frank Aiken Papers, P104/1244 (2)).
[96] Ryle Dwyer, *Tans, Terror and Troubles*, 354.
[97] Blake, *The Irish Civil War and What It Still Means for the Irish People*, 38.

demoralization of the rank and file, leading many to conclude that the war itself was finished. After the fall of Cork many IRA men simply returned to their homes.[98] On 5 August Collins reported to the cabinet that in the west of the country only four IRA units presented a problem and recommended that outside the Waterford–Cork–Kerry–Limerick area the civic guard should be introduced to restore law and order.[99] On 19 August Lynch told his men to organize themselves into active service units and to operate in the open.

The Provisional Government had quickly realized that military considerations must dictate broader policy and that the fight should be extended south and west as quickly as possible. A war council of three was appointed by the cabinet on 12 July with Collins as the leading figure. His personal charisma had been a factor in explaining why many IRA units kept their allegiance to the Provisional Government, and was one reason he was chosen as commander-in-chief.[100] William Cosgrave was appointed chairman of the Provisional Government and minister of finance in Collins' absence, but remained clearly under his influence. Mulcahy was appointed general chief of staff, with Eoin O'Duffy as commander of the crucial south western division. Other senior government figures, such as Fionan Lynch (vice commander of the south western division), Kevin O'Higgins (assistant adjutant general), Joseph McGrath (director of intelligence), and Diarmuid O'Hegarty (director of organization) also took up military positions. The anti-treaty press made much of these changes, Count Plunkett declaring that the Free State elite were indulging 'in frenzied shuffles and redistribution, in the interests of their inexperienced cliques, of posts instituted for tyrants' and had effectively set up 'a military dictatorship'. Anti-treaty propaganda represented the Provisional Government as 'a colonial junta' deriving its powers not from the people but from the British. It also emphasized the 'mercenary' nature of the Free State army, which was carrying out a war of reconquest on the part of the British.[101]

Under Collins a relentless process of centralization was put in train. The parliament was prorogued on 30 June and did not meet until 9 September.[102] Against the strong resistance of senior civil servants on 21 August Collins also imposed an oath of loyalty on all civil servants, including post office employees, and salary payments to anti-treaty members of the third Dail and to the registers of Parish Courts were soon discontinued.[103] On 11 July the circuit judges were recalled in mid-circuit and two days later the Supreme Court was abolished. This resulted in the resignation on 26 July of George Gavan Duffy, minister of foreign affairs, who believed that the new state's judiciary should evolve from the republican courts.[104] Then the cabinet took the decision to formally rescind the

---

[98] Hopkinson, *Green against Green*, 165.
[99] Collins to Cosgrave, 5 August 1922 (NA, D/T, S3361).
[100] Walsh, *The Civil War*, 7.
[101] George Noble Count Plunkett, 'To the People of Ireland', *Poblacht na hEireann*, 15 July 1922.
[102] P.G. Minutes, 18 August 1922 (NA, G1/3).
[103] P.G. Minutes, 22 July 1922 (NA, G1/2).
[104] Younger, *Ireland's Civil War*, 467.

Dail decree that established the republican courts, the only Dail decree ever to be rescinded. Collins did continue to pay the salaries of the four judges on the Supreme Court, but after 31 July only two of them received payment. All four were unanimous that the suppression of the Dail courts in July had been illegal.[105] However, O'Higgins declared that the old British legal system was sounder and more experienced than its republican rival.[106] The abolition of the 'illegal' Parish and District Courts followed logically from the abolition of republican Supreme and Circuit Courts, and was imperative once the Dail courts had shown a predilection for favouring IRA prisoners in their verdicts.[107] The fact that some of the registrars of the District Courts were also republicans was recognized by one minister, Patrick Hogan, as a particular problem that could be overcome by appointing people with sounder views from the pre-existing District and Parish Courts.[108]

Rigorous censorship of the media, including the prohibition of certain films in cinemas, was also put in place. As early as 29 June it was decided that references in the newspapers to the military situation in Dublin should be censored.[109] The importation, distribution, or sale of any newspapers not passed by the official censor was also prohibited. After deciding that the attitude of the Dublin newspapers was unsatisfactory, the editors of the *Freeman's Journal* and the *Irish Times* were soon called in for interview and later editions showed 'a considerable improvement'.[110] The anti-treaty IRA had made a fundamental mistake by leaving Dublin in the hands of their enemies, thereby allowing the Provisional Government to present themselves to the outside world as the lawful government in overall control of the situation.[111] Government propaganda reflected this fact. The following guidelines were issued to the press:

The Army must always be referred to as the 'Irish Army', the 'National Army', 'National Troops', or simply 'Troops'.
The Irregular Forces must not be referred to as the Executive Forces nor described as 'forces' or 'troops'. They are to be called 'bands' or 'bodies'.
Irregular leaders are not to be referred to as of any rank, such as 'Commander', etc, or are not to be called officers.
No news as to movements of troops may be published.
No news may be published as to movements of newly-enrolled members of the army, movements of foodstuffs or trains, or transport, or equipment for army purposes.
Articles or letters as to the treatment of the Irregular prisoners may not be published.
Censors may propose to substitute words or phrases, such as 'irregular' for 'Republican'; 'fired at' for 'attacked'; 'seized' for 'commandeered'; 'kidnapped' for 'arrested'; 'enrolled' for 'enlisted'.

---

[105] 'Memo on Supreme Court' by Judge Douglas, n.d. (UCD, de Valera Papers, P150/163).
[106] Townshend, *Ireland: The Twentieth Century*, 119.
[107] 'Local Courts', July 1922 (UCD, P24/72).
[108] Hogan to Blythe, 28 July 1922 (UCD, P24/73).
[109] P.G. Minutes, 28 June 1922 (NA, G1/1).
[110] P.G. Minutes, 7 July 1922 (NA, G1/1).
[111] Blake, *The Irish Civil War and What It Still Means for the Irish People*, 36.

Letters, news, or articles dealing with proposals for peace, or negotiations with the
irregulars should not be passed without submitting them to the Chief Censor.
The term 'Provisional Government' should not be used. The correct term being 'Irish
Government'.[112]

Collins' death, reportedly on his way to a meeting with anti-treaty IRA men in
Cork on 22 August, led many to believe that the Free State cause had been dealt a
fatal blow. On 24 August Joe McKelvey, a member of the IRA Executive, wrote to
Ernie O'Malley that the Free Staters are 'terribly cut up' about Collins' death and
seemed absolutely lost without him.[113] Ironically however, his death actually lead
to the stabilization of the Provisional Government's broader policy, and nowhere
was this more apparent than with respect to Northern Ireland. At the beginning
of the year Collins was confident of his ability to secure Irish unity under the
terms of the Treaty and favoured dealing directly with Sir James Craig instead of
relying on the British representative on the Boundary Commission.[114] He hoped
to entice the North into an Irish state through the mechanism of a constitutional
convention that would draw up a constitution for the whole island. To this end
non-recognition of the northern parliament was essential. However, between 6
December 1921 and 31 May 1922 73 Protestants and 147 Catholics were killed in
Belfast, and Collins also tried to play the role of protector of northern Catholics
through his negotiation of two pacts with Craig. On 22 April, however, Collins
told Churchill that Craig and his supporters had completely violated the second
pact 'in practically every detail'.[115] On 4 May he stressed to his cabinet the urgent
need to prevent any extension of the Stormont parliament's powers. What was
required was a scheme of general non-cooperation and a plan 'making it impossible for them to carry on'.[116] The failure of the second pact with Craig had been
followed by another wave of violence in the North, and in May Collins and
Mulcahy agreed to cooperate with the anti-treaty IRA in Dublin in a joint
offensive across the border. At the same time Collins got his government to
agree to a public statement to the effect that the Treaty was signed between
Great Britain and Ireland, and the interpretation of its clauses did not lie with
Sir James Craig.[117] On 3 June it was decided that a policy of 'peaceful obstruction'
should be adopted towards the Belfast government, although Collins' peace
policy in this period was probably 'a mere public front'.[118]

Indeed historians differ with regard to Collins' long-term intentions on
partition. Regan suggests that Collins' involvement with the northern IRA,
who generally supported the Treaty, merely reflected his desire to prevent the

---

[112] 'The Pen is Mightier than the Sword' (NL, NIC 53).
[113] McKelvey to O'Malley, 24 August 1922 (UCD, Mulcahy Papers, P7/B/88).
[114] Provisional Government to Colonial Office, 21 January 1922 (NA, D/T, S1801/A).
[115] Collins to Churchill, 22 April 1922 (NA, D/T, S5462).
[116] 'Confidential memo from Collins to all Ministers', 4 May 1922 (NA, D/T, S5462).
[117] P.G. Minutes, 25 May 1922, NA G1/1.
[118] M. Hopkinson, 'The Craig-Collins Pacts of 1922: Two Attempted Reforms of the Northern
Ireland Government', *Irish Historical Studies*, 27/106 (1990), 149.

anti-treaty IRA capitalizing on the emotive issue of partition.[119] Coogan, on the other hand, argues that had he lived and stabilized the south, Collins fully intended achieving the goal of a united Ireland by military means if necessary.[120] Either way the conflict in the south and Collins' eventual death opened a window of opportunity to those who wanted to normalize relations with the northern government, which after all had a common interest in stability. On 1 August a committee to review the Provisional Government's policy on Northern Ireland was established, consisting of Patrick Hogan, J. J. Walsh, Desmond FitzGerald, Ernest Blythe, and Michael Hayes.[121] On 19 August it agreed to recommend a peace policy and this was accepted by the cabinet.[122] Collins' death had removed the last person in the Provisional Government with a strong protective interest in northern Catholics. A month later Seamus Woods, officer in command of the third northern division of the IRA, wrote to Mulcahy, now commander-in-chief, citing a meeting with Collins on 2 August 1922, where Collins indicated that he intended to deal with the North 'in a very definite way', and lamenting the fact that the Provisional Government now seemed to be encouraging Catholics to recognize the northern parliament.[123]

The conventional phase of the civil war had thus witnessed the capitulation of the anti-treatyites in conventional fighting and the centralization of power in the person of Collins. The course of the fighting thus far confirmed a general finding of comparative research, which is that insurgencies not buoyed up by early military successes generally fade away. Hart paints a very clear picture of the disintegration of the Cork IRA faced with the prospect of shooting their fellow-countrymen. He notes that by October 1922 there were only 1,300 men on brigade rolls in the whole of Cork: a loss of almost 90 per cent of the county's pre-treaty strength.[124] Only a quarter of the county's revolutionary deaths resulted from the civil war.[125] Nevertheless, Cork was still one of the three most violent counties during the civil war. Ironically, Collins' death was followed by the development of a more intransigent political outlook on the part of his successors, and this was to be the most important political factor in the whole civil war. On 26 July Collins had reflected that the British government would be making a profound miscalculation if they interpreted the results of the June election as an enthusiastic vote for the symbols of 'a sham imperialism'.[126] In contrast Cosgrave, his successor, told a peace intermediary in October that 'we stand for the Treaty and at the elections the country made it plain that they did so also'.[127] Peace could only be

[119] Regan, *The Irish Counter-revolution*, 63.
[120] T. P. Coogan, *De Valera: Long Fellow Long Shadow* (London, 1992), 319.
[121] P.G. Minutes, 1 August 1922 (NA, G1/3).
[122] P.G. Minutes, 19 August 1922 (NA, G1/3).
[123] Wood to Commander-in-Chief, 29 September 1922 (NA, D/T, S5462).
[124] Hart, *The IRA and Its Enemies*, 263.
[125] Ibid., 121.
[126] Collins, Memo, 26 July 1922 (UCD, Mulcahy Papers, P7/B/28).
[127] Cosgrave to Loftus, 31 October 1923 (NA, D/T, S4522).

established on the basis of its terms, without revision.[128] Indeed the day after Cosgrave's election as president of the Executive Council on 9 September, British intelligence noted that 'there are no signs of double dealing at present, a feature noticeable with the preceding Ministry'.[129] On the other hand, there remained doubts about Cosgrave's ability to see the conflict through to the end. General Boyd, officer in command of the British troops in Ireland, informed his superiors that Cosgrave, 'though a capable and sincere man, would not be able to carry through by himself the task of establishment of order'.[130] To an army man it might have seemed obvious that an eminently civilian politician would be incapable of seeing the civil war through, but the chief paradox of the civil war was that civilians would prove more adept at fighting than the militarists, and the uncompromising role played by Cosgrave over the following months would be a dramatic illustration of this fact.

THE GUERRILLA PHASE

The 'guerrilla phase' of the civil war begins with the death of Collins and the assumption of power by a group of men who were determined to exclude the republican viewpoint entirely from the chambers of power. The conventional phase of the fighting had initially been undertaken by people with heavy hearts, who were determined to work the Treaty in order to avoid a break with Britain, but who also regarded it in the nature of an experiment, one to be judged according to whether it secured 'the freedom to achieve freedom' that Collins had hoped. The guerrilla phase in contrast saw the development of a new political programme that drew much of its vigour from the policy of deliberately closing down every avenue of peace in the interests of driving their opponents into the political wilderness. Superficial changes, such as calling the head of government 'the president' rather than 'the prime minister', and removing the King from the postage stamps, testified to the Sinn Fein origins of this new elite, but between the convening of parliament on 9 September 1922 and the imperial conference of 1926, the overriding logic of policy seemed to be to tie 'southern Ireland' more firmly to the Empire it had repudiated in 1918.[131] On the anti-treaty side, once Liam Lynch accepted the inevitability of conflict there was no man more committed to the defence of the republican ideal.[132] On 7 October British army intelligence would report that the political leaders of the republican side were ceding power to the Bolshevik and the gunman, while the frequent resort to

---

[128] *Irish Times*, 1 January 1923.
[129] 'Dublin District Weekly Intelligence Summary, No 178, for week ending 10 September 1922' (NA, D/T, 1784).
[130] 24th (P) Infantry Brigade, Weekly Intelligence Summary for Week ending 26 August 1922: 'Civil War: Intelligence Report to British Government by General Boyd' (NA, D/T, 1784).
[131] O'Brien, 'The Irish Free State: Secret History of Its Foundation'.
[132] Lyons, *Ireland since the Famine*, 464.

reprisals and ill-treatment of prisoners was alienating the general public from the Provisional Government.[133]

With this process of polarization also went a change in the nature of the fighting itself. With conventional hostilities ostensibly over by September, the struggle was now carried on by ambush and counter-ambush, jarring men's nerves and driving the pro-treaty side to extremes of cruelty.[134] The Provisional Government responded to the shift with the same measures that the British had employed between 1919 and 1921: emergency powers, internment, and official and unofficial reprisals, giving substance to the charge that their project was essentially a neo-colonial one.[135] O'Halpin suggests that the National Army was more than willing to go beyond its legal powers, especially concerning the murder of 150 prisoners in custody, but the drastic measures it took were also very effective in lowering republican morale.[136] Regan in contrast suggests that the executions, although effective in preventing the wholesale assassination of Free State personnel, were also intended by the politicians on the Free State side to kill off any hope of general reconciliation.[137] The anti-treatyites' reaction to the executions, particularly through the destruction of the property of Free State supporters, then seemed to fulfil Mary MacSwiney's prophecy that their cause could only triumph if the duress they subjected the Irish public to exceeded the 'immoral duress' that had forced them to accept the British Empire.[138] In county Longford for example, 55 per cent of the houses burned down during the civil war were destroyed between the end of January and the end of March 1923, largely in reaction to the increased number of executions by the government.[139] In other words in the new year, which kicked off with 34 official executions in January alone, the guerrilla war had all the semblance of a post-colonial dogfight, and if both sides had entered the conflict as reluctant adversaries, its final phase was testimony to their combined capacity for antagonism. Perhaps it was fortunate that the destructive potential of this stalemate was ultimately limited less by the scruples of the combatants than by the unequal balance of power in the field.

The appointment of William Cosgrave, who also retained his finance portfolio, as chairman of the new Provisional Government in August 1922 was an important moment in the consolidation of a genuinely pro-treaty regime despite Griffith's death only two weeks earlier. Cosgrave was a 'reluctant revolutionary' who had been a supporter of Griffith's monarchist strand within Sinn Fein from the outset, and had issued a pamphlet denouncing de Valera's 'document number

---

[133] 'Dublin District Weekly Intelligence Summary No 181 for Week Ending October 7 1922' (NA, D/T, 1784).

[134] Lyons, *Ireland since the Famine*, 465.

[135] Tonwshend, *Ireland: The Twentieth Century*, 271; Blake, *The Irish Civil War and What It Still Means for the Irish People*, 43.

[136] O'Halpin, *The Irish State and Its Enemies*, 31.

[137] Regan, *The Irish Counter-revolution*, 122.

[138] MacSwiney to de Valera, 10 February 1923 (NL, Ir 320 P78).

[139] M. Coleman, *County Longford and the Irish Revolution, 1910–1923* (Dublin, 2003), 145.

two' earlier in 1922.[140] Although a volunteer in the 1916 Rising, Cosgrave had also been a member of Dublin Corporation since 1909, chairman of its financial committee from 1916 to 1922, and minister of local government both of the Dail of 1919–21 and of the provisional government.[141] De Valera described him as 'a ninny' but one that would be 'egged on by the Church' against republicans.[142] As part of the new cabinet O'Higgins left his army post and became minister of home affairs, Mulcahy was now both minister of defence and chief of staff, while Desmond FitzGerald took over external affairs. Other appointments, such as Joe McGrath to industry and commerce, Ernest Blythe to local government, Eoin MacNeill to education, Patrick Hogan to agriculture, with Eamonn Dugan and Fionan Lynch as ministers without portfolio, and J. J. Walsh continuing as postmaster general, were also made from the administrative cream of the pro-treaty elite rather than from the IRA and the IRB.[143] As Regan remarks, in a time of potential defections and uncertainty Griffith and Collins had had to rely on the more dedicated pro-treatyites within Sinn Fein for ministerial positions, avoiding even the most aggressive 'stepping stone' pro-treatyites.[144] Many of these had a 'literal' attitude to the Treaty, in contrast to Collins, who had tried to manipulate its terms in order to accommodate the republican perspective.[145]

Two days after the death of Collins Churchill had asked his successors for an assurance that there would be no change in their attitude towards the Treaty. In response, the cabinet decided that those clauses in the new constitution dealing with external relations, the senate, and justice could not be altered by the new Dail.[146] All those elected to the new Provisional Government on 9 September signed acceptance of the Treaty as was required by its terms. Another sign of the new government's departure from the 'stepping stone' approach to the Treaty was their attitude towards the oath. Unlike in the House of Commons, where the members took an oath in the presence of the House and of the public, the Irish oath was to be taken in secret in the office of a subordinate official before the deputy was allowed to enter the chamber. This suggested to some that the real purpose of the procedure was to exclude the republicans from the Dail and deny them the oxygen of publicity.[147] Only one anti-treaty TD, Laurence Ginnell, attended the meeting on 9 September, and was expelled after enquiring whether the parliament was *Dail Eireann* or a partition assembly. Later in the month, when the new constitution was being debated by the Dail, the Labour leader Thomas Johnson enquired of the government which articles of the draft constitution they considered necessary to preserve the Treaty position and which could

---

[140] Regan, *The Irish Counter-revolution*, 82; Coogan, *De Valera: Long Fellow Long Shadow*, 345.
[141] Fanning, *Independent Ireland*, 18.
[142] Curran, *The Birth of the Irish Free State*, 253.
[143] Regan, *The Irish Counter-revolution*, 81.
[144] Ibid., 82.
[145] M. Hopkinson, 'From the Treaty to Civil War, 1921–2', in J. R. Hill (ed.), *Ireland, 1921–84: A New History of Ireland*, vol. 11 (Oxford, 2003), 8.
[146] P.G. Decision, 26 August 1922 (NA, G1/3).
[147] O'Brien, 'The Irish Free State: Secret History of Its Foundation'.

be revised. On 22 September O'Higgins replied that the preamble and those articles dealing with the status of the state (1 and 2), the role of the crown in the legislative process (5, 8, 12, and 16), the taking of an oath (6 and 17), the powers and salary of the governor general (7 and 14), and the appeal to the Privy Council were all considered necessary.[148] O'Higgins' attitude to the constitution contrasted with that of Collins, who had told his constitutional committee earlier in the year that the Treaty was a new thing 'and not a sort of widening of existing powers derived from the English Parliament'.[149]

The corollary of such a strict adherence to the terms of the Treaty was even less tolerance of the republicans, and the new government quickly moved to the view that drastic measures were needed to meet their challenge. Collins himself had been against executions, but his death removed the one brake on his colleagues' desire for sterner measures against the IRA.[150] The Dail approved the use of military courts on 28 September, and on 10 October the government issued a proclamation to the effect that such courts were being set up with the power of inflicting death upon those who were guilty of taking part in attacks on government forces, looting and arson, and possession of explosives and firearms.[151] A proposal by the Labour leader to treat captured IRA prisoners as prisoners of war and to appoint legal officials as presidents of the military courts was defeated in the Dail by 47 votes to 15. In the Dail Mulcahy declared that such official executions would prevent his men carrying out unofficial ones. On 17 November, Kevin O'Higgins, the minister for home affairs, told the Dail that four young Dublin men had been shot that morning, following a secret court martial. They had been found guilty of the possession of firearms. The first news the men's relatives received was an official form with the wording 'Remains of—coffined and buried' with the name of the dead man inserted in the blank.[152] On 26 November E. Culverwell, a professor of law at Trinity College, told Cosgrave that the secret nature of the courts created unease even among those convinced of the necessity for stern methods to deal with the IRA.[153] Two days earlier Erskine Childers had also been executed for the possession of a pistol, originally given him by Collins. It was rumoured that his wife had been deliberately kept ignorant of the date of his execution and that Childers was refused the cleric of his choice for his last rites.

The executions that followed were usually at the discretion of the local commanders, and the authorities wished that personal responsibility should be as widely spread amongst senior officers as possible.[154] Over the following six months the executions would be evenly distributed throughout the state: between

[148] O'Higgins to Johnson, 22 September 1922 (NA, D/T, S4650/1).
[149] 'Constitution of the Irish Free State' (NA, D/T, S1125/15).
[150] Regan, *The Irish Counter-revolution*, 106.
[151] S. MacSuain, *County Wexford's Civil War* (Wexford, 1995), 81.
[152] Blake, *The Irish Civil War and What It Still Means for the Irish People*, 47.
[153] Culverwell to Cosgrave, 26 November 1922 (NA, D/T, S8141).
[154] Blake, *The Irish Civil War and What It Still Means for the Irish People*, 53.

17 November and 26 April 35 would take place in the eastern command area, 20 in the western command area, 19 in the southern command area, and 7 in the Curragh. The most controversial execution was the shooting of four unconvicted members of the IRA Executive, Rory O'Connor, Liam Mellowes, Joseph McKelvey, and Richard Barrett, one from each province, in Dublin on 8 December, in reprisal for the shooting of two pro-treaty TDs the previous day. They had all been arrested before the public safety bill came into force so their execution had no legal basis. The following day Mulcahy proclaimed that a conspiracy existed to assassinate the members of the nation's parliament and this had already claimed two victims. The Free State authorities had got hold of documents revealing that on 27 November Lynch had ordered that all the TDs who had supported the government's execution policy were to be assassinated. A captured document, apparently signed by Thomas Derrig as 'adjutant general' of the anti-treaty forces, was sent to Cahir Davitt in the army command's legal staff. It contained an order to execute all the members of the Provisional Government, all who voted in the Dail for the special powers act, all the members of the Army Council, and most of the army command's legal staff. Davitt was summoned to the adjutant-general's office where the Army Council had been meeting on the evening of 7 December.[155] The meeting decided to execute the four leaders. Apparently it was the fear of his supporters caving in that led Mulcahy to ask for the consent of the cabinet for the execution of the four men.[156]

The army's communiqué on the executions of the four men contained the term 'reprisal', which drew a protest from Archbishop Byrne of Dublin that the execution of the four IRA leaders were 'unjustifiable from the moral point of view'.[157] However, republicans believed that the bishops' pastoral issued at Maynooth on 10 October had provided the government with the specific moral sanction they required.[158] The pastoral had emphasized the duty of the population to support the government and banned republican soldiers from receiving the sacraments of communion and confession. To the end of the conflict many priests would refuse to preside over the funerals of dead IRA men. As early as June 1921, when de Valera visited Maynooth to ask the bishops to give formal recognition to the Republic set up in 1919 and allegedly given a strong mandate in the election the previous month, the bishops had showed their reluctance to endorse the republican cause.[159] Once the Treaty was signed, the Catholic hierarchy came out wholeheartedly in favour of the settlement and were instrumental in shaping public opinion during the Christmas recess. Then the bishops' pastoral on 26 April, which was read out at all masses, advised the public to accept the Treaty and denounced the IRA. The Provisional Government had consulted the Church about Article 10 in the constitution providing for free primary education and

---

[155] D. Keogh, *Twentieth-Century Ireland: Nation and State* (Dublin, 1994), 14.
[156] Blake, *The Irish Civil War and What It Still Means for the Irish People*, 51.
[157] Keogh, *Twentieth-Century Ireland*, 15.
[158] Murray, *Oracles of God*, 83.
[159] Ibid., 19.

Cosgrave in particular enjoyed close relations with several prominent clerics.[160] The joint pastoral published in the newspapers on 11 October was timed to coincide with the amnesty offer made the week earlier, and with the application of the recent Public Safety Bill, which would apply from 15 October. It was read out at all masses on 22 October.[161] The pastoral declared it a matter of 'divine law' that the 'legitimate authority in Ireland just now' was the Provisional Government; that there was 'no other government, and cannot be, outside the body of the people'; that 'the guerrilla warfare now being carried on by the Irregulars is without moral sanction; and therefore the killing of National Soldiers in the course of it is murder before God'.[162] Although the executions were opposed in private by various bishops, Cosgrave reminded Archbishop Byrne on 18 November that their pastoral letter had provided his government with a moral basis for stern measures, and that the issues were no longer merely political, but a question of what is right or wrong according to divine law.[163]

To the end of the conflict there is no record of a specific Episcopal condemnation of any of the Free State misdemeanours during the civil war, and the Church–State alliance survived the executions and the further reprisal killings that were to take place, notably in Kerry in early March, when seventeen IRA prisoners were killed in unofficial reprisals within a fortnight.[164] Nevertheless, the anti-treatyites took the pastoral with the utmost seriousness and tried to exploit a clause that stated that its contents were binding on the faithful subject to an appeal to the Holy See.[165] One of the significant effects of the pastoral (which stated that the Provisional Government was 'the government set up by the nation') was to provide the spur for the formation of a republican government that might give some substance to their claim that the Provisional Government was a usurpation and give legal and moral sanction to the activities of the IRA.[166] At the instigation of Count Plunkett, a Catholic Appeal Committee was set up on 12 October in order to appeal to the Pope against the bishops' pastoral, which 'subject a large number of Irish Catholics to severe penalties on political grounds'.[167] The appeal was delivered in December to Pietro Gasparri, secretary of state to the Vatican, and asked the Pope to revoke the decision to deprive republicans of the sacraments and stop the Irish hierarchy penalizing the republicans on political grounds. It argued that there were now two rival governments in Ireland, each claiming legitimacy. One, the government of the Republic, had been established by the Irish people themselves in 1918 and 1921, and another that derived its authority from the English parliament. Since the Treaty ignored Ireland's right to self-determination and its right to maintain its territorial

[160] Regan, *The Irish Counter-revolution*, 83.
[161] Fanning, *Independent Ireland*, 20.
[162] Murray, *Oracles of God*, 75.
[163] Ibid., 87.
[164] Ibid., 74.
[165] Ibid., 76.
[166] Ibid., 88.
[167] *Irish Times*, 11 November 1922.

integrity what ensued was not a war between parties but a defence of a nation's rights.[168] The appeal, however, failed to reverse the Catholic Church's attitude to the republicans who remained blamed for all the destructiveness of the civil war.[169]

The formation of a Republican Government served other purposes besides preventing the Free State government from establishing itself as the legal successor of the Second Dail. It would also provide a rallying point for the anti-treaty activists and establish a claim to the funds of the Republic, most of which were still in the United States.[170] The funds were the crucial reason for de Valera's acceptance of a need for a Republican Government and they could be used to purchase much-needed arms.[171] The establishment of a government also followed logically from the IRA Executive's declaration in September that the Third Dail was an illegal assembly, since the Second Dail, which they considered the legitimate parliament of the country, had not been dissolved. As de Valera commented, any other response to the convening of the Third Dail would leave the anti-treatyites 'at sixes and sevens'.[172] De Valera's actual preference was for the anti-treaty party to take control, acting as the legitimate Dail, but he realized that the IRA would not give it the support without which the government would be a farce. He also privately confessed that his side 'will be turned down definitely by the electorate in a few months time'.[173] The solution was to ask the army to authorize him to establish a Republican Government, which it did late in October, when it publicly called on de Valera to form a presidential government after its Executive meeting on 16/17 October.[174] The available anti-treaty deputies met secretly for the first time in Dublin on 25 October and constituted themselves as a government. The personnel chosen were Austin Stack (minister of finance), P. J. Ruttledge (home affairs), Sean T. O'Kelly (local government), Robert Barton (economic affairs), and Liam Mellowes (minister of defence). Mellowes was in prison at this stage and would be executed on 8 December.

The process of government formation revealed de Valera's limited influence on the IRA leadership during the war. In February 1923 he would reflect that he was condemned to view the war 'as through a wall of glass, powerless to intervene effectively', and from September to February, when he called for a peace based on document no. 2, de Valera's preferences were clearly subordinate to those of Lynch.[175] On 12 October he had informed the IRA Executive that if the Treaty could be worked without Ireland appearing to agree to give away her sovereignty and accept partition, he would be in favour of working it.[176] Then on 19 October

[168] (UCD, de Valera Papers, P150/1655).
[169] Murray, *Oracles of God*, 90.
[170] De Valera to Chief of Staff and Members of the Executive, 12 October 1922 (NL, Ms 31,528).
[171] Murphy, 'The Irish Civil War 1922–1923', 300.
[172] De Valera to Murchadha, 6 September 1922 (UCD, Mulcahy Papers, P7/B/331).
[173] De Valera to Murchadha, 13 September 1922 (UCD, Mulcahy Papers, P7/B/258).
[174] *Irish Times*, 30 October 1922.
[175] De Valera to Ellis, 26 Feburary 1923 (NL, Ir 320 P78).
[176] De Valera to Chief of Staff and Members of the Executive, 12 October 1922 (NL, Ms 31,528).

1922 he told Joe McGarrity that he would make peace on the basis of document No. 2, 'and I do not want the young fellows who are fighting for the Republic to think otherwise'. However, at the same time de Valera arranged with Lynch that documents from his defence department would be signed by both himself and Lynch, and this remained the practice for the rest of the war.[177] As a result, on 7 November a notice appeared in the press, signed by de Valera, stating that the principles the republicans were defending in the civil war were not open to compromise, and that victory or utter defeat and extermination were now the alternatives.[178] The Provisional Government exploited this weakness in the political anti-treatyites' position by citing it as reason not to entertain peace terms: on 28 September Ernest Blythe had announced that the Irregular IRA leaders were not honourable men and the political leaders had not the power to make peace proposals.[179]

De Valera's relationship with Lynch was put under further pressure when faced with the dilemma of how to counter the executions. Although (in an order dated 27 September) Lynch at first ordered no reprisals if the Public Safety Bill was passed, the proposal to assassinate members of the Dail was made long before the executions began on 31 October, and bore fruit with Lynch's proclamation of 17 November, when, in response to the executions that day, Lynch had listed all members of the Dail who had voted for the Public Safety Act, hostile newspapermen, editors, High Court judges, senators, Unionist representatives, and 'aggressive Free State supporters' as legitimate targets.[180] However, after the IRA Executive meeting held on the 16/17 October had agreed unanimously to execute all the members of the Dail who voted for the Public Safety Bill, Lynch had not issued a general order for such actions, but instructed the Dublin first and second brigades that nine members of the Provisional Government were to be assassinated and two members of the parliament arrested. He proposed to de Valera that the speaker of the Dail be informed of the threat and that the Labour TDs also be notified that if they continued their attendance at the Dail, similar action would be taken against them.[181] De Valera replied that while the efficacy of reprisals was open to doubt, he saw no other way of stopping the others and protecting their men. The speaker should indeed be informed of their 'eye for an eye' policy.[182] After the IRA burnings of the following weeks, however, de Valera told Lynch that the policy of an eye for an eye was not going to win the people round and without the people they could never win.[183] Lynch replied that the burnings were helping their cause with the people, and rejected the accusation that their policy was an eye for an eye, since they had recently released hundreds of prisoners without harm.[184]

---

[177] Pakenham and O'Neill, *Eamon de Valera*, 201.
[178] *Irish Times*, 7 November 1922.
[179] *Irish Times*, 28 September 1922.
[180] De Valera to each member of the Executive Council, 13 December 1922 (NL, Ir 320 P78).
[181] Lynch to de Valera, 25 November 1922 (UCD, de Valera Papers, P150/1749).
[182] De Valera to Lynch, 27 November 1922, ibid.
[183] De Valera to Lynch, 12 December 1922, ibid.
[184] Lynch to de Valera, 14 December 1922, ibid.

De Valera, however, wanted to know what the ultimate objective of Lynch's policy was, and warned him that his leadership had too low an estimate of the strength and determination of their opponents and too high an estimate of their own.[185]

For the Government the simple lesson to be drawn from the executions of 8 December was that they had prevented the implementation of Lynch's 'orders of frightfulness' and no more TDs were assassinated during the civil war. However, when the government met with the Army Council on 11 January and ministers presented memoranda on how the lawless state of the country could be dealt with, both O'Higgins and Hogan advocated more systematic executions.[186] Their eagerness contrasted with the army's own stance. That day an army poster in Kerry had stated that three men from Tralee and one from Dingle had been found guilty of possession of weapons. It warned that IRA activity in the county had to cease or the stay on the execution of their sentences would be removed.[187] The men were never executed. At the government meeting on 11 January, however, O'Higgins and Hogan got their way: committees of officers were established at battalion level throughout the country to sentence prisoners, resulting in more localized executions.[188] The executions in Kerry were resumed on 20 January when four men, James Daly, John Clifford, Michael Brosnan, and James Hanlon, were shot in Tralee. Key figures within the civilian leadership were clearly convinced that behind the irregular campaign lay the menace of social revolution and this fear informed their more extreme proposals. On 1 February Kevin O'Shiel, a government legal adviser, informed Cosgrave that the IRA campaign could pave the way for the coming of Bolshevism. In his view the 'Irregulars' had placed themselves outside the pale of civilization and had to be dealt with 'by methods usually not adopted by civilised governments'. He asked for the summary execution of those found in arms.[189] Cosgrave was also convinced that the bulk of the IRA were not motivated by patriotic motives. In March he told the *Daily Express* that he was faced with four types of opposition: the political malcontents such as de Valera and Mary MacSwiney, 'the military-political section' composed of men who were both military officers and TDs, 'blatant opportunists and job hunters', and criminals.[190]

Despite this cynicism, the policy of executions continued to be applied in a selective way and no more than 77 men had been officially executed by the end of the war. As Keogh suggests, in a comparative context this is small scale: at the end of the Hungarian civil war more than 5,000 people were killed in the White terror, not to mention the 12,500 Finns who died in White prison camps in the summer and autumn of 1918.[191] Where the methods were extreme, as in Kerry, this

---

[185] De Valera to Lynch, 15 December 1922, (UCD, de Valera Papers, P150/1749).
[186] Regan, *The Irish Counter-revolution*, 120.
[187] Ryle Dwyer, *Tans, Terror and Troubles*, 365.
[188] Regan, *The Irish Counter-revolution*, 121.
[189] O'Shiel to Cosgrave, 1 February 1923 (UCD, Mulcahy Papers, P7/8/100).
[190] *Irish Times*, 12 March 1923.
[191] Keogh, *Twentieth-Century Ireland*, 11; on Hungary, see J. Rothschild, *East Central Europe between the Two World Wars* (Seattle, 1974), 153; on Finland, see R. Alapuro, 'Coping with the Civil War of 1918

seemed to be the result of outsiders (mainly Dubliners and Northeners) trying to impose order on an uncooperative society. Ryle Dwyer suggests that 40 IRA men were killed in custody in the county during the civil war.[192] In Cork, on the other hand, where most of the national troops were natives, no comparable cycle of reprisals set in.[193] Only one of the 77 official executions took place in that county. One factor that may also have militated against wholesale executions was the army's common belief that the rank and file of the IRA were essentially decent men who had been 'duped' by their leaders. One officer who visited Tralee jail wrote to his superiors:

I must say that I was surprised at the type of Irregular that I found. They are quite different from any other prisoners I have seen and are mainly farmers sons. I firmly believe that when things become normal that most of these prisoners could be released and they would give no further trouble. They are mostly men who have been led astray and who really did not know what they were doing. They simply followed certain leaders who led them astray. This is the explanation for the tough fight they put up in Kerry. They are mostly men who thought they were fighting as in the old days and who were poisoned with Irregular propaganda. Now that they are beginning to see the light they are quite friendly towards our troops and I believe that most of these men will one day join either the Army of the Civil Guard.[194]

Either way, in the new year the solidity of the republican force began to disintegrate. A lull in the executions in February, combined with calls from IRA prisoners for peace to be discussed, signalled the beginning of the disintegration of the IRA's resistance, which would culminate in a ceasefire on 30 April, more than a fortnight after Lynch had been killed running from Free State forces. At a minimum the IRA had tried to force the Provisional Government to collapse, but more perceptive members realized that behind the Free State government lay the might of the British army. The executions had killed off the prospect that one day the IRA would be reunited in a final push for full independence, meaning that a divided and impoverished country would be unable to accomplish such a goal. One officer, Frank Barrett from Clare, wrote to Lynch on 11 February:

Until recent developments (Deasy and Limerick gaol) I had no doubt but we could have defeated the Free State army, and compelled the Free State government to capitulate. My hopes of ever doing this now are not at all bright. Anyhow to do so will exhaust our last resource and England is there always. We cannot now join with the Free State army in anything. What then is going to defeat England?[195]

---

in Twentieth Century Finland', in K. Christie and R. Cribb (eds.), *Historical Injustice and Democratic Transition* (London and New York, 2002), 169.

[192] Ryle Dwyer, *Tans, Terror and Troubles*, 364.

[193] Hart, *The IRA and its Enemies*, 121.

[194] 'Report on Operation carried out in the West Cork and South Kerry Areas', May 1923 (NA, D/T, S3361).

[195] Frank Barrett to Lynch, 11 February 1923 (UCD, P69/39/18).

An open breach between de Valera and the IRA Executive then occurred on 17 February when in an interview he asked the British to allow Ireland to chose in a plebiscite between the Free State and the alternative (document no. 2) that he put forward January a year ago.[196] De Valera felt that the anti-treatyites needed to make clear that they accepted certain fundamental conditions, which the press made it appear they denied, and the statement was an attempt to formulate 'a moral basis' for their position.[197] However, the rank and file of the IRA had never been interested in document no. 2, and Lynch was oblivious to the need to justify their position in democratic terms. By February de Valera was already reorganizing Sinn Fein for post-civil war politics, and had begun formulating his own peace proposals that would eventually bring the IRA campaign to an end. In the process document no. 2 would be abandoned. The IRA Executive would not meet until April, but a combination of limited popular support and the executions was forcing the most ardent republican purists to accept reality. On 13 February 1923 Cosgrave had declared that de Valera's followers amounted to more than 3,000 or 4,000 people throughout the country, and his cause had not a ghost of a chance of success.[198] On 7 March Tom Barry remarked that

It has been our hope in the past that we could prevent their governing, that popular opinion would force their abdication, that the decent elements in the Free State Army would revolt, that they could not hold out financially, that the people would come over to us. But none of these things happened. One thing we forgot in our calculations was that the Free State government was a government only when it suited itself to call itself and act as such. To all intents and purposes it is a body of men who will do anything to win.[199]

Behind such judgements lay an increasingly hopeless military situation. An army report on the state of the country in March stated that armed opposition in anything like column strength could be found only in a few places, and where such columns existed it was mainly due to the mountainous terrain. IRA activity in Cork was almost non-existent while in Kerry the IRA were no longer interested in fighting.[200] An army report for mid-April further commented that in areas where resistance had been most formidable four or five months ago, government troops had now established themselves securely and were gradually but surely winning round the confidence of the people.[201] Where the army was inefficient, however, the IRA continued to dominate local areas, such as in Kerry and Mayo. In Wexford too the columns of Thomas O'Sullivan in the New Ross area, and Bob Lambert around Wexford town, caused extensive destruction and still controlled large areas of the countryside in the spring. In fact, because of a lack of support from Waterford Command, inefficient army methods, and non-cooperation

---

[196] *Irish Times*, 17 February 1923.
[197] DeValera to Chief of Staff and the Ministry, 8 February 1923 (UCD, Moss Twomey Papers, P69/92 (129)).
[198] *Irish Times*, 13 February 1922.
[199] Barry to Executive Council, 7 March 1923 (UCD, de Valera Papers, P150/1647).
[200] 'Report on the Military Situation', 31 March 1923 (NA, D/T, S331).
[201] 'Army Report for Week Ending 15 April 1923', ibid.

from the public, IRA activity in the county actually increased as the conflict wore on.[202] The South Wexford IRA brigade report for January had painted a remarkable picture:

In the 4th Battalion area we are in the strongest fighting position and the enemy seems to have concentrated on this. They have large cycling columns, 70 to 80 men, sometimes accompanied by lorries. These columns go out at 3 a.m. and lie behind ditches on the off chance of our men walking into it. They have a few houses which they raid in every area with clocklike regularity. Enemy do not move about this area, except in very strong bodies and they are always noticed going out of town, so that if some signal could be arranged from Wexford it would be very helpful. A peculiar feature of enemy activity in this area is that they have made only one serious attempt at a 'round up' on a large scale.[203]

More generally, police reports in the spring made a distinction between the state of the country, which was unsatisfactory, and the overall military situation, which was encouraging, but the former was precarious precisely where the military situation was not cleared up. In Leitrim, for example, although IRA activity was significant only in the border area with Sligo, most of the county remained in a disturbed condition well into 1924. The Garda report for September 1923 said that the southern portion of the county was 'practically lawless'. The following month it was considered 'utterly lawless'. In November the whole of the county was in an 'exceedingly unsatisfactory condition'. In December the report stated that in the southern portion 'complete lawlessness prevails'.[204] The report for February 1924 commented:

Armed Irregulars are moving about both in South and North Leitrim. The Irregulars have the support of the majority of the inhabitants who shelter and give them food. Until these bands of armed Irregulars are completely broken up and their leaders arrested there can be no hope of a return to normal conditions. Their very presence and the ease with which they would appear to move about produce a most demoralising effect on the public mind.[205]

The establishment of military posts throughout the county and the arrest of prominent IRA leaders brought an improvement in the situation in the spring of 1924, but the county was still considered unsatisfactory in May, a year after the civil war ended. In that month there were 36 prosecutions of IRA men in the county.

In so far as the civil war had been seen by the government primarily in terms of the reassertion of law and order, and IRA activity as essentially criminal in nature, the civil war could not be said to have ended with the IRA ceasefire at the end of April. In legal terms the civil war came to an end on 31 July 1923 when the High Court ordered the release of certain prisoners in army custody on the grounds that a state of war no longer existed. However, immediately afterwards the Irish

---

[202] Hopkinson, *Green against Green*, 245–6.
[203] 'South Wexford Brigade General Report', 17 January 1923 (UCD, Moss Twomey Papers, P69/13/4–1).
[204] 'Garda Siochana Reports on Economic Situation' (NA, D/T, S3435).
[205] 'Confidential report for Month of February 1924' (NA, D/T, S3435).

parliament passed an internment law that in effect continued in existence until the Emergency Powers Act of 1926. This Act enabled the government both to proclaim a state of emergency and to provide for the further use of internment. The evidence suggests that such powers were necessary. The Garda reported in November 1923 that the suppression of the irregular 'revolt' could not be said to be complete when so many bands of IRA men roamed around the country, some of them under the leadership of men who had been returned to the Dail as TDs the previous August.[206] At the end of the month a cabinet minute divided the state into three classes of area: (a) 13 counties where normal conditions obtained, (b) 6 counties where the Garda could enforce law and order with the support of the military stationed in larger centres, and (c) 7 counties or portions of counties namely, Cork, Leitrim, South Clare, south Galway, Tipperary, Offaly, and Roscommon, where owing to the presence of bands of IRA men, the Garda could not take responsibility for the restoration of order.[207] It would take another year before normal conditions existed in all three areas. In November 1924 the cabinet declared an amnesty on the grounds that 'the highest interests of the State' would be served from discontinuing criminal proceedings for crimes committed during the civil war period.[208] This marked the real end of the Irish civil war.

CONCLUSION

With the death of key figures on both sides, the resort to brutal measures in the winter, and the lack of consensus on what caused the civil war afterwards, one conclusion is that this was 'a war without winners'.[209] However, Girvin argues that the defeat of the IRA was necessary if the pro-treaty government was to govern, and through a mixture of force and cajolement the Free State elite managed to reconcile them to democratic government afterwards.[210] Since the existence of an authoritative state is usually regarded as a precondition for the development of a democracy, 1922 could actually be regarded as 'the birth of Irish democracy'.[211] Since the Provisional Government's self-presentation was based on their success in accomplishing the practical tasks of statehood, it is difficult to accept that there were no winners in the civil war.[212] In 1927 Cosgrave told the *New York Herald* that his government had vindicated democracy, and that 'the history of the last five years is a guarantee that the principles enunciated by Lincoln at Gettysburg will never perish in Ireland'.[213] The values and objectives of Cosgrave

---

[206] 'Official Memo to All Members of the Executive Council', 28 November 1923 (NA, D/T, S3435).
[207] Minutes of Meeting of Executive Council, 30 November 1923 (NA, D/T, S3435).
[208] 'Civil War Amnesty Resolution', 4 November 1924 (NA, D/T, S4120).
[209] Keogh, *Twentieth-Century Ireland*, 17.
[210] B. Girvin, *From Union to Union: Nationalism, Democracy, and Religion in Ireland—Act of Union to EU* (Dublin, 2002), 63.
[211] Garvin, *1922: The Birth of Irish Democracy*.
[212] See K. O'Higgins, 'Three Years Hard Labour' (NA, D/T, S10632).
[213] *New York Herald*, 18 March 1927.

and O'Higgins certainly differed in important ways from those of Collins and his lieutenants, but they must occupy centre stage in any analysis of the winners and losers in the civil war.

On the other hand, since there was probably an implicit consensus in Irish society on the desirability of a democratic state, the issue is whether the civil war was a necessary means of achieving this end. Any stable democracy has, as a core element, political consensus among the dominant factions on the desirability of existing institutions and the rules of the game for regulating political conflict. Historically, such elite consensus has come about either through elite settlements or through processes of electoral competition in which the main parties eventually converge on an equilibrium point.[214] The problem with the 'birth of democracy' thesis is that the civil war was a dramatic illustration of the failure of attempts at an elite settlement in early 1922, and in itself destroyed the basis for consensus for some time. The fact that the 'enthusiastic democrats' were also more willing to resort to drastic methods than the 'reluctant democrats' in 1922–3 might be one other reason the Fine Gael tradition has been so equivocal in celebrating the civil war.[215] Moreover, the parties converged on a consensus only in the late 1930s and this consensus was engineered by Fianna Fail. That consensus had constitutional, religious, and economic dimensions, but culminated in an agreed policy of neutrality in the Second World War, suggesting that the Treaty was not the permanent basis for Irish political development that Cosgrave and co. had suggested. This may explain why, if Cumann na nGaedheal had been so successful in establishing a democratic system between 1922 and 1932, that system was dominated by Fianna Fail for the next half-century. Cumann na nGaedheal were the actual winners of the civil war, but their subsequent failure to capitalize on the strong position they were in 1923 cannot be understood within the 'birth of democracy' thesis.

In any case there was a democratic culture in pre-independence Ireland so the vista of a heroic elite forcing democratic values down the throat of a recalcitrant society should not be taken at face value.[216] Regan suggests that there was a strong consensus within nationalist Ireland before 1921 on the right to private property, individual rights, and Church–State relations, so the question was: why was there so much violence between 1916 and 1923?[217] One answer is that the civil war had its roots in the conception of republican legitimacy, which was established by the 1916 Rising.[218] One Kerry IRA man, Pat 'Belty' Williams, later recalled that to him the ordinary citizen did not count after 1916, 'an attitude born of continued association and indoctrination as a member of the guerrilla force'.[219] Hart refers

---

[214] See J. Higley and M. Burton, 'Elite Settlements and the Taming of Politics', *Government and Opposition*, 33/1 (1998), 98–115.
[215] See A. Dolan, *Commemorating the Irish Civil War* (Cambridge, 2003).
[216] See Kissane, *Explaining Irish Democracy*, 165–95.
[217] Regan, *The Irish Counter-revolution*, 375.
[218] See Hart, 'Definition: Defining the Revolution', 26.
[219] Quoted in Ryle Dwyer, *Tans, Terror and Troubles*, 353.

to this as the fundamental tension in republican thinking between two conceptions of popular sovereignty—of the 'people' (expressed through elections) and
of 'the nation' (revealed historically and spiritually in heroic actions). The
radicals in the IRA were willing to act without electoral legitimacy in 1922, but
only to defend the rights of the nation.[220] Another argument is that the overall
contours of the Irish question, the failure of Home Rule, partition, the Treaty
settlement, and the establishment of the Free State itself were all determined by
the use or threat of force, and nationalist commitment to constitutional politics
could only have been weakened by this confluence of pressures.[221] Both points are
valid but neither explains the limited nature of the violence during the civil war,
or why the IRA's resistance to the Free State was so feeble. Part of the answer lies
in the swiftness of the Free State's victory in conventional hostilities, but the IRA's
unwillingness to fight itself conditioned that victory. More apposite is the fact
that with the Free State having a monopoly on the sources of power, British
military aid, the moral sanction of the Church, and the finances of the banks, it
must have been difficult for the anti-treatyites to formulate any realistic war aims,
besides retreating to the countryside and hoping to force the government to
capitulate. What they would have done if that had happened is hard to imagine.
The Provisional Government, on the other hand, had as their prerogative the
desire to build up the authority of the state and secure the economic base of the
country, and with the most powerful sections of the society cooperating with
them in a small country, this practical task was eminently realizable. This basic
inequality in the factors of power affected how both sides saw the conflict and
must have been dispiriting to an essentially political leader like de Valera.
Although his wilder statements in 1922 suggest a politician clutching at straws,
he came out of the conflict with a clearer sense of his own leadership than he
entered into it with. On 19 April 1923 he told P. J. Ruttledge that the phase begun
in 1916 had run its course, and that those who would continue to work for Irish
independence must prepare themselves for a long patient effort at reorganization
and education.[222]

[220] Hart, *The IRA at War 1916–1923*, 24.
[221] Regan, *The Irish Counter-revolution*, 377.
[222] M. Ryan, *Liam Lynch: The Real Chief* (Cork, 2003), 168.

5

Explaining the Intractability
of the Conflict

While there have been numerous accounts of the origins of the civil war, less attention has been paid to the intractability of the conflict and why, in particular, it did not reach a negotiated conclusion. As a conventional military contest the war was essentially over by September 1922, but the subsequent proposals that were intended to establish what de Valera termed 'a peace by understanding' failed to bring it to a peaceful settlement. The common roots of both sides in the Sinn Fein movement, the personal ties among the political elite, and the existence of scores of well-meaning interlocutors ought to have provided a basis for negotiations. However, the longer the conflict progressed, the less realistic peace proposals seemed, and by April 1923 the common ground among the political elite had entirely disappeared among exchanges over the need for IRA decommissioning. This chapter documents the efforts made to bring the fighting to the end, and illustrates the process of political polarization that took place among the Irish political elite after June 1922. It concludes that the nature of the issues underlying the conflict was the primary reason the conflict proved so intractable. That this was so suggests that the traditional interpretation of the conflict, as a war fought between two essentially compatible variants of Irish nationalism, ought to be revised.

From the point of view of peacemakers, the main obstacle to a negotiated peace was simply the obduracy and intransigence of the leaders on both sides who preferred a policy of violence and force to that of negotiation and persuasion. This was certainly the view of V. S. Pritchett, a British correspondent based in Dublin during the war. He believed that after six years of revolution, 'the politicals were suffering from strain and many were out of their minds'. Personal relations among the political elite had become embittered: 'there was continual talk of "principle", but personal jealousy and vengeance were at the bottom of these actions'.[1] In August 1922 the Labour leader Cathal O'Shannon lamented the fact that on both sides he found people whose minds were so 'warped and twisted with party passion' that they could not imagine any organization not taking one

---

[1] V. S. Prichett, *Dublin: A Portrait* (London, 1991), 5.

side or the other.[2] Such a view, which emphasizes the role of elite psychology in explaining the intractability of the conflict, is too simple. The nature of the issues underlying the conflict, the internal politics of each side, the military balance in the field, even the role of third parties, can also have a fundamental bearing on the manner in which any conflict is concluded.[3]

At first glance so great were the constitutional differences dividing the two sides in Ireland that attempts to transcend them were doomed to failure. Indeed the civil war had been preceded by at least six months of failed efforts to maintain the unity of the nationalist movement that had been divided into two by the Treaty. On the anti-treaty side de Valera, had tried to rally support for his alternative 'document no. 2', which envisaged a new Irish state, internally a republic, but 'externally associated' with the British Crown for matters of common concern. On the pro-treaty side, Michael Collins had tried to win the allegiance of the anti-treatyites by producing a constitution that would be acceptable to his republican critics. This would be a vindication of his argument that the Treaty, although falling short of full independence, was a 'stepping stone' to greater freedom. Both attempts to 'split the difference' over the Treaty resulted in failure. The anti-treaty IRA continued to refuse to recognize the Provisional government chaired by Collins, while by late June Collins' colleagues had become convinced that military action was necessary in order to assert the authority of the Provisional government. In the course of the conflict both sides would refer to their opponents' behaviour in the spring of 1922 as reason for not negotiating further.

At the heart of the resulting civil war was the question of governmental legitimacy. Although the Provisional government claimed to have received a mandate to implement the Treaty in the June 1922 election, the anti-treaty forces contended that the election was not the free expression of the public's will, and the authority of the Provisional government remained contested as a result. The pro-treaty view was that the Provisional government derived its powers from the Irish people, while republicans countered that they derived them from Lloyd George and Winston Churchill.[4] The more the anti-treaty forces refused to submit to the authority of the Provisional government, the more concerned the Provisional government was to assert that authority, and the less reluctant they were to entertain terms that suggested that the anti-treaty critique of the Free State had a legitimate basis. Early on in the conflict the press was instructed to refer to the anti-treaty forces as 'bands' or 'irregulars', and to the Provisional government as 'the government'. The corollary of this policy of criminalization was that opposition to the Treaty was a product of general lawlessness, and not of any defect in the Treaty settlement. Having adopted that position, it was

---

[2] *Voice of Labour,* 12 August 1922.
[3] R. Licklider, 'How Civil Wars End: Questions and Methods' in idem (ed.), *Stopping the Killing: How Civil Wars End* (New York and London, 1993), 14–16.
[4] *Poblacht na hEireann,* 17 August 1922.

impossible for the Provisional government to entertain terms that suggested revision of the Treaty.

INTRACTABLE ISSUES

With this in mind it is not surprising that one issue that quickly became crucial to peace talks was that of arms decommissioning. From the government's perspective, the demand for decommissioning was a token of its commitment to imposing democratic values on a recalcitrant society. For republicans the demand was made primarily to prevent the anti-treatyites challenging the Treaty settlement in negotiations. It quickly became apparent that neither side was disposed towards compromise on the issue. The first fighting was intended to dislodge the anti-treaty IRA from their positions in Dublin city centre. An initiative was launched by an ambulance officer stationed opposite the anti-treaty headquarters in the Hammam Hotel. J. F. Homan had met an influential bishop who suggested that the hostile propaganda directed at the anti-treatyites was the main obstacle to peace. A friendly message from the other side, 'as fellow Irishmen', might create an atmosphere 'in which really friendly negotiations could begin'. On 1 July Homan met Collins, who asked him to tell his opponents that 'neither I, nor any member of the government, nor any officer in the army... not one of us wished to hurt a single one of them, or even humiliate them in any way that can be avoided'. All, including officers, were free to return to their homes without a formal surrender, provided they deposit their weapons in the national armory.

The next day Homan approached de Valera, who was only willing to endorse terms that allowed the insurgents to return to their homes with their rifles. Collins thought this proposal unreasonable, even though he accepted that the arms in Dublin represented only a small part of what was available to the anti-treatyites. Homan sought the advice of James Douglas, an influential businessman and soon to be senator, who felt one strong move could bring peace provided de Valera could bring the hardliners with him. They proposed that the republican military leaders give a public assurance that on the withdrawal of government troops they would cease fighting and return to their homes, leaving only one army in the country. Douglas was confident this would induce the cabinet to accept de Valera's terms. Homan returned to the Hammam but de Valera had departed. Homan was advised to speak to Cathal Brugha, now commanding the small garrison. Brugha, however, stated that the fighting men would agree to leave with their arms and join their comrades elsewhere and no more: 'we are out to achieve our object or die', he declared. Homan was persuaded he could do no more.[5]

Collins' insistence of decommissioning notwithstanding, the battle for Dublin did not kill all hopes for peace. Liam Lynch was allowed safe conduct out of the

---

[5] 'Peace Proposal—J. F. Homan, Clontarf' (NA, D/T, S8138).

city in the hope that he would remain a voice of moderation in the south. On 7 July he signed the agreement with two Free State commandants in Limerick declaring a truce between their divisions stationed in the city. Their hope was that a uniting of their forces would force army GHQ to look for compromise, but this policy was rejected by headquarters.[6] On 18 July, the IRA Executive informed the Cork Harbour Board that they would be willing to accept the Treaty if the constitution was redrafted by a constituent assembly, but the Provisional government expressed no interest in the Cork peace moves.[7] Nevertheless, there was still hope for peace in the allegiance both sides felt towards the Dail Eireann, but the Second Dail had been adjourned on 8 June until 30 June. The Third Dail, elected on 16 June, was to meet on 1 July, but was prorogued until 15 July. On 12 July this Dail was prorogued for another fortnight. Up to the end of July Collins may have been contemplating a second election on the Treaty as a way of enticing his opponents to limit themselves to constitutional opposition.[8] However, he also believed that it was only in the Waterford–Cork–Kerry–Limerick area that he confronted a 'definite military problem', and clearly wanted to wait until the decisive battles had been won before convening the Dail.[9] On 5 August he advised the cabinet that:

if Parliament did not meet until the 24th our military position would be very favourable. We would have occupied sufficient additional posts in the South to dominate entirely the position there and would be able to indicate so definitely our ability to deal with the military problem there that no parliamentary criticism of any kind could seriously interfere with that ability.[10]

Popular myth has it that Collins' death, on his way to a meeting with neutral and opposing officers in Cork on 22 August removed the one person who would have brought the two sides together. However, to the end Collins had insisted that the anti-treatyites meet two demands: '(1) Going home without their arms and; (2) Behaving decently in support of the administration and in acceptance of the people's verdict'. These terms should be made 'clear and straight and strong' before the public, which is exactly what the Provisional government was to do.[11] For Collins himself decommissioning was not merely a symbolic issue. He remarked that prisoners had been offered their freedom provided they pledged not to 'use arms against the Parliament elected by the Irish people, or the government for the time being responsible to that Parliament'. They mainly refused to do so, and there was little point in negotiating with people 'that mean to take up arms again against the government of the Irish people'.[12] The official statement on the prorogation of the Dail on 12 July had stated that tolerance of an armed IRA organization would mean economic ruin as well as

---

[6] E. Neeson, *The Civil War: 1922–1923* (Dublin, 1973), 140–4.
[7] O'Maoldhomhnaigh to Daly, 18 July 1922 (UCD, de Valera Papers, P150/1638).
[8] M. Valiulis, *General Richard Mulcahy and the Founding of the Irish Free State* (Dublin, 1992), 174.
[9] Army Report, 5 August 1922 (NA, D/T, S3361).
[10] Ibid.
[11] 'Notes', n.d. (UCD, Mulcahy Papers, P7/B/28).   [12] Neeson, *The Civil War*, 221.

the re-establishment of British government in the country.[13] Collins had also advised that government propaganda should highlight the economic costs of the anti-treatyite actions, 'to get the minds of the people focused on these and off such controversial matters as the national position'.[14] This does not suggest he envisaged terms that would infringe the Treaty in the short term. On the other hand, he told Cosgrave that 'the men who are prepared to go to the extreme limit are misguided, but practically all of them are sincere'. For this reason 'we must avoid anything that savors of personal abuse'.[15] This contrasts with Cosgrave's remark at the beginning of the war that the occupants of the Four Courts should not be portrayed in the press as republicans, but rather as 'a band of armed free-booters invested with no lawful authority from any quarter whatsoever'.[16]

The Provisional government had wanted to pursue a quick victory with a minimum of bloodshed, but in August the anti-treatyites switched to guerrilla tactics, which 'brought about a new and ruthless campaign of terrorism in parts of the country, and produced a policy of the iron heel and mailed fist on the part of the pro-treaty authorities who determined to stamp these guerrillas out once and for all'.[17] After Gavan Duffy's public disagreement with the Provisional government over the closure of the republican courts, on 11 August the cabinet agreed that the reasoning behind any particular line of action should not be published by individual members of the government.[18] Then the cabinet insisted from 5 September onwards that its members adhere strictly to collective respon-sibility, and that any minister associated with peace moves would report on them to the cabinet. On the same day, however, Mulcahy, now chief of staff, accepted a secret meeting with de Valera, who reportedly believed enough of a fight had been made for the Republic and had changed his views. The meeting failed. Mulcahy wanted peace on the basis of the Treaty, de Valera on the basis of revising it. Mulcahy claimed the meeting led him to support the establishment of military courts with the power to execute in order to hasten a surrender.[19] British intelligence reports had speculated that Collins' death would either result in a loss of nerve on the part of the government, or cause the army to lose its temper and take drastic action—the latter proved to be the case.[20]

The possibility still remained that a resolution to the conflict could result from the meeting of the Third Dail. The previous two months had seen a variety of calls for the Dail to be convened, many based on the assumption that anti-treaty members would attend. British intelligence reports were pessimistic about the Provisional government's chances of receiving a mandate from the Dail for the

---

[13] Official Statement, July 12 1922 (NA, D/T, S1332A).

[14] Collins to Fitzgerald, 12 July 1923 (NA, D/T, S595).

[15] Collins to Cosgrave, 25 August 1922 (UCD, Mulcahy Papers, P7/B/29).

[16] Cosgrave to Griffith, late June 1923 (NA, D/T, S1322B).

[17] Neeson, *The Civil War*, 251.

[18] P.G. Minutes, 11 August 1922 (NA, G1/3).

[19] Valiulis, *General Richard Mulcahy*, 174.

[20] 24th (P) Infantry Brigade, Weekly Intelligence Summary for Week Ending 26 August 1922 (NA, D/T, S1784).

continuance of the civil war in such circumstances.[21] A proposal was launched in Cork by a prominent clergyman who often acted as a mediator in labour disputes in the city. Revd Dr Thomas O.S.F.C. sent the following proposals to the cabinet, and also to de Valera, Lynch, and Sean Moylan, an IRA leader from Cork:

(1) It is agreed that all military forces are the servants of the Nation and subject to the representatives of the people.
(2) It is agreed that the Republican Members of the Dail are free to attend the forthcoming Meeting without interference or molestation.
(3) It is agreed that the Republican forces shall accept and abide by the decision of the forthcoming meeting of the Dail and meantime that all military activities on both sides shall cease.[22]

Thomas pointed out that the scheme could only be successful if the IRA Executive could meet, which would require guaranteed safe passage for the leaders and that the opinions of the arrested leaders be ascertained. However, on 30 August the Provisional government had passed legislation stating that any member of the Dail involved in the anti-treaty campaign should be arrested, and any member already in prison would not be released for the purpose of attending the Dail.[23] Thomas's terms were discussed by the cabinet on 6 September, and it was decided that no action would be taken.[24] On the republican side, Lynch now believed that the IRA Executive was the only body competent to deal with the issue of peace.[25] However, at the end of August he had refused a request by de Valera for a meeting of the Executive, stating that it would be some time before a meeting would be called.[26] In response to peace negotiations that had developed in Cork as a result of Collins' last visit, Lynch had also decided that there could be no negotiations except on the basis of recognition of the Republic.[27] Republican TDs should not attend the Third Dail as the Second Dail and the IRA Executive were the only bodies to bring about peace.[28] There was thus no hope for peace on the basis that the anti-treatyites would recognize the Third Dail. Conversely, in the eyes of the Provisional government the Second Dail had ceased to be a representative body the moment the election result in June was declared.[29] On 9 September Cosgrave convened the Dail, which retrospectively vindicated the military actions taken by the Provisional government since June. Four days later the Provisional government advertised six terms of peace, again including government control of all arms in the country.[30]

[21] Weekly Dublin District/Intelligence Summary No 176 for Week Ending 2 September 1922 (NA, D/T, 1784).
[22] 'Civil War 1922–4 Peace Negotiations by Father Thomas, O.S.F.C.' (NA, D/T, S8140).
[23] P.G. Decision, 30 August 1922 (NA, D/T, S6236).
[24] P.G. Minutes, 6 September 1922 (NA, D/T, S8140).
[25] Lynch to Assistant Chief of Staff, 7 September 1922 (UCD, Ernie O'Malley Papers, P17a/153).
[26] Lynch to de Valera, 30 August 1922 (UCD, Mulcahy Papers, P7/B/33).
[27] Lynch to Assistant Chief of Staff, 27 August 1922 (UCD, Ernie O'Malley Papers, P17a/153).
[28] Lynch to O/C 1st Southern Division, 6 September 1922 (UCD, Ernie O'Malley Papers, P17a/17).
[29] *Freeman's Journal*, 7 August 1922.
[30] *Irish Independent*, 13 September 1922.

Lynch's views had clearly hardened since the early days of the war when he was determined to prevent the fighting spreading south. Throughout September a succession of clandestine meetings instigated by pro-treaty officers close to Collins took place in Cork. They proposed restoring army unity under a new Executive and if necessary persuading the anti-treaty element in the National Army to organize on their own. They were motivated partially by fears that ex-British officers were getting a hold on the army. Their proposals involved abolishing the minister of defense, disbanding both armies, and the formation of a volunteer force under an agreed Executive. That such an arrangement would be something of a military dictatorship was conveyed by the proposal that the army was to be the servant of the government, 'only in so far as the better government of the country is concerned'.[31] Lynch interpreted the proposals as a sign of the government's weakness, believing that only a constitution that destroyed the Treaty and placed Ireland outside the Empire would 'settle the matter'.[32] Thus, precisely at a time when 'the spirit of compromise had vanished from the leaders of the pro-treatyites, and was replaced by a ruthless intransigence which refused to consider the anti-treaty viewpoint at all', the anti-treatyite military leadership committed itself to achieving its ultimate demand, 'the isolated Republic'.[33]

INTERNAL ELITE POLITICS

The failure of peace proposals in the early stages of the civil war is clearly explained by the nature of the issues that underlay the conflict. The demand for decommissioning, the division over which parliament should be sovereign, and the overall question of whether Ireland should be in the Empire were all funda-mentally divisive, and it is difficult to see what proposals could have been made that could have reconciled the two positions. Ultimately though, issues cannot be considered separately from the elites that articulate them, and the internal politics of each side must be considered in any analysis of the intractability of the conflict beyond September 1922. In the spring peacemakers had been motivated by the conviction that the interests of their country lay in securing a basis for army unity between opposing forces in the IRA, and by the close ties that existed between former comrades in the Irish Republican Brotherhood. Neither factor survived the course of the war. Paradoxically, the politicians in the Provisional government were less convinced that common ground could be established than the military men, who had been slower to move towards confrontation. Ironically these politicians would grow in influence throughout the war. A policy of compromise had only been accepted by the cabinet in the spring of 1922, whereas it seemed to

---

[31] 'IRA Executive Meetings etc' (NL, Florence O'Donaghue Papers Ms 31 258).
[32] M. Hopkinson, *Green against Green: The Irish Civil War* (Dublin, 1988), 185.
[33] Neeson, *The Civil War*, 267.

be militarily necessary, and as long as Collins and Mulcahy held sway. Once Cosgrave became chairman of the Provisional government, the 'stepping stone approach' to the Treaty, with whatever that entailed, was discarded.

Cosgrave's position on the Treaty was revealed by his response to a peace proposal made late in September by a professor of law at Trinity College Dublin. E. Culverwell informed Cosgrave that the main difficulty de Valera had with the Treaty was the King's right to veto domestic legislation. De Valera believed that once economic legislation passed by an Irish parliament affected English commercial interests, 'you will see that British Ministers will advise the King and he will veto the bill'. Nevertheless, de Valera added that if the constitutional practice of the Free State did follow that of Canada, as prescribed in the Treaty, and the King did not exercise his veto, then de Valera would alter his position. Culverwell urged that 'a basis for peace should be found in an undertaking by the members of the Provisional government that if the Treaty were violated by the King's veto being used in domestic legislation against the advice of his Irish Ministers then they would resist such action by force if necessary'.[34] De Valera himself disputed this version of their interview, stating that he would only accept a King if he had been chosen by the freely exercised vote of the Irish people.[35] In any case Cosgrave was not impressed. He claimed the constitution gave the state all the powers de Valera said it lacked, and that de Valera no longer counted on the republican side as he had lost hold of the military element.[36] At the end of October, when asked to consider another scheme whereby the new constitution would be amended to placate the republicans, as Collins had attempted to do in the spring, Cosgrave reiterated his fundamental position:

There is a big chasm between Mr. de Valera and myself and it is not easy to see how this chasm is to be bridged. The laying down of arms by those who are not properly authorized to bear them is an absolute essential of peace. So far as I can ascertain Mr. de Valera is not in a position to 'deliver the goods' as the Americans say and I do not know of any person that is.[37]

Cosgrave also assured Churchill that the replacement of Lloyd George's coalition with a purely Tory government would not lead to a weakening of the Treaty settlement:

We are not concerned with party issues in Great Britain and we know nothing of the merits of the domestic questions upon which your ministry has quitted office but we do know that in our regard your ministry represents a combination of vision and boldness in statesmanship unparalleled in the unhappy relations of our two countries and that you have done a big thing too close to us yet to be truly valued but which if not blindly undone or stupidly whittled away contains the fertile seeds of great generations. We share your faith in the Treaty which our nations have made and ratified and in its fulfillment we look to

---

[34] Culverwell to Cosgrave, 27 September 1922 (NA, D/T, S8141).
[35] De Valera to Culverwell, 13 October 1922 (UCD, de Valera Papers, P150/1647).
[36] Cosgrave to Culverwell, 2 October 1922 (NA, D/T, S8141).
[37] Cosgrave to Major Loftus, 31 October 1922 (NA, D/T, S4522).

find goodwill and unity in Ireland and peace at last between Great Britain and Ireland and the fruits of peace.[38]

If the Treaty was to be a permanent basis for Irish political development then it follows that negotiations with republicans bent on revising that Treaty were fruitless. This raises the question of what the Provisional government's long-term strategy for dealing with their opponents was? On 28 September 1922 Kevin O'Shiel advised Cosgrave that

there appears to be no doubt at all that the morale of the Irregular forces, is at a very low ebb and that their organization, both here in the City and in the country, is for the moment, at any rate, badly broken. I have heard from many quarters (and I am sure you have) that there are large numbers amongst them completely wearied of the whole business and only too anxious to get a chance to return to their homes. Without such an amnesty this large section may fight on in desperation feeling that there is no hope for them and that even should they return to their homes they do so without any guarantee of security.[39]

As early as 10 July the cabinet had committed itself to a policy of releasing arrested rank-and-file republicans provided they sign a form of undertaking with regard to future conduct. It was later agreed that this would not apply to IRA leaders or people with past criminal records.[40] On 5 October the Provisional government proclaimed an amnesty for those who agreed to hand in their arms and voluntarily withdraw from the IRA campaign. The offer was published in the national newspapers, displayed at all post offices, and sent to clergymen and local government officers.[41] On the other hand, in late September the Provisional government had also passed the special powers bill giving them the power to execute people for a variety of offences, including the possession of firearms. These powers were first used in mid-November when four young men from Dublin were charged with the unlawful possession of firearms and executed. Then on 24 November Erskine Childers was executed for the possession of a pistol originally given him by Michael Collins.

If it had become clear that those whose acceptance of the Treaty was influenced by Collins' 'stepping stone' interpretation now had more in common with those on the anti-treaty side, it was also true that those whose rejection of the Treaty was based on the premise that 'document no. 2' could provide a realistic alternative were soon sidelined by the republican leadership. On 16 and 17 October the IRA Executive held its first meeting since the war began at Nugents Ballybacon in south-west Tipperary. Twelve members attended, alongside four more who were co-opted to replace those in prison. Although a letter from de Valera was read by Lynch arguing that the Executive had to clarify its position on majority rule and on peace terms, it was decided that the IRA Executive alone would be responsible for the issue of peace and war.[42] On 15 September the authorities had got hold of

---

[38] Cosgrave to Churchill, 26 October 1922 (PRO, CO 739/2 21922).
[39] O'Shiel to Cosgrave, 28 September 1922 (NA, D/T, S1785).
[40] P.G. Minutes, 10 July 1922 (NA, G1/1).   [41] *Irish Times*, 5 October 1922.
[42] J. M. Curran, *The Birth of the Irish Free State 1921–1923* (Mobile, Ala., 1980), 254.

important documents on the republican side showing that de Valera did not share Lynch's optimism about the likely success of their campaign.[43] According to Liam Deasy, once de Valera had seen that Lynch and his men had to burn Fermoy Barracks and abandon their fixed positions in early August, he thought his side had no hope of military victory.[44] Later that month, he travelled south and tried to persuade senior IRA leaders that having made a show of arms in protest, the most honourable thing to do now was to withdraw from a war the IRA could not win.[45] As a result of the Executive decision, however, de Valera would not be responsible for peace negotiations. Moreover, the Army Council of the IRA, composed of Liam Lynch, Ernie O'Malley, Liam Deasy, Thomas Derrig, and Frank Aiken, was instructed by the Executive to negotiate terms of peace 'such as will not bring the country within the British Empire'. This meant that they would automatically reject terms that sought to establish a *via media* between the two sides. Finally, it was decided that the final decision on peace rested with the old Executive, which had been formed before the war began. This included four men who were now in jail, Peader O'Donnell, Joseph McKelvey, Liam Mellowes, and Rory O'Connor. Their views would have to be ascertained before terms could be accepted.[46] Taken together, these decisions were to determine the IRA's response to peace moves until the following April. The meeting also appointed a five-man Army Council to discharge its functions when it could not meet, with Lynch also heading this body.

On 9 November de Valera publicly announced that the republicans were not contemplating acceptance of the amnesty, and 'that victory for the Republic or utter defeat and extermination are now the alternatives'.[47] It was at this time that another proposal was launched by a Catholic priest, Canon Eamon O' Kennedy, president of St Flannan's College, who suggested that given the right terms, the western divisions of the IRA would transfer their allegiance to the Provisional government. These divisions had not been consulted when the Republican Government was set up and their officers 'deeply resented de Valera's 'victory or extermination' proclamation, which raised doubts in their minds 'as to the capabilities and wisdom of those who set up this government'. If it were to be 'a fight to the finish', the overall constitutional issue, Republic or Free State, should not matter. O'Kennedy advised the Provisional government that a large majority of the soldiers of the second, third, and fourth western divisions in counties Galway, Mayo, and Sligo 'would probably be prepared to accept the Treaty and give full allegiance to the government'.[48] O'Kennedy outlined a scheme whereby the anti-treatyites would be reinstated into the National Army. A commission composed of an equal number of anti-treatyites and pro-treatyites would be

[43] Cope to Churchill, 16 September 1922 (PRO, CO 739/2).
[44] M. Ryan, *Liam Lynch: The Real Chief* (Cork, 1986), 149.
[45] L. Deasy, *Brother against Brother* (Cork, 1998), 76.
[46] 'IRA Executive Meetings etc' (NL, Florence O'Donaghue Papers, Ms 31 258).
[47] Neeson, *The Civil War*, 280.
[48] 'Civil War 1922–4, Peace Proposal; Eamon Kennedy' (NA, D/T, S8142).

established to oversee the allocation of posts. Appointments at officer level were to be made from the ranks of the pre-truce IRA. No officer currently with the anti-treaty forces would be given less rank than that held by him prior to the truce. Anti-treatyites would also be encouraged to seek appointments in government departments and recruitment to the newly established police force should cease.

It was the first time since September that proposals for army unification were made, and the response would be clearly indicative of the Provisional government's long-term policy. Eoin MacNeill, minister for education, discussed the proposals with the canon and his brother, and believed a general amnesty possible, but thought the re-instatement of anti-treaty officers problematic, especially under officers they were now fighting against. There was a possibility of recognition of rank based on positions before the IRA split, and also of officers being put on half-pay, but not of real duties. The rank and file had no claim on the army, although subject to conditions recruitment in the civic guards was possible. As long as a state of armed revolt existed, however, the government could not give an undertaking 'to provide appointments for officers and others in revolt'. The whole plan depended on the 'completeness of the reversion to peace and order'.[49] These proposals were discussed by the cabinet on 20 December and rejected. The government, in the words of Cosgrave, would not 'subject any public service of the state to the demands of a commission composed of two-fifths of those now in arms against the state'.[50]

This peace move naturally caused a considerable amount of consternation among the IRA leadership. An IRA bulletin later remarked of the terms that 'it will be noted, as showing a curious mentality, that of the eight conditions set out, no fewer than five are concerned with offers of pay and jobs'.[51] In February 1923 Cosgrave was reported in the press saying that western divisions of the IRA rejected de Valera as president of the Republic. However, the IRA leadership blamed Cosgrave himself for the terms, saying they were communicated to the officers in the western area by one of his 'emissaries', Dr Michael Fogarty, bishop of Kilaloe, who was well known for his anti-republican opinions. The aim of the offer was to undermine discipline by 'bribing' officers with offers of pay and jobs. The government responded by saying that the terms originated with the officers themselves and the government had not seen the proposals before they reached them in their final form. They added that the obvious purpose of the anti-treatyites' propaganda was to encourage their men to ignore the offer of amnesty in February by suggesting that better terms were obtainable in December and could still be secured.[52] A few days later Dr Fogarty announced that he never sent proposals of peace to any quarter, either in Cosgrave's name or in anyone else's.[53] On 20 December the cabinet had refused a request made by Canon Kennedy to

[49] Eoin MacNeill, memo, 30 November 1922, ibid.
[50] Cosgrave, memo, n.d., ibid.
[51] IRA GHQ Daily Bulletin no 116, 14 February 1923 (NL, Florence O'Donaghue Papers, Ms 31 261).
[52] *Irish Independent*, 17 February 1922.
[53] Ibid., 20 February 1922.

provide safe conduct through the west for a peace intermediary in Tuam, recording that it was hardening in its determination to use all means possible to suppress disorder.[54]

Lynch had clearly become worried about the impact of peace proposals on his men. On 11 December he had informed de Valera of the dangers of anything but a permanent truce, since a ceasefire would result in the disintegration of morale among an IRA devoid of finance and barracks. The only terms that could be accepted by him were those agreed by the IRA Executive in October.[55] This also meant that peace would have to be agreed with the British government at the same time as with the Irish government.[56] On 27 December Lynch then informed his officers that on at least four occasions the Free State had approached IRA officers with a view to learning their views. He reiterated that no terms could be accepted short of independence, as sanctioned at the last meeting of the IRA Executive. His opponents were, he maintained, trying to get the anti-treatyites talking, while the Free State consolidated its position, as had happened in the spring of 1922:

> After signing of Treaty, our Civil and Military forces talked with the enemy while he was developing his army and procuring his supplies: this because we relied on their honesty to save national position and honor. Their bad faith, dishonest methods, and barbarous acts, have definitely proved they will stop at nothing at trying to make the Free State a reality.[57]

By the end of December it was clear that the government would win the war, but it remained to be seen at what price. In December the four imprisoned members of the IRA Executive were executed in reprisal for the assassination of Sean Hales, a pro-treaty TD in Dublin. Archival evidence does not enable us to judge whether the Provisional government knew that the last IRA Executive meeting had ruled that the consent of these men was necessary before the IRA accepted peace terms.[58] In January thirty-four more prisoners were executed. Some argued that the executions hastened the end of the war, but they were part of a process of polarization taking place on many levels, which led many to fear for the future. If civil war continued as it was, reconciliation would be impossible, and it was this fear that motivated the next proposals. In response to calls from county and urban district councils throughout the country, the writer George Russell, known as A.E., published a letter entitled 'Peace at Last', using the name of a Polish patriot, Koscivszko, who had declared a Polish Republic after the partitions of the late eighteenth century.[59] A.E. proposed to solve the arms issue by getting the anti-treatyites to accept the verdict of a general election provided it was conducted fairly. Over a three-week period the anti-treatyites would store all their weapons and ammunition in three buildings, each guarded by fifty republicans

---

[54] Executive Council Minutes, 20 December 1922 (NA, G1/3).
[55] Lynch to de Valera, 11 December 1922 (UCD, de Valera Papers, P150/1749).
[56] Lynch to de Valera, 18 December 1922, ibid.
[57] Lynch to O/Cs, 27 December 1922 (UCD, Moss Twomey Papers, P69/92 (95)).
[58] 'IRA Executive Meetings etc' (NL, Florence O'Donaghue Papers, Ms 31 258).
[59] *Irish Independent*, 8 January 1923.

and ten Free State soldiers. Three men would be in charge, one for each building, and they would guarantee to deliver the arms to the president elected after a general election, which would take place not later than May. The military authorities expressed no clear opinion on the details of A.E's scheme, but said that it was the first time that they might be persuaded to consider a proposal on its merits. The political response was less friendly. The cabinet could not possibly consider such proposals and were inclined to place little faith in them.[60]

Although A.E.'s terms might have provided an honorable 'get-out' for the anti-treatyites, and provided a possible solution to the decommissioning issue, Lynch still believed that his forces had a chance of winning. On 12 January IRA headquarters announced that

We are in position to state that the recent rumours concerning peace negotiations on the part of individual Republican leaders have no foundation. They have their origin in the same quarter which seeked [SIC] to manufacture public opinion by sending day after day, anonymous letters to the Daily Press, namely Mr. Desmond Fitzgerald's Publicity Department. The trick is as old as British government in this country. Mr Desmond Fitzgerald, through some of his agents, raises a kite, and when they find it won't fly, Mr. Cosgrave, with a fine show of being the strong man, makes a pretence of knocking it down.[61]

Nevertheless, Lynch soon held a meeting with Tom Barry and Tom Crofts (officer in command of the first southern division). After a visit to Dublin both had returned to the first southern division's HQ near Ballyvourney on 9 February, and held a division council meeting at Cronin's in Gougane Barra on 10 Feburary. The following day they drafted a letter to Lynch requesting a meeting of the IRA Executive. Both had recently been drafted onto the Executive and warned Lynch of the IRA's extremely weak position in the south. Another first southern division council meeting took place, with Lynch present, in Coolea on 26 February and lasted for three days. Each of the 18 divisional officers expressed the view that they had fought to a standstill, but the majority were still willing to carry on the fight, even without hope of victory.[62] Tom Barry suggested that the IRA's total strength in the country did not exceed 8,000 men. This convinced Lynch of the need to call an Executive meeting.[63] As a result, with both sides on the verge of carrying out even more desperate measures, Lynch advised de Valera of the need to exchange minimum terms with the government.[64] However, these terms were never agreed upon by the two men. The latter persisted in his belief that only document no. 2 could provide a basis for peace, whereas Lynch was still trying to organize the shipment of artillery pieces from Germany, which he thought would turn the course of the civil war.[65] On 10 February Lynch instructed his officers not to enter

[60] Ibid.
[61] IRA Daily Bulletin, No 89, 12 January 1923 (Fianna Fail Archives, FF/12).
[62] M. Ryan, *Tom Barry: IRA Freedom Fighter* (Cork, 2003), 191.
[63] Ryan, *Liam Lynch: The Real Chief*, 154.
[64] Lynch to de Valera, 2 February 1923 (UCD, de Valera Papers, P150/1749).
[65] T. Davis, 'The Irish Civil War and the "International Proposition" of 1922–23', *Eire-Ireland* 29/2, 77–92.

into negotiations, but to accept only in writing, and without comment, any suggested basis of peace. Officers who violated this instruction would be court-martialled. Individuals, laymen or clergy, who persisted in approaching his men with peace terms and 'influencing them to accept terms of peace which would mean the surrender of the Republic' should be placed under arrest and retained in custody.[66]

With their military position crumbling, however, individual IRA men still sought ways of ending the conflict. The arrest of the Cork IRA leader, Liam Deasy, on 18 January, had resulted in him signing a form declaring that he would 'accept and aid in an immediate surrender of all arms and men as required by General Mulcahy'.[67] By the new year Deasy had concluded that the IRA campaign should have ended with the fall of the Four Courts, and now lamented the lack of popular support for his side.[68] After his arrest he was sentenced to death by court martial on 20 January, but was granted a stay of execution if he called for the unconditional surrender of the anti-treatyites. His sentence had been due to be carried out the following morning, but after agreeing to the government's terms, he was transferred to Arbour Hill prison where he contacted numerous members of the IRA Executive, including Lynch, through Father Tom Duggan, who was then secretary to the bishop of Cork and sympathetic to republicans. Those who replied to his appeal for an unconditional surrender all refused in unqualified terms.[69] Nevertheless, his appeal had a demoralizing effect on the anti-treaty side, some of whom were 'thunderstruck' by the call for an unconditional surrender.[70] Deasy was reprimanded by Lynch, and the leaders of the large first southern division unanimously rejected his appeal. De Valera urged Lynch to issue a communiqué stating that Deasy's appeal had been issued after receiving notice of his execution the following morning, and that Deasy had been stripped of all rank.[71] The same day Lynch wrote to Deasy stating that he should have realized that his men would fight to the death rather than accept such terms.[72] Nevertheless, Lynch was told by one IRA officer that 'great numbers of our men all over the country will avail of the amnesty and hand in their arms'.[73] After the war, in January 1925, Deasy would be tried by the IRA Executive with cowardice and treason. Found guilty, his death sentence was later commuted to permanent expulsion from the IRA.

In February further division among the anti-treatyites was caused by the publication of a newspaper article by de Valera in which he called for a peace based on document no. 2. One IRA officer remarked that 'it was not for document no. 2 or compromise between political parties that men are in the field', and

---

[66] Lynch to O/Cs, 10 February 1923 (UCD, Moss Twomey Papers, P69/2 (67)).
[67] Hopkinson, *Green against Green*, 230.
[68] Deasy, *Brother against Brother*, 96.
[69] Ibid., 122.
[70] McLouhglin to Deasy, 7 February 1923 (UCD, Mulcahy Papers, P7/B/100).
[71] De Valera to Lynch, 5 February 1923 (UCD, de Valera Papers, P150/1749).
[72] Lynch to Deasy, 5 February 1923 (UCD, de Valera Papers, P150/1749).
[73] Barrett to Lynch, n.d. (UCD, Moss Twomey Papers, P69/39 (126)).

de Valera's action was roundly criticized for creating the feeling that men had died in vain.[74] Lynch himself remarked that his men generally did not understand such documents.[75] However, de Valera persisted in his public stand that document no. 2 was becoming practical politics as far as the British government was concerned.[76] On 19 February he reported to the IRA Executive that recent rumors concerning Lord Midleton, Lord Donaghmore, and Bonar Law's interest in instigating negotiations with de Valera could only boost public support for their position. Again de Valera advised that they make document no. 2 their objective and try to get the British government to state publicly that they were willing to reopen negotiations, something that would 'kill' the Free State.[77] Three days later, however, he confessed to Tom Derrig, the adjutant general, that the maximum his side might be able to achieve in negotiations could be as low as zero.[78] Peace moves nonetheless continued. Prisoners in Limerick, Clonmel, and Cork jails petitioned the authorities to allow prisoners to be released to discuss terms of peace with their leaders. It was believed that Lynch intended having the men who left Cork jail on parole arrested.[79] Clearly, the IRA was divided between those willing to discuss terms, and those that felt that any compromise was a betrayal of national ideals. With Lynch in overall command, it was clear which approach would hold sway. Deasy later recalled that Lynch's view of the war from his hideout in Ballymun in Dublin was very dependent on the written reports submitted to him by local IRA leaders, and these reports were often exaggerated and misleading.[80] On 2 March Lynch wrote that if the IRA Executive ever decides their ideals cannot be achieved, they must 'leave a clear road' for the present and future generations: 'surrender of arms or accepting the present position, that is the Free State, cannot do this'.[81]

The dilemmas facing the IRA leadership at this stage were best expressed by an anonymous republican:

I think we have in our ranks a number of men who do not believe we can get the isolated Republic in our generation but who do believe that we should not take less; that we should go on fighting 'till there are very few left as a protest and then give it to the next generation to finish. I think Deasy had that type of mind. I have met some of the type since; they are all very cheerful over it; quite satisfied to go down themselves; not tired of the fight like some others may be but it is the isolated Republic or nothing. Well I don't quite agree with that. I believe we could get an honourable basis of Peace now, within a very short time all the isolation we can desire will work out automatically, largely through an entirely different economic and social system, which I can see coming and which I believe the history of the past twelve months is hastening. But what would happen if a Peace was planned which

---

[74] Barrett to Twomey, 10 February 1923 (UCD, Moss Twomey Papers, P69/39/118).
[75] Ryan, *Liam Lynch: The Real Chief*, 150.
[76] De Valera to Ruttledge, 19 February 1923 (UCD, de Valera Papers, P150/1736).
[77] De Valera to IRA Executive, 19 February 1923 (ibid., P150/1647).
[78] De Valera to Derrig, 19 February 1923 (ibid., P150/1758).
[79] 'Memorandum', 1 March 1923 (UCD, Mulcahy Papers, P7/B/284).
[80] Deasy, *Brother against Brother*, 96.
[81] Lynch to Barrett, 2 March 1923 (UCD, Moss Twomey Papers, P69/39 (115)).

some might think could be honourably accepted, but which the fighting men who have borne the brunt of the fighting considered 'letting down the Republic'? Railing at their want of understanding, their failure to grasp essentials would not do any good. They could be the men of faith, the men who count, and who can be relied upon to stick it out. They will not yield to any individual until they are convinced that the Republic is safe. It is up to the government and army Executive to convince them before any peace terms are decided upon. Nothing is practical politics unless it is practical politics to them.[82]

The problem for pragmatists on the republican side, however, was that there was no sign that the Provisional government was about to negotiate. This was obvious from Cosgrave's response to the Neutral IRA initiative in February. Cosgrave had been advised by Professor Culverwell, who had been in contact with the Neutral IRA, that the movement was 'really a genuine one', and the reasons for cooperating with them seemed more compelling than ever: the economic cost of the war was rising all the time; the government's recent call for fresh army recruits suggested the conflict would last for another year; and the executions were alienating even those who supported the government. Moreover, the effect of the executions was to make the more determined anti-treatyites oppose peace moves they would otherwise support.[83] Cosgrave was not per-suaded and informed Donald Hannigan and M. J. Burke, two members of the Association's Executive, that the executions were having a deterrent effect.[84] By the end of February Cosgrave was aware that IRA military activity had all but collapsed. On 13 February he had announced that 'many persons have presented themselves to the government professing to bear offers of peace terms from various and widely scattered groups of Irregulars in Cork, Waterford, Limerick, Tipperary, Killen, Galway, Mayo, Roscommon, Kerry, Wexford, Dublin, and Sligo'.[85] A week later it was reported that seventy prisoners in Tralee jail had signed a statement approving of Deasy's action. Kevin O'Higgins, announced that 'there has been a considerable crumbling in the rank and file, and of course, the prisoners, who are freer than the men outside, are practically all lined up on the side of amnesty'. Press reports also stated that many anti-treatyites who had been active in the strongly republican areas of Kerry and West Cork had availed of the amnesty and were returning home after surrender.[86]

At this stage the unequal balance of forces in the field was clearly an important factor in explaining the intractability of the conflict. A proposal involving Arch-bishop Harty of Cashel and a number of priests and laymen was made in February. They addressed their proposals to Tom Barry, who had resigned his Executive position over Lynch's refusal to call a meeting of the Army Council after Deasy's appeal, and had travelled south to propose an alternative to Deasy's

[82] 'Proposals for Peace', n.d. (ibid., P69/15 (29)).
[83] Culverwell to Cosgrave, 6 February 1923 (NA, D/T, S8141).
[84] 'Interview between the President and D. Hannigan and M. J. Burke of Neutral I.R.A.', 27 February 1923 (NA, D/T, S8139).
[85] *Irish Independent*, 13 February 1923.
[86] Ibid., 20 February 1923.

terms. His move was reported to have the backing of J. J. Walsh the postmaster general, 14 pro-treaty Sinn Fein TDs, the Senate, the Labour Party, and the business community.[87] They centred around the prospect of another general election following a truce. Harty's proposals were

(1) The immediate cessation of hostilities by the calling off of all activities and operations by the I.R.A.
(2) The dumping of all arms and munitions by the republican forces under the charge of battalion commandants, the battalion commandants to be responsible that the arms will not be used against the Free State government or forces.
(3) Subsequent to a General Election the arms and munitions to be handed over to the elected government of the country.

On 10 February the proposals were put before a meeting of the first southern division who decided to request an Executive meeting to discuss the terms. On 26 February the next meeting of the first southern division concluded: 'impossibility of carrying on and this matter to be clearly put to executive meeting'.[88] Barry communicated these proposals to the IRA Executive on 7 March on behalf of Archbishop Harty's peace committee, which consisted of three other senior clerics and three laymen, including Frank Daly of the Cork Harbour Board. Barry endorsed the proposals, citing the decline in IRA morale since the Deasy episode. He proposed that the IRA dump its arms rather than carrying on 'until we are wiped out without gaining our objective'.[89] Lynch, however, refused to hold a meeting and told Barry to discontinue his involvement in peace moves.[90] The IRA Executive as a whole rejected the proposals and on 12 March Kevin O'Higgins reiterated the government's own demands, which were: (a) the acceptance of majority rule, and: (b) weapons under the control of the elected representatives of the people.[91] The Archbishop's terms did not infringe the Treaty, but O'Higgins failed to clarify in what respect his proposals did not meet his terms. The Provisional government had clearly turned its back on negotiation. They knew that the anti-treaty leadership was divided: the political group was 'war mad', including what might be called 'the Army politicians', whereas all who had ever fired a shot were 'heartily sick of it'. Crucially, the Provisional government believed that the large first southern division would break away from the Executive if it did not stop the war. Entering negotiations would only boost the flagging morale of their opponents.[92] In this vein, an army report for the month of March advised that 'if peace moves are finally killed it will be hard for the leaders to get the offensive of a few months ago going again'.[93] From this stage onwards, the

[87] Department of Intelligence to Lynch, 9 February 1923 (UCD, de Valera Papers, P150/1793).
[88] Hopkinson, *Green against Green*, 233.
[89] Barry to Executive Council, 7 March 1923 (UCD, de Valera Papers, P150/1647).
[90] Ryan, *Liam Lynch: The Real Chief*, 155.
[91] *Irish Independent*, 12 March 1923.
[92] Memorandum, 1 March 1923 (UCD, Mulcahy Papers, P7/B/284).
[93] Army Reports, 31 March 1923 (NA, D/T, S3361).

government's attitude towards peace talks was conditioned by their knowledge of the fact that their opponents were disintegrating. In mid-April a notebook found on the arrested Austin Stack contained a draft memorandum to be signed by all the available members of the IRA Executive, proposing 'a general laying down of arms'.[94]

A meeting of the IRA Executive finally took place between 23 and 27 March, firstly at James Cullinnane's in Blianta, and then at John Wall's Glenanore in the Nire Valley. It was the first time they had had a chance to assess the situation together since October.[95] De Valera was initially refused admittance, but later joined the meeting on the understanding that he had no vote. De Valera argued that an acceptance of Irish sovereignty and the abolition of the oath were the two prerequisites for peace.[96] At this stage the total strength of the IRA in the field was about 8,000, whereas the Free State could count on 38,000 combat troops.[97] By six votes to five, however, the meeting rejected Barry's motion 'that, in the opinion of the Executive, further armed resistance and operations against the Free State government will not further the cause of the independence of the country'. Lynch pointed out that the Executive had no power to make peace or war, and that the members currently imprisoned had to be released for that purpose. The question of document no. 2 did not arise, as the only terms that the Executive could make peace on were those of the October meeting.[98] Lynch voted against Barry's motion. A majority of the Executive also rejected de Valera's call for negotiations and still clung to the hope that mountain artillery could be imported to the country. It was agreed that another meeting would take place on 10 April, and that de Valera would in the meantime try to find out what chances there were of securing peace on the basis of his principles. Knowing that the artillery would never materialize before the next meeting, de Valera was apparently convinced that peace would have to be negotiated.[99]

ENDGAME

As late as the end of March the internal politics of the republican side dictated that the IRA would not accept terms that involved a recognition of the Free State and the abandonment of the Republic. Lynch's ascendancy, however, was soon to end. He was killed by Free State soldiers on 10 April. Frank Aiken, who was close to de Valera, was elected chief of staff. Aiken, Barry, and Liam Pilkington were also appointed as an army council. These changes had a dramatic influence on the course of the conflict. Aiken later recalled the circumstances that would lead to an IRA ceasefire:

[94] Ryan, *Tom Barry: IRA Freedom Fighter*, 195.
[95] Hopkinson, *Green against Green*, 237.
[96] Ryan, *Tom Barry: IRA Freedom Fighter*, 193.
[97] Ibid., 193.   [98] *Irish Independent*, 9 April 1923.
[99] F. Pakenham and T. P. O'Neill, *Eamon de Valera* (Dublin, 1970), 218. This version of events is disputed by Coogan in *De Valera: Long Fellow Long Shadow* (London, 1993), 351.

At this time, military resistance to a vastly greater Free State Army had spent itself and we were faced with the fact that there were twenty thousand Republicans in jail, whilst only a few hundred men were left in arms throughout the country. Added to this seventy-eight of our soldiers had already been executed and further batches were awaiting their legal murder, having already been notified. This slaughter would have continued whilst the Free State had the slightest pretence of armed resistance to justify it.[100]

Following a meeting held at Poulacapple, County Tipperary, on 20 April, the IRA Executive authorized de Valera's 'government' to make peace on the basis that: (1) The sovereignty of the Irish nation and the integrity of its territory are inalienable; and (2) that any instrument purporting to the contrary is null and void. It was agreed that all members of the Executive would accept majority rule, 'as a rule of order', if the Free State accepted conditions 1 and 2. In February de Valera had declared that these principles should form the basis of national policy if the British government refused to accept the result of a plebiscite on the Treaty.[101] A proposal to continue the war if the Provisional government did not accept peace terms divided the IRA Executive, six for and six against. A further meeting of the Executive held on 26/27 April instructed de Valera to offer terms to the government.[102] De Valera published his proposals on 27 April, declaring his 'government's' willingness to negotiate an immediate ceasefire on the following basis:

(1) That the sovereign rights of this nation are indefeasible and inalienable.
(2) That all legitimate governmental authority in Ireland, legislative, executive, and judicial, is derived exclusively from the people of Ireland.
(3) That the ultimate court of appeal for deciding questions of national expediency and policy is the people of Ireland—the judgement being by majority vote of the adult citizenry, and the decision to be submitted to, and resistance by violence excluded not because the decision is necessarily right or just or permanent, but because acceptance of this rule makes for peace, order, and unity in national action, and is the democratic alternative to arbitrament by force.
(4) That no individual, or class of individuals, who subscribes to these principles of national right, order and good citizenship, can be justly excluded by any political oath, test, or other device, from their proper share and influence in determining national policy, or from the Councils and Parliament of the nation.
(5) That freedom to express political or economic opinions, or to advocate political or economic programmes, freedom to assemble in public meetings, and freedom of the press, are rights of citizenship and of the community which must not be abrogated.
That the military forces of the nation are the servants of the nation, and subject to the foregoing, amenable to the national assembly when freely elected by the people.[103]

All these principles had been present in de Valera's 8 February declaration 'to the people of Ireland', when he declared that forms of government were, compared to

---

[100] *Irish Press*, 3 June 1935.
[101] De Valera, 'To the People of Ireland', 8 February 1923 (UCD, Moss Twomey Papers, P69/92).
[102] 'IRA Executive Meetings etc' (NL, Florence O'Donaghue Papers, Ms 31 258).
[103] *Dail Debates*, 9 May 1923, 676–8.

these principles, 'mere lifeless machinery'.[104] A further note, titled 'Suspension of Offensive', signed by Aiken, declared an end to IRA operations as from noon 30 April, excepting defensive measures to protect men and munitions. Two days earlier three more IRA prisoners had been executed in Tralee.

De Valera described his proposals as 'a sort of national super-constitution, made by ourselves in a truly Sinn Fein way without reference to any outsiders and adopted by agreement as a fundamental code of rules by which our political differences in the future might be judicially resolved without recourse to arms or violence'.[105] However, Cosgrave was determined to stick to his public declaration that he would not sit down and negotiate with de Valera, and he regarded the only alternative, Austin Stack, as an equally impossible person.[106] De Valera himself knew that his opponents would not negotiate with him on the pretence that he had 'a continental mind', and would be too slippery at the negotiating table.[107] Senators Douglas and Jameson were asked by de Valera to act as intermediaries and agreed to do so. They were asked by the government to establish which republican leaders would be bound by any peace terms, and what proportion of the IRA rank and file would follow them.[108] Cosgrave's reply to de Valera's terms contained the same terms that had been set by Collins in August, and repeated by O'Higgins early in March: (a) 'that all political issues whether now existing or in the future arising shall be decided by the majority vote of the elected representatives of the people'; and (b) 'that the people are entitled to have all lethal weapons within the country in the effective custody or control of the Executive government responsible to the people through their representatives'. The Provisional government had decided that a policy of silence and 'a stiff upper lip' was the best response to de Valera's proposals.[109] Cosgrave warned that military action against the 'Irregulars' would continue while they retained control of their weapons, although the actual surrender of weapons would be handled 'with as much consideration as possible for the feelings of those concerned'.[110] Cosgrave informed Jameson that he would be willing to accept a scheme whereby the clergy would be instructed to collect IRA arms on behalf of the state.[111] However, the release of prisoners was attendant on the decommissioning of these arms and the written subscription of each individual prisoner to the terms above. Beyond that, Cosgrave promised 'a clear field' for his opponents in the coming election, 'provided they undertook to adhere strictly to constitutional action'.[112] On

[104] De Valera, 'To the People of Ireland'.
[105] De Valera, letter, May 1923 (NA, Sinn Fein, 1094/1/12).
[106] Loughnane to Curtis, 17 April 1923 (PRO, CO 739/18).
[107] De Valera to Lynch, 7 May 1923 (UCD, de Valera Papers, P150/1752).
[108] See J. A., Gaughan (ed.) *Memoirs of Senator James G. Douglas (1887–1954) Concerned Citizen* (Dublin, 1998), 102.
[109] Loughnane to Curtis, 1 May 1923 (PRO, CAB 27/216).
[110] *Dail Debates*, 9 May 1923.
[111] Cosgrave to Jameson, 5 May 1923 (NL, Florence O'Donaghue Papers Ms 31 258).
[112] Neeson, *The Civil War*, 292.

2 May, two days after the ceasefire declaration, the government executed two more IRA prisoners.

With decommissioning again a demand there was little hope the anti-treatyites would accept Cosgrave's terms. Apparently de Valera believed in May that if the IRA retained its arms the government would fear that too severe a dose of repression could spark off another civil war.[113] He also initially wanted guarantees from Cosgrave with respect to the oath, the republican funds in the United States, and the right of prisoners to be released without having to sign any forms.[114] In the end de Valera replied to Cosgrave with a document in which he implied that Cosgrave agreed with the first five of his original proposals. Indeed on 9 May Cosgrave had declared in the Dail that clauses 1, 2, and 5 of de Valera's terms were already allowed for in the constitution and did not form an issue in peace talks.[115] Clause 4, however, was rejected by Cosgrave because the government would not do away with the oath of allegiance. Moreover, de Valera included in his new proposals eight new clauses, the most important of which, clause d, required:

(1) the strict supervision and control of all arms in the hands of the F.S. forces and their auxiliaries; and
(2) assigning to the republican forces at least one suitable building in each province, to be used by them as barracks and arsenals, where republican arms can be stored, sealed up, and defended by a specially pledged republican Guard—these arms to be disposed of after elections by re-issue to their current holders, or in such manner as may secure the consent of the government then elected.

Cosgrave replied that the senators had brought back 'not an acceptance of these conditions but a long and wordy document inviting debate when none is possible'. He insisted that all arms must be under governmental control, and once that happened prisoners who agreed to be bound by the terms of peace would be released.[116] No further communication with de Valera would be entertained. The two senators believed that the government was willing to do everything in their power to enable their opponents to contest the August election peacefully, but to that end they also wanted control of all the arms in the country.[117] De Valera commented that his proposals had 'been met by rigid insistence on a condition in a form which is well known by everyone conversant with the situation to be impossible'.[118] However, early in April Cosgrave had advised the Papal Nuncio Monsignor Luzio, who was suspected of 'Irregular sympathies', that decommissioning required the actual destruction of IRA weaponry and not its retention in the custody of Free State or neutral forces.[119] On 13/14 May the Republican government and the new IRA Army Council met in

---

[113] Lord Longford and O'Neill, *Eamon de Valera*, 225.
[114] Gaughan (ed.), *Memoirs of Senator James G. Douglas*, 105.
[115] *Dail Debates*, 9 May 1923, 681.
[116] Ibid.
[117] Gaughan (ed.), *Memoirs of Senator James G. Douglas*, 107.
[118] De Valera to Douglas and Jameson, 9 May 1923 (NL, Florence O'Donaghue Papers, MS 31 258).
[119] Loughnane to Curtis, 17 April 1923 (PRO, CO 739/18).

Santry, Co. Dublin, and debated whether to accept Cosgrave's terms or quit. They unanimously decided on the latter.

In view of the IRA's current reluctance to decommission, de Valera's offer is of the first historical importance. Popular myth has it that the IRA has always refused to decommission its weapons, but de Valera's terms were broadly accepted by the IRA leadership in May.[120] In 1933 Frank Aiken recalled that when de Valera's terms were sent to all IRA units in the country, as well as to all jails and prison camps, not a single protest was made to the IRA Executive, which had unanimously backed the terms.[121] However, the IRA were only willing to decommission their arms if no oath barred citizens from taking part in the Dail.[122] Aiken's ceasefire message to the IRA had mentioned Cosgrave's demand for decommissioning, and declared that they would keep their arms until they saw 'an honorable way of reaching our objectives without arms'. Officers in charge of commands and brigades had been thus ordered to ensure that, while remaining on the defensive, volunteers should take adequate measures to protect themselves and their munitions.[123] For Cosgrave the oath was an unalterable part of the Treaty, and in his view the public had indicated their desire to accept it in an election. On 24 May O'Higgins also told Cosgrave that, 'the present government has no intention of jeopardizing the important benefits of the Treaty position by altering that clause in the constitution which makes the taking of the oath a condition precedent to taking a seat in the Oireachtas'.[124] The government's rounding up of IRA men continued after the ceasefire, and knowing how easily prisoners could return to hostilities, they did not want to give these men an opportunity of visiting the hidden arms dumps.[125] The problem for Cosgrave, however, was that the failure of the negotiations meant that a serious public order problem would persist after the ceasefire. Throughout the 1920s the police had to mop up arms and munitions dumped by the IRA in 1923, a process that peaked in 1926 when 273 rifles, 299 revolvers, 47 pistols, 1,243 shot guns, and 588 bombs were recovered.[126]

From the losers' point of view, the government's inflexibility reinforces the argument that the pro-treaty elite, although forced into the civil war by the IRA in June 1922, were subsequently unable to respond creatively to the conflict.[127] Whether Aiken could really have delivered on the commitment to decommission in May is open to question, but sections of the IRA had been veering towards negotiations since December. From the government's perspective, large numbers of the IRA had availed of the amnesties before May 1923, and as early as March 1924 army intelligence could remark that the bulk of the 'Irregulars' seemed to

---

[120] E. Moloney, *Sunday Tribune*, 27 November 2000.
[121] Aiken to De Valera, 23 September 1933 (UCD, de Valera Papers, P/150 1823).
[122] Aiken to Brennan, 26 February 1932 (UCD, Frank Aiken Papers, P104/1322 (1)).
[123] S. MacSuain, *County Wexford's Civil War* (Wexford, 1995), 109.
[124] O'Higgins to Cosgrave, 24 May 1923 (NA, D/T, S2210).
[125] Ryan, *Tom Barry: IRA Freedom Fighter*, 196.
[126] Appendix 111 (NA, D/T, S5864B).
[127] 'Voice Recording Made for the Bureau by the Hon. George Gavan Duffy, President of the High Court', 20 January 1952 (NA, Gavan Duffy Papers, 1125/15 no. 17).

be adopting constitutional methods.[128] Both these facts could be said to vindicate the government's long-term policy. Strictly-speaking, Cosgrave stuck to the terms set by Collins the previous August, but had he lived Collins' response might have been different. In support of that view William O'Brien quoted one of Collins' last memos, which mentioned the advisability of keeping an avenue to peace open, and indicated that Collins would appreciate any effort made in that direction.[129] Sadly, in the maelstrom of the Irish civil war it was difficult for either side to think well of their opponents, and there is no way of knowing whether Collins would have remained untouched by this syndrome. For the most part Collins did not experience the wilder side of the IRA campaign against the Free State. O'Brien reflected that

Their criminal recklessness of the life and limbs of non-combatants, their forced levies, their bomb throwings and burnings, and railway raids in every form of blind destructiveness that could imperil the peoples means of communication, their sources of employment and even their daily food—shook the foundations of morals and civilization to their base and might well seem to justify the sacred fury with which any suggestion of a truce with such men on any terms other than unconditional subjection or extermination was denounced as treason to the first principles of society.[130]

The crucial issue is whether the course of civil war politics might have been pre-empted in May 1923. Cosgrave had been advised by Kevin O'Higgins to insist on decommissioning as 'the only possible proof that could be given of bona fide acceptance of the right of the people to decide domestic and international issues'.[131] Peace talks had come to and end and the differences between the two sides boiled down to two issues, arms and the oath, so important at the beginning of the war.[132] Once again, the nature of the issues that underlay the conflict proved intractable. A compounding factor was the feeling of distrust. De Valera suspected the government, fearing a straight electoral contest in the summer, hoped that 'war conditions with raiding, terrorism, etc, will continue right up to the elections'.[133] In turn the government doubted de Valera's intentions. An army report on the Limerick area in May gave the following interpretation of de Valera's peace move:

The one sentence 'It is all over' seems to sum up the situation as far as superficial irregular activities are concerned. For the past few weeks little or nothing worthy of note has been attempted by them and it was plainly evident to anybody studying the situation that the rank and file were getting war-weary and were adversely affected by the numerous arrests of prominent leaders. It may therefore be safely assumed that the Proclamation of the 'President' and the 'Chief of Staff' were welcome news to the majority of the dupes.

---

[128] 'Extracts from Confidential Reports Furnished by the Police on the State of the Country during the Month of March 1924' (NA, D/T, S3435).

[129] W. O'Brien, 'The Irish Free State: Secret History of Its foundation'.

[130] W. O'Brien, *The Irish Revolution and How It Came about* (Dublin, 1923), 450.

[131] O'Higgins to Cosgrave, 24 May 1923 (NA, D/T, S2210).

[132] Neeson, *The Civil War*, 239.

[133] De Valera, letter, May 1923 (NA, Sinn Fein Papers, 1094/1/12).

Perhaps in their simplicity the minor fry fondly imagined that the government forces would begin to treat with their leaders and that a 'Settlement' would be arrived at. De Valera and Aiken in all probability had a more subtle move in contemplation. The Pact succeeded fairly well last year and if the release of the prisoners could be effected and a mutual cessation of hostilities could be arranged, it would afford Irregulars a convenient space of time for re-organizing their forces and attempting to secure fresh supplies of Armament. They would then be in a position to renew the struggle on an intensified scale at a later period.[134]

That there was no hope of reconciliation was made even clearer by the response, months later, to a proposal made by the IRA leader Dan Breen, who suggested that in return for a full amnesty the anti-treatyites would destroy their dumped munitions, and accept the Treaty decision, acting in the future on democratic lines. Breen's ultimate aim was to reunite people from Sinn Fein but his terms were rejected by the government. On 1 February 1924 Cosgrave told Mulcahy that

The attitude of certain prominent people on the government side is being enquired after. In fundamental matters this attitude has not changed. The position is that prominent members of the government have stood for the execution of certain Irishmen with good national records and without simply because by their particular action they challenged the life of the Nation. The attitude in these matters has not changed since the 8th of December 1922.[135]

There was little hope that the government would respond favourably to a proposal that the two wings of the old Sinn Fein party reunite: another official memorandum commented that the people of the new anti-treaty Sinn Fein party was comprised of 'all orders of society who have a grudge against the great mass of the people'.[136]

CONCLUSION

The failure of peace proposals during the Irish civil war bears eloquent testimony to the intensity of the Treaty divide among the nationalist elite. The proposals had tried to establish ways in which the anti-treatyites would recognize the authority of the Provisional government, and in which the Provisional government would tolerate republicanism in return. They failed on both counts. For most of the war the anti-treatyites were led by a man who, blind to military realities, refused to give up on the idea of 'the isolated Republic'. According to Todd Andrews, Lynch would not hold an Executive meeting of the IRA because he knew de Valera wanted to make a compromise peace.[137] For Lynch honourable failure was mostly preferable to the compromises that a return to peaceful politics would entail.

---

[134] Army Report Week Ending 5 May 1923 (NA, D/T, S3361).
[135] Memo, 1 February 1924 (NA, D/T, S585).
[136] 'Notes on Penetration', ibid.
[137] Ryan, *Liam Lynch: The Real Chief,* 156.

Deasy believed that Lynch's promise on 28 June 1922 to support the Four Courts garrison if they were attacked, and the broken treaties he had signed in Limerick with Donncha O'Hannigan and then Michael Brennan, confirmed his determination to fight to the finish.[138] On the Provisional government side, Collins' early insistence that the anti-treatyites decommission their arms as part of any settlement was never departed from. If there was to be peace, the anti-treatyites had to find a way of recognizing the Free State and accepting decommissioning, and the Provisional government had to be prepared to risk British displeasure by abolishing the oath. Right to the very end of the conflict there was no evidence that either would happen.

If the ascendancy of Lynch was an obvious reason so many proposals failed, Cosgrave's role as the Provisional government's 'front man' during peace discussions meant that the search for means of bridging the gap between the two sides was also abandoned on the government side. In December 1922 he had objected to the reopening of peace discussions 'on the basis of the maximum offer which had been made in June', when only a 'drawn' conclusion was possible.[139] In other words, this eminently civilian politician would reject proposals for army unity, of whatever kind. When asked to consider a reversion to the Collins–de Valera pact of the previous spring, he replied that Irish democracy 'was too well founded to tolerate the imposition of a new political aristocracy'. The people, he maintained, had to be free to dispense with 'politicians who may have rendered good service but whose period of usefulness has for some time been eclipsed'.[140] Such a dismissal of anti-treaty political pretensions may have been short-sighted, but in view of their disastrous showing in the June 1922 election, it was not surprising.

The more realistic of the proposals had tried to find a formula whereby the anti-treatyites could find their way back into the political system as a constitutional opposition. De Valera's terms seemed to presage an acceptance by the anti-treatyites of majority rule as the means by which questions of national policy would be decided, but the IRA was still unprepared for this. At the end of May a circular entitled 'Our Duty in the Future' spelt out its leadership's interpretation of their ceasefire:

The dumping of arms does not mean that the usefulness of the IRA is past, or release any member of it from his duty to his country. On the contrary a disciplined Volunteer force, ready for any emergency will be a great strength to the Nation in its march to Independence. It is clearly our duty to keep the Army Organization intact.[141]

It would be three years before the political leadership of the anti-treatyites would assert the primacy of politics over the military wing, and then it would take the form of a split. It would be another twelve years before the ambiguity of their

---

[138] Deasy, *Brother against Brother*, 75.
[139] 'Civil War 1922–4, Peace Proposal; Eamon Kennedy', 'Memo by President' (NA, D/T, S8142).
[140] Cosgrave to Mid-Tipperary ex-IRA men, n.d. (NA, D/T, S8139).
[141] Deputy C/S to All Officers, 28 May 1923 (NA, Sinn Fein: de Valera Papers relating chiefly to the organisation of Sinn Fein 1922–3, S1297).

attitude towards their former comrades would disappear, and this would result in the proscription of the IRA in 1936.

One factor that was not of crucial importance in peace discussions was the attitude of the British government. Once assured that Cosgrave's government would honour the terms of the Treaty, the British government seemed satisfied to let the Provisional government determine the conduct of the civil war. There is no evidence that the Provisional government's stance on decommissioning reflected British influence. When asked of their attitude towards the executions, it was stressed that the feeling in British official circles was that the Provisional government should be 'the sole judges of whatever measures they find it necessary to take'.[142] Indeed British attitudes towards the Provisional government were a mixture of relief and gratitude rather than over lordship, as is conveyed by the following memo:

The various sources of secret information at our disposal not only in this office but in the War Office, have yielded no single indication of bad faith on the part of the Free State government. The members of the government have risked their lives and suffered loss in their property and families in order to make good their obligations under the Treaty to establish a constitutional government in Ireland. The most conclusive proof of all this is that they have not hesitated to execute some of their former comrades.[143]

Although the internal politics on the anti-treaty side were obviously key to explaining why the IRA ceasefire came about, ultimately the nature of the issues underlying the civil war were of paramount importance in explaining the intractability of the conflict. Senator Douglas believed that a peace agreement could have been achieved in May if de Valera had limited his ambitions to finding an agreed means of converting his movement into a peaceful one before the August election.[144] However, de Valera acted as if he was the head of a rival government, and wanted an agreement on wider political issues signed by both himself and Cosgrave. In particular, he refused to compromise on the issue of the oath, while the government was unwilling to revise any of the Treaty's terms in advance of the election. As Douglas remarks, the tragedy was that both sides esteemed the ideal of full independence in equal measure, but differed fundamentally over whether the Treaty was an appropriate means to that end.[145]

Closer also emphasizes the impossibility of effective conflict resolution when opposing sides have different interpretations as to what their conflict is about.[146] On the pro-treaty side Cosgrave was unable to consider the anti-treaty position in isolation from the methods used to defend it. On 15 December 1922 he told the Cork Harbour Commissioners that if peace was to be established at the cost of allowing people to commandeer goods, arrest citizens, and break agreements

[142] Curtis to Loughnane, 19 December 1922 (PRO, CO 739/2).
[143] 'Obligations of His Majesty's Government in the Matter of Compensation to Irish Loyalists', 23 April 1923 (PRO, CAB 27/216).
[144] Gaughan (ed.), *Memoirs of Senator James G. Douglas*, 102.
[145] Ibid., 108.
[146] L. A. Coser, *Continuities in the Study of Social Conflict* (New York, 1967), 38.

made with other nations, the sooner he was informed that he did not represent public opinion the better.[147] On the anti-treaty side, Lynch told Deasy on 8 February 1923 that compromise on the issue of independence could not be contemplated with a government with such a record of pledge-breaking. They were being asked to consider terms that offered 'material advantage' and these Irish republicans could only despise.[148] On one side was a largely 'constitutionalist' mentality, which emphasized the need for a state to provide for social order, to uphold the rule of law, and to protect individuals from the assaults of others. On the other was an 'ideological' outlook, which concerned itself with the need for the state to comply with a general theory of political legitimacy, in this case the doctrine of self-determination. Cosgrave was a perfect representative of the former mentality, Lynch of the latter. De Valera probably had a foot in both camps.[149] Up to 1921 it was possible for these two outlooks to co-exist, but once the fighting began, a clear process of ideological polarization took place. War polarizes ideas, and so great was the gulf soon separating the two sides of this tiny elite, that it is remarkable that they were ever reconciled.

[147] *Freeman's Journal*, 15 December 1922.
[148] Lynch to Deasy, 8 February 1923 (UCD, de Valera Papers, 1749).
[149] Garvin, *1922: The Birth of Irish Democracy* (Dublin, 1996), 145.

6

Civil Society under Strain:
Intermediary Organizations
and the Civil War

It is often argued by political scientists that a strong and vibrant civil society is an essential pre-condition for the successful functioning of a democratic system. Of the many functions civil society can have, that of mediating political conflicts and creating sources of cross-cutting cleavages is one of the most important.[1] It is less clear, however, whether a strong civil society is a sufficient source of democratic stability in conflict situations, or whether the most that civil society can achieve is the amelioration of conflicts. Civil society, although a necessary feature of any democratic system, can itself do little to guarantee political stability when a political system is beset by fundamental conflicts. In that context the fate of any regime is decided above all by military factors. Yet what then is the role of civil society during civil wars? Is it to augment the power of the state or to steer a middle ground between the state and the insurgents? Although there is already a large and burgeoning literature on the phenomenon of civil society, enthusiasts for the idea of civil society seldom apply themselves to a realistic analysis of these questions.[2] What follows is an examination of the role of civil society in the civil war. A host of civil society organizations consciously tried to mediate between the contending parties throughout the war, a war they considered needlessly destructive. Their intervention has been neglected by most historical accounts but it was a factor in the calculations of both sides. How successful was this intervention and what does the fate of neutral bodies tell us about the relationship between the contending parties in 1922–3 and the wider society?

---

[1] L. Diamond, 'Toward Democratic Consolidation', in L. Diamond and M. Plattner (eds.), *The Global Resurgence of Democracy* (second eds.) (Baltimore and London, 1996), 232.

[2] J. Cohen and A. Arato, *Civil Society and Political Theory* (Cambridge, 1992); R. Fine and R. Shirin (eds.), (London, 1997); John, A. Hall (ed.), *Civil Society: Theory History Comparison* (Cambridge, 1995).

THE CONCEPT OF CIVIL SOCIETY

The concept of civil society is a protean one, put to many uses. Keane describes it as an 'ideal-typical' concept employed to mean different things in different contexts. For some, civil society is primarily an analytical concept used to analyse and interpret 'the empirical contours of past, present, or emergent relationships between social and political forces and institutions'. For others civil society is a pragmatic term, to be used 'as a guide in formulating a social and political strategy or action programme'. For others yet again, civil society is a normative term used to highlight 'the ethical superiority of a politically guaranteed civil society compared with other types of regime'.[3] It is primarily in the first sense of the term that civil society is used here, as a concept that describes a legally protected but spontaneously generated set of social and political institutions. Although civil society is conceived of as a realm of collective action separate from the state, it is not synonymous with 'society' as a whole. Firstly, civil society is concerned with public rather than private ends. Secondly, civil society relates to the state in some way, 'but does not aim to win formal power or office in the state'.[4] Civil society, in short, is a legally protected arena of collective action that relates to the state in some way.

Despite the present popularity of the term, the concept of civil society is seldom used in Irish history or political science. The most suggestive use lies in Garvin's argument that the division over the Treaty can be understood as a conflict between Irish civil society, 'in the shape of the voters, priests, journalists, labour leaders and other social leaders', and 'the public band' tradition represented by the anti-treaty IRA.[5] According to Garvin, civil society 'governed itself by means of impersonal and mechanical public rules such as laws and constitutions, whereas the public band governed itself by informal and personal links of comradeship and trust'.[6] A key feature of civil society is that 'actors in civil society need the protection of an institutionalised legal order to guard their autonomy and freedom of action'.[7] In this vein, on 12 September 1922 William Cosgrave told the Dail that the military actions taken by his government since 28 June were not for 'the mere formula of the supremacy of parliament', but 'a formula for the security of the people, of the security of their lives, and the value of their money in the country'.[8] The Provisional Government saw itself as the protector of civil society, in other words.

On the other hand civil society also provides a basis for a limitation of state power. As suggested by Keane, 'the exercise of power is best monitored and

[3] J. Keane, *Civil Society: Old Images, New Visions* (Cambridge, 1998), 36–7.
[4] Diamond, 'Toward Democratic Consolidation', 229.
[5] T. Garvin, 'Unenthusiastic Democrats: The Emergence of Irish Democracy', in R. Hill and M. Marsh (eds.), *Modern Irish Democracy: Essays in Honour of Basil Chubb* (Dublin, 1993), 15.
[6] Ibid.
[7] Diamond, 'Toward Democratic Consolidation', 230.
[8] *Dail Debates*, 12 September 1922, vol. 1 col. 195.

controlled publicly within a democratic order marked by the institutional separation of civil society and state institutions'.[9] Civil society always implies an arena of collective action capable of launching political initiatives independently from the state. The relationship between the state and civil society is thus a complex one. Civil society requires the state to uphold a legal order, but it must also have the autonomy and resources to act as a counterweight to the state. It is not surprising that relations between the state and civil society can then become irksome, even to a government defending an established legal order. On 12 July 1922 Michael Collins revealed to Desmond FitzGerald his fears of convening the Third Dail in this way:

I think that it is not disputed that we are in for as hot a time as any young government could possibly be in for. The Dail chamber will resound with much verbal thunder against us, and everything will be done by our opponents there to undermine our influence in the country and endeavour to make us look despicable. No doubt there will be much sympathy for the bold heroes in Mountjoy and Kilmainham from those who are happy in their heart of hearts that they would not be successful.[10]

In the long run, however, a strong civil society may legitimate state authority when that authority is based on the rule of law.[11] Much depends of the practice of self-limitation by governmental agents, and the extent to which state actors are perceived to be operating within a shared set of rules. In some contexts, where the state either acts outside the accepted legal framework or is contemptuous of the autonomy normally enjoyed by groups or by individuals, the relationship between the state and civil society becomes antagonistic, with the latter typically standing for a residual civility based on an eschewal of violence and a defence of political pluralism.[12] Neither extreme was true of the Irish case. The Provisional Government did not operate outside a recognized legal framework, nor did it attempt to undermine the basis for political pluralism. On 17 July 1922 its members voted unanimously not to take action against persons engaged in anti-treaty political propaganda who were not found in arms.[13] On the other hand, tension between civil society and the state did exist, as civil society organizations tried to influence government policy.

What kind of civil society should we then expect to find in Ireland during the civil war? Firstly, it is important that civil society organizations be bound by a set of shared rules or laws. For that reason organizations like the anti-treaty IRA were not part of civil society since they operated outside the legal order. Secondly, civil society organizations must be committed to the principle of non-violence. As a result, both the combatants in the civil war and their ancillary organizations are not covered by our conception of civil society. Thirdly, civil society organizations

---

[9] Keane, *Civil Society: Old Images, New Visions*, 11.
[10] Collins to FitzGerald (NA, D/T, S595).
[11] Diamond, 'Toward Democratic Consolidation', 228.
[12] Ibid., 229.
[13] P.G. Minutes, 17 July 1922 (NA, G1/1).

must be capable of launching political initiatives independently from the state. For this reason it is appropriate to consider local government bodies as part of civil society, since they provided a platform from which independent political initiatives could be taken. Lastly, civil society organizations must not aim at capturing state power for themselves. Typically, political parties are not considered part of civil society. In Ireland, however, the Labour Party had no ambition to enter government in 1922, and its role was to provide a counterweight to the Provisional Government in the Dail. Given its links with the trade union movement, it can be considered part of civil society. Aside from Labour, civil society consisted of a myriad of organizations, many of them local government bodies, which were associated with peace moves through the civil war.

A classic example of how a civil society organization can bolster the authority of the state lies in the attitude of the Catholic Church towards the Provisional Government. The Church did not seek to occupy a neutral position in the conflict. Rather it specifically used its influence with the public to garner public support for the Provisional Government. At a conference of the Catholic Truth Society of Ireland at the Mansion House, Dublin, on 11 October 1922 Dr O'Doherty, the bishop of Clonfert, outlined succinctly the position of the Church, which was: (a) that the legitimate rulers of the state, while acting in that capacity, are the instruments and Ministers of God Himself, and (b) that the sacred duty of the citizen is respect and reverence for the legitimate civil authorities.[14] On 22 October 1922 the Pastoral Letter of the Irish Catholic hierarchy excommunicated the anti-treaty forces by banning them from receiving the sacraments of Penance and Holy Communion while they opposed the Provisional Government. The hierarchy remained strongly supportive of the Provisional Government, emphasizing 'the duty of every citizen to support the civil and military authorities by every available means'.[15] Murray reflects that the overwhelming impression created by the public and private discourse of bishops and clergy in 1922–3 is one of a strong attachment to the institutions of the new state, a willingness to excuse the excesses of the state's security forces, and a tendency to blame the anti-treatyites for all the evils of the civil war.[16]

The position of the Church was not reflective of the attitude of Irish civil society during the civil war. Whether we are referring to local government bodies or to other civic organizations that existed before the outbreak of the civil war, like the Cork Harbour Board, or to organizations that came into being as a result of the civil war, like the People's Peace League, Irish civil society maintained a neutral position and tried to bring about a negotiated end to the conflict. This inevitably meant that they incurred the displeasure of the combatants, and a considerable amount of energy was expended both by the Provisional Government and the IRA Executive in dampening down talk of peace. As a result civil

[14] *Irish Times*, 12 October 1922.
[15] Ibid.
[16] P. Murray, *Oracles of God: The Roman Catholic Church and Irish Politics, 1922–1937* (Dublin, 2000), 90.

society was doomed to failure in a conflict conducted by a close-knit but acrimonious nationalist elite. The fate of individual 'peace proposals', however, forms the subject of the previous chapter. What concerns us here is the nature of the relationship between civil society and the state, as well as the relationship between civil society and the anti-treatyites. At the very least this chapter documents the existence of a third force in the conflict, one that remained opposed to what Professor Alfred O'Rahilly, a member of the committee that drafted the 1922 constitution, called 'the entire vicious circle of violence and force'.[17]

CIVIL SOCIETY AND CIVIL WAR

The Irish civil war began on 28 June 1922 when the Provisional Government began shelling IRA positions in the centre of Dublin. In time fighting spread to the countryside, and by September anti-treatyite tactics had taken the form of a guerrilla campaign. In its early stages there was still some hope that a meeting of the Dail would bring the fighting to an end. The Second Dail had been adjourned on 8 June, and had been due to meet on 30 June. The Third Dail was to convene the following day. However, the Second Dail never met and the Third Dail was prorogued by the Provisional Government until 15 July. Then on 12 July the Dail was prorogued for another fortnight. On 29 July the Dail was then prorogued until 12 August. All in all, the Dail was prorogued five times, and did not meet until the second week of September. With the Dail not in session, civil society organizations could argue that the Provisional Government lacked proper sanction for the military actions that had been taken since 28 June.

One of the first attempts to get the Provisional Government to suspend their military operations came from a delegation of women from a Mansion House meeting held in Dublin at the end of June. This is a curious fact, in light of the claim later made by P. S. O'Hegarty that politically active Irishwomen, 'the furies', were inherently extremist.[18] The delegation was met first by Cosgrave and then by Collins. Louie Bennett, a supporter of the Treaty and a senior member of the Irish Women Workers Council, argued that it was wrong to act before the Dail could convene. Peace moves were going on, and people were hopeful that the fate of the Four Courts would not be decided by military means. Cosgrave replied that the only terms that he would accept from the anti-treatyites were unconditional surrender, and his colleagues in the Provisional Government approved this policy on 1 July. Collins suggested that a cessation of hostilities would endanger the lives of members of his government.[19] On the same day, Ernest Blythe, the minister of local government, reported to the cabinet that he had received a visit from the lord mayor of Dublin, Laurence O'Neill, the archbishop of Dublin, and Cathal

[17] *Irish Times*, 16 December 1922.
[18] P. S. O'Hegarty, *The Victory of Sinn Fein* (Dublin, 1998), 73–5.
[19] (NA D/T, S1438).

O'Shannon of the Labour Party, proposing a ceasefire. Their overtures were rejected, despite de Valera's support for them.[20]

Criticism of the Provisional Government nonetheless continued. A protest at the prorogation of the Dail was also made by the Women's International League, 'a body representative of the various women's organisations in Dublin'.[21] A meeting held in Tralee by the Kerry Farmers Union and Commercial Representatives also called for a meeting of the Dail to restore peace.[22] Another similar meeting was held by 'the People's Rights Association' in Cork. The Cork People's Rights Association was composed of representatives of public bodies, labour, and commerce, in the county, and was drawn from many areas, including Youghal, Clonakility, Bandon, Bantry, Mallow, Passage, Macroom, Kinsale, Fermoy, and Midleton. Sixty representatives attended the Cork conference on 17 July, which was, according to the republican newsletter, 'completely non-republican'.[23] They represented the South of Ireland Cattle Association, the Cork Food Council, the Cork Mental Hospital, the Cork Chamber of Commerce and Shipping, the Cork Industrial Association, the Cork Harbour Commissioners, and the Cork Industrial Development Association.[24] The conference unanimously passed the following resolution:

Resolution adopted at a Conference of Representatives of all Public Boards of Cork City and County 17 July, 1922.

1. *Against War;* We believe we are voicing the views of the people of Munster when we declare ourselves not satisfied that such a disastrous fratricidal strife is unavoidable and when we appeal to those who fought so nobly for freedom to consider whether we are all drifting towards the greatest calamity in Irish history.

2. *Dail;* We demand the immediate assembly of Dail Eireann as the Sovereign-Body of this country and as the only authority now recognised by both sets of belligerents.

3. *Armistice;* We ask for an immediate cessation of hostilities and we request Dail Eireann to call an Armistice. Pending the meeting of the Dail we call upon the Government in Dublin and G.H.Q. Clonmel to cease-fire.

4. Should the proposal for an Armistice prove unsuccessful we request the Dail immediately to exercise its authority and order a cessation of hostilities.

We hereby form here a Peoples' Rights Association.[25]

The association then requested public bodies to endorse the resolutions and to appoint a delegate to attend a conference at a date to be fixed subsequently. It then called on all the available members of the Second and Third Dails to meet in conference on Saturday 29 July at the Harbour Office in Cork 'to discuss the most effective means of securing the immediate assembling of Dail Eireann and the proclamation of an armistice'.[26] That plan having failed, a subsequent meeting of

---

[20] P.G. Decision, 1 July 1922 (NA, D/T, S1437).   [21] *Voice of Labour*, 22 July 1922.
[22] *Poblacht na hEireann*, 29 July 1922.
[23] Ibid., 24 July 1922.
[24] *Evening Echo*, 17 July 1922 (UCD, FitzGerald Papers, P80/711 (1)).
[25] 'Civil War 1922–24: Resolution by the People's Rights Association in Cork' (NA, D/T, S8143).
[26] *Irish Times*, 27 July 1922.

the conference decided to send a delegation to Dublin to ask for an immediate convocation of the Dail. The delegation consisted of a pro-treaty delegate, Sean Hales, an anti-treaty delegate, Lord Mayor O'Callaghan, and the chairman of Cork Trades Council. The deputation met with Eoin MacNeill, the minister of education, on 24 July. MacNeill replied that a meeting of the Dail was impractical, and that it would meet as soon as the conditions of the country made it possible to do so. MacNeill's response was approved by the cabinet.[27]

The anti-treaty press interpreted the Cork peace moves as indicative of a shift in public opinion against the government among prominent pro-treatyites and non-republicans in the county.[28] Indeed the People's Rights Association had received a reply from Liam Lynch, stating that if the government ceased its attacks, 'defensive action on our part can cease'. Lynch promised that he would guarantee the allegiance of his army to the Second Dail or any other 'elected assembly'. On 18 July Frank Daly, chairman of the Cork Harbour Board, received a set of terms that conveyed the IRA headquarters' views on the People's Rights appeal. Remarkably, it stated that they were willing to recognize the position created 'by the signing and the acceptance of the Treaty', and called for a constituent assembly to approve a constitution that should be validated by the Irish people, regardless of British opinion. With suitable amendments to the constitution, notably to the preamble, both it and the Treaty could be validated by the assembly. Under these terms the 4 May truce could also be restored and the army negotiations continued.[29] In turn on 1 August the association sent Collins a letter containing two questions:

1. Do you agree to arrange for such a cessation of hostilities as General Liam Lynch intimates he is prepared to accept?
2. Do you agree to call forthwith a meeting of the Second Dail, to be followed by a meeting of the Third Dail, as previously arranged, and to allow the Sovereign Assembly of the people to decide on the necessity or policy of a bitter and prolonged civil war?

Collins answered on 4 August that peace would come when the anti-treatyites 'see fit to obey the wishes of the people, as expressed through their public representatives; when they will give up their arms and cease their depredations on the persons and property of Irish citizens'.[30] A further meeting of the association was held on 5 August. Professor O'Rahilly referred to Collins' declaration that he would carry on the war until the IRA surrendered their arms, and added that 'undoubtedly he had received no mandate from Parliament not even from the Parliament recently elected to which he professed to be responsible'.[31] Following the fall of Cork on 12 August, the association submitted further proposals, reflecting the weakened anti-treaty position. They included an amnesty for all

[27] 'Civil War 1922–24: Resolution by the People's Rights Association Cork' (NA, D/T, S8143).
[28] *Poblacht na h-Eireann*, 21 July 1922.
[29] Maoldhomhaigh to Daly, 17 July 1922 (UCD, FitzGerald Papers, P80/712 (5)).
[30] 'Civil War 1922–24: Resolution by the People's Rights Association Cork' (NA D/T, S8143).
[31] *Poblacht na hEireann*, 14 August 1922.

prisoners, handing over arms to a joint committee, and framing a new constitution. They were rejected by the Provisional Government.[32]

The Cork moves served as a precedent for the mobilization of public opinion against the war. Wexford and Roscommon County Councils also demanded an immediate session of the Dail, and Waterford County Council passed a resolution condemning 'the wanton war of destruction that was being waged without the sanction of Dail Eireann'.[33] Darrell Figgis, the independent TD, addressed a letter to the Provisional Government demanding, in the name of Irish Farmers, an immediate session of the Dail in order to ensure 'the proper constitution of a government'.[34] In the attitude of Labour, however, the Provisional Government found its most significant civic opponent. During the People's Rights Association conference the Labour TD, Robert Day, who had topped the poll in the June elections in the city, voiced the opinion that 'for the strife at present there was no authority or mandate from the people of Ireland'.[35] A joint meeting of the National Executive of the Labour Party and the Executive of the Dublin Workers Council had been held at the Mansion House on Saturday, 1 July. Labour members from places as distant as Moate, Dungarvan, Carlow, and Waterford had attended, thus demonstrating that there was 'no insuperable difficulty in the way of members attending'.[36] A motion demanding the revocation of the order postponing the meeting of the Dail until 15 July was passed, and an immediate meeting of the Dail was demanded.

Labour adopted two strategies in order to get the Dail to meet. Firstly, it called for a meeting of all elected TDs to be held in the Mansion House on 20 July. The lord mayor of Dublin and 12 of Labour's 17 TDs attended, but none of the independents or Farmers Party TDs turned up.[37] The meeting was declared 'abortive' because 'the elected representatives of the two main parties were so tied up to their own parties that they would not do anything that the parties had not already agreed upon'.[38] The party received a communication on behalf of the available anti-treaty members in Dublin dated 19 July, suggesting that the conference could more efficiently pursue its objective 'uninfluenced by our presence'.[39] They received no communication from the other parties. The Provisional Government had decided that attendance would be inadvisable.[40] Labour's second strategy was more daring. On 12 August, following a meeting of Congress on 7 August, Labour sent an ultimatum to the Provisional Government demanding that the parliament meet by 26 August. Otherwise, Labour threatened that their members 'shall meet their constituents, hand back the mandate given them by the

---

[32] M. Hopkinson, *Green against Green: The Irish Civil War* (Dublin, 1988), 183.
[33] *Poblacht na hEireann.*, 17 August 1922.
[34] Ibid., 18 August, 1922.
[35] Ibid., 24 July 1922.
[36] Ibid., 22 July 1922.
[37] Ibid., 29 July 1922.
[38] Ibid., 12 August 1922.
[39] (NL, Thomas Johnson Papers, Ms 17, 139).
[40] (UCD, Richard Mulcahy Papers, P7/B/29).

electors, and resign their seats'.[41] The Labour newspaper had already criticized the Provisional Government's claim that they received an electoral mandate for the military actions carried out since June:

> When it made the Collins–de Valera Pact, the Second Dail did its utmost to prevent the electorate voting for or against the Treaty, and after the elections it has the colossal impudence to claim that the electorate, which was expressly forbidden to vote on the Treaty, gave a certain decision on what it was prevented from deciding! As to the mandate given by the electors, whatever it was it was most emphatically not a mandate for the waging of civil war.[42]

The Provisional Government had decided to ignore Labour's threat.[43] The party's interpretation of the 'pact election' was the same as that of the anti-treatyites, but Labour pulled back from their threat to resign their seats. Although the Dail had not met by 26 August, on 31 August a joint meeting of the National Executive of the Labour Party and the Labour representatives from Dail Eireann met to consider putting into force their resolution of 7 August. Sixteen of their 17 TDs were present. Having had assurances from Cosgrave that morning that the parliament would unquestionably meet on 9 September, and that the postponement of the parliament from 26 August was occasioned only by the deaths of Collins and Griffith, it was decided that the necessity for carrying out the contemplated action did not arise.[44]

There were still hopes that peace proposals would find expression in the new parliament. A peace move had been instigated by Roscommon County Council asking other local bodies to appoint representatives to meet in conference. The lord mayor of Dublin had promised his assistance and favourable replies had been received from several counties.[45] It was reported in the press that the county council movement was 'steadily gaining strength'.[46] However, the movement failed to influence the proceedings of the new Dail, which retrospectively vindicated the Provisional Government's actions since June. Moreover, on 12 September, the Provisional Government advertised its terms for peace. There could be: (a) no breach of the Treaty, and (b) the existence of armed forces not controlled by parliament would not be permitted.[47] Then on 28 September the Dail voted against a proposal, which had Labour support, for a fourteen-day ceasefire. This, however, did not kill all hope of peace. A meeting of businessmen and ratepayers met in the Rotunda hospital on 5 October to discuss the possibility of forming a national economic party to work for the promotion of peace and prosperity. They proposed that a national conference take place that would consist of six protreatyites, six anti-treatyites, one from the National University of Ireland, one

[41] *Voice of Labour*, 12 August 1922.
[42] Ibid., 22 July 1922.
[43] P.G. Minute, 24 August 1922 (NA, G1/3).
[44] *Irish Times*, 1 September 1922.
[45] Ibid.
[46] Ibid., 6 September 1922.
[47] Ibid., 12 September 1922.

from Trinity College, and six representatives of the ratepayers of Ireland.[48] It was decided to establish a National Economic Party and to hold a conference. The resolution was forwarded to the leadership of the two sides with terms to serve as a basis for a ceasefire. The association succeeded in gaining the cooperation of other local bodies that were working for peace. A combined meeting took place on 17 October at the offices of the Ratepayers Association in Henry St, Dublin, where it was decided to invite the further cooperation of other bodies. As a basis for a ceasefire the association proposed that the two sides establish a coalition government. A general election would take place, with the Treaty at issue, and with both sides undertaking 'to place no military obstacle to the carrying out of the will of the people as expressed at that election'. In his reply to the association on 17 November Cosgrave regretted that it was not possible to meet their deputation and remarked that the government's terms had already been published.[49]

On 5 October the government announced an amnesty for all those who would hand in their weapons by 15 October. Cork Workers' Council supported the offer, stating that the high unemployment in the city was directly related to the activities of armed men.[50] The Irish Womens' Workers also issued a call for an immediate truce, demanding a restoration of the 'elemental rights' of Irishwomen 'through honourable negotiation'.[51] On 24 October it was reported that 'the air continues to be filled with rumours of peace'. The previous day Dublin Corporation expressed its satisfaction that proposals for a truce had been made. Dungarvan Rural Council appointed delegates to get in touch with the 'irregular' leaders and asked the government to observe a truce to enable the negotiations to be conducted successfully.[52] A new 'non-republican' and 'non-political' organization, Clann na h-Eireann, which hoped to become a basis 'for peace with honour' with the cooperation of some distinguished clergy and the lord mayor of Dublin, was founded in Navan. It supported an Irish–Ireland programme, focusing on Irish games and Irish literature.[53] However, the optimism that seemed to be present in October was greatly diminished by a public statement signed by de Valera declaring that 'victory for the Republic or utter defeat and extermination' were now the two alternatives facing the anti-treatyites.[54]

De Valera's declaration notwithstanding, November saw further calls for peace. An immediate truce and a general election when the new register was completed was unanimously called for at the monthly meeting of the County Westmeath Executive of the Farmers Union in Moate. One of the speakers recorded his conviction that the Irish Farmers Union could eventually save the country.[55]

[48] Ibid., 6 October 1922.
[49] (NA, D/T, S1438).
[50] *Irish Times*, 6 October 1922.
[51] Ibid., 18 October 1922.
[52] Ibid., 24 October 1922.
[53] Ibid., 27 October 1922.
[54] Ibid., 31 October 1922.
[55] Ibid., 6 November 1922.

A general convention of the Gaelic League called for a week's ceasefire.[56] New Ross Rural Council called for an immediate truce. North Tipperary County Council suggested that a conference be held, chaired by Revd Dr Mannix, the archbishop of Melbourne. The Irish Women's International League also issued a call for a truce. On 20 November Dublin Corporation passed a resolution proposing that a peace conference be called. In the opinion of one member, the common people in the conflict were only playing 'the part of the bit of iron between the hammer and the anvil'.[57] In Waterford on the same day, a meeting of the Workers' Council and Labour Party passed a resolution calling for an immediate cessation of hostilities.[58] At the same time peace resolutions from the New Ross and Dungarvan Rural District Councils were circulating among the public bodies. The first suggested that the leaders of the opposing parties 'meet to arrange a truce with a view to settlement by negotiation'. The second requested all public boards to endeavour to bring about a cessation of hostilities.[59] The New Ross resolution was adopted by Wicklow Urban District Council, Youghal No. 2 Council, Longford Rural District Council, and the Cork Harbour Commissioners. Muine Beag Town Commissioners also issued a call for a truce.[60]

A People's Peace League had also been formed in November. It had called for a public meeting to be held at the Mansion House in Dublin 'to assert the will of the people as expressed at the last election'.[61] The meeting took place on 24 November and issued a proposal for peace based on the anti-treatyites and the government meeting in conference under a chairman mutually agreed upon.[62] The government noted that the meeting was called 'in terms which implied that the Government in taking action against the Irregulars is acting in opposition to the will of the people'. On 22 November the cabinet decided to instruct P. S. O'Hegarty, secretary of the General Post Office, who was prominently identified with the League, to sever his connections with the organization.[63] In December there were more calls for the conflict to be ended, in particular that there should be a truce for Christmas. The Irishwomen's International League reiterated its call for a truce in a public letter to Cosgrave and de Valera, stating that 'the great majority of the people intensely desire a pacific settlement'.[64] Wexford Corporation called for Archbishop Mannix to intervene.[65] On 7 December a conference of South and North Wexford Sinn Fein Executives, the County Wexford Farmers Association, and the local Transport Workers Union met and called for an

[56] *Irish Times*, 10 November 1922.
[57] Ibid., 21 November, 1922.
[58] Ibid.
[59] Ibid., 29 November 1922.
[60] *Freeman's Journal*, 27 November 1922.
[61] Ibid., 21 November 1922.
[62] Ibid., 25 November 1922.
[63] P. G. Minute, 22 November 1922 (NA, D/T, S8140).
[64] *Irish Times*, 1 December 1922.
[65] Ibid., 6 December 1922.

armistice, again calling for public bodies to adopt their resolution.[66] They were to receive a long reply from Cosgrave on 28 December:

I am as much in favour of Peace as anyone in Ireland. Peace to be established on a sound basis, namely under authority and subject to the authority of representative Government. Those who challenged that authority have lost what they called the 'War' and now having lost that they are gambling to win the Peace. The Government's terms are known and they are generous, bearing in mind the grave loss of life, the dislocation of business, and the destruction of property. If these were war aims the lust of the Irregulars must be well indulged by now. The time for mercy is being rapidly consumed and if advantage be not taken of it very shortly, those who are making war on the people will find too late that there is a limit to patience.[67]

Earlier in the month Limerick Corporation had carried a motion condemning the recent executions of the four anti-treatyite leaders on the IRA Executive.[68] Tipperary Board of Guardians telegraphed Cosgrave calling for 'a truce of God' to last until 8 January and passed unanimously the Peace League's Resolution. On 9 December Limerick County Council had issued a call for all parties 'in the interests of common humanity to end this strife'.[69] Peace overtures were also discussed by Dublin Corporation, who passed a resolution expressing sympathy with the parents and relatives of the executed leaders, as well as those of Sean Hales, a pro-treatyite TD from Cork, who had been assassinated by the IRA. Aghamore Sinn Fein Club called for a truce for Christmas and called on Sinn Fein clubs throughout the country to make themselves heard. Wexford District Council issued a similar call, also calling for a new election. Cork Rural District Council passed a motion condemning the death of Sean Hales and the execution of the others, as did Cork Corporation. Dundalk Trades Council called for a truce, and, in the absence of a truce, for Labour to withdraw from the Dail.[70] Around the same time a Senate Peace Committee, which consisted of five senators who were to advise as to the possibility of an immediate cessation of violence, was formed. They issued an appeal for a Christmas truce.[71] Cork Harbour Commissioners appealed for the government to appoint three members of the Dail to act in conjunction with the Senate Committee and to meet three neutral Irishmen acceptable to the anti-treatyites in order to discuss the best basis for a cessation and a permanent peace.[72] A further meeting, which received messages of support from Queenstown Urban Council and Clonakilty Board of Guardians, was held at Cork Courthouse on 14 December. Mountmellick Town Commissioners appealed for a Christmas truce, as did Longford County Council.[73] On 23 December

[66] Ibid., 8 December 1922.
[67] Ibid., 9 January 1922.
[68] *Irish Independent*, 9 December 1922.
[69] Ibid., 11 December 1922.
[70] Ibid., 13 December 1922.
[71] Ibid., 12 December 1922.
[72] Ibid., 14 December 1922.
[73] 'Civil War 1922–24' (NA, D/T, S8140).

Castlebar Rural District Council appealed for 'a peace of God' and acceptance of the people's will at a free election on the new register.

In late December/early January more calls for peace were also made by Cashel Urban District Council, Rathmines Urban District Council, Longford District Council, Tullamore Rural District Council, and Wicklow Urban District Council. So great was the demand for peace around Christmas that in the new year the People's Peace League, which was in touch with public bodies throughout Ireland, could state that 'two thirds of these public bodies favour cessation of hostilities and an immediate truce'. They demanded that there be (a) a grounding of arms, (b) a cessation of hostilities and active cooperation in the preparation of the register, and (c) an election whose result must bind both sides.[74] Further peace calls were made by Gorey District Council, North Mayo's branch of the Farmer's Association, and North Meath's *Comhairle Ceanntar* of Sinn Fein. Of the latter's special meeting on 3 January a participant noted that 'it was grand to see representatives of the two contending political parties present, united in a common desire for peace'.[75] The Peace Committee of Dublin Sinn Fein met on 7 January at the Mansion House. Nineteen Sinn Fein clubs were represented and it was decided to establish an extraordinary *Ard Fheis* committee to find a basis for peace.

By far the most hopeful peace initiative was launched by an organization calling itself the Neutral IRA Association, which was founded in Dublin in December. Two of the founding members were Sean O'Hegarty and Florence O'Donoghue, commander of Cork's number one brigade and adjutant of the first southern division, respectively. Both had been elected to the anti-treaty Executive in March 1922, but had valued republican unity above all else and refused to take sides in the civil war.[76] The Association's membership was open to those who had fought in the War of Independence and who were now neutral in the civil war. The date upon which any volunteer ceased to take part in the struggle against the British, or his personal political views, did not affect his eligibility for membership. Late in December the organization sent an open letter to Cosgrave and de Valera, stressing the advisability of a cessation of hostilities and a general election. It asserted that half of the old IRA were now neutral and argued that a continuation of the conflict would 'involve the country in economic ruin and national bankruptcy'.[77] On 31 December a largely attended meeting of the organization met to appoint an Executive and launch an organization drive. The association planned a convention with delegates drawn from already-existing battalions and brigades. At battalion conventions every ex-IRA man from the battalion who was now neutral would be entitled to attend, speak, and vote. If a motion received a two-thirds majority it would be forwarded to the brigade conventions. Resolutions that received a two-thirds majority at the brigade conventions would be

---

[74] *Irish Times*, 4 January 1923.
[75] Ibid., 6 January 1923.
[76] P. Hart, *The IRA and Its Enemies: Violence and Community in Cork 1916–1923* (Oxford, 1999), 264.
[77] *Freeman's Journal*, 30 December 1922.

forwarded for discussion at the general convention. The brigade convention would elect delegates to the general convention.[78] The response to the organization drive was very satisfactory. In Cork alone the association was reported to have between 8,000 and 10,000 members.[79]

On 12 January Tom Derrig, the IRA's adjutant general, wrote to Liam Lynch, noting that there was a growing anti-government feeling in the country, exemplified by the Neutral IRA, which he considered not entirely republican, but definitely against the executions.[80] The Neutral IRA convention in Dublin on 4 February was attended by between 150 and 200 delegates. A number of resolutions were passed, the most significant demanding that both the civil war armies be demobilized, and a new army composed entirely of men who were IRA members before the truce with the British be built up.[81] The convention declared itself vigorously against the executions, and was advised by the leadership to leave their programmes behind them as possession of the agenda might lead to them being arrested.[82] After the convention, the association, speaking in the name of its 20,000 members, communicated its proposals to Cosgrave, Mulcahy, de Valera, and Lynch. It proposed a truce of one month on the following conditions: (a) That on the republican side all military activities and acts of aggression against public and private persons and property shall be suspended; (b) that on the Free State side all military activities, arrests, trials, and executions shall be suspended. It expected replies no later than noon 23 February.[83] The association's proposals were then supported by a variety of local government bodies including Cork Corporation, Cork Rural District Council, Newcastle West Town Commissioners, Tullamore Rural District Council, Bundoran Urban District Council, Cork County Council, Ballina Urban District Council, Clonakilty Rural District Council and Guardians, Passage West Urban District Council, Trim Urban District Council, Mountmellick Trades Council, Brandon Urban District Council, Mallow Urban District Council, Kilkenny Corporation, Kantuk Guardians, Youghal Urban District Council, Youghal nos. 1 and 2 Rural District Council and Guardians, Meath County Council, Castlerea District Council, Mallow Board of Guardians and Urban District Council, Bandon Town Commissioners, Mullingar District Council, Enniscorthy District Council, Carofin Board of Guardians, Loughrea Urban Council, Wicklow County Council, Westmeath County Council, Tipperary Guardians, Charleville Rural District Council, Tullamore Urban District Council, Rathluirc District Council, Glenamaddy District Council, and Drogheda Rural District Council.

However, the association failed to elicit a positive response from the leaderships of the civil war sides. On 2 January de Valera told Lynch that the Neutral

[78] Ibid., 26 January 1923.
[79] *Irish Independent*, 26 January 1923.
[80] Derrig to Lynch, 1 January 1923 (UCD, de Valera Papers, P/150 1793).
[81] (NL, Florence O'Donaghue Papers, Ms 31,261).
[82] 'IRA Report on Neutral IRA Convention', 6 February 1923 (UCD, de Valera Papers, P150/1793).
[83] *Irish Independent*, 17 February 1923.

IRA would propose terms that would allow the Free State to function unhindered, and however much that policy could have been justified before the civil war began, nothing could be said for it now that the government had resorted to 'terrorism pure and simple'.[84] On 5 February the IRA newsletter *Poblacht na hEireann* sent the association the following warning:

Information has come to us to the effect that an attempt is about to be made to use the meeting of the delegates of the ex-IRA Mans Association to spring upon them terms of settlement which would guarantee the functioning of the Free State and which would be utterly impossible for Republicans to accept.... If the members of the ex-IRA Mens Association really wish to bring peace to the country they will take care that they are not made tools of by the politicians of Merrion St.[85]

Tom Derrig believed that the Neutral IRA's proposals for a truce would be tantamount to surrendering the Republic, and told de Valera that he distrusted them as much as he distrusted Mulcahy during the Four Courts negotiations. De Valera was suspicious of Florrie O'Donoghue's leanings in particular.[86] On the other side, Cosgrave met Donal Hannigan and M. J. Burke of the Neutral IRA's Executive on 27 February. They told him that most of the men from the first southern division, in response to the arrest of Liam Deasy three weeks earlier, were 'going home and will not take up arms again'. Although Lynch had denounced his plea, on 9 February the government offered an amnesty for all those who surrendered their arms. Hannigan and Burke suggested a three-week truce without arrests would encourage more people to give up the fight and enable the IRA Executive to meet. Their belief was that the western divisions were also for peace, but warned that 'if they are going to go down they will go down dying hard'. In their view the fight was becoming more embittered, and the public in the south and west of the country would not continue to support the government 'if the situation is not cleared up quickly'. In the long run, 'unless some honourable basis or way out is found for the republicans they will never recognise the Government'. Unless a deal was made with moderates like de Valera, the army men would act on their own. Peace would be acceptable to the southern men 'on the lines that some attempt is made that republican T.D.s be given a constitutional position in the Dail'. Cosgrave doubted the sincerity of his opponents, claiming that the anti-treatyites believed that 'they are justified in breaking any pact they may make with us, the same as they broke the Truce with the English'. A truce would place the government at a tactical disadvantage; his opponents would gain if the peace talks failed or succeeded, because the government would have gone back on its pledge that it would not negotiate. Moreover 'every bona fide republican would accept the Truce, but any lunatic who could be prevailed upon by de Valera or Stack to throw a bomb would do so, and we have to put our hands

---

[84] De Valera to Lynch, 21 January 1923 (UCD, de Valera Papers, P/150 1749).

[85] *Poblacht na hEireann*, 5 February 1923.

[86] Derrig to de Valera, 19 Feburary 1923; de Valera to Derrig, 22 February 1923 (UCD, de Valera Papers, P/150 1758).

up and give them a free hand'. He estimated that at most the leadership could control 90 per cent of its forces, but the remainder could do a lot of damage. In any case the government had arrived at the position it wanted. There was no need to negotiate. The impact of the executions was positive: once the people had seen that the Government was 'in earnest' they 'came along', and were cooperating more than ever. He declared that without moral support the anti-treaty cause was doomed: 'apart from the slaughter of little children they can't do more than they have done'.[87]

Early in March the Neutral IRA Association released a statement admitting that 'the suggestion of a truce by us has not been accepted by either side, notwithstanding the fact that it has received the general support and approval of public bodies, thereby clearly demonstrating that the will of the people is for peace'. It committed itself to no further proposals and by the end of the month the organization had begun to wind down.[88] The Neutral IRA initiative was the last significant peace move by a civil society organization during the civil war. In April, Monsignor Luzio, the Papal Nuncio, arrived in Ireland to help create an atmosphere of peace, but he was unsuccessful, despite the fact that his visit was also approved of by many public bodies. On 30 April 1923 de Valera wrote to the monsignor encouraging his efforts, stating that the people had been 'sighing and longing for peace with a yearning which none but themselves really know'.[89] Although Luzio met with both Cosgrave and de Valera, his visit provoked the government to write to the Pope, complaining that it only encouraged the forces of anarchy in Irish society, and the monsignor was soon withdrawn.[90] On 21 April Luzio had thanked the numerous public bodies that supported his visit for their support and stated that they had already demonstrated the public's desire for peace.[91] Two days later, however, Kevin O'Higgins declared that Luzio was simply 'a distinguished foreign churchman' visiting Ireland on an ecclesiastical mission.[92] By this stage anti-treaty resistance to the Free State was clearly crumbling, and de Valera was formulating his own peace proposals, which would also fail to bring the conflict to a negotiated conclusion. The civil war ended on 30 April when the IRA were instructed by their leadership to dump arms. Civil society organizations played no part in its conclusion.

THE LIMITS OF CIVIL SOCIETY

This analysis of the role of civil society during the civil war makes it clear that there were two issues at stake in 1922–3. One was the conflict between the

---

[87] 'Interview between the President and D. Hannigan and M. J. Burke of Neutral IRA', 27 February 1923 (NA, D/T, S8139).
[88] *Irish Independent*, 9 March 1923.
[89] De Valera to Luzio, 30 April 1923 (UCD, de Valera Papers, P/150 1809).
[90] P.G. Minutes, 17 April 1923 (NA, G2/1).
[91] *Irish Times*, 21 April 1923.
[92] Ibid., 23 April 1923.

Provisional Government and the anti-treaty IRA over the implementation of the Treaty, and took place among a political elite where close ties and past associations had resulted in bitter enmity. The other was a conflict between the contending parties and Irish civil society over the desirability of the civil war itself. In this second conflict, concerned citizens and neutrals who believed that the Sinn Fein political elite was leading the country to rack and ruin figured prominently. An argument has been made, as earlier indicated, to the effect that the civil war conflict was simply one between Irish civil society and the 'public band' tradition.[93] This suggests that the Provisional Government functioned as the 'protector' of civil society during the civil war. Although a useful characterization of the initial split, such a view obscures the fact that in their efforts to mediate between the opposing sides during the civil war, civil society organizations found themselves opposed not just to a militaristic IRA, but also to an equally belligerent Provisional Government. The shift in the stance of civil society was reflected by Tullamore Rural District Council's protest to the Provisional Government on 6 September 1922:

We are of the opinion that this Council when giving a mandate to Dail Eireann in December last to approve of the Treaty as an alternative to terrible war, should be sufficient indication that war for the Treaty with ourselves was never contemplated and never would have the approval of the Irish people.[94]

It is clear that many peacemakers believed that the Provisional Government did not have the full force of public opinion behind them in their prosecution of the war. Patrick Belton, chairman of the People's Peace League, thought that during the June general election the will of the people was expressed in support of the Collins–de Valera electoral pact to secure unity and peace. In Belton's opinion it was the political leaders and those 'itching for a fight' who differed in the conflict. The people were not disunited.[95] In a similar vein, Alderman Corish, a Labour TD from Wexford town, told a peace conference in Wexford that the people who were governing Ireland claimed that they were acting in accordance with the will of the people, but he said that they were not doing any such thing.[96] Around the same time Professor O'Rahilly told a similar conference in Cork that 'the people were of one way of thinking, but people who thought that the policy of violence and force—call it executions and assassinations—would settle the whole question were merely partisan'.[97] Thomas Johnson best articulated the exasperation of 'neutrals' with the Sinn Fein elite:

The great question is, how can unity and cohesion be restored or are we to throw up our hands in absolute despair and declare that all is lost? Can we believe that men who have done and suffered so much for their country have so far forgotten themselves that in the

[93] Garvin, 'Unenthusiastic Democrats'.
[94] O'Kelly to Cosgrave, 6 September 1922 (NA, D/T 1726).
[95] *Freeman's Journal*, 25 November 1922.
[96] Ibid., 16 December 1922.
[97] Ibid., 15 December 1922.

mad pursuit of war, they will refuse to listen to the wailings of a ruined country? A momentous victory of arms may drive opponents such as we have beneath the surface, but can Peace be there established? If the leaders on both sides can find no better way of settling the affairs of the Nation than by a War of hatred and revenge, for that I fear is what is has developed into, then in God's name they ought to stand down, and let others try and govern without devastating the country.[98]

Johnson supported the plan to hold a conference drawn from public and administrative bodies, which would demand, in the name of the people, a cessation of hostilities.

Certainly, the government acted at times as if its interests and those of civil society were diametrically opposed to each other. For example in July 1922 Griffith wrote to Frank Daly of the Cork Harbour Board, complaining that the action of the People's Rights Association was

Nothing short of approval of the Irregulars and the responsibility therefore is as much with the representatives as it is with the Irregulars. I mean responsibility for every action, from the murder of Protestants and ex-policemen down to the economic distress that is arising and will become more and more severe as the action of the Irregulars is persisted in.[99]

The Provisional government took exception to the assumption of the Association that it was mediating between two legitimate adversaries. Griffith complained of the tone of the Association's communiqué, which used such terms as 'General Liam Lynch, Chief of Staff', and labelled the Provisional government's action to 'secure obedience to law' nothing other than 'a bitter and prolonged civil war'.[100] No doubt he would have preferred if the organization had followed the government's instructions to the press, which were that the anti-treatyites should be referred to as 'bands' or 'Irregulars', and the Provisional government as 'the government'. When it came to the Neutral IRA, Kevin O'Higgins stated that those who were neutral were either 'moral cowards' who knew the anti-treatyite campaign was wrong and were afraid to say so or 'physical cowards' who thought it was right but were afraid to participate. He doubted whether any significant number of the Neutral IRA men had actually participated in the war against the British, and offered to pay for lists to be published in the Irish newspapers setting out the names of the Neutral IRA men and the units to which they claimed to be attached.[101] Local bodies were also targeted for abuse by some members of the Provisional government. Indeed on 1 February 1923, Kevin O'Shiel recommended to Cosgrave that his government take steps against the 'disloyal' and 'corrupt' local bodies who were encouraging the republicans by 'treasonous' or 'defeatist' resolutions.[102] In one case at least such steps were actually taken. In December the Carlow Board of Guardians passed a resolution calling for a national peace

---

[98] (NL, Thomas Johnson Papers, Ms 17,139).
[99] Griffith to Daly, July 1922 (NA, D/T, S8143).
[100] E. Neeson, *The Civil War 1922–1923* (Dublin, 1973), 222.
[101] *Irish Times*, 13 March 1923.
[102] (UCD, Mulcahy Papers, P7B/100).

conference, demanding the stopping of executions, the release of untried prisoners, and the granting of political status to political prisoners. Two months later, the proposer of the motion, Patrick Kane, who was associated with the Neutral IRA, was arrested and lodged in Carlow workhouse, which was occupied by Free State soldiers.[103] By the end of the civil war all the local government offices in Cork and Kerry were occupied by the Free State Army.

On the other hand, this clampdown extended only to state institutions and not autonomous organizations per se. For example on 17 July 1922 the Provisional government decided that no useful purpose would be served by taking action against the proprietors of the *Cork Examiner* whose issue of the fourteenth was 'entirely Irregular'.[104] The following month, the Provisional government also received news that a Franciscan monk, Fr Matthew, had told a congregation in Wexford on 6 August that 'your prayers are requested for the eternal repose of the soul of Harry Boland, murdered in Dublin'. The Provisional government was happy with the assurance of his superior that the monk 'will cause no further trouble with your government'.[105] Then in August 1922, the Provisional government was approached by directors of the Great Western Railways who asked for a definite policy on anti-treaty IRA men and women, mainly clerical and wages staff, that had taken part in the early stages of the IRA campaign. The official response was that this was a matter for the railway company.[106] However, they were more concerned when an article appeared in the 22 August edition of the *Freeman's Journal* stating that Rory O'Connor had been granted six months' leave of absence from Dublin Corporation, and that the joint committee of Grangegorman Mental Hospital had decided to reinstate two attendants who left their posts on 29 June, on the plea that they were called to the colours by O'Connor. After a meeting of the Grangegorman board had recommended leniency towards the two men, citing the possibility of a strike among the staff if they were dismissed, the Provisional government decided it was too late to intervene. There was, however, a much stronger reaction in the new year when 16 out of 80 councillors on Dublin Corporation passed measures giving half pay to dependents of internees who refused to sign the form of undertaking.[107] Dublin Corporation had been a thorn in the side of the Provisional government since July 1922 when it passed a resolution that captured anti-treaty IRA men should be treated as prisoners of war, and later established a committee to enquire into the treatment of these men. In January 1923 the government decided that an order be served by the commander-in-chief on the city Treasurer and the Deputy Treasurer in Dublin, directing that no money be paid in respect of half-wages to its employees at present in prison.[108]

[103] *Poblacht na hEireann*, 19 February 1923.
[104] Cosgrave and Griffith to Collins, 17 July 1922 (NA, D/T, S1385).
[105] Enright to Cosgrave, 23 August 1922 (NA, D/T, S1622).
[106] P.G. Decision, 18 August 1922 (NA, D/T, S1616).
[107] *Freeman's Journal*, 25 January 1923.
[108] Meeting of Executive Council, 23 January 1923, extract from minutes (NA C.1.35).

It would also be a mistake to conclude that civil society organizations were in all cases trying to steer a middle course between the government and the IRA. Several local bodies refused to endorse the peace proposals emanating from Cork, Wexford, and Roscommon. Others simply marked them 'read'. In some cases even when a local body passed a resolution critical of the government, the reality was that the council was deeply divided on the issue. At a meeting of Tralee Rural District Council in January for example, a resolution condemning the actions of the government regarding the recent executions, stating that the actions of the Irish government exceeded the worst tyranny of the British during the War of Independence and calling on the Kerry TDs to resign, was passed. However, of the nine councillors who attended the meeting it was reported that seven later called to Ballymullen Barracks and repudiated the resolution, signing a statement dissociating themselves from its substance and wording.[109] Indeed the evidence suggests that local politics were dominated by exactly the same issues that had divided the Dail in the first half of 1922. When New Ross Urban Council met to discuss peace moves on 2 January 1923, the following argument took place:

MR MURPHY   The farmers and the labourers struck too soon on the question of Irish sovereignty. They thought they could ignore it. The sovereignty of Ireland was underneath the whole thing.

CHAIRMAN   It wasn't them, but the ignoring of the definitely expressed wishes of the Irish people and of Dail Eireann.

MR MURPHY   It was not a free expression.

CHAIRMAN   It would have been free if the result was in accordance with your views, and because it was not you decided it was not free. It was as free as anything in the world could be.

MR. MURPHY   The sovereignty of Ireland was older than the British Empire. Men cannot express a free wish with revolvers to their heads.[110]

The odd council was explicitly supportive of the government's policies. In Clare County Council for example, under the chairmanship of Commandant-General Michael Brennan, the Provisional government had an enthusiastic supporter. The council refused to participate in Roscommon County Council's plan to establish a peace conference composed of public bodies.[111] On 4 November 1922 a meeting of the council adopted a resolution, reiterating the terms of peace—requiring the handing in of arms, the renunciation of the principle of armed resistance to the will of the people, absolute unswerving allegiance to the people's government, and the acceptance of a national constitution under the Treaty.[112]

Clare's position was typical only of a minority of local bodies that were fully behind the government. The majority of those that publicized their position adopted a neutral stance, which suggests that the public mood was for peace. What is nonetheless very revealing of the limitations of civil society in a conflict

[109] *Irish Independent,* 7 January 1923.
[110] S. MacSuain, *County Wexford's Civil War* (Wexford, 1995), 101.
[111] *Irish Independent,* 2 September 1922.
[112] Ibid., 6 November 1922.

of this kind was that those organizations that had been traditionally prominent in the articulation of nationalist opinion were least effective in mobilizing opinion against the civil war. For example, a peace initiative emanated from the *Ard Fheis* of the Gaelic League, which was held early in December. It was believed that the League was 'practically the only existing organisation which embraces within its ranks so many of the opposing political parties both of which are working side by side towards the same goal'. It was felt that 'the fact that enthusiastic supporters of both parties supported the motion renders the peace prospects still brighter'.[113] The convention decided to appoint two members to interview leaders on both sides with a view to bringing them together in the interests of peace, and a peace committee was later formed. However, the initiative came to nothing and the Gaelic League did not figure in the peace moves that developed in the new year. On 7 January 1923, the ruling body of the Gaelic Athletic Association met to consider a proposal made by the Cork County Board that it launch a peace initiative.[114] It was decided that the chair of the GAA would first ascertain the views of the members with a view to holding a convention on Sunday 4 February. Having heard the report, however, the president of the chair of the association decided that no useful purpose would be served by calling a convention and the plan was abandoned.[115] By then GAA activity in Connacht and Munster had virtually come to a halt as a result of the civil war. Indeed in Clare the execution of County Secretary Pat Hennessy and fellow-GAA man Con MacMahon by the government in January 1923 meant that for the next two years the county would have a pro- and anti-treaty county committee. A similar fate awaited the peace efforts of the Dublin Sinn Fein peace committee, which felt that it had a special responsibility for creating peace. The committee managed only to organize Sinn Fein opinion in the Dublin region and had eventually to concede that its plan for an extraordinary *Ard Fheis* was dependent on a cessation of hostilities taking place. It was therefore dependent on the success of other peace moves.

The most obvious case of a nationalist organization failing to effectively mediate the conflict was that of the Neutral IRA. The organization based its peace efforts on the assumption that the government wanted to secure a place for republicans in the system as a means of furthering general reconciliation. However, although Cosgrave would later facilitate the entry of his opponents into the Dail as a constitutional opposition, he described the Neutral IRA plan as meaning that 'that the people who roast children, burst watermains, murder our men, will have to get a constitutional position in the state'.[116] In the attitude of Eamon de Valera, the Neutral IRA faced another difficulty, as he initially refused to meet them, and a meeting did not take place until May 1923, and then only with his director of intelligence. At the meeting their representatives wondered why de

---

[113] *Irish Independent,* 11 November 1922.

[114] *Freeman's Journal,* 8 January 1923.

[115] *Irish Independent,* 22 January 1923.

[116] 'Interview between the President and D. Hannigan and M. J. Burke of Neutral IRA', 27 February 1923 (NA, D/T, S8139).

Valera did not meet them when their movement was at its strength, and claimed that with his support they could have obtained peace and even eliminated the oath of allegiance.[117] From the outset de Valera had feared that the Neutral IRA would be built up by the government as a reserve force, with the intention of creating an armed body like the Italian *fascisti*.[118] He advised the Neutral IRA Executive in February to throw in their lot behind his policy of following the Sinn Fein way and scrapping the Treaty, but ignored Florrie O'Donoghue's request for an interview to clarify what he meant.[119] The IRA leadership accurately predicted that if the organization's peace move failed, the majority of its members would fall in with the anti-treatyites.[120] Indeed the meeting in May showed an organization buckling under the strain of civil war politics. According to de Valera's informant, the representatives of the 'Neutral IRA' now claimed they were 'definitely republican, detest the Free State, and will do anything in their power to safeguard the republic'. They still claimed a membership of 25,000, few of them supporters of the Free State. They offered to support Sinn Fein at the next election and would circularize all public bodies to that end.[121] Such protestations were no doubt welcome news to the anti-treatyite political leadership who were keen to get the support of an organization that was now contemplating the establishment of an 'Irish Republican Party'.[122]

Precisely because of the inability of nationalist organizations to effectively intervene in the conflict, it was all the more important that organizations like the Labour Party could articulate the interests of civil society. Nationalist opinion was hopelessly polarized over the Treaty and if civil society was to articulate a transcendent vision of the future it fell to the admittedly small Labour Party to do so. However, Labour had tried and failed to prevent the Treaty split resulting in civil war during the spring of 1922. Then its proposal that a Council of State be formed by the Dail was supported by de Valera, but not by the Provisional government whose authority it would undercut. In the throes of the civil war Labour opposed the Provisional government's execution policy and made representations to ensure that the trials of condemned prisoners would be conducted as far as possible in accordance with legal precedents. However, Labour failed to reverse the execution policy. At a meeting with Cosgrave and Mulcahy on 21 February 1923, members of the Labour Party Executive argued in support of the Neutral IRA's proposals that the disintegration of republican opposition was more likely to proceed in the absence of more executions. Further executions, however, would have the effect of stiffening opposition, and what was needed was a continuance of the lull in executions, combined with an extension of the amnesty policy. Mulcahy, however, believed that further executions would have

---

[117] Department of Intelligence to President, 11 May 1923 (NA, Sinn Fein Papers, 1094/6/1).
[118] De Valera to Count Plunckett, 19 January 1923 (UCD, de Valera papers, P/150 1652).
[119] O'Donoghue to de Valera, 6 February 1923 (UCD, de Valera Papers, P/150 1793).
[120] Director of Organization to Lynch, 25 January 1923 (UCD, de Valera Papers, P150/1793).
[121] Department of Intelligence to President, 11 May 1923 (NA, Sinn Fein, 1094/6/2).
[122] O'Hegarty to O'Donoghue, 22 March 1923 (NL, Florence O'Donaghue Papers, Ms 31,261).

a discouraging effect on the 'Irregulars'.[123] The executions, which had practically ceased for the month of February, were resumed. On 26 February Thomas Gibson was executed in Portlaoise. A further twenty-one prisoners would be executed before the war ended.

A civil society organization had once again failed to protect standards of civility during the civil war. Labour played no real part in the negotiations that took place at the end of the war, although it did stress the advantages to the government of terminating the conflict by negotiation rather than repression.[124] Thomas Johnson approved of the main points of de Valera's peace proposals but was unable to influence either side in May 1922. Labour's failure, however, was emblematic of the failure of a whole host of peacemakers during the Irish civil war. The Treaty split had clearly polarized nationalist opinion and the tradition-ally pre-eminent nationalist organizations of Irish society were paralysed by the experience of civil war. Other organizations had raised their heads in protest at the war, only to be never heard of again. The Neutral IRA, for all its promise, rapidly became disillusioned with the Provisional government, and ended up firmly on the side of the republicans. Labour at least would still survive, but could not deny the fact that its role had been honourable but ineffectual. To the end the Catholic Church refused to collectively condemn the executions, the mistreat-ment of IRA prisoners, or the murder of men in custody. In any case, no amount of protest could disguise the fact that Irish civil society was operating under strain in the civil war and could not effectively influence the course of the conflict.

CONCLUSION

As civil society theorists would expect, the ambition of Irish civil society during the civil war was to mediate the conflict. In this it was unsuccessful. Neither the IRA campaign of destruction nor the government's execution policy was termin-ated by the influence of civic organizations. Military considerations remained at the forefront, and an end to the war did not arrive until anti-treaty opposition had all but disintegrated. The civil war demonstrated that civil society, however well organized and articulate, was ineffectual in mediating the conflict over the Treaty. The mobilization of public opinion against the war did demonstrate that Irish civil society possessed a considerable degree of autonomy from the state, but had no influence on 'political society'. Indeed the weakness of Irish civil society in 1922 was emphatically proven by the fact that those organizations that had influenced 'political society' in the decades before independence, such as the GAA, were paralysed by the civil war conflict. As in other situations 'the idea that civil society could provide a substitute for the organised public institutions of the state proved unrealistically optimistic'.[125]

---

[123] Memo on meeting (UCD, Mulcahy Papers, P7/B/100).   [124] *Irish Independent*, 16 April 1923.
[125] P. Evans. 'The Eclipse of the State? Reflections on Stateness in an Era of Globalization', *World Politics*, 50/1 (1997), 79.

In retrospect, so great were the differences between the two sides that a basis for peace could not be found. If Cosgrave had declared in September 1922 that there could be no breach of the Treaty, the following month the IRA Executive would decide that peace could only be established on terms that left Ireland outside the Empire.[126] War polarizes ideas and no amount of civic activism could bridge the divide. Peace moves also cut across the interests of the main actors. In the summer of 1922, the call for the Dail to be convened went against Collins' well-documented policy of not convening it until the decisive battles in the south-west had been won. Once the Dail had met, the idea that a conference composed of delegates from public bodies should convene in September 1922 to give voice to public opinion suggests that the Dail itself was not a suitable forum for the articulation of public opinion. The government was hardly likely to look favourably on that initiative, and would have raised questions about the representative nature of the public bodies themselves, many of whom had fallen under the control of hardline republicans in 1920. On the other side, Lynch feared that the Neutral IRA would either launch a publicity campaign to get the IRA to accept a truce on unfavourable terms or try to 'get at' individuals, ignoring the leadership.[127] De Valera was keen to get the support of the Neutral IRA for Sinn Fein in May 1923, but hardly failed to realize at the outset that such a 'constitutional republican' body could also threaten his political ambitions.

On the other hand, de Valera's keenness to get the support of the Neutral IRA suggests that civil society was an important arena of political action during the civil war. It helped demonstrate that there was a *via media* between the civil war parties, and voiced the public's sense that the war was needlessly leading the country towards economic ruin. It also showed that the country was capable of coming up with alternatives to the Treaty that fell short of the demand for the 'isolated Republic'. Where civil society mattered was in creating a space in which the non-aligned could find a voice, and in repeatedly expressing what was a widespread demand for peace. This had little affect on the course of the war, but it suggests that society as a whole was not polarized by the conflict. In the midst of a severe social and political crisis the basic structure of the society revealed itself, and its constitutionalist disposition became clear. It was surely an important portent of future developments that in large counties such as Cork and Wexford, political opinion, polarized at the national level, had remained remarkably united throughout the course of the conflict. In Wexford where the two Treaty sides' combined share of the first preference vote in the pact election was less than 25 per cent, Gory Rural District Council (30 December), Gorey Commissioners (2 January), New Ross Urban Council (2 January), Wexford Corporation (8 January), Enniscorthy Rural District Council (10 January), Wexford Rural District Council (24 February), and New Ross District Council (n.d.) all passed resolutions in favour of peace.[128] Indeed, the very activism of civil society organizations

[126] (NL, F. O'Donoghue Papers, Ms 31,258).
[127] Lynch to O/C's, 1 March 1923 (UCD, Moss Twomey Papers, P 69/92 (90)).
[128] Mac Suain, *County Wexford's Civil War*, 100–5.

at a time of acute national crisis demonstrated that political life would continue to develop in a society that was pluralist and democratic. As early as 1924 clerical school managers, the Executive of the Gaelic League, and the Irish National Teacher's Organisation were pressurizing the government to reinstate public servants that had taken the anti-treaty side in the civil war. In Kerry, in 1924, a Gaelic football match was organized to assist in the selection of the county team between pro-treaty players and anti-treaty players. John Joe Sheehy, an anti-treaty Republican, and Con Brosnan, a captain in the National Army, came together to represent the county football team. Kerry's united team competed in the All-Ireland football final in 1924. Irish civil society, which developed in the 'long' nineteenth century that preceded the end of British rule, was an important component of a developed and democratic society, and would remain in place well after the civil war.

7

Protective Democracy and the Establishment of the Free State

On 11 January 1923, during one of the worst months of the civil war, Kevin O'Higgins submitted a memorandum to the cabinet outlining steps that could be taken to counteract the lawlessness then prevailing in the Irish countryside. What was interesting about the memorandum was not the draconian measures proposed by O'Higgins, although these were extreme, but rather the conception of the state that lay behind his intervention. In the circumstances then prevailing, O'Higgins remarked that 'the Government is simply a Committee with a mandate to make certain conditions prevail, to make life and property safe, and to vindicate the legal rights of their fellow citizens'.[1] The central assumption of his remark, that the fundamental purpose of the new Irish state was to protect the property and rights of Irish citizens, signalled a dramatic reorientation of Irish nationalist politics away from the revolutionary exuberance of the years 1916–21, and formed the bedrock of the Provisional Government's propaganda campaign during the civil war and after. It showed the extent to which a section of the Irish nationalist elite had absorbed the basic tenets of the British 'protective' model of democracy developed by Jeremy Bentham and James Mill in the early nineteenth century, and was a token of their fierce determination to counter what they saw as an attack on 'all idea of morality, law and social order' in the area of the Irish Free State between June 1922 and May 1923.[2] That this reaction was successful spelt the end of what many regard as the Irish 'revolution', and so complete and unswerving was the Provisional Government's fidelity to the values of Victorian Britain, that it suggests that the revolutionary events between 1916 and 1921 had actually little impact on the ethos of a fundamentally conservative society.[3] Protective democracy, even with strong clericalist and authoritarian undertones, may have been a very circumscribed version of the democratic ideal, but in the Ireland of the early 1920s it encountered very little effective resistance.[4]

[1] O'Higgins memorandum, 11 January 1923 (UCD, Mulcahy Papers, P7b/96).
[2] O'Higgins to Cosgrave, 5 April 1923, 'Civil War: Conference of Cabinet Committee' (NA, D/T, S3306).
[3] On this theme see J. Regan, *The Irish Counter-revolution 1921–1936: Treatyite Politics and Settlement in Independent Ireland* (Dublin, 1999).
[4] On protective democracy see C. B. Macpherson, *The Life and Times of Liberal Democracy* (Oxford and New York, 1977), 23–43.

The elaboration and defence of the protective model of democracy in the Irish state took place under the strain of civil war, and under the aegis of a political elite profoundly sceptical of the civic virtue of the population to which it owed its right to rule.[5] Initially employed as a means of discrediting their republican opponents at the beginning of the civil war, the argument that the basic purpose of the state was to protect the property and liberties of Irish citizens assumed the status of a coherent outlook as the Provisional Government became faced with what they regarded as a concerted effort to undermine the moral fabric of Irish society. In their minds two seemingly incompatible ideas became fused. The first was the idea that what was at issue in the Irish civil war was not the terms of independence offered by the Treaty signed in December 1921, but the right of the Irish public to have the deciding say in national affairs. The second idea was that Irish society was still not quite ready for democracy, and that the task of democratic state-building required in the first instance the ruthless imposition of centralized authority. As a result, throughout the 1920s democratic rhetoric often concealed authoritarian actions, but such behaviour was always justified in terms of democratic principles. Paradoxically, although the victory of the Provisional Government in the civil war led to a certain depoliticization of Irish society, it also grounded the institutions of the Irish state in the defence of some individual freedoms (if not others). As such the civil war was a crucial turning point in Irish political development, not only in enabling the Provisional Government to exert its authority over Irish society, but also in determining the basis on which subsequent governments would lay a claim to popular legitimacy.

THE IMPOSITION OF ORDER

The Provisional Government established by the Treaty on 7 January 1922 had a dual transition to handle. On the one hand, they were entrusted with a transition to self-government, and in the shadow of the threat posed by the IRA, they began building up a new national army, overseeing the work of the established civil service, and developing the Dail departments, which had slowly subverted the work of the British administration in Ireland since 1919. However, despite over seven months of peace since the truce with the British in June 1921, it quickly became apparent that economic distress was widespread throughout the country. On 8 March 1922 Cosgrave got the cabinet to agree to transfer a sum of £275,000 to various county councils for the relief of unemployment.[6] Over the following months unemployment relief payments were authorized for Louth, Wicklow, Carlow, Monaghan, Kilkenny, Laois, Kildare, Sligo, Westmeath, Tipperary, Dublin, Limerick, Waterford, Clare, Cavan, and Meath.[7] On 12 May the system of

[5] T. Garvin, *1922: The Birth of Irish Democracy* (Dublin, 1996), 179.
[6] P.G. Minutes, 8 March 1922 (NA, G1/1).
[7] P.G. Minutes, 7 April, 10 May, and 22 May.

unemployment insurance was then extended as it was to be in July.[8] The possibility that the blame for the erosion of an economy that had recently seen boom
years could be put on opposition to the Treaty was alluded to by Churchill in a
letter to Collins on 12 April:

There is no doubt that capital is taking flight. Credits are shutting up, railways are slowing
down, business and enterprises are baffled. The wealth of Ireland is undergoing a woeful
shrinkage. Up to a certain point no doubt these facts may have the beneficial effects of
rousing all classes to defend their own material interests, and Mr De Valera may gradually
come to personify not a cause but a catastrophe.[9]

At this time there was no legal police force operating throughout the country, the
collection of rates and taxes was hampered by the disordered conditions existing
in most counties, and in many instances local brigades of the IRA were financing
themselves by commandeering supplies from shopkeepers and traders. In republican areas like Cork income tax was still being collected by the IRA as late as the
first week of August 1922.[10] On 27 January the Provisional government had
decided to cut financial assistance to those IRA units who were not loyal to the
government, but this only left the majority of IRA units to their own devices.[11]
According to Keogh, between 29 March and 19 April 1922 money was seized from
no less than 323 post offices.[12] The Provisional government soon came under
pressure from the banks to reimburse the money that had been lost in IRA raids
on their country branches.[13] On 26 April, in response to the IRA's occupation of
the Four Courts, the Catholic hierarchy intervened in the Treaty debate to
denounce the actions of the IRA in terms that would later influence the Provisional government's interpretation of the civil war:

We beg the young men connected with the military revolt to consider religiously our
solemn teaching on the fundamental maxim of social morality. Otherwise they will involve
themselves and their followers in conscientious difficulties of the gravest character. For
when in prosecution of these principles they proceed to make shameful war upon their
own country they are parricides and not patriots; when they shoot their brothers on the
opposite side they are murderers; when they commandeer public or private property they
are robbers and brigands, and are bound to restitution—all sins and crimes of the most
heinous kind.[14]

The Provisional government's second task was to supervise a transition to
democracy. In the course of the Treaty negotiations it had been agreed that an
election would soon be held in the Free State although no precise date was fixed.
On 30 January 1922 the Provisional government decided to hold an election at

[8] P.G. Minutes, 12 May.
[9] Churchill to Collins, 11 April 1922 (UCD, de Valera Papers, P150/1618).
[10] P.G. Decision 7 August 1922 (NA, D/T, S1590).
[11] P.G. Decision, 27 January 1922 (NA, G1/1).
[12] D. Keogh, *Twentieth-Century Ireland: Nation and State* (Dublin, 1994), 6.
[13] P.G. Minutes, 4 May 1922 (NA, G1/1).
[14] 'Statement Issued by the Cardinal Primate and the Archbishops and Bishops of Ireland on the
Present Condition of Their Country', 26 April 1922 (UCD, FitzGerald Papers, P80/279).

the earliest possible date, although it was aware of the fact that the register was not up to date.[15] In the previous election in 1921 practically all the constituencies in nationalist Ireland had been uncontested, and the 'Second Dail' was completely dominated by members of the Sinn Fein party. Senior members of the Provisional government believed that the Dail needed to renew its representative character, but the IRA's control of the larger part of the Free State meant that an election could not be held without its consent. Nevertheless, Collins was confident of his government's ultimate ability to restore ordered conditions to the country. On 28 April he told an American correspondent that

Even under the happiest circumstances a period of transition in every country is invariably accompanied by eruption of disorder and spasmodic circumstances. There are many recent examples of this truism. In Poland, Germany, Estonia, Finland, and in practically all the European countries that underwent change as the result of the European war, there were many months of fierce civil war which was only put down after vigorous fighting and appalling loss of life. Our transitional period is not being attended by scenes anything like as bad as that, nor is it likely to be. We may be depended upon to deal with the disorder in our midst just as effectively, and just as thoroughly, as those several governments dealt with it in their sphere. Our methods may be different but the results will be equally satisfactory.[16]

On 20 May, after weeks of negotiation on the part of a Dail peace committee, Collins signed the electoral pact with de Valera. However, whatever about Collins' intentions, his cabinet decided that the signing of the pact in no way implied a lesser commitment to the Treaty, and the two parties to the pact interpreted the agreement in diametrically opposite ways.[17] Much rested on the negotiations on army unification. In April Collins had resisted a proposal that the IRA would continue to be outside the control of the newly elected Dail, stating that 'no government in the world could exist unless its Executive controlled the Army'.[18] However, on 4 May the Ministry of Defence and the IRA Executive began negotiations that would result in both almost agreeing to a scheme whereby a reformed IRA Executive would continue to be responsible to its own convention! The negotiations collapsed but the Ministry of Defence's last communiqué on the issue informed the Executive that the continuation of the negotiations would be the responsibility of the coalition government that would meet on 1 July.[19]

Archival evidence does not enable us to judge the precise time at which the Provisional government irrevocably turned its backs on such negotiations, but as late as 26 June 1922, two days before the civil war began, it was clear that the Provisional government intended summoning the new parliament, the third Dail, on 1 July, and in that context, it is difficult to see how the Provisional government could have turned its backs on the coalition agreement.[20] Following the

[15] P.G. Minutes, 30 January 1922 (NA, G1/1).
[16] Interview given 28 April 1922, 'Michael Collins: Statements and Speeches' (NA, D/T, S10961).
[17] P.G. Minutes, 25 May 1922 (NA, G1/1).
[18] Collins to Daly, 13 April 1922, 'Peace Proposals 1922' (NA, D/T, S2978).
[19] B. Kissane, *Explaining Irish Democracy* (Dublin, 2002), 135.
[20] P.G. Minutes, 27 June 1922 (NA, G1/1).

assassination of Field Marshal Sir Henry Wilson on 22 June, however, the Provisional government received a letter from Lloyd George stating that the 'ambiguous position' of the IRA in the Four Courts could no longer be tolerated by the British government, and that, following the 16 June election, the pro-treaty position was now supported by 'the declared will of the Irish people'. On 26 June Lloyd George also regretted in the House of Commons that the Provisional government had not done more to protect life and property.[21] The following day the Provisional government served notice on the occupants of the Four Courts and Fowler Hall, and instructed Arthur Griffith to draft a notice to the press pointing out that such action had been compelled by 'a series of criminal acts' on the part of the IRA, chief among them the kidnapping of their assistant chief of staff, J. J. O'Connell.[22] On 29 June a government notice then appeared in the press stating that the Provisional government was not going to allow 'the profession of ideals and principles be permitted as an excuse for undermining the people's right to security of the person, and freedom to live their own lives in their own way, as long as they do not trespass on the rights of others'.[23]

It quickly became clear that the clampdown in Dublin heralded a move towards full-scale civil war. After the collapse of the Four Courts on 30 June, it was decided by the Provisional government that the attack on the other IRA strongholds in Dublin should be 'vigorously continued', strict censorship on newspapers was imposed, and on 3 July Griffith told a peace intermediary that his government was 'determined to re-establish the security of life, liberty, and property within its territory'.[24] The following day the Provisional government decided to raise the numbers in the national army to 20,000 men.[25] On 7 July a government notice appeared in the *Freeman's Journal* defining the IRA campaign as 'a conspiracy to over ride the will of the nation and subject the people to a despotism based on brigandage ... regardless of the people's inalienable right to life, liberty, and security'.[26] To counter the idealized image of the Irish people invoked by the anti-treatyites the government's propaganda represented them as enemies of the Irish nation.[27] On 12 July Collins wrote to Desmond FitzGerald, who was in charge of publicity, encouraging him to emphasize the economically destructive nature of the IRA campaign in his propaganda.[28] On 20 July the following statement appeared in the press:

Rather than bow to the overwhelming verdict, the opponents of the Treaty have declared war against their country. Everywhere they are laying the country waste. Railways, canals, bridges, roads, buildings are being destroyed; money and property are being seized;

---

[21] J. M. Curran, *The Birth of the Irish Free State, 1921–1923* (Mobile, Ala., 1980), 227.
[22] P.G. Minutes, 27 June 1923 (NA, G1/1).
[23] *Irish Independent*, 30 June 1922.
[24] Griffith to Despard, 2 July 1922 (NA, D/T, S1332).
[25] P.G. Minutes, 28 June–3 July 1922 (NA, G1/1).
[26] *Freeman's Journal*, 6 July 1922.
[27] C. Townshend, *Ireland: The Twentieth Century* (London, 1999), 108.
[28] Collins to FitzGerald, 12 July 1922 (NA, D/T, S595).

personal liberty is at an end, even the life of citizens who refuse to be coerced into assisting the Irregulars is unsafe.[29]

Later that week, the government decided to focus its propaganda on the 'campaign of destruction' being waged by the IRA, with particular attention being paid to interference with railways, destruction of roads and bridges, injury to industries, and destruction of property.[30] From the beginning de Valera and Childers were represented by the government as leaders with particular responsibility for the civil war.[31] Later in the summer, the government published documents dated 25 and 29 August and 11 September, signed by Liam Mellowes, that suggested that the IRA wanted to create further economic distress in order to prevent 'Irish Labour becoming respectable', and the Provisional government remained convinced that the anti-treaty IRA were behind the continuing Labour unrest in the country.[32]

The decision to pursue a civil war policy was something of a volte-face on the part of some members of the Provisional government. Before the election, Collins had been asked whether it might be possible to have something in the nature of a coalition government, 'as to let some of the leaders of the opposition to act as unofficial advisers to the Cabinet'? Collins replied in the affirmative.[33] Later he stated that 'acceptance of the Treaty by members of the Provisional government is a clause of the Treaty'.[34] Collins then justified the prosecution of the civil war in terms no different from those of his colleagues. Having given the IRA one last opportunity to obey the people's will in June, he wrote, 'the government took the necessary measures to protect the rights and property of the people and to disperse the armed bands which had outlawed themselves and were preying upon the nation'.[35] However, sources within the Irish state were aware that the scheme for army unification with these 'armed bands' clearly contravened democratic principles, an official memo reflecting that 'the people' would never have accepted any lessening of their 'full and absolute' control over the armed forces.[36]

The argument that the Provisional government, by initiating civil war, was simply protecting the rights and liberties of Irish citizens also raised the question of whether these rights amounted to something more than the rights of private property and the operations of the free market? Throughout the summer the Provisional government came under severe criticism for their refusal to summon the Dail, leading to the claim by the People's Rights Association in Cork that

---

[29] *Irish Independent*, 20 July 1922.
[30] P.G. Decision, 26 July 1922 (NA, G1/1).
[31] C. Younger, *Ireland's Civil War* (London, 1968), 464.
[32] 'Policy of the Irregulars' (NL NIC 68).
[33] Interview with *New York Herald*, 2 May 1922 'Michael Collins: Statements and Speeches' (NA, D/T, S10961).
[34] Interview with *Sunday Express*, June 1922 ibid.
[35] M. Collins, *The Path to Freedom* (Dublin, 1996), 11.
[36] 'Typescript Notes to be Studied by each Minister on the Irregulars, Armed Forces, and the Blowing up of the Four Courts', n.d. (UCD, McGilligan Papers, P35c/159).

they were themselves disregarding the people's rights. One neutral publication argued that

The further prorogation by the government of the meeting of Parliament, which had been fixed for the 26th August, seems to show us as complete a disregard for democracy as does the policy of the Irregulars.... It is acting as an absolute dictator, acting as if it had a clear and unchallenged mandate from Parliament, which it has not. Not alone has it not such a mandate, but it has no mandate at all. We hold that every postponement which has taken place has been unconstitutional, and that they could all have been avoided.... That government remained in existence, during the period between the elections and the meeting of the new Parliament, purely in order to carry on routine business, but without any real authority to take any fresh executive decision, and the real duty thrust on it was the summoning of the new Parliament at the earliest possible date. That duty it has not performed. And until it does perform it tramples on the constitution and on the principle of democracy.[37]

Much rested on the interpretation of the June election, and whether, in the circumstances of the pact, a mandate could have been given for any definite line of action. After all, there had been a high degree of vote transfers between the two wings of Sinn Fein in constituencies where there was only one pro- or one anti-treaty candidate.[38] Nevertheless, responding to the Labour party's threat to resign its seats if the parliament was not convened, on 22 August an exasperated minister of agriculture, Patrick Hogan, stated that 'at least they will know that the government is prepared to see to it that the right of the electors to give a mandate, and the right of Parliament to act on the mandate so given will be fully and finally established'.[39] This was a crucial argument, since the Provisional government had avoided asking the Dail to give it a mandate for the civil war. Later Cosgrave told Stanley Baldwin that 'the Nation as a whole endorsed the Treaty and all that it stood for'.[40] The key assumption was not only that a mandate for the Treaty had been given in the pact election, but that this mandate was also for civil war. Paradoxically, however, the Provisional government rejected the idea that it had started the civil war. In line with the hierarchy's statement of 26 April, the IRA were considered to be involved in a 'revolt' against the government. Indeed official statements throughout the civil war referred to the anti-treatyites as 'a minority', 'a section of the community', or in O'Higgins' case, 'a clique of neurotics', despite the fact that pro-treaty Sinn Fein had themselves only a minority in the Third Dail.[41] The use of the term 'Irregulars' to refer to the IRA also conveyed the sense that the conflict was now being fought between a properly constituted army and an undisciplined band of freeloaders, obscuring the fact

---

[37] *The Separatist*, 2 September 1922.
[38] M. Gallagher, *Irish Elections 1922–44: Results and Analysis* (Limerick, 1993), 16.
[39] Patrick Hogan, Draft Reply to Labour Party, 22 August 1922 (NA, D/T, S1332B).
[40] Cosgrave to Baldwin, 27 June 1923 (NA, D/T, S3135).
[41] C. Townshend, 'The Meaning of Irish Freedom: Constitutionalism in the Free State', *Transactions of the Royal Historical Society*, 6th series, 8 (1998), 67.

that Mulcahy had initially authorized the IRA convention in February, and committed himself publicly to maintaining the IRA as the army of the Republic.

The reasons the Provisional government did not summon the Dail until 9 September 1922 have never been adequately explained. Clearly pro-treaty Sinn Fein would not have been guaranteed a majority in the Third Dail, and may not have received the mandate for conflict they needed if the Dail had met on 1 July. Their rejection of the coalition agreement after a Dail meeting would lose the Provisional government domestic support, whereas acceptance of it would alienate the British.[42] In view of the likelihood of conflict, neither prospect was attractive. Once the war had started, on 20 July an official press statement announced that the chief duty of the government was to create the conditions in which it was physically possible for parliament to meet.[43] The following week, a government announcement stated that the rapid progress of its forces in the south and west gave good grounds for believing that no further postponement would be necessary. Five members of the government and sixteen members of the Dail were involved in the civil war on their side, and their withdrawal from military duties in order to attend the Dail would impede or prolong military operations.[44] For Collins though, the logic was purely military—a postponement

would confirm to the general public our determination to clear up this matter definitely and it will have the important effect of preventing the Irregulars in the South feeling that as soon as we came definitely up against them, we hesitated to face them boldly and turned aside from the job, and called parliament. To risk any such idea arising in the minds of the Southern Irregulars with the resultant rise in morale on their part would be a serious matter.[45]

Some leading officials were also uncertain about the loyalties of the Labour Party, which might hold the balance of power in the Third Dail if all TDs were to attend. On September 4 Kevin O'Shiel advised Cosgrave on the position Labour hoped would mature:

With the closing down of factories, workshops, and places of employment consequent on the destruction of transport, wholesale brigandage, and general war conditions, the ranks of the unemployed will have grown to almost three times their present number. When men feel want, and when, in particular, they see their wives and children suffering from the effect of hunger, their patriotism will fade before their primeval instincts for food and clothing. Then with Parliament providing an excellent platform Labour will come along and attack the government and their criticism will receive infinitely more attention than at present. It will make demands to the government and should such demands not be granted, it will call a national strike which then may certainly be obeyed. Such a contingency at such a moment would, of course, most gravely imperil the very foundations of the government and of the state.[46]

[42] See Regan, *The Irish Counter-revolution*, 73.   [43] *Irish Independent*, 20 July 1922.
[44] *Freeman's Journal*, 28 July 1922.
[45] To Acting Chairman from Commander in Chief, 5 August 1922, 'Civil War 1922–23; Army Reports' (NA, D/T, S3361).
[46] O'Shiel to Cosgrave, 4 September 1922 (NA, D/T, S600).

Although in hindsight these fears seem wildly exaggerated, given the radicalization of Irish labour since the Great War, and taking into account the growing unemployment problem, which Thomas Johnson himself credited with swelling the ranks of the anti-treaty IRA, they were not entirely without foundation. Before the Dail was convened on 9 September, the Provisional government decided to adopt a 'friendly attitude' to the Labour Party.[47] It proved a short-lived flirtation. One of the first acts of the Provisional government in March 1922 had been to cut the cost of living bonus, which was paid on a twice-yearly basis to all civil servants, including postal workers. After an independent commission enquired into the issue, further cuts were announced by the government in September, leading to a postal strike. At once the postmaster general, J. J. Walsh, threatened striking workers with dismissal, and after a majority of the Dail voted on 11 September against recognizing public servants' right to strike, the army were ordered to disrupt pickets, protect civilian blacklegs, and sort and deliver the post. The strike came to an end on 28 September with a government commitment to a new commission, but by using the army to deny the workers a right to strike, the incident demonstrated to the Labour leadership that a government publicly committed to protecting individual liberty was also capable of scrapping 'every principle of individual liberty' when it suited them.[48]

PROTECTING THE SOCIAL FABRIC

What made the 'protective' interpretation of the civil war more than a convenient way of portraying the IRA as something other than idealists was the fact that by September 1922 the vista of a fallen society had become more than just a rhetorical device to the Provisional government. Crucially, the manner in which the war was fought after 11 August, with army units protecting urban centres from a lawless countryside, dovetailed nicely with the protective preoccupations of the pro-treaty elite. Indeed as early as 5 August General Eoin O'Duffy had found it necessary to issue a proclamation stating that troops had been authorized to fire on persons committing a variety of offences: such as destroying bridges and railways lines, blocking roads, felling trees, and looting.[49] In this context the army was being dragged into responsibilities that would in normal circumstances be the prerogative of the police—such as guarding banks from armed robbery, escorting shipments of cattle to the docks, and protecting railway lines. A 'protective corp' of the army was established for the latter task. In October, Patrick Hogan received a deputation from the Cattle Traders Association and Farmer's Party, who proposed to load cattle for export on the Dublin docks themselves, despite the ongoing dockers' strike. The minister accepted

[47] P.G. Minutes, 26 August 1922 (NA, G1/3).

[48] A. Guillbride, ' "A Scrapping of Every Principle of Individual Liberty": The Postal Strike of 1922', *History Ireland*, 8/4 (2002), 35–9.

[49] *Irish Independent*, 5 August 1922.

responsibility for their plan, stating that the government's duty was to offer protection to any class of person going about their work.[50]

On 11 September O'Higgins quoted in the Dail a letter from a republican prisoner, in which the prisoner looked forward with relish to the abduction of bank officials and railway clerks. This drew the comment: 'in that single document you have embodied the disintegration that is at present proceeding apace in the country, the moral disintegration'.[51] Indeed, the army itself felt vulnerable to the general collapse of moral standards, having found it necessary in July 1922 to warn the owners of licensed premises that any pub where a member of the army was found drunk would be fined.[52] At this time the prospect of a fallen society was also preoccupying the Catholic hierarchy. Their statement of 26 April 1922 had declared that the IRA were making war on their own country, and this phrase reappeared in the Provisional government's press release of 20 July 1922.[53] On 11 July the Provisional government had concluded that the IRA's tactic of subverting the economic foundations of the country would be much more difficult if a 'proper civic spirit' could be aroused among the public, and it was suggested to seek the cooperation of influential doctors, clerics, and bankers in the matter.[54] In early August Cosgrave addressed a letter to each parish priest, suggesting what they could do to help the government and army in the present crisis.[55] Then with the sense of crisis deepening in the autumn, on 4 October the Provisional government decided that it would be advisable for the bishops to issue a statement regarding 'the low moral standards' throughout the country.[56] The bishops' statement of 10 November 1922 accordingly portrayed a society on the verge of moral disintegration:

In this lamentable upheaval the moral sense of the people has, we fear, been badly shaken. We read with horror of the many unauthorised murders recorded in the press. With feelings of shame we observe that when country houses and public buildings were destroyed the furniture and other fittings were seized and carried away by people in the neighbourhood. We remind them that all such property belongs in justice to the original owners, and now must be preserved for, and restored to them by those who hold them.

We desire to impress on the people the duty of supporting the National government, whatever it is, to set their faces resolutely against disorder, to pay their taxes, rents and annuities, and to assist the government in every possible way to restore order and establish peace, unless they learn to do so they can have no government, and if they have no government they can have no nation.[57]

---

[50] Hogan Memo, 12 October 1923 (NA, D/T, S3351).
[51] K. O'Higgins, *Dail Debates*, vol. 1 col. 98, 11 September 1922.
[52] P.G. Decision, 22 July 1922 (NA, G1/1).
[53] *Freeman's Journal*, 20 July 1922.
[54] P.G. Decision, 11 July 1922 (NA, G1/1).
[55] P. Murray, *Oracles of God: The Roman Catholic Church and Irish Politics, 1922–1937* (Dublin, 2000), 69.
[56] P.G. Decision, 4 October 1922 (NA, G1/3).
[57] *Irish Times*, 10 November 1922.

Then on Sunday, 22 October, a document read out at all masses announced that a 'section of the community' had 'wrecked Ireland from end to end', endorsing the official view that the conflict was between a lawfully elected majority and an unrepresentative minority.[58] There was now a perfect fit between the outlook of the hierarchy and their political counterparts, O'Higgins later complaining that Irish democracy lacked a proper basis because the social principles behind it were 'not Catholic in the measure to be expected'.[59]

By the new year the civil war was being waged on a much wider scale than in the summer, at least in the eyes of the Provisional government. For Patrick Hogan the issue was one of anarchy against order:

Our position now is that the effective Irregular war has definitely taken the form of a war by different sections, different interests, and different individuals, with no common basis except this—that all have a vested interest in chaos, in bringing about a state of affairs where force is substituted for law. Not only is there a variety of interests and motives, but there is a variety of methods. Houses and farms are burned in a wages dispute; men are shot in a similar dispute; haggards are burned in a land dispute, and men are murdered in a similar dispute; trains are attacked; post offices robbed; banks raided; individuals robbed without patriotic pretences or in the name of the Republic, men are murdered for personal reasons or in the name of the Republic and so on.[60]

It was thus not possible to disentangle the social from the political manifestations of 'irregularism', and one example of the former was the emergence of a serious problem of poteen drinking, particularly in the western counties of Donegal, Mayo, Sligo, Kerry, and Clare. Indeed by February 1923 the sale of poteen was considered 'universal' throughout the country, and it was subsequently decided that the distilling of liquor, the possession of ingredients, and the possession of stills should be charges tried by the Military Court.[61] To the government the IRA was also clearly behind the widespread reappearance of land grabbing. In March 1923, an army report from the Carlow and Kildare area detailed the involvement of the IRA in land grabbing in these counties, and urged the cabinet that it was 'high time to teach those robbers a lesson and give the people some measure of confidence in the power of the State to protect them and some measure of security in their property'.[62] Another report the same month suggested that two 'Irregular leaders', Cronin and McElistrim, who had been trying to purchase lands legally before the civil war began, were behind the recent land seizures in County Kerry.[63] On 23 April the minister of agriculture reported to the cabinet that he believed acute agrarian disorder would soon manifest itself, and credited an organization called the 'Back to the Land Association' with this possibility.[64]

[58] E. Purdon, *The Civil War 1922–23* (Cork, 2000), 49.
[59] T. de Vere White, *Kevin O'Higgins* (London, 1948), 181.
[60] Hogan to Cosgrave, 11 January 1923 (UCD, Mulcahy Papers, P76/96 (2)).
[61] 'Illicit Distillation Army Action: Proclamation by the Army Council 1923' (NA, D/T, S2091).
[62] Carlow and Kildare Divisional Report, 29 March 1923 (NA, D/T, S3361).
[63] Army Reports (NA, D/T, S3361).
[64] Executive Council Minutes, 23 April 1923 (NA, G2/2).

A major strike begun among 1500 agricultural labourers in Waterford on 17 May saw the army helping the farmers to get their supply convoys through the picket lines.[65] This strike soon collapsed but the reoccurrence of labour unrest in the country was felt by the army to have 'a political push' behind it.[66]

The use of the army to support the Waterford farmers showed that de Valera's ceasefire proclamation on 30 April did not herald the end of the official campaign to counter the moral collapse of Irish society. Although by September 1923 it was reported that 530 out of 870 police stations had been established in the state, the return of 50,000 demobilized soldiers and around 11,000 internees to civilian life was bound to trouble the authorities.[67] On 26 September 1923 a civil servant warned the cabinet that the number of armed robberies would reach its 'high water-mark' with the return of so many to civilian life who had been used 'to conditions which have torn moral standards to threads'.[68] Indeed the Garda figures on serious crime between 1 July 1923 and 31 December 1923 recorded 260 armed robberies and 119 armed raids.[69] Accordingly, the 1923 Public Safety Act, passed on 2 July, was specifically intended to cover the period between the cessation of war and the arrival of normal conditions.[70] It legalized the continued detention of republican prisoners. Army intelligence believed that while the IRA were unlikely to challenge the state again in arms, 'anyone who studies the forces in motion, the Irregulars, the Communists, cannot fail to recognise a highly inflammable situation'.[71] By January 1924 Cosgrave was satisfied that 'the crime wave' was at an end, but remarked that 'strikes, direct action and all such activities may necessarily by considered practical politics if looters, arsoners, and gunmen got twelve months internment with four meals a day for their leisure on failing to accomplish their task'.[72] Paradoxically, he urged an amnesty for those convicted of crimes during the civil war in order to avert further social disorder. However, the following month O'Higgins still commented on the 'chronic law-lessness' prevailing in Leitrim, Cork, Tipp, Mayo, Clare, and Sligo and added that:

Taxpayers in these areas are not receiving that protection which it is the elementary duty of a government to afford.... It is not now a question of defending the State and its foundations but a question of vindicating the rights of private citizens and affording them that protection against outrage which they are entitled to look for from the government in exchange for the taxes which it levies.[73]

---

[65] E. O'Connor, *Syndicalism in Ireland 1917–1923* (Cork, 1988), 123

[66] General Report No. 8, for fortnight ending 28 July 1923 (NA, D/T, S3361).

[67] *The Round Table*, September 1923.

[68] Memo by H. M. Murray, 26 September 1923, 'Civil War: Conference of Cabinet Committee' (NA, D/T, S3306).

[69] 'Returns showing number of serious crimes reported to the Garda during the six months from the 1st July 1923 to 31st December 1923 in Saorstat Eireann' (NA, D/T, S3527).

[70] Townshend, 'The Meaning of Irish Freedom', 66.

[71] Hogan to McMahon, Chief of General Staff, 7 August 1923 (UCD, Richard Mulcahy Papers, P7/C/6).

[72] Cosgrave, Memo on Amnesty, 5 January 1924 (NA, D/T, S581).

[73] O'Higgins to Executive Council, 7 February 1924, Garda Siochana: Reports on Economic Situation 1923–25 (NA, D/T, S3435).

Cumann na nGaedheal Election Advertisement, August 1923

FIGURE 1.

	The Challenge	
The Government and Order	V.	The Irregulars and Anarchy
The ballot and majority rule Law and good order Security for life and property Right to Life Right to Work With work to do	Challenged by	the gun, petrolcan, and torch and minority dictation chaos and disorder. murder, arson, armed robbery and loot burned houses, ruined roads and railways broken bridges and ruined trade unemployment and starvation
The Cosgrave government has beaten Anarchy.	The Cosgrave government is alone strong enough to kill it	Vote for the Cumann na nGaedheal candidates and help to kill Anarchy W. Cosgrave K. O'Higgins R. Mulcahy

Source: *Irish Times*, 25 August 1923.

In short the IRA ceasefire did not bring the state of emergency to an end, and the government's propaganda in the August 1923 election made great play of the continued threat to societal interests posed by that organization. In the election campaign, the government's tactic was to frighten the voters into thinking that the 'safety of the state' was at stake. As is shown in the election poster (Figure 1), the anti-treatyites were represented as anarchists and terrorists, and the government as the protector of life and property. The voters were asked simply to vote for the only party that could guarantee social and political order. Initially, after the IRA ceasefire, the military had reported that the 'irregulars' were turning their attention from militarist to constitutional methods, and if that circle was completed, the army would have completed its work.[74] Later, the strong showing of republican candidates in the August election was interpreted by the army as a boost for the IRA's clandestine attempt to rebuild its forces behind the 'pseudo political' Sinn Fein clubs, and the authorities were greatly alarmed by an alleged republican plot to capture local government bodies at the forthcoming elections and paralyse the administration.[75] Unless steps were taken to tackle the issue, the army warned that there would be 'a regular landslide in some parts of the country in favour of the Irregulars'.[76] Accordingly, Ernest Blythe, the minister of local government, urged the cabinet that the 161 rural district councils be abolished, lest the forthcoming local elections give every 'crank and impossibilist'

[74] General Weekly Report, no. 4, for week ending 10 June 1923 (NA, D/T, S3361).
[75] Chief of Staff to Minister of Defence, 12 October 1923, Military Situation Report for the Month of September (NA, D/T, S3361).
[76] Ibid.

in the country a platform'.[77] The councils were in turn abolished, and in 1925 the government passed further legislation ensuring that no appointment or salary increase would be made with regard to local government officers, unless they made a declaration swearing allegiance to the Irish Free State and its constitution.[78]

The previous year the minister of local government had told the Dail that the rural councils had no roots in Irish tradition and were a foreign imposition.[79] In truth local government had been central to nationalist politics since the local government reform of 1898, and between 1918 and 1921 there was a concerted and successful attempt to get the local bodies to transfer their allegiance from the British Local government Board to the First Dail. The existing urban local councils (January 1920) and the county and rural district councils (June 1920) had been elected during the War of Independence, and had become dominated mostly by Sinn Fein supporters and IRA members. During the civil war many of these local bodies had passed resolutions in favour of peace negotiations and some saw this as symptomatic of the population's general lack of civic responsibility.[80] For example, in July 1922 Dublin Corporation's decision to give Rory O'Connor six months leave of absence provoked Collins to remark that 'it is bound to have a damaging effect upon the Troops if they see Public Bodies acting in this weak-kneed, bad-spirited way'.[81] Later, in the summer of 1923, a number of councils, particularly in the south-west, began passing resolutions calling for the release of political prisoners and the abolition of the oath of allegiance, suggesting that the pattern established during the civil war might be repeated. On the issue of civic responsibility the government's attitude was clear-cut:

The duty of the Irish citizen today is to strengthen the State and the intelligence of the State by every means in his power. He should be the arms and eyes of the State. He is not confronted by a conflict of parties; nor can he with a clear conscience do as those who the Americans describe as 'mugwumps' do, sit on a fence and cry 'A plague on both your houses'. He who is not with the State today is against it: he who is not loyal to the authority of the State is loyal neither to his own self-interest nor to his moral duty. He who would cheat the State of its due is robbing his neighbour as surely as if he put his hand in that neighbour's pocket and stole what belongs to him. The mind that does not realise these things is part of the slave mind inherited from the days of the tyranny.[82]

The transfer of the spending powers of the rural councils to county councils controlled by centrally appointed officials would also prevent local governments responding to local economic conditions, and could adversely affect the

[77] Minister of Local Government to Executive Council, 20 July 1923 (NA, D/T, S3646).
[78] To Secretary Executive Council from Secretary Department of Local Government, 13 May 1924, ibid.
[79] *Dail Eireann*, 3 June 1924, 1786.
[80] *The Round Table*, June 1923.
[81] Collins to Executive Council, 23 July 1922 (NA, D/T, S1397).
[82] 'Civic Virtue', propaganda leaflet (UCD, FitzGerald Papers, P80/318).

labouring and poorer classes, but this did not trouble the minister of local government who told the Dail:[83]

As a matter of fact, I consider that this question of democracy, or the absence of it, should not be taken into consideration, or influence our view to any great extent in considering the question of local government at all. The relationship between the administration of local government and the public is a business rather than a political relationship and those who administer local government should be pledged rather by the principles by which commercial concerns are judged rather than by the principles which should guide statesmen or politicians.[84]

Along with the abolition of the republican courts, the local government 'reform' showed how far Ireland's new governing elite had moved from any conception of participatory democracy, and were firmly tied to a Victorian conception, which favoured the symbolic and executive elements of the state over the representational and the legislative.[85] That this process of retrenchment, which would culminate in the abolition of the referendum in 1928, extended beyond the formal institutional arena, can be appreciated by considering the fate of the National Land Bank after 1921. It had been founded in 1919 with the purpose of helping individuals and societies to purchase land under the British government's land reform schemes, and alongside the Irish Agricultural Organization Society (1894) and the Irish Farmers Union (1920) was one of a number of bodies formed with the intent of rural self-help.[86] Its rule book allowed ordinary members to acquire £1 shares in the bank, gave them the right to elect five of its directors, and gave them a veto power over decisions taken at the general meeting. Such rules were part of a wider process of democratizing civil society, which took place in the decades before independence.[87] No individual member was allowed to hold an interest exceeding £200 in the shares of the society. After independence, however, it was decided that this would not apply to the minister of finance, who could vote by proxy at general meetings and have a vote for each £1 share in his possession. This situation was formalized by the passing of the Loans and Funds Bill by the Dail in 1923. Then in 1924 the board of the society was reduced from nine directors to five, and on it figured James MacNeill, a brother of the minister of education, Ernest Blythe, and George McGrath (a representative of Collins, former minister of finance) who had been made directors on 30 June 1922. Erskine Childers and Robert Barton had been on the board in 1920. On 27 October 1926 a general meeting of the society proxy decided to convert the bank into a company.[88] So much for the democratization of civil society.

[83] Cahirciveen Rural District Council—Minutes of Meeting, 1 September 1923 (NA, Department of the Environment, Co. Kerry UDC, 1922–34).

[84] *Dail Debates*, 3 June 1924, 1785.

[85] D. Washbrook, 'The Rhetoric of Democracy and Development in Late Colonial India', in S. Bose and A. Jalal (eds.), *Nationalism, Democracy and Development: State and Politics in India* (Oxford, 1999), 38.

[86] See Kissane, *Explaining Irish Democracy*, 108.

[87] Ibid., 103–12.

[88] *Banc na Talman Teo* R 1508 (NA, Registry of Friendly Societies, 1508).

RECONSTRUCTION

On the other hand, Cosgrave's government could undeniably claim credit for having laid the groundwork for a stable political system in the wake of the civil war. By any standards these years were years of considerable legislative achievements—such as the 1923 Land Act, which created 100,000 new proprietors, the creation of an unarmed police force, and the passing of over 100 bills into law. In October 1924 Kevin O'Higgins told the Oxford Union that the country was now more 'normal' than at any time since 1912 or 1913.[89] O'Higgins himself tended to reduce the concept of the Irish revolution to the idea of the Irish people getting their own parliament, but the Irish also had to show their fitness for that responsibility.[90] Key to this was their acceptance of the authority of the state. By October 1924 the Provisional government had clearly secured the state's monopoly of force, and their determination to do so was evident from their insistence on IRA decommissioning as a pre-condition for peace throughout the civil war. Moreover, since legislation is the primary function of the modern state, the Provisional government also succeeded in reasserting the legal framework of the society, at the cost of abandoning the republican courts that had been set up between 1919 and 1921.[91] Moreover, for statehood to exist, there must be a generalized cognition and perception of the state, and Collins' strategy from the outset in July 1922 was to establish sufficient police and military barracks in order to break the hold local brigades of the IRA had on the public's perception of events at the centre.[92] There is no doubt that this had largely been achieved by October 1924. Finally, since the modern state is primarily a territorial entity with fixed and clearly demarcated boundaries, the choice of a peace strategy towards Northern Ireland (and the acceptance of the Boundary Commission's findings in 1925) also contributed to this sense of 'stateness'.[93]

This concern with the authority of the state was also wedded to the longer-term process of co-opting their civil war rivals into the polity, and encouraging them to demonstrate a sense of civic virtue they had defaulted on in 1922. At the end of the civil war, as many as 10,000 republicans were in prison camps, but 90 per cent of these were released by the end of 1923, with all being set free before the autumn of 1924. Of the 300 people tried and sentenced by courts martial in 1923 all but ten had their sentences remitted in 1924. In November 1924 the cabinet decided to declare an amnesty for civil war offences, on the grounds that 'the highest interests of the State' would be served from discontinuing or refraining

[89] K. O'Higgins, 'Three Years Hard Labour', address delivered to the Irish Society of Oxford University on 31 October 1924.

[90] J. Knirck, 'Afterimage of the Revolution: Kevin O'Higgins and the Irish Revolution', *Eire-Ireland*, 38 (2003), 239.

[91] B. Parekh, 'Ethnocentricity of the Nationalist Discourse', *Nations and Nationalism*, 1/1 (1995), 25–53.

[92] J. P. Nettl, 'The State as Conceptual Variable', *World Politics*, 20 (1968), 559–92.

[93] On this concept see J. Linz and A. Stepan, *Problems of Democratic Transition and Consolidation: Southern Europe, South America, and Post Communist Europe* (Baltimore and London, 1996), 16–38.

TABLE 1. Return of 'Dumped' Arms, Ammunition, and 'War Material' Discovered and Seized by the Police from Year 1923 to July 1931

Year	Rifles	Revolvers	Pistols	Shot Guns	Bombs
1923	31	53	12	38	72
1924	63	155	24	427	24
1925	244	306	54	1,190	206
1926	273	299	47	1,243	588
1927	112	102	21	42	21
1928	86	72	16	22	98
1929	92	81	5	6	190
1930	47	61	—	8	12
1931	37	27	6	3	51
Total	985	1,156	1,85	2,979	1,262

Source: Appendix 111, 'Anti-State Activities: Joint Pastoral of Hierarchy and Events Leading up to Its Issue' D/T S 5864B.

from instituting criminal proceedings for crimes committed during the civil war period, thus effectively bringing the conflict to a close.[94] A proposal to arm the police was rejected by the cabinet on 24 January 1927, O'Higgins maintaining not only that the force was functioning successfully, but that the moral support of the people for the police might be lost if they were armed.[95] His assassination on 10 July 1927 did lead the government to introduce another Public Safety Act, allowing for internment, the suppression of seditious newspapers, and trial by court martial, but the only effect of the act was to intern one prominent member of the IRA for one month. The power to set up courts martial was never exercised, and the act was repealed in December 1928 as a gesture of peace and goodwill.[96] The official figures on the capture of dumped IRA arms and munitions between 1923 and 1931 (Table 1) also show a steady decline in the amount of war material discovered and seized by the police. Remarkably, in 1926 the authorities seized 1,243 shotguns, compared to only 42 the following year.

Perhaps the best test of whether there was a conciliatory attitude on the part of the government towards their former civil war enemies is the work of the Advisory Committee on Arrested or Interned Employees Paid out of Public Funds between 1924 and 1925. The committee consisted of Kevin O'Shiel, Diarmuid O'Hegarty, and Henry Friel, and was charged with investigating the case of public servants against whom complicity in the civil war had been alleged, and with advising the cabinet whether there were any special circumstances that gave grounds for complicity being overlooked. In the course of its deliberations the

[94] Civil War Amnesty Resolution, 4 November 1924 (NA, D/T, S4120).
[95] Secretary, Department of Justice to Executive Council, 3 January 1927 (NA, D/T, S5260).
[96] 'Anti-State Activities: Joint Pastoral of Hierarchy and Events Leading up to the Issue', (NA, D/T, S5864B).

views of many interested parties, such as Catholic school managers, the Gaelic League, and various educational bodies were made known to the committee, but it is clear that some senior government figures were also in favour of leniency—albeit within strict boundaries. On 24 March 1925 the Executive Council ordered that all civil servants declare 'full and true allegiance' to the Free State as established by law, and reinstated civil servants had to sign a form to that effect. J. J. Walsh, the minister of posts and telegraphs, argued that

the time has come when, in the interests of the Nation, a good deal of allowance can be made for the actions of men at a time of doubt and agony, when the right path was by no means clear, and who could in most cases plead the orders of those who had been their Superior Officers in the National Organisation before the Treaty. The attempt to subvert the State by force has failed and is not, I think, likely to be renewed. Most of the rank and file who helped in that attempt now realise they were misled, and I think it would be good work for the nation to reinstate all who are willing now to sign the Civil Service Declaration of loyalty to the government elected by the people.[97]

The first interim report, which was sent to the cabinet on 11 July 1924, detailed 124 cases where it was considered that there were no grounds for complicity. The second report, however, dated 4 September 1924, reported on cases where complicity had been established, and where the possibility of overlooking such complicity had been explored. In each case the public servants, all school teachers, were given an opportunity of appearing before the committee to present their case, and the report noted that 'it was intended that we should report favourably on as many cases as possible consistent with regard for pubic safety'. Of the 44 teachers reported on in this report the committee recommended leniency in 16 cases. The third interim report, dated 8 December 1924, recommended that 88 out of 154 persons be reinstated, 56 on the grounds that complicity was not established, and 32 on the grounds that it could be overlooked. The fourth interim report, dated 4 July 1925, reported on only 9 cases, in none of which was it recommended that complicity should be overlooked. Finally, the last interim report, dated 23 March 1926, reported on 5 cases where complicity had been established, and where it had already been recommended that it not be overlooked. The final report now recommended leniency in 3 of these cases, and brought the work of the committee to an end.[98] Although it would be too strong to argue that the implementation of the committee's recommendations showed a willingness to 'forgive and forget' on the part of the government, it did favour leniency where the civil war offences were minor, and where the supplicants were willing to accept the new political dispensation. Moreover, after the entry of Fianna Fail into the Dail in July 1927, a number of officers of the First Dail were also reinstated into their positions, including one believed by Cosgrave to be

[97] Walsh to Cosgrave, 13 April 1925 (NA, D/T, S3406A).
[98] Advisory Committee on Arrested or Interned Employees Paid out of Public Funds, First Interim Report, Second Interim Report, Third Interim Report, Fourth Interim Report, Final Interim Report (NA, D/T, S3406 A&B).

responsible for a number of serious offences during the civil war.[99] Although government policy was to favour its civil war veterans in public appointments, and encouraged private companies to do the same, the pro-treatyite elite were still sensitive to the Fianna Fail charge that people with anti-treaty convictions were victimized when it came to state appointments. Often cited was the case of Professor Hugh Ryan, who was in charge of the Chemistry Department of UCD. Though he was an anti-treaty candidate in elections for a National University seat, he was nevertheless appointed chief state chemist.[100] C. S. Andrews, a prominent republican later recruited into the civil service, reflected that the official policy in this area was less vindictive than might have been expected. In his view, the government was intent on inducing the anti-treatyites 'to participate in the normal political process, on their terms no doubt, or else to leave the country'.[101]

If by 1927 the issue of war and peace in the Free State had been decided in favour of the latter, the political atmosphere remained highly charged. The emergence of Fianna Fail as the principal opposition party in the state in 1926, and its shift to the left on economic issues, gave the government more incentive to play on public fears of what might ensue if Fianna Fail came to power, one poster during the June 1927 election campaign declaring that a Fianna Fail government would mean 'Army and Police disbanded and in their place the undisciplined gunmen of 1922 ... Repudiation of the National Loan and Savings Certificates ... A levy on bank deposits'.[102] This portrayal of the anti-treaty alternative as a threat to established economic interests was a variation of the tactic, recommended by Michael Collins during the civil war, of blaming the anti-treatyites for the economic cost of the war, in order to deflect public attention away from issues relating to the Treaty. On the other hand, Cumann na nGaedheal also felt it necessary to defend its record on economic policy: during the September 1927 campaign among its achievements it mentioned the Shannon electrification scheme, the establishment of the Agricultural Credits Corporation, the development of the sugar beet market, the opening of eighty new factories, and the building of 11,000 houses for the workers. Since 1922 the government had made life and property safe for 'the plain people of Ireland', something which would be threatened if Fianna Fail came to power.[103] The government's outlook on economic policy nonetheless remained resolutely tied to a liberal conception of the state. On St. Patrick's Day 1926 Cosgrave declared that

National greatness is built upon the individual tenacity and courage of ordinary people. The State is the expression of the collective efforts of all its citizens. When the ordinary work of the businessman, the craftsman, the farmer and the labourer is well done, when

---

[99] Cosgrave to Coogan, 12 November 1929, 'Dismissals from the Civil Service 1923–26' (NA, D/T, S2715).
[100] Michael Hayes, Comments on '1916–1926: The Years of the Great Transition', n.d. (UCD, Mulcahy Papers, P7b/185).
[101] C. S. Andrews, *Man of No Property* (Dublin and Cork, 1982), 64.
[102] *The Nation*, 11 June 1927.   [103] *Irish Times* 2 September 1927.

each feels that on the quality of his work depends his self-respect, then national self-respect and international credit are assured.[104]

During the next election campaign in 1932, with support for Fianna Fail growing, Cumann na nGaedheal was once again forced to defend its economic record, one poster listing their achievements in increasing employment, fostering industry, building roads and houses, reducing rates, extending land reform, and decreasing taxes.[105] In contrast, Fianna Fail stressed the need for protectionist measures in order to alleviate the effects of the world depression. These economic differences had been brought to a head by Britain's decision to introduce pro-tective tariffs of up to 100 per cent for imports from non-Commonwealth countries. The Free State could be guaranteed a preferential rate of just 10 per cent if it remained in the Commonwealth, but the livelihood of the exporting sectors would be placed in jeopardy if the anti-treaty party won the election. Cosgrave told voters that he opposed Fianna Fail's plan to downgrade the office of governor general, 'when the vital economic interests of this country are in such a condition as they are at this moment'.[106] Clearly, although membership of the Empire provided a vital outlet for Irish exports, the government was vulnerable to the charge that it had abandoned Collins' interpretation of the Treaty as a 'stepping stone' to greater freedom, and by 1932 three splinter parties had emerged from its ranks. Nonetheless, it seemed determined to stand by the basic provisions of the Treaty, losing interest in the North after the Boundary Commission fiasco in 1925, deleting the provision for referenda from the consti-tution in 1928 in order to prevent Fianna Fail removing the oath, and abiding by a legislative protocol that read 'The Executive Council present to your Excellency for signification in the King's Name of the King's Consent, the following Bills—'. Their public image could not have been helped either by Lord Glenavy's, the leader of the Senate, declaration that Irish republicanism should be forgotten about, and the Irish should stand shoulder to shoulder with England in her efforts to carry British civilization throughout the world.[107]

In effect, the Cumann na nGaedheal governments were open to the charge that their period of office after 1922 had actually reinforced social and polit-ical hierarchies, even as the state claimed to be the agent of liberation from such hierarchies.[108] In particular the government could not duck the allegation that its economic policy was promoting privileged interests at the expense of the com-mon good during an era of world depression. In September 1927, J. J. Walsh publicly complained that the party had 'gone over to the most reactionary elements of the state', and warned that a government could not depend on the votes of 'ranchers and importers' and at the same time develop industry and

[104] President's St Patrick's Day Broadcast, 17 March 1926 (NA, D/T, S5111).
[105] *Irish Times*, 8 February 1932.
[106] Ibid., 5 February 1932.
[107] Hon. Daniel F. Cohalan, 'Democracy or Imperialism—Which?', Speech before the Brooklyn Local Council Friends of Irish Freedom, 28 January 1925 (NL).
[108] G. Smyth, *Decolonisation and Criticism: The Construction of Irish Literature* (London, 1995), 92.

agriculture.[109] The attempts to rationalize agriculture by standardizing agricultural produce, establishing centralized credit agencies, and transferring ownership of the grazing ranches to large farmers under the Land Act of 1923 were also seen by the left as ways of squeezing out the small farmer from the national economy, and Fianna Fail made much of the plight of the small man under the Cosgrave government.[110] The essentially laissez-faire credo of a government that was itself busily reducing the wages and increasing the working hours of its own employees was also cold comfort for those left on the margins of the post-civil war economy. In his St Patrick's Day broadcast to the United States in 1927 Cosgrave had declared that

We realize there is no short road to national prosperity. Panaceas, catch cries, throwing the blame on others, are not the means by which material prosperity or general welfare is achieved. It is accomplished only by well-directed hard work, thrift, adoption of the most efficient methods of production and distribution, and by the willing cooperation between the government and its people in all that makes for economic advancement.[111]

After all, in the British utilitarian tradition, if the state had guaranteed the security of life and property without which economic life could not prosper, it should be in the citizens' interest to support that state.[112] The problem in Ireland was that even if the Free State had been established in defence of economic interests, once economic circumstances changed (as they did in the late 1920s), those same interests could point to other options. According to official figures, the number of days lost to strikes went from 54,292 in 1928 to 310,199 in 1931, and the formation of a new socialist republican organization, *Saor Eire*, in 1931 led the government to discern in these developments a situation that fundamentally challenged the foundations of the state.[113] The Department of Justice believed that the new radicals were a strange mixture of political and social revolutionaries, and Cosgrave once more looked to the Catholic hierarchy for support in its effort to counter what he saw as a threat to the moral senses of the people.[114] On 10 September 1931 he told Cardinal McRory that

We are confronted with a completely new situation. Doctrines are being taught and practised which were never before countenanced amongst us and I feel that the Church and the Church alone will be able to prevail in the struggle against them. Only through the powerful influence of the Church will innocent youths be prevented from being led into a criminal conspiracy, escape from which is impossible because it involves the certainty of vengeance and the grave danger of death. The Church alone, in my view, can affect the consciences of parents and others in regard to the dangers to which our young people are

---

[109] Walsh to Cosgrave, September 1927 (NA, D/T, S5470).

[110] E. Burns, *Imperialism in Ireland* (Dublin, 1931), 63.

[111] Cosgrave, 'Message to the American People on the Occasion of St. Patrick's Day', 17 March 1927 (NA, DT, S5111/3).

[112] D. Held, *Models of Democracy* (Cambridge, 1987), 68.

[113] Gerhard, *The Irish Free State and British Imperialism* (Cork, 1976), 5.

[114] 'Revolutionary Organisations, Anti-State Activities April 1929–Oct 1932, 5 April 1930 (NA, D/T, S5864A).

exposed through Communistic and subversive teachings. The Church moreover, can bring powerful influence to bear on those who through inadvertence or otherwise have in the past, by unreasonable or uninformed criticisms of State institutions and State servants as apart from political leaders, parties or programmes, contributed in some degree towards preparing the ground for the spread of the doctrines mentioned.[115]

On the one hand, the bishops' pastoral of October 1931, which denounced *Saor Eire* in vituperative terms, clearly signalled that the alliance between Church and State was still very much alive. On the other, the statement also clearly suggested that discontent could find its proper expression through the polls, so the alliance between Church and State was not between Church and Cumann na nGaedheal. Indeed within a year a Fianna Fail government would be elected, but it was unfortunate that one of the last significant acts of the Cosgrave government, the seventeenth amendment to the constitution in 1931, should result in it banning twelve left-wing organizations, mostly of a propagandist rather than military nature.[116] For the pro-treatyites Irish liberalism had always to rest on sure moral foundations, and since these organizations were threatening to undermine those foundations, especially among the young, it followed that it was necessary to curtail liberal freedoms in order to protect them. This was the dilemma at the heart of that strange mixture of British liberalism and Catholicism characteristic of the Irish nationalist elite. In September 1927 Cosgrave had actually told an audience in Kilkenny that 'the real purpose of the Public Safety Act is to assert the authority of the Ten Commandments in this country'.[117]

Ultimately, however, the seventeenth amendment showed that the pro-treaty elite had no long-term democratic answer to the basic issue of public order in an economically depressed society. In so far as they had defended the values of liberal democracy during the civil war, this was achieved through the paradox of withholding the conventions of democracy until after the state of crisis passed.[118] The problem was that as long as their economic policy was laissez-faire, these crises would never pass and representative democracy itself would remain un-consolidated. Initially, Cosgrave and his colleagues had a clear idea of how to bring the Irish revolution to an end. During the civil war O'Higgins remarked that the political aspect of the pro-treaty position 'was that we could not hope to hold the people indefinitely on a course which demanded such exacting standards of self-immolation, if no concrete results were in sight or reasonably probable'.[119] Once the anti-treaty IRA had 'seceded' from the Ministry of Defence, and became

---

[115] Cosgrave to Cardinal Joseph McRory, 'Anti-State Activities: Joint Pastoral of Hierarchy and Events Leading up to Its Issue', 10 September 1931 (NA, D/T, S5864B).

[116] These organizations were Friends of Sovet Russia, Irish Communist Party, Irish Labour Defence League, Women's Prisoners Defence League, Anti-Imperialist League, Workers Union of Ireland, Irish National Unemployed Movement, Cumman na mBan, Prisoners Dependents Organization, Irish Working Farmers Committee, Fianna Eireann, and Workers Revolutionary Party of Ireland.

[117] *The Nation,* 10 September 1927.

[118] O'Connor, *Syndicalism in Ireland 1917–1923,* 163.

[119] K. O'Higgins, Typescript copy of an article or letter to a US newspaper, n.d. 1922–3 (UCD, McGilligan Papers, P35C/160).

dependent on illegal hold-ups, levies, and commandeering to finance itself, it then became easier to portray them as enemies of the people's rights. Indeed Cosgrave remarked that they were dealing with 'the dregs of society, people who had no regard for life or property, or all the people held dear'.[120] Ernest Blythe reflected that by 1922 the Irish had overcome one traditional enemy of democracy, oligarchy, but were then faced with another, namely anarchy. In his view, those who occupied the Four Courts, who robbed motor cars, and who took life during the civil war, were anarchists who were guilty of 'the highest offence' known against democracy—'against the rule of the people'.[121] Yet the defeat of the IRA was not the only motivation of the Provisional government. Clearly the protection of property, the assertion of the rule of law, and the defence of the state itself were part of a wider nationalist project 'for the establishment of all the signs by which a nation is to be held worthy of consideration among the States in the world'.[122] Chief among these was the establishment of an authoritative state, on which the lives and liberties of the individual in any case depended—as O'Duffy put it, 'should the state go or even suffer in prestige, then the economics will have been in vain'.[123] Yet as the seventeenth amendment showed, too much concern for the prestige of the state in the face of the myriad of evils, real or imaginary, that it encountered might also result in the diminution of those freedoms the state had been founded to protect.

CONCLUSION

As a means of discrediting republican opposition to the Treaty, as a way of securing those individual rights without which economic life could not prosper, and as a principle that justified the reassertion of central authority in the wake of a sustained revolt against British rule, the concept of protective democracy was the foundational principle of the Irish state. It required in the first place that the state protect the citizens of the state from each other, in particular from the anti-treaty IRA, but it also required that the state itself be protected from civil society, and this resulted in the weakening of local government, the abolition of the referendum, and the repeated enactment of emergency legislation. One Cumann na nGaedheal poster from the 1932 election actually asked the public to vote for the party in order to 'protect your state', and the weakening of local government in the 1920s has always been presented by the Fine Gael tradition as a way of counteracting corruption and the influence of sectional interests on local government.[124] A crucial strategy of the British colonial state elsewhere had been to

[120] F. Blake, *The Irish Civil War and What It Still Means for the Irish People* (Dublin, 1986), 53.
[121] 'Democracy and Its Enemies: Oligarchy and Anarchy', c.1925 (UCD, Blythe Papers, P24/553).
[122] *Irish Times*, 17 July 1922.
[123] O'Duffy to O'Higgins, 'State of National Emergency: The Garda Armed or Unarmed', 6 December 1926 (NA, D/T, S5260).
[124] See G. FitzGerald, *Reflections of the Irish State* (Dublin, 2002), 69–70.

represent civil society as inherently divisive, and for men like O'Higgins, the defence of the Irish state was also intimately linked to his view of a disorderly and corrupting native political culture.[125] However, although his defence of the protective model of democracy in Ireland was not free of contradictions, it could call on two justifications that have a long lineage in European political theory. On the one hand, the Cosgrave governments could have cited Machiavelli's argument that one should distinguish between the kind of politics necessary for the liberation of a state from corrupt and oppressive conditions and the kind of politics necessary for the functioning of a state once it had been properly established. The place of democracy in the former was quite limited, but more than appropriate to the latter.[126] On the other hand, since in this model authority is bestowed on the government for the precise purpose of advancing the ends of the governed, should these ends not be defended adequately by the state, the people can dispense with the governments if they wish.[127] From this perspective, the decision to hand over power in 1932 was the ultimate justification for the model imposed over the previous decade.

Of course it could be objected that neither Cosgrave nor his Fianna Fail successors provided a satisfactory answer to the question of how to contain the coercive power of the state, so that its agents do not interfere with the social and political freedoms of its citizens. The 1922 constitution was informed by two rival traditions, one believing that the people possessed inalienable rights over and above those of the state, and the other maintaining that only a strong centralized state could protect minority rights and strengthen the influence of the individual citizen.[128] Arguably, the tension between the two was always resolved in favour of the latter perspective. Moreover, however much the founders of the Free State faced dilemmas typical of the European experience as a whole, their perspective was also informed by an indigenous conviction that the Irish were not quite ready for democracy, and a Victorian belief that democracy was not about reflecting the rights of citizens, but was a means of strengthening the state and guaranteeing the social order.[129] In November 1923 John Marcus O'Sullivan reflected that

Unfortunately, our whole political training has tended to the creation of bad habits. We do not possess that instinctive obedience to the law so necessary to the stability and success of modern government. Too long the law was the expression, not of our, but the oppressor's will; and too long were we accustomed to regard it as an instrument, a weapon—to be used, if in our favour, to be evaded, if against our immediate aims. It was never something to which respect was due.[130]

---

[125] See Washbrook, 'The Rhetoric of Democracy', 40.
[126] Held, *Models of Democracy*, 47.
[127] Ibid., 52.
[128] J. Praager, *Building Democracy in Ireland* (Cambridge, 1989), 38, 76.
[129] Washbrook, 'The Rhetoric of Democracy', 38.
[130] J. M. O'Sullivan, 'Phases of Revolution', lecture delivered before the Ard Chumann of Cumann na nGaedheal, 21 November 1923 (UCD, McGilligan Papers, P35c/159).

Grounding the democratic rights of the people in the protective embrace of the state, while at the same time suspecting that the public were not quite ready for democracy, could have draconian consequences, as was obvious in Eoin O'Duffy's attempts to arm the Gardai in 1927. The problem for the Gardai, according to O'Duffy, was that of enforcing the principles of citizenship amongst a population the vast majority of whom 'know or care little about such principles'. Since the basis of the state was 'the surrender by the citizens of his individual rights to a central authority who is depended by him to defend those rights', it followed that there could be no objection to arming the police in a situation where the state was failing in its protective duty.[131]

The analysis of the formation of the Irish Free State put forward in this book suggests that it was the project of a triple alliance between the British government, the Catholic Church, and the Irish middle class in which none had an overriding interest in promoting an expansive conception of democracy. After all, the problem with the protective model is that there is no enthusiasm in it for democracy, as 'a morally transformative force', and what is left is 'nothing but a logical requirement for the governance of inherently self-interested conflicting individuals who are assumed to be infinite desirers of their own private benefits'.[132] In the Irish context, the one outstanding consequence of the victory of the triple alliance in the civil war was the eradication of any sense of idealism—republican, socialist, or feminist—from the political landscape, which was an attribute of the pervasive sense of disillusion that accompanied the consolidation of the Irish state. Indeed the lessons learnt from the Irish 'revolution' by the founding fathers of the Free State were eminently conservative ones. In 1923 John Marcus O'Sullivan wrote that

The anarchy that accompanies most revolutions, and of which we have had our share, is easy enough to understand when we bear in mind that not on general principles alone does the State live. More important, from the point of view of stability are the power and prestige of the government, the vigour of the soul of the nation, made up of its traditions, habits of obedience to constitutional authority, reverence for and acceptance of national institutions. The strength of the race largely depends on the strength and soundness of these things, and not merely on the profession of generous ideals, a profession which, unless it is bound up with that aggregate of sentiments, good habits and even prejudices which make up the national mind, can at best be but a lip service, and can provide the State with no adequate defence against the many forces that threaten it with destruction.[133]

It can be debated whether the founding philosophy of the Free State was an enduring one, but the state's courting of Church support, the promotion of interests over ideals in the electoral arena, and the curtailment of civil liberties through the various Public Safety Acts were not to disappear when Fianna Fail came to power. Crucially, the argument that the pro-treaty elite were defending

[131] O'Duffy to O'Higgins, 'State of National Emergency: The Garda Armed or Unarmed', 6 December 1926, (NA, D/T, S5260).
[132] Macpherson, *The Life and Times of Liberal Democracy,* 43.
[133] O'Sullivan, 'Phases of Revolution'.

the public's economic interests in the civil war was not lost on de Valera, with the result that Fianna Fail never neglected the materialist dimension to electoral politics in their ascent to power. On the other hand, the revision of a Treaty, which was the mainstay of Cumann na nGaedheal overall policy, suggests that Fianna Fail had a different conception of how to secure the state, and that possibility will be explored in the next chapter. What seems clear, however, is that the civil war brought the Irish 'revolution' to an end, and that that strange mixture of self-interest, morality, and state paternalism, so characteristic of the Cumann na nGhaedheal elite, was to be an infectious one. As O'Higgins put it, 'the nation, after all, is simply a collection of homes'.[134]

---

[134] T. de Vere White, *Kevin O'Higgins* (London, 1948), 179.

8

'Defending the Republic' and the Rise of Fianna Fail

The transformation of the defeated opposition in the civil war into the respectable party of government that was the Fianna Fail of the late 1930s is one of the most remarkable events in Irish political history. Not only did defeat in the civil war see the moderate section of the anti-treatyites enter the Third Dail on 11 August 1927, after coming to power in 1932, the leadership of the party embraced the very principle they had opposed in the civil war, majority rule. As a result by 1934 the gulf between those republicans who accepted the leadership of de Valera and those who refused to accept the authority of the Free State *tout court* became unbridgeable. The result was the end of the informal alliance that had seen the IRA support Fianna Fail in the 1932 and 1933 elections, the use of military tribunals to suppress the IRA, and the Fianna Fail government's proscription of the organization in 1936. This was certainly a metamorphosis and by asserting, in an increasingly authoritarian fashion, the prerogatives of the 26-county state over those of the 32-county Republic, Fianna Fail found itself exposed to the charge that it was a recent 'convert' to the principles of democracy. In the debate on the passing of the Offences against the State Act in March 1939 Fine Gael pointed out that the underlying assumption of the legislation was that the primary duty of the government was to preserve order and this was considered a 'magnificent volteface' on the part of the government by one Fine Gael TD.[1]

Of course the view that Fianna Fail had become 'converted' to the principles of democracy after 1923 is inseparable from the interpretation of the civil war as one that saw the imposition of majority rule on an unaccountable and potentially despotic anti-treaty minority. If the moving spirit of the pro-treatyites in the civil war had been democratic, the related assumption is that the anti-treatyites eventually accepted that ideology, culminating in their entry into the Free State parliament in 1927. This seems to imply that the original ideology of the anti-treatyites was completely undemocratic, and underwent a total metamorphosis between 1923 and 1932. In this respect there was a curious symmetry in the 1930s between the views of Fine Gael and the IRA, both of whom believed Fianna

---

[1] Deputy Fitzgerald Kenny, *Dail Debates*, 2 March 1939, 1342.

Fail had sold out on its core beliefs. Fanning emphasizes de Valera's commitment to the majority rule principle from 1923 onwards, but does not address the issue of how he could move from one set of principles to another without losing popular support.[2] On the one hand, if the anti-treaty embrace of democracy in 1927 was only tactical, it becomes difficult to explain their continued commitment to democratic rule even when their exercise of power does not lead to the Republic.[3] On the other hand, the conversion perspective ignores the extent to which 'constitutional republicanism', the basic outlook of Fianna Fail, was rooted in an interpretation of the civil war that was no less constitutionalist than that of the victors. This interpretation was common both to moderates like de Valera and to military men like Liam Lynch, and may well help to explain how the party managed subsequently to embrace democratic politics without losing credibility among republicans. In the light of current trends in Irish historiography, it should also be recalled that when de Valera proposed an independent commission to establish the causes of the civil war in 1936, the idea was rejected by Cosgrave not by Fianna Fail.[4]

This is not to deny that political circumstances; military defeat in 1923, the absence of an anti-treaty perspective in the national press, and the conservatism of the electorate played a role in shaping Fianna Fail's reformist strategy. Nevertheless, the overwhelming bulk of the evidence suggests that Fianna Fail's interpretation of the civil war in the 1930s was clearly consistent with the position taken by most anti-treatyites in 1922. Moreover, although de Valera gradually led the party to accept the principle of majority rule as the decisive 'rule of order' in southern Irish politics, this never amounted to the frank acknowledgement of the legitimacy of the Free State that would have implied an acceptance of Fine Gael's view of the civil war. As late as 1936 de Valera was arguing that the Free State had been founded out of an 'executive *coup d'état*', and only the passing of a new constitution the following year would see the establishment of a state in accordance with the Irish people's wishes.[5] It is a short step from such a view to the argument that the undoing of the Treaty in the 1930s was as much a triumph of Irish democracy as its implementation in 1922, and the issue is obviously crucial to our understanding of Irish political development. No doubt there was much double-think in Fianna Fail's version of the events of 1922–3, but their interpretation of the civil war played a key role, not only in allowing the party to represent itself to the electorate as a viable party of government, but also in enabling its leadership to maintain its pre-eminent role as 'Fianna Fail: The Republican Party'.

[2] R. Fanning, 'The Rule of Order: Eamon de Valera and the IRA, 1923–1940', in J. P. O'Carroll and J. A. Murphy (eds.), *De Valera and His Times* (Cork, 1983), 160–73.
[3] J. Augusteijn, 'Political Violence and Democracy: An Analysis of the Tensions within Irish Republican Strategy, 1914–2002', *Irish Political Studies*, 18/1 (2003), 13.
[4] *Irish Times*, 15 August 1936.
[5] 'Civil War 1922–24: Historical Summary by President de Valera' (NA, D/T, S9282).

DEFENDING THE REPUBLIC

A characteristic feature of republican thinking in Ireland is the tendency to ascribe all the pitfalls of Irish political life to the malevolence of British governments. In 1922 this manifested itself in the argument that the civil war was not a civil war as such, but a continuation of the struggle that had begun against the British in 1916.[6] The clear evidence that the Treaty was welcomed by a broad strand in Irish public life was ignored in favour of a view that ascribed the outbreak of the civil war to an imperial strategy of divide and rule, and not to the IRA's indifference to public opinion. Nationalist inability to prevent the split in Sinn Fein from resulting in civil war was also attributed to British pressure, since it was Lloyd George's ultimatum that ultimately led to the attack on the Four Courts on June 1922.[7] On 29 June 1922 Peader O'Donnell told his fellow Donegal citizens that the British, with their 'damnable genius for dividing the peoples they rule', had 'seduced' a section of his former comrades to do their dirty work for them.[8] Radical republicans' own contribution to the descent into civil war, the occupation of the Four Court's for example, was discounted in favour of the view that the anti-treatyites' most earnest wish had been to avoid conflict, and that they were the primary victims of the course of events between May and July 1922.

With this in mind it was perhaps no surprise that the person who seemed to embody the essence of the moderate anti-treaty position, and the most important military leader who advocated a constitutional policy after the civil war, was Frank Aiken. After the signing of the Treaty Aiken and his officers in the fourth northern division declared themselves to be against the holding of an IRA convention since it would inevitably cause a split. When the convention was held, no officer from their division attended, and Aiken had written to Rory O'Connor advising him to postpone it until the constitution was published. He hoped that Collins' constitution would open a political avenue to anti-treaty republicans that events were slowly closing down. With the formation of the new IRA Executive, Aiken's divisional staff remained loyal to the Dail Ministry, although on 6 July Aiken also informed Mulcahy that he would not attack the anti-treaty Executive forces. On 8 July 1922 Aiken met with Liam Lynch and advised him to cease fighting. Soon after, having received orders from Mulcahy's GHQ to attack the Executive forces in his area, a meeting of his officers on 14 July agreed that if the Provisional Government did not give the anti-treatyites a constitutional way of working for the Republic, such as through removing the oath, they would not support the government. Having let Mulcahy know his views on the issue, Aiken was arrested by the National Army and, escaping,

---

[6] 'The Case of the Republic of Ireland', n.d. (UCD, de Valera Papers, P150/1653).
[7] 'Who Caused the Civil War?: Extracts from Some Speeches, Documents, and Records, Which the Free State Ministers Forget' (Dublin, n.d.), 6.
[8] 'Appeal to the People and Volunteers of Tirconnaill', 29 June 1922 (NL, NIC 29).

subsequently took the anti-treaty side in the civil war.[9] Later in the summer, Aiken appealed to members of the IRA fighting with the National Army to 'down tools' rather than fight with men unwilling to take the oath.[10]

For Aiken civil war only became necessary when all political avenues of working for the Republic were closed, and this was a constant theme of Fianna Fail thinking until the oath was removed in May 1933. The anti-treatyites' initial response to the Treaty was to eschew military action in favour of a political campaign against the agreement. The Republican newspaper *An Phoblacht* was launched on 3 January, plans for an anti-treaty party Cumann na Poblachta were drawn up on 8 January, and at the end of the month de Valera was elected President of the Irish Race Congress in Paris. The moderation of the anti-treaty majority at the Sinn Fein *Ard Fheis* on 21/22 February showed that they were not primarily interested in military action at that stage.[11] At the heart of their interpretation of why the civil war happened was the breaking of the Collins–de Valera pact. De Valera maintained that he had avoided campaigning on the Treaty issue in the run-up to the June election, so as not to break the pact, and this was true of the anti-treatyites as a whole.[12] He also argued that hundreds of thousands of republicans voted for pro-treaty candidates, leading to their seeming victory.[13] Collins' apparent renunciation of the pact and subsequent prosecution of the civil war was attributed to the spirit of 'party' taking hold of the pro-treatyites, as well as to British pressure.[14] Liam Lynch later reminded the TDs in the Third Dail that the pact was broken by a group that was a minority in that Dail, and that the Dail was elected specifically to avoid civil war.[15] Collins' breaking of the pact was mainly seen as one in a series of acts of betrayal that, together with an electoral register that excluded a quarter of the voters and 'the poisonous clamour of the lying press', saw the 'muzzled' anti-treaty candidates suffer 'a temporary reverse' at the election. Nevertheless, the election, in so far as it gave a mandate at all, had given a mandate for the declared object of the pact, the unification of the National Army under a coalition government. Instead 'a self-serving clique' had, in an outrageous act of usurpation, set up a military dictatorship and started the civil war.[16]

---

[9] 'To all Officers and Men: Position of the 4th Northern Division from January 1922 to July 17 1922', 17 July 1922 (UCD, Aiken Papers, P104/1240 (3)).

[10] 'To Members of the IRA Now Serving under the Provisional Government', 3 August 1922 (UCD, Aiken Papers, P104/1246 (4)).

[11] B. P. Murphy, 'The Irish Civil War 1922–1923: An Anti-Treaty Perspective', *The Irish Sword*, 20/80 (1997), 295.

[12] (UCD, de Valera Papers, P150/1736).

[13] 'The People's Will and the Path to Peace', 25 November 1922 (NL, Joseph McGarrity Papers, Ms 17,440).

[14] Copy of newspaper report on de Valera's remarks on the repudiation of the electoral pact, 13 September 1922 (UCD, de Valera Papers, P150/1651).

[15] Lynch, Letter to TDs (UCD, P53/43).

[16] 'Manifesto to the People of Ireland, 15 July 1922, Adopted at a Conference of the Available Deputies of the Republican Party', NL.

The essence of the pro-treaty position was that the Provisional Government's prosecution of the war was a defence of the people's will as expressed in the June election. A leading editorial in the *Freeman's Journal* on 25 November 1922 called on the republicans to accept the verdict of the June election and to abandon their struggle. This led the IRA's director of publicity to respond with a set of arguments that were by then common currency among the anti-treatyites'. In it he noted that the electorate had supported the Republic for three years since 1918, that the plenipotentiaries in London had broken theirs oaths and terms of reference, and that Griffith and Mulcahy had publicly committed themselves to maintaining the IRA as the army of the Republic until the people, in a free election, disestablished the Republic. The crucial argument was that with a restrictive register and with the pact providing that the Treaty was not at issue in the June election, a mandate could not have been given for the Treaty. Therefore the Republic had not been disestablished. Rather the mandate was for the coalition agreement and this expression of the popular will was frustrated not by the republicans, but by a minority party in the new parliament who seized power two days before the new parliament was to meet.[17] It was later claimed that out of 1,789,293 names on the electoral register, only 398,337 voted for pro-treaty Sinn Fein in June, and that this 22.5 per cent did not express the will of the people.[18]

This interpretation of what happened was forged in the heat of intense conflict, and it would be well over a decade before de Valera submitted it to paper. It was not just an *ex post facto* rationalization of republican opposition to the Free State. Moreover, the view that the breaking of the pact was just one in a series of duplicitous acts by a Provisional Government determined to implement the Treaty even at the cost of civil war was widely shared among anti-treatyites. Rory O'Connor for example claimed that after the pact was signed, Collins and Mulcahy consented to the republicans remaining in the Four Courts, while the latter made a secret alliance with O'Connor against the Northern government. Apparently, Mulcahy's motive for allowing the republicans to remain in the Four Courts was that while they remained there, IRA activity in the North would be attributed to the anti-treatyites alone. As O'Connor recalled,

The lies and hypocrisy of the Free State leaders are astounding, especially by those who took part in the army negotiations for Unity and know the whole inner history of these negotiations. We were never requested to evacuate the Four Courts; on the contrary, at one meeting of the Coalition army council, at which Mulcahy, O'Duffy, Mellowes, Lynch, and myself were present, we were only asked to evacuate the Ballast Office, Kildare Street Club, the Masonic Hall, and Lever Bros. At that stage we actually discussed co-ordinated military action against N.E. Ulster and had agreed on an Officer who would command both Republican and Free State troops in that area. We were also to send from the South some hundreds of our rifles for use in that area. The reason given was that it would never

---

[17] Director of Publicity to editor of *Freeman's Journal*, 25 November 1922 (UCD, P80/281 (14/1)).
[18] *Sinn Fein*, 8 September 1923.

do if rifles which had been handed to the 'Government' for use against the Republic, and which, of course, could be identified—were found in use against Craig. It should be remembered that at this time the 'Government' was publicly declaring that it was the 'mutineer' section of the army which was fighting the Ulster people.[19]

Subsequently, the manner in which the war was prosecuted by the Provisional Government led the anti-treatyites to reject the argument that the conflict was simply one between constitutionalists and would-be dictators. Commenting on the favourable attitude of the *Irish Independent* towards the Government, de Valera told his director of publicity that their editorials gave the anti-treatyites an excellent opportunity for showing: (1) that the republicans were the constitutionalists, and (2) that the other side definitely caused the split in December and the breaking of the pact.[20] This attitude was shared by republican hardliners, who normally had little time for constitutional politics. On 29 December 1922 the author A.E. (George Russell) published an open letter to the anti-treatyites calling on them to abandon their struggle on the grounds that the majority of the people regarded them, not the government, as the cause of their suffering.[21] This provoked one republican to write a response reflecting the general anti-treaty view that the whole Treaty project was unconstitutional:

Prior to occupation of army buildings by the Irish Republican army certain Deputies to An Dail attended a meeting of the so-called 'Parliament for Southern Ireland' and elected a body which purported to be 'the Provisional Government for Southern Ireland'. These deputies were elected at the 1921 elections with the very definite mandate from the nation they would attend no other Parliament than the duly constituted Parliament of the Republic which was an Dail, and that they support and defend the Government thereof; they even took an oath to that effect. It must be kept in mind that the issue in these elections was the acceptance of the British Government of Ireland Act 1920 and whether the Deputies elected would attend either the Parliament of Northern Ireland or Southern Ireland, or whether they would attend the Parliament of the Republic.... Therefore the actions of the other Deputies who attended the mock parliament was in direct contravention of the expressed will of the people, and therefore it was illegal, hence the Provisional Government elected by them was nothing but a usurping dictatorship.[22]

To the anti-treatyites the civil war was a defensive struggle, not simply in the sense that the Provisional Government had started the war, but to the extent that it was being fought to defend the lawfully established Republic. To them the constitutional party was the party that stood by the Republic as the expression of the free will of the Irish people.[23] Since the Republic and its institutions were bound to be undermined by the Treaty, it was not surprising that the anti-treatyites should see themselves as victims of the Provisional Government's

---

[19] R. O'Connor, quoted in 'Who Caused the Civil War?', n.d. (Fianna Fail Archives, FF /22).
[20] De Valera to Director of Publicity, n.d. (UCD, de Valera Papers, P150 /1736).
[21] *Freeman's Journal*, 29 December 1922.
[22] Anonymous letter (UCD, O'Malley Papers, P17a/152).
[23] 'Who Are the Constitutionalists?', *Sinn Fein*, 15 August 1923.

aggression. This view fitted nicely with the view that the civil war was not a civil war at all, but the age-old struggle of the Irish people against British rule, now being administered through the agency of the Provisional Government. In No- vember 1922 de Valera was angered by an editorial in the *Manchester Guardian*, which endorsed Bonar Law's view of 'the absurd myth of continued English dictation' in Ireland. De Valera repeated his challenge to the British government, to declare their willingness to abide by the result of a free plebiscite of the Irish people to decide between the Free State and the Republic.[24] The anti-treatyites believed that public acceptance of the Treaty was not an expression of the will of the people, but 'the fear of the people', and they were fighting to defend the popular will once Britain's threat of war was removed.[25] The course of events since January had also sharpened their conviction that in the implementation of the Treaty, it was the will of the British government, rather than the freely expressed voice of the Irish people, that was the determining influence.[26]

On the other hand, evidence of a strong constitutionalist strain in anti-treaty thinking is not quite the same thing as an acceptance of the popular will as the deciding factor in national affairs. A republican document issued in response to the bishop's pastoral in October 1922 stated that the will of the people can only be expressed by a rational judgement, but even if the Treaty had been at issue in the June election, because of the limited register, the influence of the press, and the threat of immediate war if the Treaty were rejected, such a vote would not have expressed the real will (*judicium rationale*) of the people, so the vote could not have disestablished the existing Republic.[27] Another republican document later argued that the right of a people to exercise its will sprung directly from its sense of nationhood, but a power derived from nationhood could not be exer- cised to abolish that nationhood, any more than a judge who owed his official position to the existence of the law could use his office to abolish the law.[28] Another anti-treaty document invoked the law of God as the authority behind the Republic, maintaining that the elected deputies were honour bound to uphold it even in the face of public opposition:

Once such a government is thus established, 'the will of the people' immediately imposes on the people themselves, both individually and collectively, obligations which are im- perative; they are morally bound to support and maintain it. But their Deputies are, as a necessary precaution against treachery, actually sworn to maintain and support it against all attempts at subversion and overthrow. Further the Deputies are thus bound even against the very constituents who elected them, unless and until, those constituents again merge themselves in, and become part of a constitutionally ascertained majority of the people.[29]

---

[24] De Valera to editor, 1 December 1922 (UCD, de Valera Papers, P150/1662).
[25] *Sinn Fein*, 15 August 1923.
[26] Murphy, 'The Irish Civil War 1922–1923': An Anti-Treaty Perspective', 298.
[27] 'The Case of the Republic of Ireland', n.d. (UCD, de Valera Papers, P150/1653).
[28] *Sinn Fein*, 6 October 1923.
[29] 'The Truth about a Deputy's Oath' (NL, NIC 81).

With de Valera the public profession of a constitutionalist position during the civil war was accompanied by a private acknowledgment that the majority of the people were not on their side. On 12 October 1922 he informed the IRA Executive that he held majority rule to be a fundamental principle of order and progress, and 'were it not for the most exceptional circumstances in the present case I could not possibly stand for opposing it'. He added that the fact that the anti-treatyites were acting 'seemingly in opposition to this principle' was the greatest weakness in their cause.[30] In December 1922 de Valera then wrote to Lynch, stressing the need to counter the incessant propaganda in the press accustoming the people to regard the Free State as established by their will. The problem was that the people were 'misled' and did not understand the situation.[31] In January he confessed to Joe McGarrity that the people were 'dispirited' and it was impossible 'to get back the vim and dash of a couple of years ago'.[32] In a remarkable letter to the Neutral IRA in February 1923 he admitted the basic weakness of the anti-treaty position:

Despite all the obstacles I would feel confident of ultimate success if we could at all remedy the one vital weakness in our position—we are unable to accept the majority vote of the people as the decisive judgment. No country in the world would ever be able to free itself from the grasp of an Empire if the decision to attempt it depended on the vote of the majority. If the judgment went against us, it would be pretended that the people voluntarily accepted the 'Treaty'. The press makes, however, this very reasonable attitude of ours appear to be a rejection of the democratic principles of majority rule, which is undoubtedly, a wise and good principle of order where freedom is unchallenged. For States that have to secure their freedom it would be a rule for perpetual slavery.[33]

In effect, the bottom line of the anti-treatyites remained what it had been immediately after the Treaty was signed: an election on the Treaty under the threat of external force could not be accepted as a genuine expression of popular sovereignty. Nevertheless, their interpretation of why the Treaty resulted in civil war emphasized the bad faith of their opponents. In particular, de Valera blamed Collins' deceptiveness over the pact. In his view, the signing of the pact had involved an acceptance by the anti-treatyites of the people's decision as the final court of appeal, and thus the abandonment of the republican position. Nevertheless, he accepted it as a bridge towards unity, but one that could only work if Collins stood up to Lloyd George over his constitution.[34] With this in mind it is not surprising that what later became important for Fianna Fail was not whether a Republic had been constitutionally established prior to 1921, but whether the anti-treaty position in the civil war could be justified in constitutional terms. No doubt for the rank and file, the defence of the Republic during the war was precisely that: a fight to defend a state that had come into existence in 1916. For

---

[30] De Valera to C/S and Members of Executive, 12 October 1922 (NL, Ms 31,528).
[31] De Valera to Lynch, 26 December 1922 (UCD, de Valera Papers, P150/1749).
[32] De Valera to McGarrity, 10 January 1923 (NL, Joseph McGarrity Papers, Ms 17,440).
[33] De Valera to Secretary Neutral IRA, 10 February 1923, (UCD, de Valera Papers, P150/1793).
[34] De Valera to McGarrity, 10 September 1922 (NL, Joseph McGarrity Papers, Ms 17,440).

the political leadership, however, the rhetoric of 'defending the republic' was used to emphasize the lack of constitutional propriety behind the establishment of the Free State, and to counter the incessant propaganda in the press against the anti-treaty position. Given that government propaganda relentlessly blamed the anti-treatyites for the material destruction caused by the war, it is not a surprise that anti-treaty Sinn Fein would want to exculpate themselves from blame, but as the civil war turned into an uncertain peace the anti-treaty interpretation of the war had a key role to play in helping its moderate leadership benefit from that peace.

THE CEASEFIRE PROPOSALS

Once Liam Lynch was replaced by Frank Aiken as chief of staff of the IRA, de Valera now had an ally who was guaranteed to cooperate in his desire to harness the anti-treaty IRA's rank and file as the 'organised driving power' behind the Sinn Fein party.[35] By then de Valera had spent six months preparing the anti-treatyites for a post-conflict role, and he was committing them to following 'the Sinn Fein way' as established in 1917. This would mean acknowledging the right of no external authority in Ireland, and excluding from the party those who were willing to take an oath of allegiance.[36] Both would point to an abstentionist policy. The inclusion of a demand for the abolition of the oath in return for IRA decommissioning as part of his ceasefire proposals in April 1922 later proved to be the bedrock of Fianna Fail's position, since it was unanimously agreed to by the IRA Executive and accepted by the rank and file in the summer of 1923. Like Aiken, de Valera had maintained that the oath had barred the anti-treatyites from peacefully pursuing the republican ideal the previous summer, and 'the prime justification for attempting the use of force was that peaceful methods were practically barred'.[37] It followed that if the oath were removed from the constitution there would be no further justification for militant opposition to the state.

The peace terms de Valera offered the Provisional Government in April 1923 were intended to find a place at the constitutional table for that party, but also to reconcile Sinn Fein's republicanism to the imperatives of electoral competition. At the Mansion House Conference in April 1922 de Valera had promised to use his influence to win acceptance of Labour's proposal to delay the election for six months, 'not indeed as a principle of right or justice, but as a principle of peace and order', and this qualification appeared in the clause on accepting majority rule in his ceasefire proposals.[38] In his 'declaration to the people of Ireland' on 8 February 1923 de Valera stated that the cornerstones of his position were that the sovereign rights of the nation were indefeasible and inalienable, and that all

---

[35] De Valera to Barry, 14 June 1923 (UCD, de Valera Papers, P150/1752).
[36] B. Kissane, *Explaining Irish Democracy* (Dublin, 2002), 170.
[37] De Valera to Burke, 15 February 1923 (UCD, de Valera Papers, P150/1793).
[38] Ibid.

government authority in Ireland derived from the people.[39] They appeared as clause 1 and 2 of his ceasefire proposals. The demand for the abolition of the oath was essential if de Valera was to be spared the accusation of surrendering the anti-treaty position entirely, since all the other clauses were acceptable to the Government. Although de Valera had already decided to abandon the Second Dail at this stage, it is doubtful whether the proposals reflected an enthusiasm for majority rule on his part. In February 1923 he had rejected the idea of a general election if the government accepted his first two principles on the grounds that England's threat of war would prejudice the outcome.[40] Even after the ceasefire de Valera was not confident that a fair election would take place. As a result the anti-treaty strategy remained open-ended. On 31 July 1923 Aiken wrote:

While I deplore the necessity for the war that has been waged from June 1922 to May 1923 by the IRA in defence of the rights of the nation, and while I would be absolutely against our starting a new campaign while there was a chance of establishing a legitimate Government by peaceful means, it is my duty as a military officer to encourage my fellow officers to educate and train themselves in the use of the latest military tactics and weapons, so that, if war be ever again forced upon us in defence of our national faiths we would be fitted to fight, and risk our own lives, and the lives of our men, to the best advantage for our cause.[41]

By linking the demand for an abolition of the oath to the issue of IRA decommissioning, de Valera was ensuring that the anti-treaty position still rested on a key constitutional principle, even if his ceasefire message to the IRA had suggested that the Republic had been destroyed. His whole strategy in the negotiations was threatened by Tom Barry's belief that the interests of the defeated side would better be secured if the IRA were released from its allegiance to the Republican Government. In June 1923 Barry believed that the lives of the 2,500 IRA men on the run and the allegedly 15,000 men in jails would best be protected if the IRA offered the open decommissioning of its weapons in return for an amnesty. The Republican Government could not negotiate such a quid pro quo because the only terms it could accept were complete independence.[42] For his part, de Valera had been afraid that the government's strategy in the negotiations was to deal separately with the military officers of the IRA in order to rid themselves of their political rivals, and to make it appear that the fight for the Republic was simply an army mutiny with no constitutional dimension.[43] Accordingly, he strongly opposed Barry's proposal, remarking than an army that took it upon itself to champion the national cause to the extent of creating a situation that led to civil war could not then turn round and treat the

---

[39] 'To the People of Ireland', 8 February 1923 (UCD, P69/92 (120)).

[40] De Valera to Burke, 15 February 1923 (UCD, de Valera Papers, P150/1793).

[41] Letter to *Freeman's Journal* and *Irish Independent*, 31 July 1923 (UCD, Frank Aiken Papers, P104/1313(4)).

[42] Barry to de Valera, 8 June 1923 (UCD, de Valera Papers, P150/1752).

[43] De Valera to Lynch, 7 May 1923 (UCD, de Valera Papers, P150/1752).

whole thing as if it were merely 'a petty mutiny'.[44] At an IRA Executive meeting held on 11 and 12 July 1923 Aiken censured Barry with acting without the approval of the army, leading the latter to tender his resignation.

In the summer of 1923 the general process of demobilization coincided with preparations for the August election, and the government, with the national dailies strongly behind them, clearly held the stronger hand. Carty emphasizes 'the important role played by political leaders in creating and politicising issues that will evoke electoral responses' in Irish elections of this era.[45] These issues— the need for strong government, the responsibility of the anti-treatyites for the destruction of the civil war, and the continued threat posed by the anti-treatyties to established economic interests—were all a legacy of the civil war and remained central until the late 1930s: de Valera claimed in August 1936 that Fine Gael were still playing upon the prejudices of the civil war years.[46] Sinn Fein, on the other hand, proposed policies aimed at those who had played a part in the civil war on their side, such as the reform of public services to ensure that no one will be unjustly treated, the abolition of murder gangs, the closing of secret military courts, and an end to censorship, as well as policies with a general appeal, such as state intervention to reduce unemployment, the revival of the Irish language, and an offer of local autonomy to Ulster within a 32-county Republic.[47] Most of the grievances would be jettisoned when the new anti-treaty party, Fianna Fail, was formed in May 1926.

The hostility of the press, emigration, and public apathy were all cited by Sinn Fein as reason for their electoral failure between 1923 and 1926, but the key impetus for the formation of Fianna Fail in 1926 was frustration with the abstentionist policy. The possibility that a section of Sinn Fein would abandon that policy led to the IRA's decision at its convention in November 1925 to withdraw its allegiance from the Republican Government and vest control of the organization solely in its Army Council. However, the convention did not agree to expel those who advocated entry into the Free State parliament if the oath were removed, Aiken making the case that such a policy was consistent with the ceasefire proposals.[48] De Valera later recalled that he proposed a change in Sinn Fein's policy on the basis of the ceasefire proposals, and claimed that the IRA had never opposed the formation of Fianna Fail.[49] Although nobody mentioned the possibility of entering the Dail with the oath still in place, as was to happen in August 1927, the formation of Fianna Fail the following year did not end the informal alliance between elected and non-elected republicans that the convention had committed itself to.[50] Aiken was a strong advocate of continuing cooperation:

[44] De Valera to Barry, 14 June 1923 (UCD, de Valera Papers, P150/172).
[45] R. K. Carty, 'Social Cleavages and Party Systems: A Reconsideration of the Irish Case', *European Journal of Political Research*, 4 (1976), 201.
[46] *Irish Press*, 17 August 1936.
[47] *Irish Times*, 25 August 1923.
[48] Typescript, 4 November 1933 (UCD, Aiken Papers, P104/1327 (1)).
[49] Speech at New Ross, 14 August 1936 (UCD, Aiken Papers, P104/1459 (9)).
[50] 'Report of General Army Convention 14–15 November 1925' (UCD, Aiken Papers, P104/1337).

The Army should not act as if it relied solely on force of arms to achieve victory and thereby give the support of the people as a gift to the anti-Republicans North and South; it should not try to withdraw into itself and become a society of select brethren who will admire one another instead of openly giving a helping hand in its spare time to civilian organisations that are fighting honourably for the same ends.[51]

For de Valera too the formation of Fianna Fail did not occasion the democratic 'conversion' appearances would suggest, since he told the first meeting of Fianna Fail that though majority rule was an inevitable rule of order, in basing acceptance of the Treaty on it, majority rule ran counter to the fundamental rights of the nation, 'and so clashed with a matter of natural rights and justice'. There were rights that no majority was justified in destroying, such as the right to life or to be free of slavery.[52] In other words, after the civil war de Valera did not directly shift from an undemocratic position to a democratic one—he shifted from authoritarianism to ambiguity, and then to democracy. On the other hand, he also told Joe McGarrity in April 1927 that force alone could not achieve a Republic and that a successful civil war against anti-republicans backed by England could not be waged.[53]

However, normative arguments were one thing and political strategy another. Almost as vital in Fianna Fail's break with Sinn Fein as the abstentionist issue had been was the party's strategy of winning the support of different social groups on the basis of concrete economic rather than abstract nationalist issues.[54] In 1926 Sean Lemass publicly argued that the anti-treaty party needed to teach the Irish people that independence meant 'real concrete advantages for the common people and not merely an idealist's paradise'.[55] Indeed during the civil war de Valera had told Count Plunkett that 'the spur of a direct material concrete grievance' was absent in their cause, and the press and the pulpit had convinced the public that it was the anti-treatyites who were responsible for 'the material burdens being placed upon the people'.[56] From its inception Fianna Fail's emphasis was on such concrete material issues, and the phalanx of constitutional grievances was quickly reduced to the question of the oath of allegiance, a strategy consistent with de Valera's interpretation of the civil war.[57] For the June 1927 election Fianna Fail borrowed a large part of the Labour Party's programme, declaring a commitment 'to prevent extravagant expenditure, to stem emigration, to provide work for the unemployed, to better our declining trade position and to cause an industrial revival'.[58]

[51] Aiken to Chairman of Army Council, 18 November 1925 (UCD, Aiken Papers, P104/1320 (2)).
[52] Speech at inaugural meeting of Fianna Fail, at La Scala Theatre, May 1926 (UCD, de Valera Papers, P150/2082).
[53] De Valera to McGarrity, 30 April 1927 (NL Ms 17,441).
[54] R. Dunphy, *The Making of Fianna Fail Power in Ireland 1921–1948* (Oxford, 1995), 67.
[55] Ibid., 69.
[56] De Valera to Count Plunkett, 12 June 1923 (UCD, de Valera Papers, P150/1652).
[57] Dunphy, *The Making of Fianna Fail Power*, 84.
[58] *The Nation*, 11 June 1927.

Nevertheless, after Fianna Fail's entry into the Dail on 11 August 1927, the government still made great play of the responsibility of the anti-treaty camp for the destructiveness of the civil war, Cosgrave claiming that Fianna Fail's interest in social issues 'meant nothing to you until your own political extinction was at hand'.[59] Although some government advertisements for the September 1927 election mentioned policy achievements, the most effective ones were based on generating a sense of fear and ridicule stemming from Fianna Fail's civil war record. Among the leaders were: 'Help the Government to Finish the Job', 'Who Are the War-Makers?', 'Now They Are Shocked', 'The Making of Ireland—or Its Undoing', 'They Took the Oath to Save Their Party—They Would not Take It in 1922 to Save Their Country from Civil War', 'De Valera in the Dumps and the Voters on the Warpath', 'Economy—by Torch and Petrol Can', 'Digging Freedom's Grave in 1922'.[60] Not surprisingly Fianna Fail felt it had to discard its hardline republican image if they wanted to be an electoral success. In September 1927 de Valera publicly announced that 'the sinister design of aiming at bringing about a sudden revolutionary upheaval with which our opponents choose to credit us, is altogether foreign to our purpose and programme'.[61] As a response to the government's propaganda that month he actually filled a whole page of a Dublin paper with a signed promise that his intentions were peaceful and respected the will of the people.[62] The constitutional issues were now important as a 'back up weapon', which put their opponents on the defensive, but the emphasis on the oath still helped the party maintain its position as the leader of the republican opposition after 1926.[63]

Although Fianna Fail had refused an offer of formal cooperation with the IRA for the June 1927 election, with its electoral victory in February 1932, the issue of a Fianna Fail government's relationship with the IRA was bound to cause anxiety. In 1932 Ernest Blythe submitted an article to a journal for publication asking whether militant republicanism would, after the formation of the Fianna Fail government in 1932, fade away in the same way Fenianism had died out after the cooperation between the Irish Parliamentary Party and the Land League in the 1880s. Since the IRA was now emboldened by the fact that de Valera was in power, and since parliamentarism itself was in crisis internationally, Blythe rejected the analogy. Unless the government changed its attitude to the IRA, or a new force entered the field, the coming twelve months would see the IRA set up a dictatorship. Since neither the Firearms Act nor the law against drilling was being imposed on the IRA by the government, democrats would have to resort to the same methods even at the price of bloodshed.[64]

---

[59] *Irish Times*, 1 September 1927.
[60] W. Moss, *Political Parties in the Irish Free* State (New York, 1933), 126.
[61] *The Nation*, 10 September 1927.
[62] Moss, *Political Parties in the Irish Free State*, 126.
[63] Dunphy, *The Making of Fianna Fail Power*, 84.
[64] O'Farrell to de Valera, 5 March 1934 (UCD, de Valera Papers, P150/2290).

What Blythe did not know was that Fianna Fail had already turned down an offer for formal cooperation with the IRA, and was determined to stick to the 1923 ceasefire proposals. In February 1932 Aiken, now minister of defence, went into conference with Michael Brennan, chief of staff of the IRA, with a view to bringing an end to the IRA's existence as a distinct organization. He actually proposed the fusion of the IRA and Fianna Fail, suggesting that the reason that many advocated the retention of an armed anti-treaty force since 1926 was doubt over whether the Cosgrave governments would hand over power to a Fianna Fail government committed to the ceasefire declarations. Now that that had happened, he asked for a public declaration by the IRA that they were willing to accept the same proposals that had been accepted by the organization in 1923.[65] Fianna Fail asked:

(1) Whether the Irish Republican Army of today will on its part accept these proposals (Cease Fire Proposals) if a Fianna Fail government does so ?
(2) May I take it that on a removal of the oath and the acceptance publicly of the "Cease Fire" proposals by a Fianna Fail government, the IRA will place their arms at the disposal of the elected representative of the people?

Each battalion of the IRA was offered these terms for discussion by the Army Council and all turned them down. The IRA committed itself to its continued existence as a distinct organization with all arms and equipment under its control.[66] The government then refused to go into conference with the IRA's Army Council to discuss their alternative interpretation of de Valera's 'Dump Arms order'. At heart was a disagreement over the causes of the civil war, the IRA leadership believing that the oath was not the real issue in the Treaty. An internal memo on de Valera's appeal cited the first two clauses of the ceasefire proposals instead, arguing that election results did not affect the vital issue of sovereignty.[67] Another outlined a scenario whereby IRA arms would be handed over, but Fianna Fail would then be defeated at the polls before carrying out any more of their objectives. With Cosgrave back in power, republicans would then be robbed of the means of active resistance.[68] Mary MacSwiney outlined her criticisms of the new government's position:

There are few, if any, republicans who do not sincerely rejoice that the gaols are empty of political prisoners for the first time in ten years (there are still republican prisoners in the Six County Area); that the Irish people have not merited lasting disgrace by putting back into power the authors of the most infamous Coercion Act Ireland has ever known; that the men who accounted it a bond of honour to fasten England's yoke more tightly on Ireland, have at last, been driven out of office—never again, it is hoped, to get control—but while recognising that these things are good, it is necessary to emphasise that the Irish Free

---

[65] Aiken to Brennan, 19 February 1932 (UCD, Aiken Papers, P104/1322).

[66] Kissane, *Explaining Irish Democracy*, 181.

[67] 'Memo Prepared for General Army Convention', August 1932 (UCD, Moss Twomey Papers, P69/53 (374)).

[68] (UCD, Moss Twomey Papers, P69/53 (377)).

State is still a British Institution—not Irish—not Free—not a state in any real sense—and that until the whole Treaty is repudiated, every line and word of it, that British institution is usurping the place of the lawful Government of the Republic.[69]

Clearly the view that the civil war divide was reducible solely to the question of the oath was not accepted by all the anti-treatyites. On the other hand, the appeal for the IRA to decommission its weapons made perfect sense to a minority government accused of being unable to control the hardliners. During the 1932 campaign de Valera had actually complained that the government was not fighting the election on economic issues but relying instead on 'frightening' the voters.[70] In that election the government made few policy proposals, projecting itself instead 'as the sole bulwark against terror and Communism'.[71] In the campaign, the minister for justice, Mr FitzGerald Kenny, told voters in Mayo that 'Mr de Valera's policy is that armed associations like the so-called I.R.A. and Saor Eire should continue to drill arm and endeavour to impose their will by force on the people'.[72] Since 1927 Fianna Fail had been desperate to assure voters that it could be trusted with office, and the informal alliance with the IRA, accepted as necessary in 1926, was increasingly unsustainable. After the election Aiken warned Brennan that doubt in the people's minds as to whether Fianna Fail could secure internal peace could lead Labour to withdraw its support for the minority government, and only a dramatic step by the IRA could eliminate that possibility.[73] However ambiguous the embrace of a peaceful path had been in 1923, by 1932 that ambiguity could not longer be tolerated.

NATIONAL DISCIPLINE AND MAJORITY RULE

In Europe as a whole, political elites in the 1930s were forced to make a clear choice between democracy and dictatorship and the new de Valera government was no exception. As early as October 1931 de Valera had declared himself satisfied that Irish democracy would not succumb to extremist challenges, since it rested on strong foundations, such as the people's individualistic tendencies, the system of land tenure, and the Catholic faith, that were not likely to disappear.[74] Nevertheless, the first two years of the party's period in power would see it facing extraparliamentary challenges from the right and left, and as late as 1937 de Valera's former civil war enemies in the Fine Gael Party were worried about the dictatorial potential of his new constitution. Moreover, while de Valera's governments had been lenient in their treatment of the IRA in their first three years

---

[69] M. MacSwiney, *The Irish Republic* (Cork, n.d.), 36.
[70] *Irish Times*, 10 February 1932.
[71] Moss, *Political Parties*, 184.
[72] *Irish Times*, 3 February 1932.
[73] Aiken to Brennan, 19 February 1932 (UCD, Aiken Papers, P104/1322 (1)).
[74] 'Interview given by Mr de Valera to representatives of the United Press', 29 October 1931 (UCD, de Valera Papers, P150/2168).

in power, by 1936 the government was convinced that permanent repressive legislation was necessary to deal with the organization. Against this background it was not a surprise that the whole issue of the civil war and the Fianna Fail elite's role in it would return. A series of important speeches made by de Valera in 1936 were grouped together in a party document called *National Discipline and Majority Rule,* which built on the old view that de Valera had done his utmost to prevent the Treaty split resulting in civil war, and also claimed that the Fianna Fail elite had never denied the right of the people to decide on the Treaty issue.

If there was one issue that put Fianna Fail's democratic credentials to the test it was that of political subversion. In 1931 de Valera had stated that when the removal of the oath meant that peaceful political action would be open to all, and when the security forces observed strict discipline, harmony would soon reign between the various sections of Irish society.[75] On 3 March 1932 the Executive Council ordered the pardoning of the seventeen men imprisoned by the military tribunals that had been established by Cosgrave in 1931 and the remission of their sentences. The work of the tribunals was suspended, although article 2A, which allowed for their use, was not removed from the constitution. Although the relative calm of Fianna Fail's first year in office would seem to have vindicated de Valera's optimism, the return of seriously disordered conditions in 1933 forced a turn-about in policy. On 22 August 1933 the government decided to reappoint the tribunals with exactly the same powers and personnel as under the previous government. Between 1933 and 1937 these tribunals would convict over 800 people, and in 1939 the powers contained in article 2A would form the main prop of Fianna Fail's new Offences against the State Act.

According to Fianna Fail, the re-establishment of the tribunals was necessitated by the appearance in 1932 of a shirted movement with all the hallmarks of fascism. A small Army Comrades Association had been established on 2 February 1932, and was described by Eoin O'Duffy, the chief of police, as 'a formidable insurrectionary force'.[76] This was later transformed into the National Guard, founded on 20 July 1933, and banned the following month. This body in turn was replaced by the Young Ireland Association, which was formed on 9 September 1933 and banned in December 1933. Finally, the League of Youth was formed on 14 December 1933 and was soon banned under the powers given by article 2A. At its height, the Blueshirts had as many as 50,000 members, although it claimed double that figure. Initially formed with the avowed intent of protecting freedom of speech for Fine Gael politicians, its rank and file were also motivated by agrarian grievances stemming from de Valera's ongoing tariff war with the UK. This resulted in 1934 in a widespread campaign against the payment of rates and annuities, an intensive campaign of destruction of means of communication, and an extensive series of 'incidents arising from political animosities' leading to

---

[75] 'Interview given by Mr de Valera to Mr. Henri de Kerillis', 14 July 1931 (UCD, de Valera Papers, P150/2166).
[76] 'Notes on Use of Article 2A by Present Government' (NA, D/T, S2454).

violence and the destruction of property. In that year alone, the collection of government revenue was obstructed on 424 occasions.[77]

One of the most controversial questions in Irish political history is whether the Blueshirts were fascists, and the certainty that they provided de Valera with the justification for his recourse to article 2A. Not only were the various Blueshirt organizations declared unlawful, the wearing of shirts by political organization was made a criminal offence in March 1934, and between 1933 and 1935 434 Blueshirts were convicted by the military tribunal.[78] European parallels informed de Valera's attitude to the Blueshirts, and Fianna Fail constantly invoked them during the Dail debate on the wearing of uniforms in March 1934. By then emergency legislation against shirted movements had been passed in states such as Belgium, Norway, and Switzerland, and there was no obvious reason Ireland should be an exception. The movement's position was not helped by a statement during the debate by the former Attorney General John A. Costello that just as the Blackshirts were victorious in Italy and the Hitler shirts were victorious in Germany, 'the Blueshirts will be victorious in the Irish Free State'.[79] The Blueshirt leader, O'Duffy, openly derided parliamentary institutions, his supporters saluted him with a fascist-type salute, and the Blueshirts marched in military file. The Government also had possession of several Blueshirt publications, celebrating the principle of action in political life, praising their intelligence-gathering activities, and idealizing the corporative state.[80] If the plan was not to overthrow parliamentary institutions, de Valera asked what was the meaning 'of raising a private army, of adopting a Fascist salute and uniform, or organising a secret intelligence service, and trying to seduce public servants to join it?'[81]

The answer can only be given with reference to Fianna Fail's relationship with the IRA, which had decided to support it in both the 1932 and 1933 elections. A classic example of the conflict spreading through the countryside in 1933 was afforded by its leader Eoin O'Duffy's trip to Tralee on 6 October. The meeting hall was put under siege, many delegates were assaulted before and after the meeting, the Gardai were attacked with stones, sticks, and bottles, and a bomb was later found at the back of the hall. Between 15 August and 5 December 1933 17 armed attacks on individuals occurred in the area, many involving the kidnapping of Blueshirts.[82] Indeed the long-term significance of the Blueshirts was merely to delay the confrontation between de Valera and the IRA, and Fianna Fail's democratic credentials were vindicated by the fact that it repressed both simultaneously. That there would be conflict between them was apparent from a radical change in IRA policy introduced by the general IRA convention held on 17 and 18 March 1933. The IRA was no longer behind the economic war and rescinded its

---

[77] 'Abnormal Duties in 1934', 'Return of Political Outrages' (NA, D/J, JUS 8/355).
[78] Kissane, *Explaining Irish Democracy*, 186.
[79] *Dail Debates*, 28 March 1934, 2237.
[80] 'Press Cuttings on Mentality of Blueshirt movement' (UCD, de Valera Papers, P150/2343).
[81] De Valera, Speech in Tralee, 17 December 1933 (UCD, de Valera Papers, P150/2279).
[82] (UCD, de Valera Papers, P150/2279).

resolution, carried at the army convention of 1932, to adopt a supportive attitude towards the government. It would now 'pursue its policy irrespective of its reactions on the policy of the Free State Government and other political parties'.[83] In turn, in his speech in Tralee on 17 December 1933, de Valera told the crowd that people who were guilty of disorder were not patriots, but simply 'mischievous disturbers of the peace' who should be treated as such.[84] At the same time the government was resisting pressure from the local Fianna Fail organization for local courts to try 12 republicans convicted by the tribunals because of their part in the recent events in Kerry.[85] The escalation of violence in 1933 had dismayed the government, but not its rank-and-file supporters, some of whom saw it was a second round of hostilities with 'the Free State'.[86] The use of military tribunals against the IRA was objected to by many within Fianna Fail, particularly in Kerry, where civil war bitterness was greatest.[87] After the shooting of two prominent IRA men, George Gilmore and T. J. Green, by detectives in Kilrush late in 1932, a delegation of Fianna Fail supporters had visited de Valera and Gerald Boland with demands for the CID's disbandment. They were allegedly told that 'an established body' such as the Special Branch could not be disbanded so easily, and that delegations such as theirs could not dictate to the government.[88] This was part of its strategy in office of working with the existing machinery of government, culminating in de Valera's plea to his civil war opponents on 1 March 1934, to 'give up this tomfoolery of Blueshirting' and form a composite force.[89]

The potential for conflict was even more pronounced because Fianna Fail was also committed to a policy of absorbing former IRA men into the volunteer reserve of the army. On the night of 21 December 1934 Thomas Breen of Derry-shane County Clare was fired on and wounded, simply because he had left the IRA and joined the force. At least twenty such attacks had taken place over a twelve-month period in Kerry alone. The perpetrator was brought before the military tribunal and sentenced to five years' imprisonment.[90] By revising the most objectionable articles of the Treaty de Valera had hoped to reconcile the IRA to the Free State but the events of 1933–4 put paid to his optimism. In August 1936 he declared that the IRA had civil war as their end, and seems to have come to the same conclusions as Cumann na nGaedheal regarding the necessity for article 2A.[91] In the long run, the Fianna Fail government's skilful presentation of itself as both the inheritor of the republican tradition and the defender of Irish democracy put the IRA on the defensive, and left them appearing to stand for mere 'sectional'

---

[83] Kissane, *Explaining Irish Democracy*, 184.

[84] De Valera, Speech in Tralee, 17 December 1933 (UCD, de Valera Papers, P150/2279).

[85] 'Resolution of Kerry Dail Ceanntair of Fianna Fail', 28 November 1933 (UCD, de Valera Papers, P150/2279).

[86] B. Hanley, *The IRA 1926–1936* (Dublin, 2002), 139.

[87] Ibid., 137.

[88] Ibid., 138–9.

[89] *Dail Debates*, 1 March 1934, 2505.

[90] 'Notes on Use of Article 2A by Present Government' (NA, D/T, S2454).

[91] *Irish Times*, 17 August 1936.

interests.[92] Between 1934 and 1936 a total of 341 IRA men were convicted by the tribunal, and under part 4 of 2A the IRA was proscribed in July 1936 following a series of murders.[93]

Yet Fianna Fail was now reliant on the same repressive powers it had bitterly denounced in 1931. In December 1933 it justified its arrest of IRA men in Kerry on the grounds that 'the primary duty of Government is to protect the persons, the liberties and the property of citizens', exactly the same principle enunciated by Cumann na nGaedheal during the civil war.[94] On 29 April 1936 the police also seized copies of the newsletter of a new republican party, *Cumann Poblachta na hEireann*, on the grounds that they were 'seditious', in an act reminiscent of Cosgrave's attempted prosecution of Fianna Fail's newspaper, *The Irish Press*, before the 1932 election.[95] In January 1937 Sean MacEntee publicly acknowledged in the Dail that his opponents had established majority rule in the country, which drew the accusation from the party's Wolfe Tone Cumann in TCD that he was repudiating the republican position in the civil war. While denying this, MacEntee pointed out that Fianna Fail was now attracting the votes of people who opposed them during the civil war, and had resolved the differences of the civil war period.[96] At the same time the government was resisting pressure from the Old IRA association to give preference in public employment to anti-treaty civil war veterans, on the grounds that one of the first acts of the government in 1932 was to discontinue the Cosgrave government's preferential treatment of ex-members of the National Army. Although ex-IRA men did receive pensions and land allotments, on 16 October 1936 the government committed itself to equal opportunities to all with regard to employment, regardless of creed, class, or political or sectional affiliations.[97]

Fianna Fail's response to the dilemma in which it found itself after 1933 was to emphasize the constitutional lineage of their brand of republicanism, and the role the party had played in preventing a reoccurrence of civil war conditions. De Valera's speeches to the Dail on 1 and 2 March 1934, were published by the party in a pamphlet called *The Way to Peace*. It was prefaced by a quotation from Wolfe Tone, which declared the unification of the Irish people as his end and the abolition of the memory of past dissensions as his means.[98] In 1936, the year that saw the IRA proscribed, de Valera made three public speeches that marked a final parting of the ways with the organization. In Enniscorthy on 2 August 1936, he emphasized Fianna Fail's contribution to the consolidation of a democratic system. Not only had there been no vindictiveness after they came to power in 1932, the Blueshirts' effort at establishing a fascist organization had been

---

[92] Hanley, *The IRA 1926–1936*, 144.
[93] 'Military Tribunal Statistics' (NA, D/J D29/36).
[94] Official Reply to Ned Drummond, 5 December 1933 (UCD, de Valera Papers, P150/2279).
[95] MacBride to O'Ceallaigh, 2 May 1936 (NA, D/T, S1899).
[96] MacEntee to Honorary Secretaries, 27 January 1936 (UCD, MacEntee Papers, P67/453).
[97] 'Report of Cabinet Committee on Old IRA—Preferences in Employment' (UCD, Aiken Papers, P104/2893 (1)).
[98] *The Way to Peace* (UCD, Aiken Papers, P104/2868 (1)).

prevented, and the removal of the oath had opened the democratic way to all those who wanted to pursue their objectives peacefully. Any minority group that now wanted to pursue its objectives by force could only rouse the resistance of the majority and civil war would ensue.[99] The following week at Galway, de Valera appealed to young people to realize that the IRA won the support of the people only when it functioned as the army of the people, acknowledging the authority of the people's parliament and government. Until these conditions were repeated the use of the name could only be a usurpation.[100] The press would soon be banned from using the name IRA in its references to the organization. In New Ross on 14 August 1936 de Valera responded to Cosgrave's suggestion that he was a recent 'convert' to the principles he was now defending. After the Treaty was accepted by the Dail in January 1921, de Valera maintained that he urged the anti-treaty IRA in March to keep their allegiance to the Ministry of Defence, accepted Labour's proposal at the Mansion House conference to postpone an election on the Treaty for six months, and shortly after fighting began, supported a proposal by the lord mayor and archbishop of Dublin for a ceasefire that would enable the Dail to sit and resolve its differences. Crucially, he argued that at no time between the signing of the Treaty and the civil war did he and the other leaders of Fianna Fail reject majority rule as a principle of order, or the right of the Irish people to decide upon the Treaty issue.[101]

The 'Executive *Coup d'état*' thesis, formulated in 1936, was de Valera's formal working out of this position on the civil war. Immediately after the Treaty had been accepted by the Dail cabinet in December 1921, he publicly declared that 'the great test of our people has come', and urged that that there was 'a definite constitutional way of solving our political differences'.[102] Although the Treaty could be accepted by the Dail it was not within its competence to disestablish the Republic, which could only be done by the votes of the people. In this vein Griffith had promised that republican institutions would be preserved intact until the people in an election had pronounced upon the Treaty. According to de Valera, 'our presence in the Dail during the whole of the period up to June is evidence that we accepted the principle of majority rule and the right of the people to decide finally on the question at issue'.[103] At the Sinn Fein *Ard Fheis* in February 1922, it was agreed to delay the election for three months, so that when the electors went to the polls to decide between the Free State and the Republic, they would have the constitution before them. In the meantime, the electoral register should be reformed to include large numbers of young people who were excluded. At the Mansion House Conference in April it was suggested by Labour that the army be united, a strong stable executive be set up, and that there be six months' delay before the election took place. These proposals were accepted by de

---

[99] *The Way to Peace* (UCD, Aiken Papers, (P104/1459).
[100] Ibid. (P104/1459 (7)).
[101] Ibid. (P104/1459 (9)).
[102] 'Civil War 1922–24: Historical Summary by President de Valera'.
[103] Ibid.

Valera but not by the Provisional Government. Then on 20 May the pact with Collins was signed, which remained effective until polling day, and which ensured that 'the Treaty as such was not an issue in the election'. Without warning the constitution was not published until the morning of the election. After the election had taken place de Valera still expected the coalition government to be set up. Instead the Provisional Government, under British pressure, attacked the Four Courts, postponed the meeting of the Second Dail, and failed to convene the Third Dail. In effect 'by what can only be called an Executive coup d'etat they proceeded to change the established state and substitute another'.[104]

This account of the origins of the civil war was true to the extent that in the spring of 1922 de Valera had opted for a policy of delaying the decision on the Treaty so that the two wings of the IRA would be reunited. He had also maintained that once the Dail had accepted the Treaty, the issue would have to be settled by force or by votes. However, during the Mansion House Conference in April he himself rejected a proposal for a plebiscite on the Treaty, choosing instead to opt for Labour's proposal to delay the election for six months. In the meantime he hoped that passions could subside, personalities could disappear, and the fundamental differences between the two sides could be appreciated.[105] De Valera promised to use his influence with the IRA Executive to have them accept these proposals, which would involve the reunification of the IRA. Indeed he maintained that it was not the June electoral result as such, but the assassination of Sir Henry Wilson in London, that destroyed the peaceful settlement that the republican party in the Dail had been so earnestly working towards. Once British pressure had been applied, the Provisional Government then proceeded to act as if the people had formally accepted the Treaty and the constitution and had voted for the disestablishment of the Republic. This is what drove the moderate anti-treatyites into giving support for the IRA Executive's policy.[106]

This interpretation stands in sharp contrast to the pro-treaty view that de Valera actually incited the IRA towards civil war in the spring of 1922, and refused to accept the electorate's verdict on the Treaty afterwards. In September 1933 de Valera was asked by Revd John Sincox, of St. Edmund's College, Ware, how he could reconcile his present belief in majority rule with his 'wading through blood' speech in Thurles on 20 March 1922.[107] He replied that the speech was part of a campaign to secure the continued support of the majority for the Republic, and that his present government's reluctance to exceed their mandate in the area of constitutional reform was further proof of his respect for the will of the majority.[108] Indeed in the late 1930s Fianna Fail maintained that its leaders had never rejected majority rule as the decisive rule of order: one party document cited the use of the 1918 general election mandate to establish the Republic as an example.

---

[104] Ibid.
[105] *Irish Independent*, 15 April 1922.
[106] Speech at New Ross, 14 August 1936 (UCD, de Valera Papers, P104/1459 (9)).
[107] Sincox to de Valera, 16 September 1933 (UCD, de Valera Papers, P150/1612).
[108] De Valera to Sincox, 2 October 1933 (UCD, de Valera Papers, P150/1612).

It also said that in the run-up to the civil war, while the Fianna Fail elite refused to accept the right of the Dail to disestablish the Republic, they accepted Griffith and Collins' government as the government of the majority. Since the people never disestablished the Treaty in a proper election, their civil war effort after June 'was an effort to maintain the existing state which had been set up by a vote of the majority of the people'. Later elections, such as that of 1923, were held in such irregular conditions that they could not be regarded as expressions of the public will, and the first decisive election was that of September 1927, after which Fianna Fail accepted the de facto authority of the government if not the manner in which it came to power.[109]

Such arguments were grist to the mill to a party seeking majority support at the polls, but whereas there was substance to the view that the 1923 election was not a proper register of public preferences, de Valera's own attitude to the people's 'real will' was hardly democratic. On 15 February 1923 he had told the Neutral IRA:

It is obvious that as long as England's threat of war is hanging over our people an election will not truly indicate their wishes, and it would be most unfair to them to put them into the position of voluntarily appearing to give up their birthright. Unless there was almost a certainty that the people would reject the 'Treaty' by a substantial majority and thus vindicate the national claims and their own national spirit, it would be wrong to put any such issue before them.[110]

In 1926, when Fianna Fail was founded, he argued that nearly half of the electorate were still prevented from expressing their preferences in elections, and that two-thirds were opposed in spirit to the existing regime. The 'pretence at democracy' and the 'misrepresentation' of the 'real' wishes of the people was the main obstacle to any advance of national lines at that time.[111] It followed that the real will of the people would be expressed when the oath was removed. In 1934, however, he then remarked that three-fourths of the people were nationalists who wanted complete independence, but fear of the economic and military consequences still deterred them from demanding a Republic.[112] Looking back at the whole period in 1936, he then confessed that his recognition after 1923 that the majority of the people were not willing to vote for the immediate establishment of the Republic led him to change Sinn Fein's policy on the basis of the ceasefire proposals. The 'real will' was as elusive as ever, but he was convinced that Fianna Fail would one day be as great and as united a movement for Irish national freedom as Sinn Fein was after 1918.[113]

---

[109] 'Proofs That Majority Rule as a Rule of Order and as a Means of Unifying the Nation Have Never Been Denied by the Present Republican Leaders—the Leaders of Fianna Fail' (UCD, de Valera Papers, P150/1532).

[110] De Valera to Burke, 15 February 1923 (UCD, de Valera Papers, P150/1793).

[111] Speech at inaugural meeting of Fianna Fail, at La Scala Theatre, May 1926 (UCD, de Valera Papers, P150/2082).

[112] 'Interview with Dr Joseph Chapire', 29 May 1934 (UCD, de Valera Papers, P150/2284).

[113] Speech at New Ross, 14 August 1936 (UCD, de Valera Papers, P104/1459 (9)).

The Fianna Fáil thesis that their leaders had never opposed the majority rule principle is open to the simple objection that the anti-treatyites unequivocally opposed the Provisional Government's proposal for a plebiscite on the Treaty issue at the Mansion House Conference, and only consented to the June election when guaranteed a share of seats proportionate to their existing representation in the Second Dáil. In his *Way to Peace* speech in March 1934 de Valera practically admitted as much, stating that he perhaps did not learn early enough that we must take majority rule as determining policy, and be content with it 'even when we think and are convinced that it is wrong'.[114] Once the Treaty had been signed, de Valera said that it was primarily up to the cabinet to accept or reject it. Once they had accepted it, he pushed the responsibility onto the Dáil and that failing, onto the people, whose verdict he also rejected. In his own language he was looking for a 'brake' on the shift in public sentiment that occurred after the Treaty was signed. On the other hand, an open election was bound to lead to polarization, so the anti-treatyites' argument that they had tried to prevent the civil war is still plausible. Moreover, the argument that the Fianna Fáil leadership had done their utmost to prevent a reoccurrence of civil war conditions after 1922 is sustainable. As early as January 1923 de Valera wrote that internal peace was the most urgent need of the nation, and all the anti-treaty elements should combine in telling Britain that 'anything that stood in the way of internal peace had to go'.[115] In 1936 he told his New Ross audience that his ceasefire proposals had been intended to lead to government stability and the healing of civil war wounds, but the government's insistence on the oath proved to be the stumbling block.[116] After the electoral amendment bill in 1927, Fianna Fáil had to take the oath since civil war would have been the likely result if peaceful methods were not tried.[117] After its removal in 1933 de Valera believed he had removed a cause of internal disorder and made majority rule 'an effective reality'.[118] Then, within a matter of weeks of their coming to power in 1932, the Blueshirt phenomenon threatened to recreate the same conditions Fianna Fáil had been founded to avert, and only the passing of the Wearing of Uniforms Bill in March 1934 allowed the government to overcome the danger.[119] It is doubtful whether the oath was the root cause of the civil war in the first place, but between 1933 and 1938 Fianna Fáil's strategy of marginalizing anti-treaty opposition to the Free State through revision of the Treaty was generally a success.

---

[114] *The Way to Peace* (UCD, Aiken Papers, P104/2868 (1)).
[115] De Valera to Minister for Home Affairs, 6 January 1923 (NA, D/T, S1297).
[116] Speech at New Ross, 14 August 1936 (UCD, de Valera Papers, P104/1459 (9)).
[117] 'The Story of Fianna Fáil 1926–1945' (UCD, de Valera Papers, P150/2083).
[118] 'Interview given by President to Mr. Rue, New York Daily News', 10 October 1934 (UCD, de Valera Papers, P150/2284).
[119] 'The Story of Fianna Fáil 1926–1945' (UCD, de Valera Papers, P150/2083).

CONCLUSION

The anti-treaty interpretation of the civil war has been neglected in most historical accounts of the conflict, but it is impossible to understand the nature of Irish political development after 1923 without taking it into consideration. After all, if their ideals in 1922 were so incoherent and indefensible, it is difficult to explain why Fianna Fail proved so successful after 1926.[120] Their interpretation of what happened in 1922 had two strands: the first emphasized the defence of the Republic as a lawfully established government, while the second emphasized the unconstitutionality of the pro-treaty project. In this sense Regan is right to suggest that a constitutional consensus, premised on a disposition to see political conflict in constitutional terms, survived the civil war.[121] Both strands concurred on the bad faith of their opponents in deserting the Republic, but as the heat of civil war receded, it was primarily the latter strain that proved important. Identifying the oath as the main cause of the civil war had the advantage of basing their opposition to the Free State on a democratic principle, but it also enabled Fianna Fail to speak for the whole republican movement until 1933.

For a Fianna Fail party anxious to establish its democratic credentials after 1926, it was the constitutionalist rather than militarist means of defending the Republic that mattered. In none of the three speeches de Valera made in 1936 did he mention the 1916 Rising, the declaration of a Republic in 1919, or the legitimacy of the Second Dail. The historical legitimacy that could be derived from the revolutionary period cut little ice with the electorate, and only the issue of the oath figured at all in the various election campaigns between 1926 and 1933. Given the violent birth of the state the party's concern to have a constitutional self-image might be considered surprising, but apart from the fact that the public, as de Valera admitted, was largely constitutionalist in its orientation, Fianna Fail also wanted to show their supporters that republican objectives could be achieved by constitutional means, which Sean Lemass later recalled as a chief task of the party in its early history.[122] Their hope was that by removing the oath from the constitution, they would encourage all republicans to take part in the constitutional process, which reflected de Valera's view that the oath was the cause of the civil war division in the first place. Since the party's avowed aim after 1926 was to prevent a reoccurrence of civil war conditions, it was also important to stress that between January and June 1922 de Valera strove constantly 'to save the people from the dark fate that hung over them'.[123]

Of course historical truth was sacrificed on the altar of political expediency, but neither side in the Free State was really truthful with regard to the course of events that led to civil war. Publicly de Valera made no mention of the occupation

[120] Michael McDowell, *Irish Times*, 24 January 1998.
[121] J. M. Regan, *The Irish Counter-revolution 1921–36: Treatyite Politics and Settlement in Independent Ireland* (Dublin, 1999), 377.
[122] See J. Horgan, 'Arms Dumps and the IRA 1923–32', *History Today*, 48/2 (February 1998), 16.
[123] 'The Story of Fianna Fail 1926–1945' (UCD, de Valera Papers, P150/2083).

of the Four Courts as a factor in the equation, but the evidence suggests that he believed that the more extreme IRA men had created the conditions that led to civil war. On 2 March 1923 he told Lynch that he would not be associated with a policy that led the people to believe they could gain more from the British than was possible, since the civil war was the direct result of a policy of that kind.[124] Moreover, if the IRA Executive was privately held responsible for the civil war, it is a short step from this position to adopting a strategy that would ultimately marginalize their influence in the Free State. On the other hand, the Fianna Fail position would have been undercut if de Valera had conceded publicly that the civil war resulted simply from an army mutiny, and the issue of the oath enabled the party to stress the constitutional nature of their resistance. Nevertheless, de Valera's role was not as innocent as he later claimed. He had helped legitimize the IRA Executive's position by publicly rejecting an election on the Treaty, and although the public was certainly not being presented with a free choice in 1922, the decision as to whether to accept peace or to wage war is probably the most important one any public can make. In 1934 de Valera told the Dail that the rules for governing a country were more or less 'rough and ready' and could not operate if people responded with 'ifs' and 'buts', but that was de Valera's attitude to the Dail vote on the Treaty.[125] Once the civil war had started, it was not consistent, as A.E. pointed out, to decry the influence of fear on the people in the spring of 1922, and then to try to use fear to get the public to yield to your own policy.[126] Nevertheless, given the morass in which the anti-treatyites found themselves in December 1922, and bearing in mind that their interpretation of the civil war ultimately became the dominant one in the state, what was remark-able was the creative way in which that interpretation evolved over the next two decades. Indeed, in March 1939, when seeking Fine Gael support for the Offences against the State Act, de Valera went a step further, publicly stating that the Provisional government had resisted Lloyd George's ultimatum in June 1922, and instead blamed the civil war on 'a spark out there in the streets'.[127]

---

[124] De Valera to Lynch, 1 March 1923 (UCD, de Valera Papers, P150/1749).
[125] *The Way to Peace* (UCD, Aiken Papers, P104/2868 (1)).
[126] *Freeman's Journal*, 29 December 1922.
[127] *Dail Debates*, 1 March 1939, 2506.

9

Historians and the Civil War

The civil war happened too recently in Irish political memory to generate the kinds of rival interpretive schools that have marked the historiography of the American civil war. The American debate has seen historians first emphasize the role of individual leaders in producing conflict, then seen them shift attention from the 1890s onwards to the conflict situation itself—a situation over which politicians could exert little control—and finally experience a return to an emphasis on the 'needless' nature of the civil war and to the task of allocating responsibility for it.[1] Regardless of these shifts, and bearing in mind the allure of 'the needless war doctrine' to historians of southern sympathies, the dominant interpretation has, however, been the 'nationalist' one, which sees the American civil war as an 'irrepressible' conflict fought about a fundamental issue, slavery, over which reasonable and patriotic politicians could not be expected to compromise.[2] Moreover, holding that there are some conflicts that the normal democratic process is unable to resolve, many American historians have expressed satisfaction at the outcome of the civil war—the Union saved, slavery abolished, and the south eventually reconciled—so much so that some regard the civil war as a positive event in the emergence of American democracy.[3]

In comparison the Irish historical debate is fragmented and remains fixed on the role of personalities in producing conflict. So great has this emphasis on personal responsibility been that there has been little analysis of the issue of causality itself. As Carlton Younger observed in 1968, it is easy to pinpoint the events that led to the Irish civil war, but less easy to distinguish the causes of the conflict.[4] It took the Americans just over thirty years to depart from the conspiratorial mode of explaining their civil war, but the Irish debate is still framed by two books, both closely identified with the views of rival nationalist leaders, that emerged before the Second World War.[5] Naturally, if one believes that de Valera's behaviour really was a cause of the civil war, this should imply that the

---

[1] See W. Dray, 'Some Causal Accounts of the American Civil War', *Daedalus*, 91/3 (1962), 578–99.

[2] T. N. Bonner, 'Civil War Historians and the Needless War Doctrine', *Journal of the History of Ideas*, 17 (1956), 193–216.

[3] T. J. Pressly, *Americans Interpret Their Civil War* (New York, 1962), 222–3.

[4] C. Younger, *Ireland's Civil War* (London, 1968), 506.

[5] P. S. O'Hegarty, *The Victory of Sinn Fein* (Dublin, 1924; 1998); and D. MacArdle, *The Irish Republic* (London, 1938).

civil war, at least in the form it took, was avoidable. However, an emphasis on the negative role played by de Valera is not incompatible with the view that the Irish civil war was fought over an 'irrepressible' issue, that of democracy, and this combination has been typical of much recent writing.[6] De Valera himself believed that he could not have done more to avert the fighting before 28 June 1922, and once it started, saw no realistic basis for peace.[7] In short the Irish civil war may also have been an 'irrepressible' conflict, fought over competing versions of democracy and freedom, but the dominant view now is that one side of that conflict was very much in the wrong.[8] As elsewhere where history is written from the winners' perspective, 'the actions of the losers appear in hindsight to be fragmented, illogical, and incoherent'.[9] In this respect the Irish literature lacks the impulse towards sectional reconciliation characteristic of the American nationalist tradition. Nevertheless, there is a virtual consensus that the civil war strengthened the impulse towards democracy in Irish life. Indeed Brendan Clifford has remarked that the Irish should take satisfaction in the fact that they established a democracy as the outcome of the civil war.[10]

There are therefore strong elements of a nationalist interpretation of the Irish civil war already in place, closely identified (as in America) with the winners' point of view. Historians sympathetic to the pro-treaty side mostly see the civil war as the product of the existence of rival traditions within the Sinn Fein movement and locate its chief cause in the character of Irish nationalism. Once the Treaty exposed the existence of these traditions, the conflict was 'irrepressible' because the issue of democratic legitimacy was not one the Provisional government could have been expected to compromise on.[11] Curran, for example, argues that only British pressure had made a united nationalist front possible after 1916, and once this pressure was relaxed, the division between moderates and extremists inevitably reappeared.[12] This approach views the Irish civil war through the lens of democratic theory, and celebrates the state-building achievements of the pro-treaty elite. In contrast, historians sympathetic to the republican side see British pressure as the crucial variable, in the absence of which the internal

---

[6] See F. Costello, *The Irish Revolution and Its Aftermath 1916–1923: Years of Revolt* (Dublin, 2003); T. Garvin, *1922: The Birth of Irish Democracy* (Dublin, 1996); M. Laffan, *The Resurrection of Ireland: The Sinn Fein Party 1916–1923* (Cambridge, 1999). All three stress the issue of democracy as well as the destructive influence of de Valera.

[7] C. Townshend, *Ireland: The Twentieth Century* (London, 1999), 113.

[8] To the books listed in the previous two notes one can add T. P. Coogan, *De Valera: Long Fellow Long Shadow* (London, 1993); B. Girvin, *From Union to Union* (Dublin, 2002); and A. Jackson, *Ireland 1798–1998: Politics and War* (Blackwell, 1999).

[9] C. Christie, *A Modern History of South-East Asia: Decolonization, Nationalism, and Separatism* (London and New York, 2000).

[10] B. Clifford, *The Irish Civil War: The Conflict That Formed the State* (Cork, 1993), 4.

[11] The classic statement following that of O'Hegarty is Garvin, *1922: The Birth of Irish Democracy*. See also Costello, *The Irish Revolution and Its Aftermath 1916–1923*; M. Laffan, *The Resurrection of Ireland*; E. O'Halpin, *Defending Ireland: The Irish State and Its Enemies since 1922* (Oxford, 1999); Girvin, *From Union to Union*; G. Walker, 'Propaganda and Conservative Nationalism during the Irish Civil War, 1922–1923', *Eire-Ireland*, 22/4 (Winter 1987), 116.

[12] J. Curran, *The Birth of the Irish Free State 1921–1923* (Mobile, Ala., 1980), 280.

divisions would have been surmountable. From this perspective, political circumstances rather than the character of Irish nationalism were of primary
importance. This chapter tries to adjudicate between these two perspectives and
establish whether there can be a 'nationalist' interpretation of the Irish civil war
in terms of three issues: whether the divisions of 1922 had an historical pedigree, whether these divisions were 'irrepressible' once the Treaty was signed, and
whether the fruits of the war can be held to justify its occurrence. Naturally, if
such an interpretation could be justified, the society as a whole could rest more
easily with its civil war memories. On the other hand, if the civil war was
unforeseeable, if it could have been avoided even after the Treaty was signed,
and if the constitutional fruits of the civil war could have been arrived at anyway,
there is less reason for self-satisfaction. Since no individual 'revisionist' historian
falls neatly into a 'nationalist' camp, the non-emergence of a self-conscious
nationalist 'school' probably tells us as much about the legacy of the civil war
as anything else.

TWO TRADITIONS?

To establish that the Irish civil war was 'an irrepressible conflict', one would first
have to demonstrate that the civil war revealed the existence of rival traditions in
the Sinn Fein movement. Of course ever since the establishment of the Irish
Republican Brotherhood in 1858, the dominant preference of Irish nationalists for
some form of Home Rule had been challenged by a small but vocal minority who
advocated the republican ideal of complete separation. The early history of
organizations like the GAA was clearly punctuated by constant power struggles
between the two tendencies.[13] Nevertheless, we are concerned here with the issues
that touched the imagination of the Sinn Fein generation, and these arose
primarily in the context of the revolt against British rule between 1916 and 1921.
Since Sinn Fein came to pre-eminence as a result of the first democratic election
to take place in Ireland in 1918, and since much of its strategy was influenced by
the Allied victory in the First World War and the promise of self-determination
afterwards, those issues can be reduced to the question of democratic legitimacy.

For a long time the dominant view of the Irish 'revolution' was provided by
Dorothy MacArdle's 1938 *The Irish Republic*, which emphasized the strong democratic credentials of the republican cause. She accepted that the original Sinn Fein
party was not republican, but the effects of the 1916 Rising and the promise of
international justice after the war transformed the movement. The 1918 general
election was clearly seen by the public as a plebiscite on the issue of separation,
and the result was an overwhelming majority declaring for the Republic. Then the
results of the municipal and urban elections that took place in January 1920, and

---

[13] W. F. Mandle, 'The IRB and the Beginnings of the Gaelic Athletic Association', *Irish Historical Studies*, 20 (1977), 418–38.

of the June 1920 elections to rural councils, were a further vote of confidence in Sinn Fein's programme. As a result every county council, every rural district council, and every board of guardians in Leinster, Munster, and Connacht gave allegiance to the Dail government.[14] Furthermore, in his electoral address for the 19 May 1921 general election de Valera declared that the issue was 'nothing less than the legitimacy of the Republic'. In that election, all the 124 seats in the 26 counties were captured by Sinn Fein candidates in an uncontested poll, and there was total agreement on the goal of the Republic prior to the truce of 11 July 1921. On 2 April 1921 Collins himself remarked that 'the same effort which would get us Dominion Home Rule would get us a Republic'.[15] However, when the Second Dail met in public for the first time on 16 August 1921, de Valera told the delegates that the prior elections had not given a mandate for a form of government, but for Irish freedom and independence. He added, however, that though his government were not 'doctrinaire republicans' Irish independence 'could not be realized at the present time in any other way so suitably as through a Republic'.[16] There was no compromise on the Republic. Had there been, the various elections would have been treated in conference as 'a mere romantic gestures', as indeed they have been in later historiography.[17]

P. S. O'Hegarty's 1924 *The Victory of Sinn Fein* was a revisionist elegy to the leader he regarded as the noblest spirit of the Sinn Fein movement, Arthur Griffith. He recalls that at as early as 1905 or 1906 Griffith had rejected the adoption of a thoroughly separatist constitution for Sinn Fein on the grounds that the mass of the people were not separatist, and would not support such a policy.[18] In preparations for the new Sinn Fein constitution to be presented to the *Ard Fheis* in October 1917 Griffith would not agree to bind himself to a republican form of government, whereas republicans on the national council insisted on it as the only valid objective. The result was the compromise formula of 1917.[19] What explains how the public came to give their full support for Sinn Fein in the 1918 general election was Britain's coercive policy, particularly over the conscription crisis, and the shift in sentiment away from the Irish Parliamentary Party among sections such as the clergy, the businessmen, and the large farmers, who had hitherto supported Home Rule. Their emotions had been heightened by the events of the previous two years, but the onus was still on the party to explain to them what Sinn Fein actually stood for. When the Dail took the oath to the Republic in 1919, de Valera told it that he understood the pledge to mean only that he would do his best for the Irish people in any given circumstances. However, Sinn Fein carefully handpicked their candidates for the 1921 elections, and the result was a parliament that, as de Valera reminded it, represented only one section of the people: 112 of the members had already served terms of imprisonment.[20] When the invitation to negotiate came from Lloyd George in September

[14] MacArdle, *The Irish Republic*, 366.   [15] Ibid., 465   [16] Ibid., 514.
[17] Ibid., 536.   [18] O'Hegarty, *The Victory of Sinn Fein*, 21.
[19] MacArdle, *The Irish Republic*, 241–3.   [20] Ibid., 471.

1921 de Valera's acceptance of negotiations on 30 September 1921 implied in itself a willingness to compromise on the Republic.

O'Hegarty's book was published only a year after the civil war but his interpretation has been supported by three recent books, this time based on systematic archival research. In *The Resurrection of Ireland*, Michael Laffan emphasizes the diversity of views within Sinn Fein. By 1917 few Sinn Feiners were royalists who regarded an Irish Kingdom 'as a positive aim worth striving for'; yet many believed that the republican policy would only alienate the Unionists and make agreement with Britain impossible. Although voters in the 1918 general election may have been voting just to spite the government or to punish the Parliamentary Party, they had little control over how their votes would be interpreted by Sinn Fein.[21] Laffan quotes the recollection of a judge in 1948 who identified four strands of thought within the movement: those for whom the Republic was an article of faith, those who thought it a valid goal that could be obtained under the existing circumstances, those (perhaps a majority) who regarded it as no more than a symbol of independence, and a few who thought it a bogus ideal.[22] Unfortunately, the unification of so many disparate elements in Sinn Fein could not force the radicals to reassess their ideals after 1917, and 'they retained their convenient devotion to the image of an abstract "Ireland" which existed quite independently of the people who happened to live on the island'.[23]

For Laffan the Irish revolution 'depended on freak circumstances for its initial impetus', and was reined in, at least in part, 'by an organized expression of mass civilian opinion'.[24] This is substantially the argument Tom Garvin makes in *1922: The Birth of Irish Democracy*. According to Garvin, the 1918 and 1921 general elections were not democratic elections at all. In the former, many seats were uncontested, and there was much intimidation by what was becoming the IRA. There was also plenty of impersonation and stuffing of ballot boxes. The dramatic events of the previous two years turned the election into a 'stampede' of young newly enfranchised male voters, and the Dail it elected contained only one party, Sinn Fein: the remnants of the Parliamentary Party, the Unionists, and some Labour Unionists stayed away. Even worse, in 1921 Sinn Fein nominees, generally approved by a small coterie surrounding Collins and Harry Boland, were elected in uncontested constituencies as had been the norm in many parts of Ireland for decades.[25] The 1922 election, where the Labour Party, the Farmers Party, and many Independents came forward to contest the election, was the first election to produce a genuinely representative assembly, and ended the 'romantic posturing' that passed for politics in pre-treaty Ireland.[26]

---

[21] Laffan, *The Resurrection of Ireland*, 244.
[22] Ibid., 243–4.
[23] Ibid., 215.
[24] Ibid., Preface.
[25] Garvin, *1922: The Birth of Irish Democracy*, 39.
[26] Ibid., 51.

Garvin's perspective is largely supported by Michael Farry's rigorous work on the civil war in Sligo, a county where fighting during the civil war was more intense than during the War of Independence. Sligo's record during 'the Tan war' may have been poor, but the truce was seen in the county as a victory for the physical force tradition, the IRA's officers were all free for the whole of the truce period, and its organization was revitalized in the latter half of 1921. The impact of the truce on the local IRA's resources and self-image was to fundamentally condition its response to the Treaty.[27] By 1922 the local IRA men had developed a tendency to despise 'politicians', and would brook no competition from them in their desire to be the saviours of the Irish people.[28] Indeed Farry provides a clear picture of how the hold of politicians on the Sinn Fein party had been weakened during the War of Independence. For the 1918 election the Sinn Fein candidates had been chosen by its *Comhairle Ceantair*, but by the 1921 general election few Sinn Fein clubs actually existed in Sligo, and the selections were made by IRA commandants. Those selected were high-ranking IRA officers and were elected unopposed.[29] However, Farry stresses that although the divisions between the local politicians and the IRA in Sligo had already been established before the Treaty, a split was not inevitable. Instead they suggested a division was possible and one possible line of fraction was between those who were interested in politics per se and those whose main interest was in armed struggle.[30]

If civil–military relations within Sinn Fein had become problematic by 1921, from the nationalist perspective the issue of majority rule also had clear constitutional antecedents, and the rival traditions within Sinn Fein were exposed by the Treaty. Hancock saw in the 1917 compromise the existence of two fundamentally different conceptions of independence with a long lineage in Irish nationalist politics:

> On the one side was the dogma of the undying republic, won by the blood of the martyrs, living in its own right, needing no ratification by popular vote, but needing only resolution and arms. For this living Republic Sinn Fein was trustee, claiming full loyalty and obedience. Here in germ was the party state. But on the other side was nationalist democracy, equally resolute for Irish independence, but admitting the right of the Irish people to choose the symbolism and forms of government in which that independence would express itself. This theory subjected Sinn Fein itself to the suffrage of the people.[31]

Today there is virtual consensus among historians that the issue of democratic legitimacy was central to the civil war. The argument originated with O'Hegarty, who argued that the Free State's triumph in 1923 was a victory of the people against military despotism, a victory of the ballot box over the bullet.[32] In 1980 Curran argued that behind the controversy over the Treaty was a more

[27] M. Farry, *The Aftermath of Revolution: Sligo 1921–23* (Dublin, 2000), 2.
[28] Ibid., 18.
[29] Ibid., 21.
[30] Ibid., 20.
[31] K. Hancock, *Survey of Commonwealth Affairs*, vol. 1 (London, New York, and Toronto, 1937), 104.
[32] O'Hegarty, *The Victory of Sinn Fein*, 101.

fundamental division of opinion over the right of the Irish people to rule themselves.[33] More recently, O'Halpin shares the views of Garvin and Laffan that the conflict was fought between those who thought that the people should rule, and those who thought that an unaccountable elite should rule.[34] Keogh goes further and compares the IRA's acts of intimidation and vandalism in the spring of 1922 to what was to happen in Fascist Italy and Nazi Germany in the 1920s and 1930s.[35] Finally, Jackson notes that by comparison with their opponents, the Free State cause admirably preserved the ascendancy of democratically elected politicians over the fighting men, even if it was these same civilians who pushed for the more extreme measures taken during the civil war.[36]

From this perspective the civil war's basic cause was the anti-treatyites' insistence that there be no democratic appeal to the people on the Treaty issue.[37] Lee writes that

The civil war was fought ostensibly over the Treaty, and particularly the Oath. But the Treaty was merely the occasion, not the cause, of the civil war. The cause was the basic conflict in nationalist doctrine between majority right and divine right. The issue was whether the Irish people had the right to chose their own government at any time according to their judgement of the existing circumstances. The clash might have been evaded but for the Treaty, but once the issue surfaced the choice lay between democracy and dictatorship.[38]

However, it is one thing to say that the pro-treaty argument had greater democratic legitimacy in 1922; it is quite another to argue that the existence of the traditions was the cause of the civil war. Indeed Lee's argument is contradictory, since if the clash between majority rule and divine right 'might have been' averted but for the Treaty, the divide cannot be held to be the only cause of the civil war. Lee concedes that perhaps only a minority of the IRA held that their will should be mandatory on the public in all circumstances, in which case it was also the nature of the circumstances in 1922 that explains their rejection of majority rule.[39]

Indeed historians may not have emphasized the depth of the original divide had strong evidence in favour of such a thesis not been produced by the Treaty split. Laffan suggests that from the internal divisions that emerged once the Treaty was signed, and from the voting behaviour in the 1922 election, most of Sinn Fein regarded the Republic as a worthy objective that could nonetheless be sacrificed in a compromise settlement, but this is reading a normative preference for accepting the Treaty out of what becomes a practical imperative as a result of it. Indeed if the majority of Sinn Fein regarded the Republic as 'a worthy

[33] Curran, *The Birth of the Irish Free State 1921–1923*, 230.
[34] O'Halpin, *Defending Ireland*, 26.
[35] D. Keogh, *Twentieth-Century Ireland: Nation and State* (Dublin, 1994), 5.
[36] Jackson, *Ireland 1798–1998: Politics and War*, 266; on the executions see J. M. Regan, *The Irish Counter-revolution 1921–36: Treatyite Politics and Settlement in Independent Ireland* (Dublin, 1999), 121.
[37] O'Hegarty, *The Victory of Sinn Fein*, 88.
[38] J. Lee, *Ireland 1912–1985: Politics and Society* (Cambridge, 1989), 67.
[39] Ibid., 68.

objective', what was at stake in early 1922 was not whether that objective had democratic legitimacy, but whether it could be achieved given the existing geo-political circumstances; in which case, the old division between pragmatists and idealists becomes relevant to the debate. Laffan sees the 1917 formula (inspired by de Valera) as 'a fatal step', since the republican policy justified the leaders 'in ignoring or dismissing the views of most Irish people'.[40] This raises the question of what alternative programme would have been more representative of the public from 1918 on, since he himself accepts that Home Rule was decisively rejected in the 1918 election, and it would have maintained the same symbolic connections with the Crown as dominion status. Is Laffan seriously suggesting that Sinn Fein could have won their electoral victory in 1918 on the basis of the dual kingdom model, and at the same time persuaded international opinion of Ireland's right to self-determination? The other possibility is that no programme would have been truly representative of the public, since the public regarded the issue of status 'as being of relatively little importance'.[41] This may be so, but if so, why make the issue of democratic legitimacy the lynchpin of your interpretation?

What then of the argument that the civil war had clear constitutional antece-dents? Laffan's thesis is not helped by his argument that the 1917 compromise was not much of a concession on the part of the radicals, since most within the movement had objected to the wisdom not the desirability of a Republic. In other words, once it was recognized, there was little possibility of the public rejecting the Republic in a referendum, which rather casts doubts on the view that the republican principle had been foisted on an indifferent public by an unrepresen-tative elite.[42] For Lee popular sovereignty means allowing the public at any time to chose their own government according to their interpretation of the existing circumstances.[43] This justifies the standpoint the Provisional government took in 1922. For the anti-treatyites, as Regan has argued, the issue was not whether the public had the right to be sovereign, but whether they had the right to do so free of British pressure.[44] This was the logic of the 1917 formula since republicans believed that sovereignty was a prerequisite to the electorate expressing itself freely.[45] As a species of democratic theory this is bogus, but is reflected in current international law, which invalidates treaties accompanied by the threat of force. In the context of Ireland in 1922, with the expressed will of the people having been frustrated for four years, and with the Treaty being accompanied by a threat of 'terrible and immediate war' should it be rejected, this view certainly informed attitudes. In the Dail on 21 December Gavan Duffy, a Treaty signatory, stated:

---

[40] Laffan, *The Resurrection of Ireland*, 243.
[41] Ibid., 247.
[42] Ibid., 118.
[43] Lee, *Ireland 1912–1985*, 67.
[44] See J. Regan, 'Review of Tom Garvin's *1922: The Birth of Irish Democracy*', *History Ireland*, 5/2 (1997), 55.
[45] Regan, *The Irish Counter-revolution*, 69.

We found ourselves faced with these alternatives, either to save the national dignity by unyielding principle, or to save the lives of the people by yielding to a force majeure, and that is why I stand where I do. We lost the Republic of Ireland in order to save the people of Ireland.[46]

Since any public in a protracted military conflict will generally favour the power capable of bringing the fighting to a close, the decision to refer a decision on its continuance to the people inevitably involves a military victory for the side that holds the military advantage at that stage.[47] In this context democracy inevitably involves a recognition of *force majeure*, and for this reason Regan argues that a coerced agreement like the Treaty had the effect of upsetting the constitutional consensus in Irish society, by dislodging the IRA from their obligation to majority rule.[48] Costello sees an irony in the fact that de Valera and Brugha risked their lives in favour of Irish self-determination between 1919 and 1921, but were unwilling to consult the same people in 1922.[49] However, the anti-treaty argument in 1922 was not that the people had no right to be sovereign, but that they had a right to be so free of British pressure. As such the Treaty was not an exercise in self-determination, and though the position taken by de Valera and his followers in 1922 was not democratic, neither was it exclusively undemocratic.[50]

In any case, that severe differences of opinion might arise out of the 1917 formula was not foreseen at the time, and the idea that it foreordained a civil war fought between those believing they were defending popular sovereignty and those believing they were defending popular sovereignty if Britain's threat of war were removed is clearly ludicrous. It is one thing to say that the Treaty exposed the existence of rival traditions within Sinn Fein (which it did); another to argue that these traditions would have lead to civil war anyway. There was after all a middle ground between them, as expressed by the Dail's support for the pact in May 1922. As Lyons observed, the fact that the first preference vote for third parties in the pact election was also higher than that of either Treaty side suggests that the electorate wanted to cry 'a plague on both your houses'.[51] The consequence of the 'Four Glorious Years' for the movement was not only that both civil war sides would have constitutional arguments, rooted in varieties of democratic majoritarianism, at their disposal, but also that the outbreak of fighting can only be explained as a consequence of the Treaty and the failure of the political elite to combine realpolitik in international affairs with effective strategies for consolidation at home. Historians differ greatly in their judgement of when, after the truce, conflict was unavoidable, and so far nobody has located that moment in the pre-truce phase.

---

[46] E. Neeson, *The Civil War 1922–1923* (Dublin, 1973), 76.
[47] See F. Barry's review of T. Garvin's *1922* in *Irish Review*, 20 (2000), 157–61.
[48] Regan, *The Irish Counter-revolution*, 49.
[49] Costello, *The Irish Revolution and Its Aftermath*, 295.
[50] Regan, 'Review of Tom Garvin's *1922*', 55.
[51] F. S. L. Lyons, *Ireland since the Famine* (Glasgow, 1983), 459.

AN IRREPRESSIBLE CONFLICT?

If the Treaty had exposed the existence of rival traditions within Sinn Fein, and if these traditions were then invoked to justify positions taken in the civil war, a second condition for considering the conflict 'irrepressible' would be to show that these divisions could not have been overcome in the months between the signing of the Treaty in 1921 and the outbreak of civil war. Laffan remarks that the divisions of 1922, and the fighting that formed their climax, were rooted in the old conflict between those who thought a morally superior elite should rule, regardless of majority preferences, and those who really believed in majority rule.[52] Accepting the irrepressible nature of the Treaty split means adopting a conflict-situation paradigm for analysing events in the first half of 1922, a paradigm that assumes no realistic course of action could have succeeded in avoiding civil war. Such a paradigm might also imply that the efforts made to prevent the Treaty split resulting in civil war failed because of the nature of the issues themselves, rather than because of existing political circumstances. If this is true the civil war became inevitable at a very early stage, as is argued by much 'nationalist' as opposed to republican writing.

Indeed historians sympathetic to the pro-treatyite side generally locate the moment when civil war became inevitable very early on in the process of disintegration.[53] Garvin argues that the civil war was almost certainly not triggered off by the actual terms of the Treaty, or by any public actions of de Valera. The slide to civil war begins with GHQ's decision to assert central control over an increasingly undisciplined IRA on 25 November 1921.[54] Lee also argues that the Treaty was not the cause of the civil war, and locates its origins in the traditional ambivalence of republicans towards the majority rule principle.[55] Lyons goes further and argues that the Four Courts attack was not, as is sometimes said, the beginning of the civil war. The country had been drifting in that direction almost from the beginning of the year.[56] Emphasizing the importance of the IRA's convention of 26 March, Laffan sees the attack on the Four Courts as a final stage in a pattern of events that had been leading towards civil war for several months.[57] Younger, however, believes that the attack on the Four Courts was inevitable once the Provisional government had been given a mandate from the people.[58] All suggest that the existence of the anti-treaty IRA outside the control of the Ministry of Defence (and the disorder produced by it) was a sufficient cause of the civil war, a consensus that clearly absolves the Provisional government of all

---

[52] Laffan, *The Resurrection of Ireland*, 376.
[53] See H. Lacey, 'There Need Never Have Been a Civil War: What Caused the Tragedy?', *Irish Press*, 6 July 1958.
[54] Garvin, *1922: The Birth of Irish Democracy*, 56.
[55] Lee, *Ireland 1912–1985*, 67.
[56] Lyons, *Ireland since the Famine*, 461.
[57] Laffan, *The Resurrection of Ireland*, 411.
[58] Younger, *Ireland's Civil War*, 510.

responsibility for starting the conflict. Security, and the control of the means of security, was obviously paramount.

In contrast, other historians suggest that civil war only became a possibility with the Treaty split. Pakenham remarks that the outside observer in 1922 would see the Treaty gradually driving a wedge of resentment, alienation, and suspicion through every community in Ireland.[59] Regan also suggests that the process of disintegration was a top-down one, stating that all the constituent parts of the revolutionary movement 'began inexorably to divide and to disintegrate' following the leadership's division over the Treaty and the Dail vote on 4 January.[60] Hopkinson argues that civil war becomes inevitable once the anti-treaty IRA occupy most of the barracks and police stations left vacant by the departing crown forces, unless a solution to the constitutional differences dividing the two sides was found. In this regard Costello states that Britain's rejection of Collins' constitution 'guaranteed' that civil war would be the inevitable result.[61] For Neeson, the basic spur for the attack on the Four Courts was the pressure the British government brought to bear on the Provisional government not to fulfill the terms of the pact, and suggests that the Provisional government must ultimately take responsibility for the civil war.[62] Generally, however, the closer the point identified by historians comes to the actual start of the fighting, the greater the emphasis on the possibility that it could have been avoided.

Clearly, empirical advances in historical research have not lead to consensus on causality. Historians who emphasize that a predisposition towards some kind of conflict existed at an early stage in the Sinn Fein movement are attributing causal status to the character of Irish nationalism, whereas those who emphasize that conflict could have been avoided end up focusing on the political circumstances in which leaders like Collins had to operate. Hart, for example, rejects the view that the civil war was simply the result of decisions made in 1921, and that it could have been avoided if key people acted differently. Rather what was more or less inevitable, given the prior development of Irish Republicanism since 1916, was the violent defence of the Republic and the principles of the Rising by 'a self-consciously militant minority'.[63] From this perspective, the civil war was an irrepressible conflict, since the issue of democratic legitimacy was not one the pro-treatyites could reasonably be accepted to compromise on. From the opposite perspective, civil war was a predictable but not inevitable consequence of the Treaty split. In 1958 an article appeared in Fianna Fail's *The Irish Press* arguing that the civil war was essentially an avoidable tragedy brought about by the British government's role in breaking the Collins–de Valera electoral pact in June.[64]

---

[59] Pakenham, *Peace by Ordeal: The Negotiation of the Anglo-Irish Treaty, 1921* (London, 1992) 334–5.
[60] Regan, *The Irish Counter-revolution*, 50.
[61] Costello, *The Irish Revolution and its Aftermath 1916–1923*, 302.
[62] Neeson, *The Civil War 1922–1923*, 111.
[63] P. Hart, 'Definition: Defining the Irish Revolution', in J. Augusteijn (ed.), *The Irish Revolution 1913–1923* (Basingstoke, 2002), 26.
[64] Lacey, 'There Need Never Have Been a Civil War: What Caused the Tragedy?'

It is often argued that a less or more generous settlement than the Treaty would have meant a Dail united, either in rejection or acceptance, but Garvin suggests that during the Truce it was obvious to many observers that elements within the IRA were determined to use physical force against any compromise settlement.[65] De Valera's external association formula's chances of success depended on the existence within Sinn Fein and the IRA of a broad consensus on the norms of majority rule, precisely what contemporary historians deny:

The central flaw of external association as a single policy for preserving Sinn Fein's unity was that in itself it could not take account of the intimate and the ultimately destructive latticework of internal power struggles, personal antagonisms, kinships, and local and regional loyalties which transcended any issue of ideology and loyalty. The distribution of power within the revolutionary movement, and more importantly the struggle for it, contrived to make the process of reaching a compromise with British Imperialism an infinitely more complicated matter than simply securing the republic, as de Valera planned, by spectral degrees.[66]

Indeed Garvin argues that local units of the IRA saw themselves not the Dail as the best representatives of the nationalist cause and derived their mandate to act not from elections, but from deeply rooted traditions of agrarian and sectarian agitation and local defence. During the fighting against the British between 1918 and 1921 they developed a contempt for normal politics, and arrogantly assumed that the ordinary people could not be trusted to vote the right way, and were fitted only to be slaves or underlings.[67] What ended their dominance was the invasion of the political scene in 1922 by the voters, lawyers, priests, journalists, businessmen, farmers, trade unionists, and all the other elements of civil society that backed the Treaty. De Valera was caught at the faultline between this newly emergent civil society and the 'public band' tradition, but he chose to throw in his lot with the anti-treaty IRA, opposed a democratic vote on the Treaty, and ended up president of the Republican government during the civil war.

However, the pro-treaty insistence that de Valera's actions were a cause of the civil war amounts to saying that if he was not present, the civil war would not have taken place. This overestimates his influence on the anti-treaty IRA. After the Treaty debates de Valera actually urged the IRA's HQ staff and the divisional commanders to give the same loyalty to Mulcahy as they had to Brugha, but there is no evidence that the IRA listened to him.[68] The argument that de Valera's opposition to the Treaty also gave political status to what was merely an army mutiny is dependent on the thesis that the IRA's opposition to the Treaty was not ideological. However, Garvin's emphasis on the public band tradition is incompatible with the IRA's own desire to be seen as a conventional army defending the rights of a nation. The IRA only began their campaign after the 1918 election, and

---

[65] T. Garvin, 'The Aftermath of the Irish Civil War', Speech given to St. Columban's College, 20 October 1997.
[66] Regan, *The Irish Counter-revolution*, 7.
[67] Gavin, *1922: The Birth of Irish Democracy*, 44.
[68] F. Pakenham and T. P. O'Neill, *Eamon de Valera* (Dublin, 1970), 182.

came to see their fight as validated by the mandate given in that election.[69] Indeed Liam Deasy recalled that the southern IRA had fought 'imbued with the full republican ideal'.[70] It would be more convincing to argue that the commitment of many in the IRA to the defence of this republic transformed the conflict between local and central power, which had existed before the Treaty.[71] In Sligo, reactions to the Treaty clearly had a major role to play in shaping the divisions that culminated in civil war and were mere echoes of arguments made in Dublin. On the pro-treaty side the argument was for peace and a recognition that the Treaty gave a substantial measure of self-government to 'southern Ireland'. On the anti-treaty side, the emphasis was on the historic ideal of the Republic, which the elite was committed by oath to defend and which overrode any selfish desire for peace and self-government. The vehemence with which the latter viewpoint was maintained suggested that a compromise between the pragmatists and the idealists would be hard to achieve.[72]

Arguably, Garvin also overstates the intractable nature of the IRA's relationship to GHQ in 1922. Considering the radical example of the 1916 Rising, the brutality of British counter-insurgency measures between 1919 and 1921, and the fact that the Treaty project threatened the very existence of the IRA, the scale of military resistance to the National Army (as opposed to widespread lawlessness) after 28 June was unimpressive. As early as 15 July 1921 Ernie O'Malley reflected that 'the number of real republican men in the IRA is small, this is, of men who will see the Republic through to the bitter end'.[73] According to Coogan, between July 1921 and November 1921 the ranks of the IRA increased from around only 3,000 to a massive 70,000, due to the influx of 'trucileers'.[74] At the end of June 1922, however, the government estimated republican strength at only 12,000 as against less than 9,000 semi-trained recruits.[75] Hart suggests that

Liam Lynch and most of the pre-eminent 1st Southern Division, wanted above all to maintain army autonomy and its role as defender of the republic against British tyranny— thereby resurrecting the idea that the Volunteers should remain as the permanent national guardian of national freedom. So long as the army kept its guns, authority, and nerve, the Treaty could not be imposed and the nation could be reunited around the old cause. Civil war, or even precipitous renewal of war with Britain, would destroy everything.[76]

In other words, if the majority of the IRA had no real appetite for civil war, the question remains why were they not reconciled to the Free State by political as opposed to military means? Sean MacBride later believed that Collins' draft

---

[69] M. Mulholland, 'Review of P. Hart, *The IRA and Its Enemies: Violence and Community in Cork, 1916–1923*' *The Voice of the Turtle* (1999).

[70] L. Deasy, *Brother against Brother* (Cork, 1998), 21.

[71] Laffan, *The Resurrection of Ireland*, 303.

[72] Farry, *The Aftermath of Revolution*, 48–9.

[73] F. Blake, *The Irish Civil War and What It Still Means for the Irish People* (Dublin, 1986), 12.

[74] Coogan, *De Valera: Long Fellow Long Shadow*, 307.

[75] Townshend, *Ireland: The Twentieth Century*, 115.

[76] P. Hart, *The IRA at War 1916–1923* (Oxford, 2003), 104.

constitution was the key to averting civil war, and its rejection by the British government clearly played a role in ending the negotiations on army unity and in leading Collins to renounce the pact.[77] Liam Deasy also recalled that the only approach that could have reconciled the powerful southern IRA to the Free State was Collins' constitutional plan and the retention of the IRA as the army of the Republic. After the banned IRA convention of 26 March the moderate section of the anti-treatyites tried to maintain unity in the hope that a republican constitution would allow everyone to subscribe to it without the stigma of an oath to the Crown.[78] However, the British cabinet regarded Collins' preferred constitutional draft as 'a negation of the Treaty', and insisted on a modified version of the draft that 'underscores the Treaty in a most emphatic manner'.[79] As Liam de Roiste, a pro-treaty TD from Cork, observed, the anti-treaty strategy at the time of the pact was to get into power by an implied but not explicit acceptance of the Treaty position, and then try to enlarge on the Treaty's terms when circumstances permitted.[80] Indeed the majority of the IRA remained committed to a policy of conciliation with the Provisional government until the attack on the Four Courts and the renunciation of the pact.

On the other hand, since a republican constitution did not result from the conferences between the British and Irish sides in May 1922, there was no test of Regan's thesis about the ultimately divisive role of the power struggles within the movement, so we cannot know for sure whether the civil war was down to native genius rather than political circumstance. From the pro-treaty perspective the Treaty division was irrepressible, since between those seeking to run a state by ostensibly democratic means and those seeking to subvert it there is little common ground.[81] On the other hand, Fitzpatrick suggests that differences of principle were relatively unimportant and Collins and his allies had come close to avoiding civil war with the pact.[82] The pact is obviously crucial to the whole issue since it attempted to repress the Treaty division so that an election could be held. One view was that it muzzled the electorate since it was intended to prevent them from expressing an opinion on the settlement.[83] Another is that 'instead of being forced to choose at once between a government committed to the Empire and a government pledged to defend the Republic even at the risk of war', the voters were offered an opportunity of returning a coalition government 'pledged to peaceful conservation of the present national strength'.[84]

The relative success of pro-treaty Sinn Fein candidates, the anti-treatyites' loss of 22 out of 41 seats, and the fact that third party candidates received just under 40

[77] N. Mansergh, 'The Freedom to Achieve Freedom? The Political Ideas of Collins and de Valera', in G. Doherty and D. Keogh (eds.), *Michael Collins and the Making of the Irish State* (Cork, 1998), 180
[78] Deasy, *Brother against Brother*, 35.
[79] Quoted in Neeson, *The Civil War 1922–1923*, 108.
[80] See Regan, *The Irish Counter-revolution*, 70.
[81] Coogan, *Long Fellow Long Shadow*, 322.
[82] D. Fitzpatrick, *The Two Irelands 1912–1939* (Oxford, 1998), 125.
[83] Laffan, *The Resurrection of Ireland*, 388.
[84] MacArdle, *The Irish Republic*, 742.

per cent of the first preference vote in the pact election are interpreted by Laffan as a decisive vote in favour of the Treaty and against the politics of Ireland's revolutionary years.[85] In contrast, Regan suggests that any vote for the panel candidates—with the exception of the two constituencies where the pact collapsed—was a vote for the *status quo ante*, which intended to frustrate the democratic will of the electorate in the hope of regenerating unity within Sinn Fein.[86] However, during its eleven meetings the Dail committee charged with agreeing terms for the pact had not been able to agree to a preamble that accepted that the majority of the Dail and of the people accepted the Treaty. The anti-treatyites willingness to accept an agreed election was based on the principle that no issue was being determined at the election.[87] This irrepressible difference of outlook resurfaced when the electoral results became known. The pro-treatyites did not adhere to the understanding that the Treaty would not be an issue in the election, and regarded the results as a mandate for the Treaty. The anti-treatyites saw the result as a vote for coalition and peace.[88] Over 70 per cent of electors on both sides of Sinn Fein had given transfer votes to the other wing where there was no candidate available from their own side. However, the transfers usually stayed within each wing where there was a candidate from one's own side of the party.[89] In other words, many Sinn Fein voters were expressing a preference for one of the Treaty sides as well as supporting the coalition idea. Clearly the results lent themselves to both interpretations, but with the republicans getting less than 25 per cent of the first preference vote few can doubt that this victory for the Treaty side influenced decisions taken in the following weeks.[90]

For Garvin Collins' apparent renunciation of the pact on the eve of the election was an 'explosion' of his basically democratic instincts against the elitism of the IRA. The issue of democracy could not be repressed any longer, and the voters then broke the pact by voting for so many third party candidates who supported the Treaty.[91] O'Gadhra in contrast sees the pact as Sinn Fein's first attempt at establishing cross-party consensus and coalition government in the interests of avoiding civil war. He suggests that Collins came to realize that it would not work because a coalition would have been in breach of article 17 of the Treaty, which required every member of the Provisional government to accept the Treaty in writing.[92] From this perspective the pact fell apart, not because of the democratic versus authoritarian divide, but because of political circumstances. Collins' intentions clearly matter. In his speech to the Sinn Fein *Ard Fheis* on 23 May 1922 he suggested that he thought the pact more important than the Treaty.

[85] Laffan, *The Irish Revolution*, 407.
[86] Regan, 'Review of Tom Garvin's *1922*', 55.
[87] B. Kissane, *Explaining Irish Democracy* (Dublin, 2002), 130–1.
[88] MacArdle, *The Irish Republic*, 758.
[89] M. Gallagher, 'The Pact General Election of 1922', *Irish Historical Studies*, 21 (1979), 419.
[90] N. O'Gadhra, *Civil War in Connacht 1922–1923* (Cork, 1999), 28.
[91] Garvin, *1922: The Birth of Irish Democracy*, 129.
[92] O'Gadhra, *Civil War in Connacht 1922–1923*, 23–5.

Privately he hoped that the election would register a vote in favour of the Treaty.[93] Pro-treaty voters who gave their second preferences to anti-treaty Sinn Fein might have been thinking the same way. In any case, the fate of the pact was inextricably linked to that of the constitution. Lloyd George had shrewdly judged that if the British insisted on a constitution on their terms, de Valera would not be able to accept it and the pact would be broken.[94]

Although the events of late June certainly 'triggered' the civil war, by then Collins had run out of options and probably decided that a limited civil war was the price he had to pay to avoid further conflict with Britain. On the one hand, the banned IRA convention, the occupation of the Four Courts, and the split in the IRA at the June convention strengthened the arguments of those within the government who believed that a legitimate government could not tolerate the existence of a private army in its midst. When the results of the June election became known, the issue of democratic authority could not be repressed any longer. On the other hand, the vetoing of the constitution, the collapse of the army negotiations, and the failure of the pact left Collins with no basis on which he could reconcile the anti-treaty moderates to the Free State. Internal divisions and external pressure came together as the election results became known. Close analysis of the peace efforts made in the first half of 1922 suggests that the differences between the two sides were irrepressible precisely because Collins was operating in an increasingly compressed political space. It is impossible to decide on the basis of the archival evidence whether Collins himself regarded the issue of democracy as repressible, but for O'Higgins, Cosgrave, and Griffith, it clearly was not.[95] The problem for their side, however, was that the course of events since the Treaty was signed gave substance to the anti-treaty view that Britain was still in control, and many joined their colours out of a sense of constitutional grievance with the Free State. The reality of local military power, the different traditions within Sinn Fein, and the depth of the Treaty split were all necessary ingredients in the situation that led to civil war, but continued British pressure after the Treaty was signed also meant that civil war was the most likely outcome in 1922, given the impossibility of the Provisional government satisfying the anti-treaty republicans and their British partners at the same time.[96]

The civil war provides a classic example of a conflict where judgements of causality and of value are hard to separate. If the irrepressible divide between democrats and authoritarians was at the heart of the conflict, then it was right for Collins and his colleagues to renounce the pact, even if it led to civil war. Breaking the pact would only be a trigger for a civil war whose basic cause lay in the anti-treatyites' rejection of the majority rule principle. On the other hand, if the political divisions were repressible, British pressure on Collins to make his constitution adhere to the Treaty and thus destroy the pact was the cause of the

---

[93] Kissane, *Explaining Irish Democracy*, 131.
[94] Neeson, *The Civil War 1922–1923*, 25.
[95] Kissane, *Explaining Irish Democracy*, 128.
[96] Hart, *The IRA at War 1916–1923*, 27.

civil war, and it was wrong for the Provisional government to bow to their ultimatum. In other words ultimate responsibility must lie with the Provisional government who remained free agents.[97] What is clear is that there is very little difference between these perspectives and the interpretations later put forward by the protagonists themselves. From one point of view, the civil war was caused by an army mutiny that existed *in potentia* before 1922 and that was then carried out by Rory O'Connor and his followers in the spring of that year. For the anti-treatyites the civil war was caused by the disestablishment of the Republic at Britain's behest through a series of acts of bad faith on the part of the Provisional government. The manner in which that government acquired and asserted its authority in 1922 gave substance to the claim that the establishment of the Free State was unconstitutional, while the anti-treatyites' opposition to this process was regarded by the Provisional government as a rejection of democratic author-ity. Faced with such competing conceptions of legitimacy it appears that neither perspective can really be objective if it excludes the other side's viewpoint from its account of what caused the conflict.

THE CIVIL WAR AND IRISH POLITICAL DEVELOPMENT

Despite the protracted debate between pro-revolutionaries and anti-revolution-aries in political theory, almost nothing systematic has been written about the long-run effects of civil wars and the comparative costs of revolutionary and evolutionary transformations.[98] Since civil wars only emerge when peaceful political processes have broken down, perhaps it is considered axiomatic that they could not strengthen a country's commitment to parliamentary democracy. On the other hand, the Irish Republic has, rather perversely, been considered one of a number of states that were 'beneficiaries' of a civil war: Greece, France, Spain, the United Kingdom, and the United States are other examples cited by Roberts.[99] Moreover, T. D. Williams suggested that the civil war prevented continual sect-arian slaughter in the north, clerical domination in the south, and the prospect of war between classes over the distribution of wealth.[100] Perhaps since some civil wars are fought over intractable issues and are as such, unavoidable, they can also resolve certain issues, purge the society of some undesirable elements, and establish the primacy of democratic over anti-democratic forces in the society. In the 1960s Ernest Blythe remarked that 'all countries must have a civil war, sooner or later, in their evolution', which suggests that the Irish civil war was a part of a long-term process of social and political development.[101]

[97] Neeson, *The Civil War 1922–1923*, 38.
[98] H. Eckstein, 'On the Etiology of Internal Wars', *History and Theory*, 4/1 (1963), 136.
[99] H. Roberts, *The Battlefield: Algeria 1988–2002—Studies in a Broken Polity* (London and New York, 2003), 353.
[100] T. D. Williams, 'The Summing Up', in T. D. Williams (ed.), *The Irish Struggle 1916–1926* (London, 1966), 167.
[101] Neeson, *The Civil War 1922–1923*, 36.

The issue of whether the civil war strengthened the impulse towards democracy in Irish life is clearly related to the other elements of the nationalist interpretation of the civil war. If there was ambivalence within the IRA and Sinn Fein about majority rule, if the Treaty split was an irrepressible conflict because of the crucial issue of democratic legitimacy, and if the pact election gave the Provisional government a mandate to implement the Treaty, it follows that their civil war victory was a triumph of democracy. Garvin argues that the emergence of the Free State was in fact a victory for electoral democracy, a cooperative effort of those in Sinn Fein who became 'Free Staters' and the leaders of Irish Labour who were intellectually able to see through the emerging tyranny of Soviet Russia.[102] In contrast, if there had been consensus on the legitimacy of the republican ideal before 1922, if the Treaty was an essentially coerced settlement, and if the mandate in the pact election was for the avoidance of fratricidal strife, the civil war was anything but a triumph of democracy. Neeson argues that the civil war achieved absolutely nothing not capable of being achieved peacefully.[103] From the first perspective civil war can be evaluated positively, as something that purged the society of some undesirable elements, whereas from the latter civil war can be regarded as an avoidable tragedy that inflicted a deep wound on the society. Causal arguments are thus clearly linked to evaluative ones.

There is no doubt that the civil war was 'the conflict that formed the state' with an impact on Irish political culture disproportionate to the amount of fighting in 1922–3. However, the argument that the civil war was a profoundly formative event in the development of Irish political culture, and the claim that a democracy was established 'as the outcome of the civil war' must be kept separate.[104] Both require analysis, but the latter has provided a number of more specific hypotheses: that the military victory over the IRA was a necessary pre-condition for democratic government, that the breaking of the pact led to the emergence of a genuinely competitive party system, and that the civil war divide structured allegiances in a way that strengthened the Irish state. If these outcomes could only be achieved through civil war, it follows that the ends may justify the means, and a notable paradox of the Irish historiography is that historians who put the issue of democratic legitimacy at the heart of their interpretations of the civil war are those who are quickest to justify the extreme measures used to defend it. Jackson reflects that perhaps the deaths by execution of 77 'determined and idealistic' young men helped 'smooth the transition from the *ancien regime* to a settled democratic polity' on the grounds that they paved the way for de Valera to re-establish his ascendancy over the republican side.[105]

The strongest argument of the nationalist interpretation of the civil war is that the conflict strengthened the impulse towards democracy in Irish society by allowing for the military defeat of the IRA (for the first time) in the field. Girvin

---

[102] Garvin, *1922: The Birth of Irish Democracy*, 30.
[103] Neeson, *The Civil War 1922–1923*, 13.
[104] Clifford, *The Irish Civil War: The Conflict That Formed the State.*
[105] Jackson, *Ireland 1798–1998*, 273.

argues that 'without a clear and decisive victory over the republican forces, the new government would not have been in a position to govern'.[106] Civilian control over the military is a necessary but insufficient condition for democratic government, but where the military shares the democratic orientations of the population, a conflict need not materialize.[107] Further research would be necessary to establish whether the separatist tradition in Ireland was really anti-democratic, but numerous memoirs, such as Liam Deasy's, have emphasized that public opinion, in the form of election results, had little influence on the IRA after 1916.[108] On the other hand, Hart argues that the IRA were 'ademocratic' rather than 'anti-democratic', since they never envisaged carrying out a *coup d'état* to undermine the political process. For example, when the first southern division declared its opposition to the Treaty in December 1921, Sean Moylan insisted that as citizens they had a duty to express their views, but 'not with a view to dictating to politicians'.[109] Moreover, the bulk of the IRA only resorted to arms when the civil war was forced on them by the Provisional government, so the question is again why were they not subordinated to the civil power by peaceful rather than military means? To be consistent, the nationalist interpretation must explain this failure as a product of the IRA's undemocratic attitude; yet both sides were also willing to contemplate a scheme for the reunification of the army that involved its Executive being elected by an IRA convention, and these negotiations collapsed because they could not agree which side would provide the chief of staff. The possibility remains that but for the divisive role played by the British government in the spring, the issue of civil–military relations would not have necessitated civil war on the scale that ensued.

With regard to party politics Clifford argues that without the civil war, which created the two-party dynamic between Fianna Fail and Fine Gael, you would have had the same sort of thing that has been seen in numerous colonies since then—a gradual slide into authoritarianism.[110] On the one hand, this view seems justified by the fact that between 1885 and 1921 parliamentary elections were often uncontested in most of the future area of the Irish state.[111] Sinn Fein inherited this position of monopoly in 1918, and for the May 1921 general election all seats in this area, bar those for Dublin University, were uncontested. The pact, had it held, threatened to continue this tradition, and resulted in non-competitive elections in 8 of the 28 constituencies. The ratio of candidates to seats (just 1:4) in 1922 was the lowest ever since. Gallagher writes,

In this sense, the election marked a contest between two groups with very different views on the place of politics. One saw Irish society in essentially monist terms, as innately conflict-free. It wanted any differences of opinion to be resolved within the framework of

---

[106] Girvin, *From Union to Union*, 61.
[107] R. Dahl, *Democracy and Its Critics* (New Haven, 1989), 249.
[108] Deasy, *Brother against Brother*, 43.
[109] Hart, *The IRA at War*, 97.
[110] Clifford, *The Irish Civil War: The Conflict That Formed the State*, 4.
[111] Kissane, *Explaining Irish Democracy*, 147.

an all-encompassing 'national movement', and was suspicious of the very idea of political parties because the concept implied a fragmentation of the Irish people into different sections with different interests. The other took a more pluralist view, and saw the political process as existing in order to allow the peaceful resolution of conflicts that inevitably existed within Irish society. The fact that enough non-Sinn Fein candidates came forward to make the election a genuine test of the people's will ensured that the second view prevailed, and established the new Irish state as a twentieth-century liberal democracy.[112]

On the other hand, the strong vote for third party candidates in the face of widespread intimidation during the pact election suggests that the basis for pluralism was already very strong in 1922. Vanhanen has constructed an index of democratization for European states in the period between 1910 and 1949 and a statistical way of relating states' level of political development to their societal bases. He tries to measure how the 'equalization of power resources' within society leads to a competitive system. Vanhanen suggested that the degree of political participation could be measured by the percentage of the population that could vote in general elections, whereas the degree of competition could be measured by the share of the smaller parties share of the vote (i.e., all but the largest parties' per cent of the vote). These two dimensions of democratization were combined to calculate an index of democratization (ID) formed by competition (C) multiplied by participation (P) divided by 100.

From Table 2 we can see that the Irish index of democratization was higher throughout the inter-war period than the mean figures for European democracies as a whole, and dramatically so than the mean figure for European non-democracies. Notably, the Irish figure for competition in the 1920s (61.2 per cent)

TABLE 2. Political and Social Indicators for the Irish Free State and Mean Figures for European Democracies and Non-democracies, 1920–1939

	Political variables			Social variables				
	C	P	ID	IOD	IKD	FF	Mean	IPR
Irish Free State								
1922–9	61.2	34.9	21.4	33.5	46.5	40	40	6.2
1930–9	53.0	44.2	23.4	35.5	52.5	58	48.7	10.8
European democracies								
1920–9	62.6	29.2	17.6	47.8	52.0	45.3	48.4	11.8
1930–9	62.5	35.7	21.9	50.5	53.4	56.4	53.4	14.5
European Non-democracies								
1920–9	32.0	9.5	4.5	26.5	30.5	38.0	31.5	3.6
1930–9	19.6	10.3	3.0	36.0	39.2	43.3	37.6	5.8

Source: Vanhanen (1984), 144–5.

[112] M. Gallagher, *Irish Elections 1922–44: Results and Analysis* (Limerick, 1993), 1.

was almost double the undemocratic mean (32 per cent). However, the high figure for ID after 1922 could still be attributed to the collapse of the pact and the early enfranchisement of women, so the question is whether these political indicators were out of sync with other aspects of the state's development. Vanhanen's index of power resources (IPR) was a compound measure of an index of occupational diversity (IOD), an index of knowledge distribution (IKD), and the share of family farms in the total area of holdings (FF). It was calculated by the formula (IOD × IKD × FF)/10,000. For Ireland he suggests that 'its IPR was so

TABLE 3. Civil War Parties' Combined Percentage (%) Mean First Preference Vote by Region, 1922–1938

	Centre	Heartland	Border periphery	Western periphery
1922	54.40	52.86	85.37	97.79
1923	68.04	55.51	67.78	80.46
1927 June	55.28	43.31	55.44	66.69
1927 Sept.	75.06	65.82	71.67	87.33
1932	74.07	76.60	78.58	89.89
1933	85.11	72.73	75.23	92.73
1937	70.30	77.27	84.46	88.60
1938	82.86	80.84	90.42	92.12

Note: Due to boundary revisions in 1923 and 1935 the following classifications were made. In 1922 *Centre* includes Dublin Mid, Dublin North West, Dublin South, and Dublin County; *Heartland* includes Carlow-Kilkenny, Cork Borough, Cork East and North East, Cork Mid, North, South, South East, and West, Kildare-Wicklow, Laois-Offaly, Louth-Meath, Tipperary North, South, and Mid, Waterford-Tipperary East, and Wexford; *Border periphery* includes Cavan, Donegal, Leitrim-Roscommon North, Longford-Westmeath, Monagham, Sligo-Mayo East; *Western periphery* includes Clare, Galway, Kerry-Limerick West, Limerick City and East, Mayo South-Roscommon South, and Mayo North and West. In 1923–33 *Centre* includes Dublin North, Dublin South, and Dublin County; *Heartland* includes Carlow-Kilkenny, Cork Borough, Cork East, Cork North, Cork West, Kildare, Laois-Offaly, Meath, Tipperary, Waterford, Wexford, and Wicklow; *Border periphery* includes Cavan, Donegal, Leitrim-Sligo, Longford-Westmeath, Louth, Monaghan, and Roscommon; *Western periphery* includes Clare, Galway, Kerry, Limerick, Mayo North, and Mayo South. For 1937–8 *Centre* includes Dublin North East, Dublin North West, Dublin South, Dublin Townships, and Dublin County; *Heartland* includes Carlow-Kildare, Cork Borough, Cork North, Cork South East, Cork West, Kilkenny Laois Offaly, Meath-Westmeath, Tipperary, Waterford, Wexford, and Wicklow; *Border periphery* includes Athlone-Longford, Cavan, Donegal East, Donegal West, Leitrim, Louth, Monaghan, Roscommon, and Sligo; *Western periphery* includes Clare, Galway East, Galway West, Kerry North, Kerry South, Limerick, Mayo North, and Mayo South.
In 1922 Limerick City and East, Donegal, Leitrim-Roscommon North, Clare, Kerry-Limerick-West, and Mayo North and West were uncontested constituencies.
Figures for university constituencies are not included.

high (6.2) that democracy was on a firm footing right from the start'.[113] Although the individual figures suggest that the Irish state was politically overdeveloped relative to its societal base, these indicators still compare well with the European non-democratic sample, never mind the post-colonial states in Asia and Africa.

The thesis that the collapse of the pact was a pre-condition for the development of modern party politics is also relevant to Robert's argument that 'Ireland became a democracy because a party-political division developed within Irish society' as a result of the civil war. He maintains that the division between pro- and anti-treatyites created an 'entirely new political cleavage' in 1922, transcending and depoliticizing all earlier lines of division.[114] The civil war parties' share of the first preference vote, which was around 60 per cent in 1922, actually reached over 85 per cent in 1938. Their combined electoral strength was initially greatest in areas where the civil war was fought most extensively, but increased dramatically throughout the state once Fianna Fail entered the Dail in July 1927. Table 3 shows the combined first preference vote of the two civil war parties by region between 1922 and 1938. It shows that before September 1927 in the 'heartland' of Ireland, and in Dublin, their share of the vote was usually less than 60 per cent. Indeed in the heartland, where most constituencies were located, their share of the vote had dropped to only 43 per cent by June 1927. In the border counties their share of the vote dropped from over 85 per cent of the total in 1922 to less than 56 per cent in June 1927. A similarly dramatic fall occurred in the 'western periphery' from over 97 per cent in 1922 to less than 67 per cent in June 1927. It is only after June 1927 that we can speak of a two-and-a-half-party system. Fianna Fail's entry into the Dail in August 1927 was clearly crucial. The regional distribution of support suggests that the dominance of the civil war divide emerged in an west–east direction, and was an aspect of 'the invasion of the center by the periphery' between 1922 and 1938.[115] In this way 'civil war politics' became the dominant form of electoral competition throughout the state.

According to Roberts, mass mobilization around the civil war divide transformed the content of Irish political opinion and the structure of political allegiance, entailing 'a qualitative development in the state–society relationship and the reinforcement of the state as a consequence of this change'.[116] In the inter-war period voter turnout went from 47 per cent in the 1918 general election, to just under 60 per cent in 1922, to over 80 per cent in 1933, to a respectable 75.7 per cent in 1938.[117] Lipset and Rokkan suggest that parties can further national integration in two ways: (a) by establishing a national network of cross-local communication channels in a way that strengthens national identity, and (b) by helping to set the national system of government above any particular set of office

[113] T. Vanhanen, *The Emergence of Democracy: A Comparative Study of 119 States* (Helsinki, 1984), 79.

[114] Roberts, *The Battlefield: Algeria 1988–2002*, 353.

[115] T. Garvin, 'Political Cleavages, Party Politics and Urbanisation in Ireland: The Case of the Periphery-Dominated Centre', *European Journal of Political Research*, 2 (1974), 309.

[116] Roberts, *The Battlefield: Algeria 1988–2002*, 353.

[117] P. Mair, *The Changing Irish Party System: Organisation, Ideology and Electoral Competition* (London, 1987), 46.

holders, by encouraging voters to target their discontent at the governing party and not the political system as a whole.[118] However, the application of this framework to the Irish case assumes that Ireland was a tabula rasa in 1922. Against this view Sinnott argues that by 1922 Irish electoral alignments had already frozen around one of the fundamental social cleavages identified by Lipset and Rokkan. During the first 'mass mobilizing' election in 1918 Irish politics was dominated by a centre–periphery conflict, with the British government representing the centre and the nationalist Sinn Fein party representing the Irish periphery. The conflict that ensued was between a strongly nationalist and a moderately nationalist party, both with common roots in Sinn Fein: 'as such it was a conflict within the nationalist or peripheralist consensus already established, and far from being unrelated to the 1918 mobilization and institutionalization around the center–periphery issue, it developed from it and in turn reinforced it'.[119] Moreover, the new party system reflected a long-standing cleavage in Irish society, 'between those who, for class, cultural or other reasons, assume a natural affinity between Ireland and Britain and those who do not, or would rather such an affinity did not exist'. Such a distinction manifested itself in the more anglophobe Fianna Fail tradition and the less anglophobe pro-treaty, Fine Gael tradition.[120] According to Garvin,

It is often lamented that the Civil War deprived Ireland of conventional European 'left versus right' politics, in favour of two factions based on ancestral hatreds. I would suggest that even without a civil war, Irish society did not naturally lend itself to this kind of polarization. To imagine the impossible, had there been no Civil War and had Collins succeeded in uniting both wings of the IRA as one force and had accepted that it could not be used to destabilize Northern Ireland, presumably a Sinn Fein party under Griffith, Collins and de Valera would have governed as a centre-right party, with farmers on the right, and Labor on the left. Sinn Fein would eventually almost certainly have divided into two main groups—on the pattern of India after independence—the one more republican and separatist, the other more 'Commonwealth' and rightist.[121]

In summary, the three specific hypotheses about the positive role of the civil war on Irish political development are open to a host of objections. The general issue of how to assess its impact on Irish democracy ultimately comes down to whether to apply a 'genetic' as opposed to a 'structural' theory of democratization to Ireland. In arguing for the former, Rustow argued that patterns of conflict and the choices made in conflict situations are usually central to any democratic transition.[122] In this vein Townshend has argued that amidst the storms of the Irish civil

[118] S. M. Lipset and S. Rokkan, *Party Systems and Voter Alignments: Cross National Perspectives* (New York, 1967), 4.

[119] R. Sinnott, 'Interpretations of the Irish Party System', *European Journal of Political Research*, 12/3 (1984), 303.

[120] T. Garvin, *The Evolution of Irish National Politics* (Dublin, 1981), 135.

[121] T. Garvin, 'The Emergent Irish State—Did We Turn Our Backs on the North?', speech at St Columbans College, Navan, 20 October 1997, 5.

[122] D. Rustow, 'Transitions to Democracy: Toward a Dynamic Model', *Comparative Politics*, 3 (1970), 344.

war 'a working democracy was built', which suggests that the pro-treatyites took advantage of the chaos of 1922 to impose democratic institutions on a recalcitrant society.[123] On the other hand, explaining why Irish democracy survived the civil war in terms of the values of a particular group of people at a particular historical juncture leads to the conclusion that Irish democracy survived the inter-war period because of the presence of a heroic and far-sighted elite, which was presumably usually absent on the continent. A compromise would be to accept that fundamental social changes make democratization possible, but the manner in which the transition took place in Ireland, involving a violent revolt from below, created problems for democratic consolidation afterwards. Here the contribution of the pro-treaty political elite, in terms of the assertion of civilian control over the army during the army mutiny of 1924, the creation of an unarmed police force, and the insistence of meritocratic standards in the public service, was key.

All the other European civil wars of the twentieth century (Finland, Greece, Hungary, and Spain) resulted in authoritarian or semi-authoritarian political systems. Civil wars demand the forcible establishment of unity, and there can be only one dominant authority above the clash of interests underlying such conflicts. To legitimate this authority, a unifying ideology is also required, one that stresses the absolutist nature of political obligations and goals.[124] In Ireland however, the pro-treatyites, who were militarily dominant by the end of the civil war, did not have an ideology that would justify an authoritarian clampdown, whereas their opponents certainly had. They may not have been 'enthusiastic democrats', but they were liberals, and their ambition to construct a legal rational state apparatus uncorrupted by the society surrounding it was totally at odds with the impulse towards authoritarianism elsewhere in Europe at that time.

Townshend suggests that the key was that the pro-treatyites were 'constitutionalists', not in the sense of an exaggerated obeisance to the written constitution, but in the sense that they based their regime on appeals to the public that they knew would have widespread resonance.[125] In contrast, Regan argues that the ambition of this elite was to end the Irish revolution by restoring power to the rising Catholic middle class who had been poised to inherit it with the advent of Home Rule.[126] Both views are not incompatible, since 'countering' the revolution in the name of public opinion meant sidelining those organizations associated with it, and a democratic state was a product of that process.[127] Perhaps Ireland was simply fortunate in that the most talented section of the political elite won out in the innumerable power struggles of the civil war. Those Dail deputies who

---

[123] Townshend, *Ireland: The Twentieth Century*, 108.
[124] Karl Dietrich Bracher, *The Age of Ideologies: A History of Political Thought in the Twentieth Century* (London, 1985), 113.
[125] C. Townshend, 'The meaning of Irish Freedom: Constitutionalism in the Free State', *Transactions of the Royal Historical Society*, 4th series, 8 (1998), 45–70.
[126] Regan, *The Irish Counter-revolution*, 87.
[127] Ibid., 101–26.

had ministerial experience, or who had held senior positions in the Sinn Fein movement, were among the most unequivocal supporters of the Treaty, and of the eleven appointed to Cosgrave's government in September 1922 six had held ministerial positions before the Treaty.[128]

The paradox, however, was that pushing for extreme measures against the IRA was a token of how committed the pro-treaty side were to the cause of civilian ascendancy within the state, but whether this response left a positive legacy is open to question.[129] Indeed the contribution of the pro-treaty elite must be considered alongside the fact that they bore the strain of civil war with less grace than their opponents, who generally did not shoot their prisoners or fire on unarmed policemen. William O'Brien suggested that the pro-treaty elite could not have been human if the dangerous conditions in which they lived their daily lives in 1922/3 did not add a degree of additional bitterness to their loftier motives.[130] Regan suggests that refusing the anti-treatyites prisoner of war status was an open invitation to murder prisoners, and the official policy of executions could easily have been interpreted by the rank and file as a licence to carry out further murders at the local level.[131] However, Girvin believes that the government's ruthlessness in the civil war and after was 'absolutely necessary' to secure the state and its democratic institutions, which rather suggests that the military outcome depended on the 77 executions.[132] O'Halpin catalogues the excesses of the pro-treaty forces, noting the use of systematic internment, the murder of 150 men in custody, and reprisal executions, but also concludes that the government had to meet IRA terror with state terror.[133] This suggests at least a moral equivalence between state violence and private violence, a view endorsed by Younger:

Some writers have it that the seventy-seven executions carried out by Mr. Cosgrave's government scarred Ireland forever. There is no doubt that they have left an ugly mark, but history will set them back in the context of the Civil War as a whole, indeed, as a not very significant factor in the growth of a nation, for whatever passions were fired by the executions and blaze still in the minds of individual men and women, the Civil War, every murderous shot of it, every bridge blown and train derailed, every building shattered, every life destroyed, every heart grieved and every lie snarled by one side or the other, was the real trauma that Ireland suffered.[134]

Of course state terror may have been superior to IRA terror, not in political theory, but in the minds of the Irish public, and O'Halpin suggests that the absence of protests from non-republican sources and the results of subsequent elections suggest that the general public acquiesced in such measures.[135] However,

[128] Ibid., 82.
[129] Ibid., 101–26.
[130] O'Brien, *The Irish Free State: Secret History of Its Foundation*, unpublished manuscript.
[131] Regan, *The Irish Counter-revolution*, 101–26.
[132] Girvin, From *Union to Union*, 61.
[133] O'Halpin, *Defending Ireland*, 37.
[134] Younger, *Ireland's Civil War*, 477.
[135] O'Halpin, *Defending Ireland*, 35.

in the nine constituencies that were contested in both the 1922 and 1923 elections, the republican vote increased in all but one in 1923, despite the fact that the anti-treatyites were in no position to campaign in the election. The first real democratic contest between the two sides was in June 1927, when the two sides' vote share was almost identical.

Lee remarks that 'if the civil war illustrated with a vengeance the potential for autocracy lurking in Irish political culture, it illustrated even more emphatically the potential for democracy', but Irish historians have done little to define the parameters of either democracy or authoritarianism as they existed in 1922 or afterwards.[136] Regan suggests that the problem with the use of a democrat versus authoritarian divide for 1922 is that there were lapses in the pro-treatyites' observance of democratic principles, and Collins in particular realized that a fastidious adherence to them would endanger the whole pro-treaty project. His failure to publish the constitution before the morning of the 1922 election, his ambiguous approach to the pact, and his decision not to consult the Dail before launching the civil war are consistent only with a very loose definition of democratic propriety.[137] The ambiguity of the pro-treaty position in the summer of 1922 is conveyed by Curran's remark that 'only when victory was assured could the government afford the restraints of parliamentary rule'.[138] According to the Labour leader, Thomas Johnson,

These people had obtained authority without criticism, perhaps, and that sense of authority had grown to a sense of arrogance and dictatorship. They did not take the people into their counsels, but decided it was enough to report what they had done, and get from them commendatory resolutions. Contempt for the people and, perhaps he should add, fear that they would not be able to carry a majority inspired their attitude.[139]

The philosopher Karl Popper observed that in contrast to other systems liberal democracy created conditions that allowed challenges to its own existence to emerge. The paradox was that in order to surmount those challenges democratic liberties and constitutional norms had to be suspended in order that democracy could survive. The subsequent history of an Irish state that professed great loyalty to constitutional principles, but regularly put its constitutional provisions in abeyance when dealing with subversives, was a direct consequence of the civil war.[140] The use of military courts, internment, and (occasionally) executions did not end in 1922, suggesting that the civil war reinforced an impetus towards authoritarianism in Irish political culture, a point that might be generalized even further. Walker suggests that the experience of upheaval, suffering, and destruction in 1922–3 made conditions ripe for a conservative if not authoritarian resurgence, and to an extent this materialized.[141] According to Garvin:

---

[136] Lee, *Ireland 1912–1985*, 68.
[137] Regan, *The Irish Counter-revolution*, 68.
[138] Curran, *The Birth of the Irish Free State 1921–1923*, 240.
[139] *Voice of Labour*, 12 August 1922.
[140] O'Halpin, *Defending Ireland*, 1.
[141] Walker, 'Conservative Nationalism', 116.

The Irish Civil War had a profound effect on Irish political development, in ways that have been so pervasive and deep as to be taken for granted by we Irish who grew up in the world created by that war. North-South relations, relations with Britain and the Commonwealth, attitudes towards veterans of the Great War, Church-State relations and the entire fabric and quality of public life were affected by the conflict to an enormous extent. While a superficial recovery occurred between 1932 and 1945 under de Valera, it was in many ways a hollow thing, a pretence that the events of 1922–23 had not really happened. A crippling of Irish public political culture occurred which necessitated an exaggerated reliance on Church and central State structures for the supply of political and cultural coherence. The historical dependence on the overarching structures of the Church, the State, the Fianna Fail party and the GAA only began to fade in the 1960s, as a general social pluralism began to melt the sociological glaciers generated by the Great Freeze of the post civil war period. This historical crippling is one which, I believe, we are still trying to overcome.[142]

CONCLUSION

Partition, the Treaty, the public band tradition, the 1916 Rising, and de Valera's vanity have all been invoked as the principle causes of the Irish civil war, but the most natural response is to believe that it reflected the existence of rival traditions within Irish nationalism. This would provide an obvious answer to the crucial question of how such a bitter civil war could have been fought amongst a people whose political history under the Union was mainly one of maintaining consensus and glossing over internal differences. However, the possibility that rival traditions tore the movement apart only becomes obvious in retrospect, once the Treaty was signed, much in the same way that the localism and factionalism within the IRA became a real problem once the Treaty undermined the authority of the Ministry of Defence. The nature of the settlement was clearly crucial. Neeson remarks that as a model for resolving differences de Valera's external association formula had appeared too early in the annals of imperial history, when imperial membership meant only one thing and freedom separ-ation, to resolve the Anglo-Irish conflict.[143] If the formula had potential for peace in 1922, however, this would support the widely held argument that the failure of the negotiations to produce a compromise that satisfied Irish national aspirations was the major cause of the civil war.[144]

Another good reason for doubting that the existence of 'two traditions' was a sufficient rather than a necessary cause of the civil war was the sense of shock with which the conflict was experienced by the Irish public, in such a way as to shatter its belief in its own uniqueness. The dramatic loss of confidence in key leaders, the jockeying for power on both sides, and the extreme methods the conflict gave rise to all formed a brutal counterpoint to the view that the Irish were a spiritually pure people in a world of godless materialism.[145] In such a context the belief that

[142] Garvin, 'The Aftermath of the Irish Civil War'.
[143] Neeson, *The Civil War 1922–1923*, 69.
[144] Mansergh, 'The Freedom to Achieve Freedom?', 181.
[145] See O'Hegarty, *The Victory of Sinn Fein*, 126–31.

the civil war was a reflection on the unruly character of Irish nationalism was a natural response for a people long accustomed to hearing that they were unfit for self-government. Notably, in contrast to MacArdle, who believed that the revolt against British rule brought out the best in the Irish people, O'Hegarty related the lowering of moral standards among the public at large during the War of Independence to the civilian leadership's failure to maintain control over the IRA.[146] Yet the contrary argument, that political circumstances themselves dictated that the Sinn Fein revolution would combust in an internal flagration, is also a strong one. Comparative analysis suggests that transitional states, where a change of regime or of a political system has just occurred, are the most likely to experience civil war.[147] Add to that the fact that the withdrawal of a common enemy is bound to raise the question of who should inherit the Empire's legislative and military power, and another stark probability suggests itself. Indeed violent succession crises of various kinds followed soon after the First World War in many post-imperial European states, and the Irish conflict was not unique.[148] Civil war is also likely when those entrusted with the task of state-building have a weak power-base compared to other forces in the new state.[149] The Irish case lends support to all three propositions.

On the civil war's impact on Irish political development generally, a notable paradox has always existed in the literature. Writers like O'Hegarty saw the civil war as a triumph of democracy, but then commented on the loss in 1922 of the decency, selflessness, and idealism that had initially sustained the Sinn Fein movement.[150] Today historians who subscribe to the nationalist interpretation of the origins of the civil war, like Garvin, are also sceptical about its salutary effects. Although celebrating the achievements of the pro-treaty elite in *1922: The Birth of Irish Democracy*, Garvin had earlier described Irish democracy as a political marriage between republican elites who were cynical about the people and an electorate who would only vote for the immediate advantages offered to them by these elites.[151] Obviously, if historians who believe that the survival of Irish democracy was at stake in the civil war also believe that nothing much was ultimately achieved by the conflict, there can be no nationalist interpretation of the conflict. There is no space here to enumerate the standard wisdom about the negative consequences of the conflict: the bitterness that marred parliamentary debate, the disappearance of women from the public realm, the censoriousness of many state policies, the copper-fastening of partition, and the neglect of many

---

[146] Ibid., 37.

[147] H. Hegre, T. Ellengsen, S. Gates, and N. P. Gladitsch, 'Towards a Democratic Civil Peace? Democracy, Political Change, and Civil War, 1816–1992', *American Political Science Review* 95, (2001), 16–33.

[148] J. Coakley, 'Political Succession and Regime Change in the New States in Interwar Europe: Ireland, Finland, Czechoslovakia, and the Baltic Republics', *European Journal of Political Research* (1987), 14, 187–207.

[149] J. Cohen, B. R. Brown, and A. F. K. Organski, 'The Paradoxical Nature of State Making: The Violent Creation of Order', *American Political Science Review*, 75 (1981), 901–11.

[150] O'Hegarty, *The Victory of Sinn Fein*, 129.

[151] T. Garvin, *Nationalist Revolutionaries in Ireland* (Oxford, 1987), 165.

pressing social issues.[152] Lee suggests that the impact of the civil war on Irish political development depended on the nature of Irish political culture and the need both the largest parties felt for a cause that would highlight the differences between them, but whether such intense adversarial competition within an overarching nationalist consensus left a positive legacy depends very much on one's view of how well the political system served the public.[153] The fact that the Treaty did not provide a permanent basis for Irish political development, and the fact that partition remained contested, has meant that issues relating to the internal structure of Irish society were, until the 1960s, marginalized (to say the least). The contribution of the civil war to Irish democracy was ambiguous at best, compared to the undoubted fallout in terms of a stunted political pluralism and a fallen idealism. Fintan O'Toole has suggested that there are two ways in which a society that thinks it is special can react to the discovery that it is capable of brutality. One is to pretend that nothing has happened and take refuge in a fantasy of spiritual purity. Another is to become petty and cynical, expecting nothing from the political process. The tragedy of the Irish case is that they did both these things at the same time.[154]

[152] See Garvin, 'The Aftermath of the Irish Civil War'.
[153] Lee, *Ireland 1912–1985*, 69.
[154] F. O'Toole, 'Civil War Shattered a Belief in Our Own Uniqueness', *Irish Times*, 18 December 1998.

10

Conclusion

Eight decades or more after the end of the Irish civil war there is little sense in which an agreed interpretation of the conflict has emerged among historians, their readers, or the general public. Such was the formative nature of the civil war that the time span in public memory between 1922 and the early twenty-first century seems necessarily short. More than the tradition of collective action started by O'Connell in the 1820s, more than the idealism of 1916, and more than the presence of an overarching authority in the Catholic Church, the civil war has had a formative influence on the development of the Irish state that has not been matched by any other factor. Indeed, the key issue in the civil war—how Irish republicanism could be reconciled to a democratic but 26-county state— remains a source of contention in the early twenty-first century, and the current growth of Sinn Fein ensures that it will remain so. Politicians know this and are keen to trace the legitimacy of their own political traditions to the divisions of 1922. During the Fine Gael party's annual pilgrimage to *Béal na Bláth*, the scene of Collins' death, on 19 August 2001, former party leader Michael Noonan referred to Collins as 'the father of Irish democracy'.[1] In contrast, Fianna Fail's Charlie McCreevy told a meeting in Cork in April 2004 that the men and women of 1916, rather than those who took power in 1922, were the real founders of the Irish state, and gave the Irish people the freedom they enjoy today.[2] So profound is this difference of opinion, and so key are assumptions of personal heroism to the whole debate, that the task of the historian, when summing up his contribution to the field, might be to depersonalize the question of causality, and emphasize the constricting conditions in which political elites were forced to operate.

THE ISSUE OF CAUSALITY

At the very least the civil war, along with partition, should be seen as a product of the universal difficulty of carrying out secession from what is internationally regarded as a democratic state, as opposed to an antiquated empire. Successful secession, as opposed to decolonization, is an extremely rare event in inter-

---

[1] *Irish Times*, 19 December 2002.
[2] Ibid., 12 April 2004.

national politics, and in 1918 the British political elite did not emerge victorious from the First World War to contemplate humiliation on their own backyard.[3] Even when the seceding territory is not adjacent to the core of the state, the territorial contraction of states often comes about, not just at the cost of radic-alizing nationalism, but at the breaking of the constitutional consensus of the metropolitan elites.[4] With Lloyd George, in 1921 the British elite moved very far from the fractious days of the Home Rule crisis, but not to the point of forcing Ulster Unionists into an all-Ireland state, or allowing the 26 counties to break away from the Empire. As Collins recognized, their priorities were basically imperial, but one should also remember that apart from the consensual separ-ation of Norway from Sweden in 1905, the western European state system had largely been impervious to secession since the formation of Belgium in 1830. The Irish (partial) break-away from the UK in 1922 was an exception to the historical trend.

Of course Irish nationalists also tried to exploit the favourable international climate for small European nations that emerged in 1918, but the confluence of factors that produced the 1918 electoral landslide were temporary in nature. They made a case for separation as decolonization, but by 1921 their international diplomacy for this interpretation had clearly failed. Indeed the evidence suggests that only the descent of the War of Independence into terror and counter-terror in 1920 (and not the electoral victories of Sinn Fein) forced the British govern-ment to contemplate fundamental compromise. By then the island had already been partitioned, and the southern public increasingly war weary. Total separ-ation from Britain now had all the connotations of secession. In that context, the Treaty settlement was an inevitable one, and the main weakness of the anti-treaty position remained their lack of a constructive alternative. Indeed their civil war propaganda largely ignored the issue of partition, conscious as they were that it could be ended only by another, more destructive, civil war.[5] De Valera's scheme of external association, which also effectively accepted partition, was a fair one, but it too acknowledged that a total break was unrealizable, and his opponents argued that he openly admit the logic of that position. Irish independence, in other words, could only come in stages, and if not achieved in stages, it would come at a human cost that pro-treaty politicians were unwilling to accept responsibility for.

Yet although the civil war would force nationalists of all persuasions to realize the tragedy latent in Ireland's revolutionary politics, the conflict also started in, and in large measure was necessitated by, the institutional vacuum in which the Treaty split occurred. Civil wars normally have their roots in various kinds of

---

[3] J. M. Regan, *The Irish Counter-revolution 1921–36: Treatyite Politics and Settlement in Independent Ireland* (Dublin, 1999), 24.

[4] I. Lustick, *Unsettled States: Disputed Lands: Britain and Ireland, France and Algeria, Israel and the West Bank* (Ithaca, NY and London, 1993), 42.

[5] G. Walker, 'Propaganda and Conservative Nationalism during the Irish Civil War, 1922–1923', *Eire-Ireland*, 22/4 (Winter 1987), 105.

objective grievance, but the combination of weak central institutions with political polarization is often what makes them unavoidable. Under the terms of the Treaty the Irish Free State would come into being no later than December of the following year. Both Griffith's Dail cabinet, which would be replaced once an election took place, and Collins' Provisional government, whose work would be completed when the Free State came into being, were thus of a temporary nature. The basic feature of parliamentary democracy, a governing executive responsible to parliament, was also absent in the first part of 1922. Effective diplomacy was conducted through informal and secretive channels, but there were no formal mechanisms for the regulation of conflict. For example, the Dail committee charged with finding terms for an agreed election in May failed in its efforts, and agreement was only achieved through the last-minute intervention of Collins.[6] By May 1922 the Second Dail itself had become merely 'a showpiece which preserved the trappings of republicanism', and did not even debate the pact before agreeing to its terms.[7]

Moreover, in June 1922, most of the territory of the state was under the control of IRA units hostile to the Provisional government, and although the IRA would show little appetite for civil war once it started, Collins' tactic of delaying confrontation over the Treaty must have encouraged many to believe they could still dictate terms of the Provisional government. As Fitzpatrick put it, when the state apparatus is undeveloped, 'both the risks entailed by rebellion, and the benefits of peaceable political participation seem minor'.[8] Compounding this lack of state authority were organizational anomalies stemming from the revolutionary period. The IRA had never been under the effective control of politicians before 1922, whereas Sinn Fein as a party had almost ceased to function during the Anglo-Irish war. The Irish Republican Brotherhood, headed by Collins, straddled both organizations with an ill-defined relationship to their leaders. As in other post-colonial contexts, 'the weakness of the various nationalist institutions, and the speed and improvised nature of their growth, made for an increased importance for individuals and the divisions between them'.[9] What followed in the civil war was thus 'the violent creation of order' on the part of the Provisional government, and one more example of the paradoxical relationship between violent conflict and state-building.

Yet if institutional factors are to be blamed for the elite's failure to prevent the Treaty split resulting in civil war, within the nationalist elite itself, the civil war was attributed either to British malevolence or to the IRA's rejection of democratic authority in 1922. The former argument has two strands: one that focuses on the pressure brought to bear on the Provisional government in June 1922, and

---

[6] B. Kissane, *Explaining Irish Democracy* (Dublin, 2002), 127.

[7] T. D. Williams, 'From the Treaty to the Civil War', in T. D. Williams (ed.), *The Irish Struggle 1916–1926* (London, 1966), 125.

[8] D. Fitzpatrick, *The Two Irelands 1912–1939* (Oxford, 1998), 117.

[9] M. Hopkinson, 'From Treaty to Civil War, 1921–22', in J. R. Hill (ed.), *A New History of Ireland: vol. 7 Ireland, 1921–84* (Oxford, 2003), 6.

the other that relates to the 'literal' way the Treaty was implemented after Collins' death. In the first respect there is no doubt that the British government played a part in thwarting Collins' stratagems, and had Collins, through the pact, succeeded in delaying the decision on the Treaty, the new state *might* 'have acquired sufficient firepower and discipline to stifle its opponents without substantial bloodshed'.[10] On the other hand, the suggestion that Collins' successors abandoned his 'stepping stone' approach to the Treaty, at Britain's behest, ignores the fact that they thought the Treaty a good bargain, and one that should be honoured. Moreover, their 'literal' approach to the settlement was a token of their desire for stability, and for prioritizing internal consolidation over and above the redress of nationalist grievance. Only the establishment of social order and the successful running of the southern state could entice the unionists into unity, and here the republicans had no answer.

In contrast, the anti-treaty IRA have been blamed with undermining the democratic process, and for creating the conditions in which military confrontation became inevitable in June 1922. Indeed, the evidence suggests that some military conflict between the more radical IRA men and the Provisional government was inevitable once the Treaty was signed. Yet, if the IRA's Executive meeting held on 18 June showed that a large minority of them were determined to restart the conflict with Britain, the majority also placed their faith in the moderate tactics of Liam Lynch. Hart notes that the strategy of the pre-war volunteers had been a deterrent one—merely by existing they would prevent partition and conscription and save the national honour—and this attitude influenced the bulk of anti-treaty IRA, who had no serious plans to pull off a *coup d'état* in 1922.[11] In other words, the moderate anti-treaty IRA obstructed rather than threatened the democratic process, and although their attitude was a key factor in that mix of circumstances that led to civil war, it was not the only one. Once the fighting began, the reluctance with which they joined the fray suggests that it may be because there was a romantic tradition of violence that, paradoxically, the fighting was so limited.

EVALUATING THE CIVIL WAR

Yet if it is possible to divest many of the actors with responsibility for the civil war, while retaining a sense of their causal significance, arguments about the legacy of the civil war, the costs and benefits associated with such a bitter conflict, are more contentious. Here the major question is whether the civil war completed or 'countered' the Irish national revolution. Girvin has pointed out the ways in which the Irish case does not satisfy the objective requirements of a revolution, but this approach is open to the objection that Sinn Fein was revolutionary in the

---

[10] Fitzpatrick, *The Two Irelands*, 125.
[11] P. Hart, *The IRA at War 1916–1923* (Oxford, 2003), 101.

context of Irish history.[12] Indeed in three ways historians have argued that the civil war completed the Irish national revolution. Curran believes that the Dail's acceptance of the Treaty 'marked the culmination of the Irish Revolution', since it brought the Act of Union to an end, and this was the objective of the most advanced nationalist movements in the nineteenth century.[13] Hart believes that the Irish revolution came to an end on 30 April 1923 with the IRA ceasefire, since it completed what the Irish people had been fighting for since 1916, the transfer of sovereignty from the British state to the Irish people. Since the Rising a situation of 'multiple sovereignty' had existed, and only the complete victory of the Free State ended that situation by locating sovereignty exclusively in the people.[14] Finally, for Girvin, the 1923 electoral victory of Cumann na nGaedheal completed the Irish revolution by endowing the Cosgrave government with democratic legitimacy.[15] Regan, in contrast, believes that in so much as violence ceased after the Treaty settlement, and new governmental institutions were then established, a 'counter-revolution' took place, albeit in the name of constitutional politics. The result of the civil war was the return of power to the small Catholic middle class that was poised to inherit in the event of a Home Rule settlement before 1914.[16] A compromise between these positions might be to adapt Gramsci's conception of 'passive revolution' to the Irish case. Superficial political changes took place, but the pro-treaty elite countered the revolution precisely at the point in which it threatened to jeopardize the existing social order. In the long run the Catholic middle classes produced by the educational reforms of the late nineteenth century did take over the apparatus of the colonial state, but no fundamental social revolution occurred. Instead, as in other post-colonial cases, the space occupied by civil society institutions like the Gaelic League came to be occupied by institutions of political society with a close affiliation with the state. As a result, nationalist politics became substantially de-radicalized.

In any case the simplest objection to the thesis that the civil war completed the Irish revolution is that it assumes a partitioned Ireland, which Sinn Fein explicitly opposed in the 1921 general election, which returned the Second Dail as a thirty-two-county parliament. However, the civil war saw the development of a peace policy towards the Stormont government almost from the start, the stiffening of the siege mentality of Ulster Unionists, and the postponement of a boundary commission, part of whose task would be to redraw the border. In the course of the Treaty negotiations and after, the Sinn Fein elite had failed to make a priority of partition, or defend the interests of northern Catholics, who proved to be an indirect victim of the southern civil war. It seems that the shock of the civil war forced them to conclude that the consolidation of independence was more

[12] B. Girvin, *From Union to Union: Nationalism, Democracy and Religion in Ireland—Act of Union to EU* (Dublin, 2002), 64.

[13] J. M. Curran, *The Birth of the Irish Free State 1921–1923* (Mobile, Ala., 1980), 278.

[14] Hart, *The IRA at War*, 22.

[15] Girvin, *From Union to Union*, 65.

[16] Regan, *The Irish Counter-revolution*, Preface.

important than any imperative to Irish unity.[17] With the death of Collins, opposition to what he considered the restoration of 'the old ascendancy' was superseded by ambiguity if not a tacit partitionism.[18] Yet fixation on the internal politics of the Provisional government in 1922 does no justice to the enormity of what happened in nationalist consciousness. After existing throughout the ages as a unified cultural unit, southern nationalism seemed to renounce the 'map image' of Ireland, and turn their back on the North. Yet the emergence of a particularly southern form of Irish nationalism before 1922 has not been treated seriously enough as a problem by historians, even if it appears to be such a remarkable aspect of the civil war. Revealingly, most of the peace terms exchanged between the two sides did not even mention the issue of partition. Perhaps since the logic of the Gaelic revival had been cultural to begin with, it was no surprise that the centre of gravity within Irish nationalism would come to lie in those areas in the south and west that were most distinct from Britain. Analogously, those areas that were most British did not feature in the nationalist imagination. On the other hand, the civil war proved to be a profoundly formative event in many ways, and a political and bureaucratic elite committed to the defence of state institutions in 1922–3 can only think of those institutions in territorial terms. Political order in the modern world cannot be conceived of in a non-territorial way, but whereas the postponement of any attention to the border question was understandable in 1922, the long-term failure of the southern state to defend the interests of northern Catholics would carry a heavy price for all parties.

Nevertheless, the typical southern response to the issue is to emphasize the 'either or' nature of the choice in 1922. Was the Sinn Fein elite to pursue an irredentist and destabilizing policy in 1922, or to commit itself to the vindication of Irish democratic traditions within the political unit that history bequeathed them with? So dominant is the 'triumph of democracy' theme within contemporary Irish history that there is no need to recapitulate the arguments here. Suffice it to say that the argument originated with P. S. O'Hegarty, who at one stage was considered too partisan a judge. On the other hand, the Fianna Fail school of revisionist history has been unable to acknowledge the undemocratic nature of the IRA's position in 1922, perhaps because of the success of their democratic career after 1932. According to Sean MacEntee in 1936,

It is a matter of practical political experience that the principle of majority rule can only be effectively applied when the psychological conditions among the mass of the electorate are suitable. In the case of the Treaty a revolutionary temper pervaded the parties on both sides. Only a short time previously the whole nation had seen what was regarded as the triumph of force where previously the votes of an overwhelming majority had been unavailing. Moreover, feeling ran high and those who were opposed to the Treaty felt that there existed a solemn compact with the dead to maintain the Republican institutions of the state, while those who were for it held that the opinion of the living should prevail.

---

[17]   M. Hopkinson, 'Civil War and Aftermath, 1922–4', in J. R. Hill (ed.), *A New History of Ireland: vol. 7 Ireland, 1921–84* (Oxford, 2003), 61.

[18]   Collins, speech at Mansion House, 9 June 1922 (NA, D/T, S10961).

The principle of majority rule could not be applied effectively to solve such a difficulty, and it was put aside as much by one section as the other.[19]

On the other hand, as Regan has argued, although the anti-treaty position in 1922 was not democratic, neither was it exclusively undemocratic, and the implementation of the Treaty was a violation of Ireland's right to freely determine its own future.[20] In other words, in 1922 the country was faced with an unenviable choice between democracy for the 26 counties and Ireland's right to self-determination, and it took the more pragmatic and less heroic of the two. The dilemma is obvious when it comes to consideration of the 1922 constitution. On 14 June 1922 Gavan Duffy wrote to Collins that apart from the 'abominable' oath, the preamble was the worst thing in the draft, since it seems to make the constitution derive its force from the Treaty.[21] In contrast, Kevin O'Shiel argued,

The strong democratic tone of the draft is obvious from such provisions as those abolishing titles of honour; making inviolable the personal liberty and the dwelling houses of citizens, freedom of conscience and the free profession and practice of religion; establishing the right of free expression of opinion and the right of all citizens to assemble peacefully and without arms, and to form associations and unions; the prohibition, except under state supervision, of the exploitation by private individuals of the natural resources of the country; the abolition of sex distinction and what amounts to virtual adult suffrage etc.[22]

The constitution showed that the relationship between Britain and Ireland in 1922 was not one of equals, but the Free State would be as democratic as circumstances permitted. As a result, since two opposed sets of rights were at issue in 1922, the civil war conflict should be evaluated as a tragic one, in contrast to the implication of the triumph of democracy thesis. Moreover, if the Treaty was an essentially coerced settlement, as the anti-treatyites have always claimed, then the pro-treatyites were not authors of their own actions, and choices not freely made should not become the object of praise or blame. The pro-treaty position was the more democratic one in 1922, but since a basic inequality in military power underwrote the whole settlement, the civil war cannot be considered a triumph of Irish democracy as opposed to British imperialism. Of course a democratic state was the outcome of the civil war, but the resilience of Irish democracy might be attributed to many other factors beyond the trenches of 1922. Whether the eventual result, an ostensibly democratic state, with a poor record on policy issues and little civic pride, was worth the violence and suffering of 1922 is an open question, but the fighting in 1922 was not lightly entered into in any case.

---

[19] MacEntee to Honorary Secretaries, 27 January 1936 (UCD, MacEntee Papers, P67/453).
[20] J. M. Regan, 'Review of Tom Garvin's *1922: The Birth of Irish Democracy*', *History Ireland*, 5/2 (1997), 55.
[21] Gavan Duffy to Collins, 14 June 1922 (NA, D/T S9855).
[22] Kevin O'Shiel, Memo on the Constitution, June 1922 (NA, D/T, S9855).

THE CIVIL WAR AND IRISH HISTORIOGRAPHY

Indeed a key paradox of the civil war lies in the fact that a conflict that no one wanted should so fundamentally affect the development of Irish politics up to now. This is partly due to the obsession with personalities. The biographical approach to the period, which emphasizes the theme of heroic (Collins) or unheroic (de Valera) leadership, continues to thrive, and rests on the basic assumption that such a destructive Irish civil war could not have happened had the two men not become rivals. Nevertheless, the history of the Treaty negotiations also shows how judgements of causality, and those of personal responsibility, can diverge in Irish popular memory of the civil war. On the one hand, since the Treaty was bound to cause divisions, Collins' decision to accept it, in the interest of avoiding further conflict with Britain, was a cause of the Irish civil war. On the other hand, since it is generally agreed that he got as much from the negotiations as was humanly possible, he is not regarded as responsible for the civil war. De Valera, on the other hand, did not cause the Treaty to be signed, but his deliberate courting of IRA support once it was signed exposed him to the charge that he was responsible for the civil war. His inflammatory speeches were acts of will or of a politician who had lost his judgement, whereas Collins' acceptance of the Treaty was involuntary in nature.

Yet even if the issue of personal responsibility could be disassociated from that of causality in this way, it is doubtful whether such distinctions would mean much to the general public. Either way, if a more balanced view of the civil war is to be achieved by Irish historians, there is a need for both a narrower and a broader focus. In the former vein, both the local studies of Hart and Farry have cast light on the factors that led IRA units to oppose the Provisional government, and developments during the truce period seem to have been key. However, despite O'Gadhra's recent work on the civil war in Connacht, the regional distribution of opposition to the Treaty, so obvious a feature of the 1923 general election, has not received enough attention. As Hopkinson suggests, political opposition to the Treaty seemed to reflect socio-economic differences, strengthening as one goes further west.[23] On other hand, since these areas were far removed from Dublin geographically, it could simply be that they were in a position to oppose the government. Either way, it may be that local studies of counties such as Mayo and Kerry will shed light on this issue.

On the other hand, there is a need for a broader perspective too, which might help explain why the civil war proved to be such a formative event in Irish political development. The translation of civil war differences into two pivotal political parties also followed the Costa Rican civil war in 1948, but there has been little comparative work on how civil wars affect states' pattern of development. Within Europe, the best comparison is still Finland, where civil war also occurred soon after independence, and was preceded by a constitutional

---

[23] Hopkinson, 'From Treaty to Civil War', 6.

crisis in which political divisions coincided with rivalry over which organizations should provide for public order.[24] The comparison seems apt but there is a crucial difference. The Finnish right interpreted their civil war in national terms, as a War of Independence against leftist forces that had been contaminated by their exposure to the Soviet Union. The left, in contrast, interpreted the war in social terms, as a defence of the gains for the Social Democrats that had followed the October revolution.[25] In Ireland in contrast, it was the anti-treatyites who interpreted the civil war in national terms, as a continuation of the War of Independence against a governing elite that had become contaminated by their exposure to Britain. On the other hand, the pro-treatyites came to interpret the conflict in social terms. In November 1922 Eoin MacNeill remarked that peace could only be discussed with a man you 'would chat and smoke and play cards with, and not a man to be avoided'.[26] The key difference then was that in Ireland the losers had nationalism on their side, and their subsequent integration into post-civil war society stems from this basic fact. As Bowyer Bell remarked, 'the hard core republicans, who remained outside the governmental system, did not become a dissident society, but only a dissenting current within Irish society'.[27] In contrast in Finland, the hard left remained a marginalized section of Finnish society for decades to come.

For political science the issue is more what light the Irish conflict sheds on general theories of civil war. On the one hand, the uniqueness of the conflict stands out. The post-colonial parallels fall down on closer inspection, whereas the European civil wars of the period all involved a strong challenge from the left, which was absent in Ireland. On the other hand, the Irish civil war provides an interesting case study of how resources and grievances affect each other. Generally, grievances in Ireland were strong enough to provide the impetus for a long-term conflict, but the skewed nature of resource distribution saved the country from a more prolonged and destructive civil war. Even at that, the polarization of views on the constitutional issues in the autumn of 1922, the uneasy relationship between de Valera and Lynch, and the failure of so many peace initiatives, are testimony to the uncompromising nature of the Treaty divide. The case study literature on civil war emphasizes how identities often evolve during civil wars, with significant consequences for their duration, and the manner in which the perspectives of Collins and de Valera became marginalized as the Irish fighting went on is a textbook example of how war polarizes ideas.[28] Nevertheless, stability did follow the civil war and consensus on the rules of the game also ensued, even

[24] See B. Kissane, 'Democratization, State Formation, and Civil War in Finland and Ireland: A Reflection on the Democratic Peace Hypothesis', *Comparative Political Studies*, 37/8 (2004), 969–85.

[25] See R. Alapuro, 'Coping with the Civil War of 1918 in Twenty-First Century Finland', in K. Christie and R. Cribb (eds.), *Historical Injustice and Democratic Transition in Eastern Asia and Northern Europe* (London and New York, 2002), 169.

[26] Memo, 30 November 1922 (NA, D/T, S8142).

[27] J. Bowyer Bell, 'Societal Patterns and Lessons: The Irish Case', in R. Higham (ed.), *Civil Wars in the Twentieth Century* (Lexington, 1972), 224.

[28] E. J. Wood, 'Civil Wars: What We Don't Know', *Global Governance*, 9/2 (2003), 253.

if it was a 'stability without compromise'.[29] What has been less remarked upon is how an agreement that what actually happened in 1922–3 did amount to a civil war was also part of the post-civil war consensus that came into its own during the Second World War. In the long run, the balance of power between the two traditions in Irish society was so strong that neither could deny the validity of the other's perspective. Electorally, Fine Gael were the long-term losers of the civil war, but their perspective dominated in other domains, such as the universities, and the institutions of the state are also largely their creation. The claims of southern democracy, as opposed to thirty-two-county republicanism, might again be put to the test, but were right entirely on one side in 1922, it is doubtful that the civil war would have had the legacy it has had.

In any case, the contemporary resonance of the issues might serve to cloud understanding, since the nature of the choice faced by the Irish public in 1922 is unlikely to be replicated. At issue was the question of Empire, and whereas one side would have preferred rejection in the name of Ireland's revolutionary traditions, the other saw an outward orientation as a guarantee of peace, prosperity, and ideally unity. In the first tradition, the purpose of political leadership in a society thrown back on its own cultural resources was to prevent the society becoming sullied by the nip and tuck of international politics. De Valera's enthusiasm for the League of Nations notwithstanding, the 1937 constitution, neutrality, and post-war isolationism all followed the logic of this tradition. The other side believed that the criteria for evaluating the fruits of independence were not specific to the country itself, and as the Republic fell behind the rest of Europe economically after 1945, it became increasingly difficult to ignore this perspective. Indeed whereas a pragmatic and constructive acceptance of the Commonwealth in 1922 was seen as a denial of Irish national traditions, membership of the European Union has now resolved the dilemma that faced the country in 1922. It has restored the Irish to the status of a European nation, and given the state an outlet for those constructive and international instincts that all small nations must cultivate if they are to engage with the world. It is customary to represent this shift as a switch to a liberal, modern, and outward-looking type of nationalism, which contrasts with that embodied by the republican tradition after 1922. However, in the period between 1917 and 1921 Irish republicanism was also outward-looking, and only the force of international circumstances forced it to chose between the isolated Republic and cooperation with the other nations of the Commonwealth on the basis of equality. Eighty-three years on, the choice is no longer necessary, but time has not diminished the integrity of the original quarrel.

---

[29] See A. Zink, 'Ireland: Stability without Compromise', in D. Berg-Schlosser and J. Mitchell (eds.), *Conditions of Democracy in Europe, 1919–1939* (Basingstoke, 2000), 263–94.

Bibliography

PRIMARY SOURCES

National Archives Dublin

Department of An Taoiseach
Department of the Environment/Local Government
Department of Justice
Cabinet Minutes
Sinn Fein Papers
Gavan Duffy Papers

National Library of Ireland

Florence O'Donoghue Papers
Thomas Johnson Papers
William O'Brien Papers

UCD Archives

Frank Aiken Papers
Ernest Blythe Papers
Eamon de Valera Papers
Desmond FitzGerald Papers
Michael Hayes Papers
Diarmuid Hegarty Papers
Hugh Kennedy Papers
Sean MacEntee Papers
Richard Mulcahy Papers
Ernie O'Malley Papers
Moss Twomey Papers

Newspapers/Journals

Freeman's Journal
Irish Bulletin
Irish Independent
Irish Times
Nationality
Poblacht na hEireann
The Free State
The Separatist
The Southern Bulletin

The Round Table
Voice of Labour

Pamphlets/Contemporary Publications

American Association for the Recognition of the Irish Republic, *Constitution of the American Association for the Recognition of the Irish Republic*, P2167, NL.

American Commission on Irish Independence, *Report on Conditions in Ireland with Demand for Investigation by the Peace Conference* (Paris, American Commission on Irish Independence, June 1919).

Anonymous, *Sinn Fein and the Peace Conference: Promises and Performances* (Dublin, 1919).

Barton, R., *The Truth about the Treaty: A Reply to Michael Collins* (Dublin, 1922).

Bright, J. H. *What's Wrong with Ireland* (Dublin, 1919).

Childers, E., *What the Treaty Means* (Dublin, 1922).

—— *Clause by Clause: A Comparison between the Treaty and Document No. 2* (Dublin, 1922).

Collins, M., *The Substance of Freedom*, 5 March 1922, LOP102, NL.

de Valera, E., *The Foundation of the Republic of Ireland in the Vote of the People* (Melbourne?, 1919).

—— *The Testament of the Republic*, LO P101, NL.

—— *Ireland and India* (New York, 1920).

—— *De Valera: Peace and War*, IR 94109 D27 NL.

Griffith, A., *Arguments for the Treaty* (Dublin, 1922).

House of Representatives, *The Irish Question: Hearings before the Committee on Foreign Affairs, House of Representatives Sixty-fifth Congress, Third Session, December 12 1918* (Washington, 1919).

Irish Labour Party, 'Statement of International Aims Presented by the National Executive of the Irish Labour Party and Unanimously Endorsed by the Special Congress at Its Sitting on Friday November 1 1918', *Ireland at Berne: Being the Report and Memoranda Presented to the International Labour and Socialist Conference held at Berne, February 1919* (Dublin, 1919).

Irish Parliamentary Party, *Ireland's Appeal to President Wilson: Irish Parliamentary Party Reiterates the National Claim*, 5 November 1918, NL.

Irish Self-Determination League of Great Britain, pamphlet, ILB 300 P7, 41 NL.

Jordan, T. H., *Pampered Ireland: Fact not Fiction* (Belfast, 1919).

MacSwiney, M., *The Background of the Irish Republic* (Chicago, 1921), 33.

—— *The Republic of Ireland* (Cork, n.d.).

Oglaigh na h-Eireann (Dublin, 1932), LO P101, NL.

O'Rahilly, A., *The Case for the Treaty*, LO P102, NL, 22.

Sinn Fein, 'Sinn Fein Statement to the International Socialist Conference at Stockholm, December 1917', His Majesty's Stationary Office, *Correspondance Relating to the Proposal for Her Majesty's Government for an Irish Settlement* (London: HMSO, 1921), Appendix B, 57.

—— 'Address to the Congress of the United States, adopted at the January Session of Dail Eireann', 1921, NL.

—— *The Case of Ireland*, Sinn Fein Series No. 12 (1919), IR 94109 P90, NL.

—— *Ireland's Request to the Government of the United States of America for Recognition as a Sovereign Independent State* (Dublin, 1919).

Spedding, R. F., *The Call of Democracy: A Study of the Irish Question* (Dublin, 1919).

SECONDARY SOURCES

Adams, G., *Free Ireland: Towards a Lasting Peace* (Dingle, 1995).

Ageron, C. R., *Modern Algeria: A History from 1830 to the Present* (London, 1991).

Akenson, D. H., 'Was de Valera a Republican?', *Review of Politics*, 33/2 (1971), 233–54.

—— and J. F. Fallon, 'The Irish Civil War and the Drafting of the Free State Constitution', *Eire/Ireland*, 5/1 (Spring, 1970), 10–26; 5/2 (summer 1970), 42–93; 5/4, 28–70.

Alapuro, R., 'Coping with the Civil War of 1918 in Twenty-First Century Finland', in K. Christie and R. Cribb (eds.), *Historical Injustice and Democratic Transition in Eastern Asia and Northern Europe* (London and New York, 2002), 169–84.

Alter, P., *Nationalism*, second edn. (London, 1994).

Anderson, B., *The Spectre of Comparisons: Nationalism, Southeast Asia and the World* (London and New York, 1998).

Andrews, C. S., *Man of No Property* (Dublin and Cork, 1982).

Ansprenger, F., *The Dissolution of the Colonial Empires* (London and New York, 1989).

Augusteijn, J., *From Public Defiance to Guerrilla Warfare: The Experience of Ordinary Volunteers in the Irish War of Independence, 1916–1921* (Dublin, 1996).

—— 'Political Violence and Democracy: An Analysis of the Tensions within Irish Republican Strategy, 1914–2004', *Irish Political Studies*, 18/1 (2003), 1–27.

Axelrod, R., 'An Evolutionary Approach to Norms', *American Political Science Review*, 80 (1986), 1095–111.

Barry, F., 'Democracy from What Point?', *Irish Review*, 20 (2000), 157–61.

Berdal, M., and D. M. Malone (eds.), *Greed and Grievance: Economic Agendas in Civil Wars* (Boulder and London, 2000).

Blake, F. M., *The Irish Civil War and What It Still Means for the Irish People* (Dublin, 1986).

Bonner, T. N., 'Civil War Historians and the Needless War Doctrine', *Journal of the History of Ideas*, 17 (1956), 193–216.

Bourke, R., *Peace in Ireland: The War of Ideas* (London, 2003).

Bowman, J., *De Valera and the Ulster Question 1917–1973* (Oxford, 1972).

Bowyer Bell, J., 'Societal Patterns and Lessons: The Irish Case', in R. Higham (ed.), *Civil Wars in the Twentieth Century* (Lexington, 1972), 217–29.

Boyce, D. G., 'How to Settle the Irish Question: Lloyd George and Ireland 1916–21', in A. J. P. Taylor (ed.), *Lloyd George: Twelve Essays* (London, 1971).

—— (ed.), *The Revolution in Ireland 1879–1923* (London, 1988)

—— *Nationalism in Ireland* (London and New York, 1991).

Bracher, K. D., *The Age of Ideologies: A History of Political Thought in the Twentieth Century* (London, 1985).

Bromage, M., *De Valera: The March of a Nation* (London, 1956).

Buber, M., *The Way of Man* (London and New York, 2002).

Burns, E., *British Imperialism in Ireland* (Cork, 1931).

Cambell, C., *Emergency Law in Ireland, 1918–1925* (Oxford, 1993).

Carty, A., *Was Ireland Conquered?: International Law and the Irish Question* (London, 1996).

Carty, R. K., 'Social Cleavages and Party Systems: A Reconsideration of the Irish Case', *European Journal of Political Research*, 4 (1976), 195–203.

Chatterjee, P., 'Whose Imagined Community?', in G. Balakrishnan (ed.), *Mapping the Nation* (London and New York, 1996).

Christie, C., *A Modern History of South-East Asia: Decolonisation, Nationalism, and Separatism* (London and New York, 2000).

Christie, K., and R. Cribb (eds.), *Historical Injustice and Democratic Transition in Eastern Asia and Northern Europe* (London and New York, 2002).

Clifford, A., *The Constitutional History of Eire/Ireland* (Belfast, 1987).

Clifford, B., *The Irish Civil War: The Conflict That Formed the State* (Cork, 1993).

Coakley, J., 'Political Succession and Regime Change in New States in Inter-war Europe: Ireland, Finland, Czechoslovakia, and the Baltic Republics', *European Journal of Political Research*, 14 (1987), 187–207.

—— 'The Election That Made the First Dail', in B. Farrell (ed.), *The Creation of the Dail: A Volume of Essays from the Thomas Davis Lectures* (Dublin, 1994), 31–46.

—— 'Competing Conceptions of Legitimacy and the Creation of the New State', *Etudes Irlandaises*, 21 (1995), 55–67.

Cobban, A., *The Nation State and National Self-Determination* (Collins, 1969).

Cohan, A. S., *The Irish Political Elite* (Dublin, 1972).

Cohen, J., B. R. Brown, and A. F. K. Organski, 'The Paradoxical Nature of Statemaking: The Violent Creation of Order', *American Political Science Review*, 75 (1981), 901–11.

—— and A. Arato, *Civil Society and Political Theory* (Cambridge, 1992).

Coleman, M., *County Longford and the Irish Revolution, 1910–1923* (Dublin, 2003).

Collier, P., *Breaking the Conflict Trap* (Washington, D. C., 2003).

—— and A. Hoeffler, *Greed and Grievance in Civil War* (Washington, D. C., 2000).

Collins, M., *The Path to Irish Freedom* (Dublin, 1996).

Constantino, R., *A History of the Philippines: From the Spanish Colonization to the Second World War* (New York and London, 1975).

—— *Neocolonial Identity and Counter Consciousness: Essays on Cultural Decolonisation* (Whitstable, 1978).

Coser, L. A., *Continuities in the Study of Social Conflict* (New York, 1970).

Costello, F., *The Irish Revolution and Its Aftermath 1916–1923* (Dublin, 2003).

Coogan, T. P., *Michael Collins* (London, 1990).

—— *De Valera: Long Fellow Long Shadow* (London, 1992).

Curran, J. M., *The Birth of the Irish Free State, 1921–1923* (Mobile, Ala., 1980).

Dahl, R., *Democracy and Its Critics* (New Haven, 1989).

Daniel, T. K., 'Griffith on His Noble Head: The Determinants of Cumann na nGaedheal Economic Policy, 1922–32', *Irish Economic and Social History*, 3 (1976), 55–65.

Davis, R., 'The Self-Determination for Ireland Leagues, and the Irish Race Convention in Paris, 1921–22', *Tasmanian Historical Research Association—Papers and Proceedings*, 24 (1977).

Davis, T., 'The Irish Civil War and the "International Proposition" of 1922–23', *Eire-Ireland*, 29 (1994), 92–112.

Deane, S., *Strange Country: Modernity and Nationhood in Irish Writing since 1790* (Oxford, 1997).

Deasy, L., *Brother against Brother* (Cork, 1998).

De Blacam, A., *Towards the Republic: A Study of New Ireland's Social and Political Aims* (Dublin, 1918).

De Vere White, T., *Kevin O'Higgins* (Tralee, 1965).

Diamond, L., 'Toward Democratic Consolidation', in L. Diamond and M. Plattner (eds.), *The Global Resurgence of Democracy*, second edn. (Baltimore and London, 1996).

Dion, S., 'Why is Secession Difficult in Well-established Democracies?: Lessons from Quebec', *British Journal of Political Science*, 26/2 (1996), 269–83.

Doherty, G., and D. Keogh (eds.), *Michael Collins and the Making of the Irish State* (Cork, 1998).

Dolan, A., *Commemorating the Irish Civil War: History and Memory, 1923–2000* (Cambridge, 2003).

Donoghue, D., 'Fears for Irish Studies in an Age of Identity Politics', *The Chronicle of Higher Education*, 21 November 1997.

Dray, W., 'Some Causal Accounts of the American Civil War', *Daedalus*, 91/3 (1962), 578–99.

Dunphy, R., *The Making of Fianna Fail Power in Ireland 1921–1948* (Oxford, 1995).

Eckstein, H., 'On the Etiology of Internal Wars', *History and Theory*, 4/1 (1963), 133–63.

English, E., and C. O'Malley (eds.), *Prisoners: The Civil War Letters of Ernie O'Malley* (Dublin, 1991).

English, R., *Radicals and the Republic: Socialist Republicanism in the Irish Free State 1925–1937* (Oxford, 1994).

—— *Armed Struggle: A History of the IRA* (Basingstoke and Oxford, 2003).

Evans, P., 'The Eclipse of the State? Reflections on Stateness in an Era of Globalization', *World Politics*, 50/1 (1997), 62–88.

Fallon, C., 'Civil War Hungerstrikes: Women and Men', *Eire-Ireland*, 12/3 (1987), 75–91.

Fanning, R., *Independent Ireland* (Dublin, 1983)

—— 'The Rule of Order: Eamon de Valera and the IRA, 1923–1940', in J. P. O'Carroll and J. A. Murphy (eds.), *De Valera and His Times* (Cork, 1983), 160–73.

Fanon, F., *The Wretched of the Earth* (London, 1963).

Farrell, B. *The Founding of Dail Eireann: Parliament and Nation-Building* (Dublin, 1971).

—— (ed.), *The Creation of the Dail* (Dublin, 1994).

Farry, M. *The Aftermath of Revolution: Sligo 1921–23* (Dublin, 2000).

Fearon, J., and D. Laitin, 'Ethnicity, Insurgency and Civil War', *American Political Science Review*, 97/1 (2003), 75–90.

Fine, R., and R. Shirin (eds.), *Civil Society: Democratic Perspectives* (London, 1997).

Fitzpatrick, D., *Politics and Irish Life 1913–1921: Provincial Experience of War and Revolution* (Dublin, 1977).

—— (ed.), *Revolution? Ireland 1917–1923* (Dublin, 1990).

—— *The Two Irelands 1912–1939* (Oxford, 1998).

Gallagher, F., *The Anglo-Irish Treaty* (London, 1965).

Gallagher, M., 'The Pact General Election of 1922', *Irish Historical Studies*, 21 (1979), 404–21.

—— *Irish Elections 1922–44: Results and Analysis* (Limerick, 1993).

Garvin, T., 'Political Cleavages, Party Politics and Urbanisation in Ireland: The Case of the Periphery-Dominated Centre', *European Journal of Political Research*, 2 (1974), 307–27.

—— *The Evolution of Irish Nationalist Politics* (Dublin, 1981).

—— 'Anatomy of a Nationalist Revolution: Ireland, 1858–1928', *Comparative Studies in Society and History*, 28 (1986), 468–501.

—— *Nationalist Revolutionaries in Ireland* (Oxford, 1987).

—— 'Unenthusiastic Democrats: The Emergence of Irish Democracy', in R. Hill and M. Marsh (eds.), *Modern Irish Democracy* (Dublin, 1993), 9–24.

—— *1922: The Birth of Irish Democracy* (Dublin, 1996).

—— 'The Aftermath of the Civil War', *The Irish Sword*, 20/80 (1997), 387–95.

—— 'Introduction', in P. S. O'Hegarty, *The Victory of Sinn Fein* (Dublin, 1998), 1–164.

Garvin, T., 'Democratic Politics in Independent Ireland', in J. Coakley and M. Gallagher (eds.), *Politics in the Republic of Ireland*, 3rd edn. (London and New York, 1999), 350–64.

Gaughan, J. A., *Austin Stack: Portrait of a Separatist* (Dublin, 1977).

—— *A Political Odyssey: Thomas O'Donnell M. P. for West Kerry 1900–1918* (Dublin, 1983).

—— *Memoirs of Senator James G. Douglas (1887–1954) Concerned Citizen* (Dublin, 1998).

Gerhard, *The Irish Free State and British Imperialism* (Cork, 1976).

Gilland Lutz, K., 'Irish Party Competition in the New Millenium: Change or Plus Ca Change?', *Irish Political Studies*, 18/2 (2003), 40–60.

Girvin, B., *From Union to Union: Nationalism, Democracy and Religion in Ireland—Act of Union to EU* (Dublin, 2002).

—— 'The Republicanisation of Irish Society, 1932–48', in J. R. Hill (ed.), *A New History of Ireland: vol. 7 Ireland, 1921–84* (Oxford, 2003), 127–59.

Greaves, C. D., *Liam Mellowes and the Irish Revolution* (London, 1971).

Griffith, A., *The Resurrection of Hungary: A Parallel for Ireland* (Dublin, 1904).

Guilbride, A., ' "A Scrapping of Every Principle of Individual Liberty": The Postal Strike of 1922', *History Ireland*, 8/4 (2000), 35–9.

Hall, J. (ed.), *Civil Society: Theory, History, Comparison* (Cambridge, 1995).

Hancock, K., *Survey of Commonwealth Affairs, vol. 1* (London, New York, Toronto, 1937).

Hanley, B., *The IRA 1926–1936* (Dublin, 2002).

Harrison, H., *Ireland and the British Empire, 1937: Conflict or Collaboration?* (London, 1937).

Hart, P., 'The Geography of Revolution in Ireland 1917–1923', *Past and Present*, 155 (1997), 142–77.

—— *The IRA and Its Enemies: Violence and Community in Cork 1916–1923* (Oxford, 1999).

—— 'Definition: Defining the Revolution', in J. Augusteijn (ed.), *The Irish Revolution, 1913–1923* (Basingstoke, 2002), 17–34.

—— *The IRA at War 1916–1923* (Oxford, 2003).

Hartnett, M., *Victory and Woe: The West Limerick Brigade in the War of Independence* (Dublin, 2002).

Healy, J., 'The Civil War Hunger Strike—October 1923', *Studies*, 71 (1982), 213–26.

Hegre, H., 'The Duration and Termination of Civil War', *Journal of Peace Research*, 41/3 (2004), 243–52.

—— T. Ellengsen, S. Gates, and N. P. Gladitsch, 'Towards a Democratic Civil Peace? Democracy, Political Change, and Civil War, 1816–1992', *American Political Science Review*, 95 (2001), 16–33.

Held, D., *Models of Democracy* (Cambridge, 1987).

Heller, J., *The Birth of Israel 1945–1949: Ben Gurion and his Critics* (Florida, 2000).

Hepburn, A. C., and E. Rumpf., *Nationalism and Socialism in Twentieth Century Ireland* (Liverpool, 1977).

Hermassi, E., *Leadership and National Development in North Africa: A Comparative Study* (Berkely, 1972).

Higham, R. (ed.), *Civil Wars in the Twentieth Century* (Lexington, 1972).

Higley, J., and M. Burton, 'Elite Settlements and the Taming of Politics', *Government and Opposition*, 33/1 (1998), 98–115.

His Majesty's Stationary Office, *Correspondence Relating to the Proposal for Her Majesty's Government for an Irish Settlement* (London, 1921).

Hobsbawm, E., *The New Century: In Conversation with Antonio Polito* (London, 2000).

Hobson, B., 'Introduction', in *Irish Free State Official Handbook* (London, 1932), 15–17.

Hopkinson, M., *Green against Green: The Irish Civil War* (Dublin, 1988).

—— 'The Craig-Collins Pacts of 1922: Two Attempted Reforms of the Northern Ireland government', *Irish Historical Studies*, 28/106 106 (1990), 145–58.

—— 'The Civil War from the Pro-Treaty Perspective', *Irish Sword*, 20/82 (1997), 287–92.

—— 'From Treaty to Civil War, 1921–22', in J. R. Hill (ed.), *A New History of Ireland: vol. 7 Ireland, 1921–84* (Oxford, 2003), 1–29.

—— 'Civil War and Aftermath, 1922–4', in J. R. Hill (ed.), *A New History of Ireland: vol. 7 Ireland, 1921–84* (Oxford, 2003), 31–59.

Horgan, J., 'Arms Dumps and the I.R.A. 1923–32', *History Today*, 48/2 (1988), 11–16.

Howe, S., *Ireland and Empire* (Oxford, 1999).

Hroch, M., *Social Conditions of National Revival in Europe: A Comparative Analysis of the Social Composition of Patriotic Groups among the Smaller European Nations* (Cambridge, 1985).

Hutchinson, J., *The Dynamics of Cultural Nationalism: The Gaelic Revival and the Creation of the Irish Nation State* (London, 1987).

Inoue, K., 'Propaganda 11: Propaganda of Dail Eireann, 1919–21', in J. Augusteijn (ed.), *The Irish Revolution, 1913–1923* (Basingstoke, 2002), 87–103.

Jackson, A., *Ireland 1798–1998: Politics and War* (Oxford, 1999).

Jackson, H. F., *The FLN in Algeria: Party Development in a Revolutionary Society* (London, 1977).

Janos, A., 'Authority and Violence: The Political Framework of Internal War', in H. Eckstein (ed.), *Internal War: Problems and Approaches* (New York, Free Press, 1963), 130–42.

Jorstad, J., 'Nations Once Again—Ireland's Civil War in European Context', in D. Fitzpatrick (ed.), *Revolution? Ireland 1917–1923* (Dublin, 1990), 159–73.

Kaldor, M., *New and Old Wars: Organised Violence in a Global Era* (Cambridge, 2001).

Kalyvas, S., 'The Ontology of "Political Violence": Action and Identity in Civil Wars', *Perspectives on Politics*, 1 (2003), 465–94.

Keane, J., *Civil Society: Old Images New Visions* (Cambridge, 1998).

Keen, D., 'Incentives and Disincentives for Violence', in M. Berdal and D. M. Malone (eds.), *Greed and Grievance: Economic Agendas in Civil Wars* (Boulder and London, 2000).

—— 'De Valera, the Catholic Church, the Treaty Split, and the Paris Irish Race Convention, 1922', *Etudes Irlandaises*, 22 (1987), 165–71.

Keogh, D., *Twentieth-Century Ireland: Nation and State* (Dublin, 1994).

—— 'A Broader Picture of 1922', *The Irish Times*, 5 October 1996.

—— 'Eamon de Valera and the Civil War in Ireland, 1922–23', in G. Doherty and D. Keogh (eds.), *De Valera's Irelands* (Cork, 2003), 45–74.

Kiberd, D., *Inventing Ireland: The Literature of the Modern Nation* (London, 1996).

Kissane, B., 'Government Changeover and Democratic Consolidation in the Irish Free State', *Journal of Commonwealth and Comparative Politics*, 39/1 (2001), 1–23.

—— 'Decommissioning as an Issue in the Irish Civil War', *Studies in Ethnicity and Nationalism*, 1/1 (2001), 8–17.

—— *Explaining Irish Democracy* (Dublin, 2002).

—— 'Democratization, State Formation, and Civil War in Finland and Ireland: A Reflection on the Democratic Peace Hypothesis', *Comparative Political Studies*, 37/8 (2004), 969–86.

Kissane, B., 'Defending Democracy?: The Legislative Response to Political Extremism in the Irish Free State, 1922–1939', *Irish Historical Studies* 134 (2004).

Knirck, J., 'Ghosts and Realities: Female TDs and the Treaty Debate', *Eire-Ireland*, 32/4 (1997).

—— 'Afterimage of the Revolution: Kevin O'Higgins and the Irish Revolution', *Eire-Ireland*, 38 (2003), 212–43.

Lacy, H., 'There Need Never Have Been a Civil War: What Caused the Tragedy', *Irish Press*, 6 August 1958.

Laffan, M., *The Resurrection of Ireland: The Sinn Fein Party 1916–23* (Cambridge, 1999).

Langan, M., and B. Schwarz (eds.), *Crises in the British State 1880–1930* (London, 1985).

Lawlor, S. M., 'Ireland from Truce to Treaty: War or Peace? July to October 1921', *Irish Historical Studies*, 22/85 (1980), 49–64.

Lee, J., *Ireland 1912–1985: Politics and Society* (Cambridge, 1989).

Licklider, R., 'How Civil Wars End: Questions and Methods', in idem (ed.), *Stopping the Killing: How Civil Wars End* (London and New York, 1993).

—— 'The Consequences of Negotiated Settlements in Civil Wars, 1945–1993', *American Political Science Review*, 89/3 (1995), 681–90.

Linz, J., and A. Stepan, *Problems of Democratic Transition and Consolidation: Southern Europe, South America, and Post Communist Europe* (Baltimore and London, 1996).

Lipset, S. M., and S. Rokkan (eds.), *Party Systems and Voter Alignments: Cross National Perspectives* (New York, 1967).

Lloyd, D. *Anomalous States: Irish Writing and the Post-Colonial Moment* (Dublin, 1993).

Lustick, I., *Unsettled States, Disputed Lands: Britain and Ireland, France and Algeria, Israel and the West Bank* (Ithaca, NY and London, 1993).

Lyons, F. S. L., 'From War to Civil War in Ireland: Three Essays on the Treaty Debate', in B. Farrell (ed.), *The Irish Parliamentary Tradition* (Dublin, 1973), 223–57.

—— *Ireland Since the Famine* (Glasgow 1983).

MacArdle, D., *The Irish Republic*, third edn. (Dublin, 1951).

McCartney, D., 'De Valéra's Mission to the United States 1919–20', in A. Cosgrove and D. McCartney (eds.), *Studies in Irish History Presented to R. Dudley Edwards* (Dublin, 1979).

McDonald, W., *Some Ethical Questions of Peace and War: Postscript in Reply to Certain Criticisms* (London, 1920).

—— *Some Ethical Questions of Peace and War* (Dublin, 1998).

MacManus, F. (ed.), *The Years of the Great Test 1916–39* (Cork, 1967), 69–80.

MacMillan, G., *State, Society and Authority in Ireland: The Foundations of the Modern State* (Dublin, 1993).

MacPherson, C. B., *The Life and Times of Liberal Democracy* (Oxford and New York, 1977).

MacSuain, S., *County Wexford's Civil War* (Wexford, 1995).

Mahajani, U., *Philippine National Revolution: External Challenges and Filipino Response 1565–1946* (St Lucia, 1971).

Mair, P., *The Changing Irish Party System; Organisation, Ideology and Electoral Competition* (London, 1987).

Mandle, W. F., 'The IRB and the Beginnings of the Gaelic Athletic Association', *Irish Historical Studies*, 20 (1977), 418–38.

Mansergh, M., 'The Freedom to Achieve Freedom? The Political Ideas of Collins and de Valera', in G. Doherty and D. Keogh (eds.), *Michael Collins and the Making of the Irish State* (Cork, 1998).

Mansergh, N., *The Commonwealth Experience: vol. 2. From British to Multiracial Common-wealth* (London, 1982).

—— *The Unresolved Question: The Anglo-Irish Settlement and Its Undoing 1912–72* (New Haven and London, 1982).

Maume, P., 'The Ancient Constitution: Arthur Griffith and His Intellectual Legacy to Sinn Fein', *Irish Political Studies*, 10 (1995), 123–38.

—— *The Long Gestation: Irish Nationalist Life 1891–1918* (Dublin, 1999).

Moss, W., *Political Parties in the Irish Free State* (New York, 1933).

Moynihan, M. (ed.), *Speeches and Statements by Eamon de Valera 1917–1973* (Dublin, 1980).

Mulholland, M., 'Review of P. Hart, *The IRA and Its Enemies: Violence and Community in Cork, 1916–1923*', *The Voice of the Turtle* (1999).

—— 'Review of Eunan O'Halpin, "Defending Ireland: The Irish State and Its Enemies since 1922"', *H Net Reviews in the Humanities and Social Sciences* (2000).

Murphy, B. P., 'The Irish Civil War 1922–1923: An Anti-Treaty Perspective', *The Irish Sword*, 20/80 (1997), 293–307.

Murray, P., *Oracles of God: The Roman Catholic Church and Irish Politics, 1922–37* (Dublin, 2000).

Neeson, E., *The Civil War 1922–1923* (Dublin, 1973).

Nettle, J. P., 'The State as Conceptual Variable', *World Politics*, 20 (1968), 559–92.

O'Brien, *The Irish Free State: Secret History of Its Foundation*, unpublished manuscript.

O'Brien, W., *The Irish Revolution and How It Came About* (Dublin, 1923).

O'Connor, E., *Syndicalism in Ireland, 1917–1923* (Cork, 1988).

O'Connor, F., *The Big Fellow* (Dublin, 1991).

O'Crohan, T., *Island Cross-Talk: Pages from a Diary* (Oxford, 1986).

O'Day, A., *The English Face of Irish Nationalism: Parnellite Involvement in British Politics 1880–86* (Dublin, 1997).

O'Donohue, F., *No Other Law* (Dublin, 1986).

O'Flaherty, L., *Tourists Guide to Ireland* (London, 1929).

O'Gadhra, N., *Civil War in Connacht 1922–1923* (Cork, 1999).

O'Halpin, E., 'A Savage Chaos', *The Irish Review*, 6 (1989), 147–9.

—— 'The Army and the Dail–Civil–Military Relations within the Independence Move-ment' in B. Farrell (ed.), *The Creation of the Dail* (Dublin, 1994), 107–23.

—— *Defending Ireland: The Irish State and Its Enemies since 1922* (Oxford, 1999).

—— 'Politics and the State, 1922–32', in J. R. Hill (ed.), *A New History of Ireland: vol. 7 Ireland, 1921–84* (Oxford, 2003), 86–125.

O'Hegarty, P. S., *The Victory of Sinn Fein* (Dublin, 1924; 1998).

O'Higgins, K., *Civil War and the Events Which Led to It* (Dublin, 1926).

O'Malley, E., *The Singing Flame* (Dublin, 1978).

O'Sullivan, D., *The Irish Free State and Its Senate: A Study in Contemporary Politics* (London, 1940).

Ottoway, D. and M., *The Politics of Socialist Revolution* (Berkeley and Los Angeles, 1970).

O'Tuathaigh, G., 'De Valera and Sovereignty: A Note on the Pedigree of a Political Idea', in J. P. O'Connell and J. A. Murphy (eds.), *De Valera and His Times* (Cork, 1983).

Pakenham, F., *Peace By Ordeal: The Negotiation of the Anglo-Irish Treaty, 1921* (London, 1992).

Pakenham, F., and O'Neill, T. P., *Eamon de Valera* (Dublin, 1970).

Parekh, B., 'Ethnocentricity of the Nationalist Discourse', *Nations and Nationalism*, 1/1 (1995), 25–53.

Paseta, S., *Before the Revolution: Nationalism, Social Change and Ireland's Catholic Elite, 1879–1922* (Cork, 1999).

Popper, K., *The Poverty of Historicism* (London and New York, 2002).

Prager, J., *Building Democracy in Ireland* (Cambridge, 1986).

Pressly, T. J., *Americans Interpret Their Civil War* (New York, 1954).

Priolly, S., *Ireland in Rebellion* (Dublin, 1922).

Pritchett, V. S., *Dublin* (London, 1991).

Purdon, E. *The Civil War 1922–23* (Cork, 2000).

Quandt, W., *Revolution and Political Leadership: Algeria 1954–1968* (Cambridge, Mass., and London, 1969).

Regan, J. M., 'Review of Tom Garvin's *1922: The Birth of Irish Democracy*', *History Ireland*, 5/2 (1997), 54–6.

—— 'The Politics of Reaction: The Dynamics of Treatyite Government and Policy, 1922–33', *Irish Historical Studies*, 30/120 (1997), 542–64.

—— *The Irish Counter-revolution 1921–36: Treatyite Politics and Settlement in Independent Ireland* (Dublin, 1999).

Roberts, H., *The Battlefield: Algeria 1988–2002—Studies in a Broken Polity* (London and New York, 2003).

Rothschild, J., *East Central Europe between the Two World Wars* (Seattle, 1974).

Ryan, M., *Liam Lynch: The Real Chief* (Cork, 1986).

—— *Tom Barry: IRA Freedom Fighter* (Cork, 2003).

Ryle Dwyer, T., *Michael Collins and the Treaty: His Differences with de Valera* (Cork and Dublin, 1981).

—— *Tans, Terror and Troubles: Kerry's Real Fighting Story 1913–23* (Cork, 2001).

Rumpf, E., and A. C. Hepburn, *Nationalism and Socialism in Twentieth Century Ireland* (Liverpool, 1977).

Small, M., and J. D. Singer, *Resort to Arms: International and Civil Wars, 1816–1980* (Beverly Hills/London/New Delhi, 1982).

Sinnott, R., 'Interpretations of the Irish Party System', *European Journal of Political Research*, 12/3 (1984), 289–307.

—— *Irish Voters Decide: Voting Behaviour in Elections and Referendums since 1918* (Manchester, 1995).

Skinner, L., *Politicians by Accident* (Dublin, 1946).

Smyth, G., *Decolonisation and Criticism: The Construction of Irish Literature* (London, 1998).

Stephens, E. M., 'The Constitution', in *Irish Free State Official Handbook* (London, (1932), 72–80.

Stora, B., *Algeria 1830–2000: A Short History* (Ithaca, NY and London, 2001).

Towey, T., 'The Reaction of the British Government to the 1922 Collins–de Valera Pact', *Irish Historical Studies*, 22/85 (1980), 65–77.

Townshend, C., 'The Meaning of Irish Freedom: Constitutionalism in the Free State', *Transactions of the Royal Historical Society*, 6th series, 8 (1998), 45–70.

—— *Ireland: The Twentieth Century* (London, 1999).

Valiulis, M. G., 'The Army Mutiny of 1924 and the Assertion of Civilian Authority in Independent Ireland', *Irish Historical Studies*, 13/92 (1983), 542–64.

—— '"The Man They Could Never Forgive" The View of the Opposition: Eamon de Valera and the Civil War', in J. P. O'Carroll, and J. A. Murphy, (eds.), *Eamon de Valera and His Times* (Cork, 1986), 92–100.

—— *Portrait of a Revolutionary: General Richard Mulcahy and the Founding of the Free State* (Dublin, 1992).

Vanhanen, T., *The Emergency of Democracy: A Comparative Study of 119 States* (Helsinski: Societas Scientarium Fennica, 1984), 144–5.

Walker, B. (ed.), *Parliamentary Election Results in Ireland, 1801–1922* (Dublin, 1978).

Walker, G., 'Propaganda and Conservative Nationalism during the Irish Civil War 1922–1923', *Eire-Ireland*, 22/4 (Winter 1987), 93–117.

Walsh, P. V., *The Irish Civil War, 1922–23*, A NYMAS fulltext resource.

Walter, B., 'The Critical Barrier to Civil War Settlement', *International Organisation*, 51/3 (1997), 335–65.

Washbrook, D., 'The Rhetoric of Democracy and Development in Late Colonial India', in S. Bose and A. Jalal (eds.), *Nationalism, Democracy, and Development: State and Politics in India* (Oxford, 1999), 36–50.

White, N. J., *Decolonisation: The British Experience since 1945* (London and New York, 1999).

Williams, T. D., 'From the Treaty to the Civil War', in T. D. Williams (ed.), *The Irish Struggle 1916–1926* (London, 1966), 117–29.

—— 'The Summing Up', in T. D. Williams (ed.), *The Irish Struggle, 1916–1926* (London, 1966).

Wilson, R., 'Imperialism in Crisis: The Irish Dimension', in M. Langan and B. Schwarz (eds.), *Crises in the British State 1880–1930* (London, 1985), 151–79.

Wood, E. J., 'Civil Wars: What We Don't Know', *Global Governance*, 9/2 (2003), 247–69.

Younger, C., *Ireland's Civil War* (London, 1968).

Zink, A., 'Ireland: Stability without Compromise', in D. Berk Schlosser and J. Mitchell (eds.), *Conditions of Democracy in Europe, 1919–1939* (Basingstoke, 2000), 263–95.

Index